FRENCH ORGAN MUSIC

FROM THE REVOLUTION TO FRANCK AND WIDOR

EASTMAN STUDIES IN MUSIC

FRENCH ORGAN MUSIC
From the Revolution
to Franck and Widor

EDITED BY

LAWRENCE ARCHBOLD

and

WILLIAM J. PETERSON

UNIVERSITY OF ROCHESTER PRESS

First published 1995

University of Rochester Press
34–36 Administration Building, University of Rochester
Rochester, New York, 14627, USA
and at PO Box 9, Woodbridge, Suffolk IP12 3DF, UK

ISBN 1 878822 55 1

Library of Congress Cataloging-in-Publication Data

British Library Cataloguing-in-Publication Data

A catalogue record for this book
is available from the British Library

Printed in the United States of America
This publication is printed on acid-free paper

For Fenner Douglass,
author of *Cavaillé-Coll and the Musicians*

CONTENTS

WIDOR AND HIS CONTEMPORARIES

INTRODUCTION

In the past ten to fifteen years the field of nineteenth-century French organ music has developed through scholarly and artistic enterprise into an important arena of musical and cultural studies. Prominent in this development was the flurry of activity surrounding the one-hundredth anniversary in 1990 of the death of César Franck, considered today one of the greatest figures in the history of organ music. And of critical importance in this story is the attention now being given to organ sound and particularly to nineteenth-century organ-building principles: above all, the reassessment of Aristide Cavaillé-Coll's monumental work is of pivotal importance. Indeed, one of the greatest of Cavaillé-Coll's instruments, that found at Saint-Sulpice, has been justly celebrated after its restoration, completed in 1991, carefully guided by Daniel Roth and executed by Jean Renaud. A special issue of *La Flûte harmonique*, published in 1991, presented readers with an intriguing and informative account of Cavaillé-Coll's achievement at Saint-Sulpice in the 1860s considered in historical context.[1] A remarkable set of recordings recently released of over twenty Cavaillé-Coll instruments is undoubtedly a milestone both in sound recording projects (instruments matched with appropriate repertoire) and in the renaissance of interest in nineteenth-century French organ music.[2] Moreover, organ builders in the past decade have paid close attention to principles of nineteenth-century French building techniques: since the widely noted 1983 installation of a Van den Heuvel instrument in the Netherlands, several organ builders—including Bedient, Wolff, Angerstein, Fisk, Jaeckel, and Rosales in North America—have on occasion demonstrated devotion to these principles, and several of their instruments can today be heard on recordings. Indeed, recordings of French Romantic organ music are circulating in great abundance, with repertoire from the time of the French Revolution to that of canonical figures such as Franck and Charles-Marie Widor and to that of post-Romantic figures such as Louis Vierne and Charles Tournemire. Complete recordings of Alexandre Guilmant's sonatas are now a reality, and even so vast a repertoire as Tournemire's *L'Orgue mystique* has been undertaken more than once.

The reevaluation of nineteenth-century organ-building principles is but one important part of the picture: scholarly reassessment since 1980 of nineteenth-century organ music, having produced significant studies of Boëly, Franck, Guilmant, Widor, and others, signals a resurgence of interest in a subject much neglected during the middle decades of the century. Even the most summary list of works could not fail to include the following: Fenner Douglass's *Cavaillé-Coll and the Musicians* (1980), François Sabatier's *César Franck et l'orgue* (1982), Rollin Smith's *Toward an Authentic Interpretation of the Organ Works of César Franck* (1983), John Near's dissertation, "The Life and Work of Charles-Marie Widor" (1985), Andrew Thomson's *The Life and Times of Charles-Marie Widor, 1844–1937* (1987), Brigitte François-Sappey's *Alexandre P. F. Boëly 1785–1858: ses ancêtres, sa vie, son oeuvre, son temps* (1989), and essays honoring the Franck anniversary year including Smith's series of articles in *The American Organist* and the collection of essays issued by *L'Orgue* (1990).[3] Important articles and essays have been published by an impressive list of authors which includes some names mentioned above, some of those included in the present book, and others as well (Ewald Kooiman and Kurt Lueders are two prominent examples). Two recent major publications, Rollin Smith's *Saint Saëns and the Organ* (1992) and Nicolas Gorenstein's *L'Orgue post-classique français: du Concert Spirituel à Cavaillé-Coll* (1993), illustrate differing methods of investigation—one focusing on a great composer and his relation to the organ and the other focusing on a broad historical period and the roles played by many individuals in a neglected chapter within the Romantic century.[4] Orpha Ochse's forthcoming comprehensive study of what it meant to be an organist in nineteenth-century France and Belgium confirms the importance of a more sociological perspective in current scholarly investigations of nineteenth-century organ culture.

It is perhaps not surprising that within this scholarly enterprise, new questions have been asked about how to evaluate the musical texts themselves. The substantial list of source-related studies and editions of music includes a facsimile of Franck's autograph of the *Choral* in B Minor (with introduction by Emory Fanning, 1981), the first *urtext* edition of Franck's major organ works (edited by Günther Kaunzinger), the first scholarly edition of Widor's symphonies for organ (edited by Near), and various series of reprints of period editions of this repertoire (supervised by such editors as Hermann J. Busch and Wayne Leupold).[5] The history of nineteenth-century organ-playing practices has advanced in many ways, too, in these years, in part through the publication of book-length organ methods by Sandra Soderlund and more recently by George Ritchie and George Stauffer, and through the publication of essays such as Leupold's chapter on organ playing in *Performance Practice*.[6] Indeed, these studies have taken a fresh look at the important connections between France and Belgium in this period, with particular emphasis on issues of performance practice. These books, dissertations, articles, and editions from scholars in France, the United States, England, Germany, the Netherlands, and Austria, considered alongside other notable contributions, have not only established the study of French Romantic organ music as a truly international undertaking, they have made effective use of virtually all of the methodological approaches found in modern musicology: biography, analysis, criticism, source study, and performance practice.

The essays in this volume are devoted above all to issues concerning organ music. In contrast to Ochse's book, which took shape during the same years as this one, the present volume illustrates a wide diversity of aims and methods. This book, to some degree, owes its inception to a panel, "Organ Music and Liturgy in France," chaired by Fenner Douglass (to whom the volume is dedicated), which took place at the 1983 national meeting in Louisville, Kentucky, of the American Musicological Society; while several of the contributors to this volume participated, few traces of that event remain here, and the scope of this present selection of recent scholarship is substantially wider. A comprehensive interest in organs, organists, organ playing traditions, and organ music stands behind Marie-Louise Jaquet-Langlais's "The Organ Works of Franck: A Survey of Editorial and Performance Problems," in which old questions concerning Franck's organ works are revisited and new questions raised. A similarly broad array of topics can be found in William J. Peterson's "Lemmens, His *École d'orgue*, and Nineteenth-Century Organ Methods," which examines in detail the central figure in organ teaching in nineteenth-century France and Belgium through analysis of the 1862 *École d'orgue* in historical context. Performance practice is also central in Daniel Roth's "Some Thoughts on the Interpretation of the Organ Works of Franck, on His Organ, and on the Lemmens Tradition," which, like Jaquet-Langlais's essay, reevaluates the relevance of Lemmens's ideas about organ playing to the music of Franck. Style criticism is a main theme in Craig Cramer's "Boëly's *Quatorze Préludes sur des cantiques de Denizot*, op. 15, and the Creation of a French 'Christmas' *Orgelbüchlein*," which explores one aspect of Boëly's considerable debt to J. S. Bach, and in Edward Zimmerman's and Lawrence Archbold's "'Why Should We Not Do the Same with Our Catholic Melodies?': Guilmant's *L'Organiste liturgiste*, op. 65," which also examines a repertoire that owes much to Bach. A more specifically liturgical focus can be found in Benjamin Van Wye's "Organ Music in the Mass of the Parisian Rite to 1850 with Emphasis on the Contributions of Boëly," which provides, above all, a much needed context in which to understand better Boëly's organ masses. An interest in manuscripts and source studies informs two additional essays on Franck: Jesse E. Eschbach's "Paris, Bibliothèque Nationale, MS 8707: A New Source for Franck's Registrational Practices and Its Implications for the Published Registrations of His Organ Works," which reveals new information about Franck's liturgical organ playing, and Karen Hastings-Deans's "From Manuscript to Publication: Franck's *Choral* No. 1," which scrutinizes Franck's compositional process in one of his greatest and most enduring works. Lawrence Archbold, in "Widor's *Symphonie romane*," conducts a close reading of the composer's last organ symphony, presenting, among other things, new ideas about the interplay of plainchant and formal paradigms. Finally, as if fixing the boundaries of the volume, the sociology of organs, organists, and organ music takes center stage in the volume's first and last articles: in Kimberly Marshall's and William J. Peterson's "Evolutionary Schemes: Organists and Their Revolutionary Music," which examines how Parisian organists and organ music survived what was unquestionably their greatest challenge, and Rollin Smith's "The Organ of the Trocadéro and Its Players," which documents, among other events, one of the most spectacular success stories in Parisian organ playing (and a landmark in the history of organ music in public culture): the inaugural concert series of the Trocadéro organ in 1878.[7]

We take great pleasure in extending our thanks to several friends and colleagues who provided us with special help and advice: to Stephen Pinel, who encouraged this project in its earliest stages, to Lenora McCroskey, for clarification of certain details regarding the liturgical aspects of French Baroque organ music; to David Fuller and Bruce Gustafson, who provided timely advice; to Daniel J. Jaeckel, Alan Lewis, and J. Stephen Repasky, who provided assistance in locating several bibliographic items; to Jeff Watson, for technical assistance; and to the staffs of the Library of Congress and the Bibliothèque Nationale for their many kindnesses during the course of writing and editing these essays. We extend special thanks to Matthew Dirst, David Gramit, and Kimberly Marshall, who, undertaking the often thankless task of translation, succeeded in overseeing their projects with both attentiveness and imagination; without their help, the inclusion of some of the most significant work in this volume would not have been possible. George Thomson kindly adjusted his schedule to permit the completion of musical examples for the volume. Ralph Locke and Robert Easton of the University of Rochester Press generously provided useful advice and many helpful suggestions in the final phase of the editing process. Indeed, a few editorial decisions deserve mention: Bibliothèque Nationale, Conservatoire, Notre-Dame, and *La Revue et Gazette musicale* all refer to Paris unless otherwise qualified; Notre-Dame refers to the cathedral; all manucripts in the possession of libraries are music manuscripts, and call numbers preceded by Mus. MS have generally been simplified to MS only; titles of compositions are given in English wherever suitable; names of stops and Italian tempo marks are given in roman type while names of registrations and most other performance nuances appear in italics; and specific octave registers are given in the system in which middle C is labeled c'.[8] With gratitude we acknowledge support from Carleton College and from Pomona College. Most of all, we want to thank our contributors, whose patience, devotion, and good will have, in the end, made this volume possible.

Lawrence Archbold   William J. Peterson
Northfield, Minnesota   Claremont, California

November 1994

xii

NOTES

[1] *Le Grand-Orgue de Saint-Sulpice et ses organistes*, ed. Kurt Lueders, *La Flûte harmonique*, numéro spécial 59/60 (1991).

[2] *L'Orgue Cavaillé-Coll: Klangdokumentationen von 28 Orgeln des Aristide Cavaillé-Coll (1811–1899)* (Motette-Ursina M10760, n.d.).

[3] Fenner Douglass, *Cavaillé-Coll and the Musicians*, 2 vols. (Raleigh: Sunbury, 1980); François Sabatier, *César Franck et l'orgue* (Paris: Presses universitaires de France, 1982); Rollin Smith, *Toward an Authentic Interpretation of the Organ Works of César Franck*, Juilliard Performance Guides, no. 1 (New York: Pendragon, 1983); John Near, "The Life and Work of Charles-Marie Widor" (D.M.A. diss., Boston University, 1985); Andrew Thomson, *The Life and Times of Charles-Marie Widor, 1844–1937* (Oxford: Oxford University Press, 1987); Brigitte François-Sappey, *Alexandre P. F. Boëly 1785–1858: ses ancêtres, sa vie, son œuvre, son temps* (Paris: Aux Amateurs de livres, 1989); Rollin Smith, *Playing the Organ Works of César Franck* (New York: The American Guild of Organists, 1994); *César Franck*, L'Orgue: cahiers et mémoires, no. 44 (Paris: L'Orgue, 1990).

[4] Rollin Smith, *Saint-Saëns and the Organ* (Stuyvesant, N.Y.: Pendragon, 1992); Nicolas Gorenstein, *L'Orgue post-classique français: du Concert Spirituel à Cavaillé-Coll* (Paris: Chanvrelin, 1993). Smith's detailed study of Saint-Saëns as an organist mitigates to a degree the lack of emphasis on that composer in this volume.

[5] *Chorale No. 2 in B Minor for organ: Fascimile of the Autograph Manuscript by César Franck* (1981); César Franck, *Complete Works for Organ*, ed. Günther Kaunzinger, 4 vols. (Vienna: Schott/Universal, 1990); Charles-Marie Widor, *The Symphonies for Organ*, ed. John Near, vols. 11–20 of *Recent Researches in the Music of the Nineteenth and Early Twentieth Centuries* (Madison: A-R Editions, 1991–forthcoming); *Orgelmusik der französischen Romantik: Die französische Orgelmusik des 19. Jahrhunderts in Faksimileausgaben der Erstdrucke*, ed. Hermann J. Busch (Sankt Augustin: Dr. J. Butz, 1988–forthcoming); *The Organ Music of Alexandre Guilmant*, ed. Wayne Leupold, 12 vols. (Melville, N.Y.: Belwin-Mills, 1984–1993).

[6] Sandra Soderlund, *Organ Technique: An Historical Approach* (Chapel Hill: Hinshaw, 1986); George Ritchie and George Stauffer, *Organ Technique: Modern & Early* (Englewood Cliffs, N.J.: Prentice Hall, 1992); Wayne Leupold, "Organ," in *Performance Practice*, ed. Howard Mayer Brown and Stanley Sadie, 2 vols. (New York: W. W. Norton, 1990), 2:374–93.

[7] The essay by Marie-Louise Jaquet-Langlais is a translation, revision, and significant expansion of her "L'Œuvre d'orgue de César Franck et notre temps," *L'Orgue*, no. 167 (1978), 5–42; that by Daniel Roth is a translation, revision, and expansion of his "Einige Gedanken zur Interpretation des Orgelwerks von César Franck, zu seiner Orgel und zur Lemmens-Tradition," *Orgel, Orgelmusik und Orgelspiel: Festschrift Michael Schneider zum 75. Geburtstag*, ed. Christoph Wolff (Kassel: Bärenreiter, 1985), 111–17; Benjamin Van Wye's article is a slightly revised version of his "Organ Music in the Mass of the Parisian Rite (1750–1850)," *L'Orgue*, no. 229 (1994), 11–20, and no. 230 (1994), 20–25; and Karen Hastings-Deans's article is a translation and revision of what first appeared, in a somewhat abbreviated form, as "Le Premier Choral: du manuscrit à l'édition princeps," *César Franck*, L'Orgue: cahiers et mémoires, no. 44 (Paris: L'Orgue, 1990), 47–64. We acknowledge with gratitude permission to include these articles in their new forms in this volume.

[8] See D. Kern Holoman, *Writing about Music: A Style Sheet from the editors of 19th-Century Music* (Berkeley: University of California Press, 1988), 7.

From the Revolution
to Franck

Evolutionary Schemes:
Organists and Their Revolutionary Music

KIMBERLY MARSHALL and WILLIAM J. PETERSON

Although maligned by some critics as a time of musical decadence, "an empty period in the history of French music,"[1] or at best, "a transitory period,"[2] few eras are as intriguing as the French Revolution. This fascination is attributable in part to the violence of the changes that transformed French life and thought. After the storming of the Bastille, reforms came swiftly: the privileges of the feudal system that had governed France for centuries were abolished, the Rights of Man were declared, the Church was secularized, and the entire domestic bureaucracy was restructured. By the beginning of the Terror in 1793, adherence to the goals of the revolutionaries was brutally enforced: 300,000 people were arrested and 17,000 were executed as enemies of the Revolution.[3]

Marat's scathing comments about the political use of cultural distractions could well be applied to music during the French Revolution:

> It is during times of crisis, when public well-being is in danger, that the conspirators . . . work to distract the people's attention from disastrous events, from their new plots, by directing it towards amusing things, pompous spectacles, celebrations.[4]

Musicians conceded to popular demands in order to survive the collapse of the institutions that had offered them patronage for centuries. As François Devienne explained in the notes to his song, *Le Bonheur de France*:

> The people need songs, celebrations. When one wishes to interest those whose imaginations are lively, and whose spirits are not yet sufficiently enlightened, it is to the senses that one must speak.[5]

Organists found themselves abruptly shaken from their tribunes and forced to find ways to preserve and justify their art in the wake of this massive restructuring. Because they were dependent on institutions that could finance the construction and maintenance of large instruments, organists were

3

especially vulnerable when these institutions collapsed. The seizure of ecclesiastical goods in 1789 and the abolition of Roman Catholic services in 1793 greatly affected both players and builders, who depended primarily on the Church for their livelihood.

François Sabatier has estimated that there were at least 2,000 organs in France in 1789; many of these were destroyed or damaged as Church property was appropriated to the State by the revolutionaries.[6] The official decrees advocating these changes occurred in two stages. The first affected primarily the convents, when on 10 October 1789 Talleyrand proposed that all ecclesiastical goods be placed in the service of the State. Of the 522 organs put to auction as a result of this measure, 418 perished. The 104 surviving instruments were bought by parish churches for a very good price.[7] The second stage affected the property of the parishes, when on 16 Ventôse of Year III (6 March 1795), the National Convention decreed that "the sale of organs belonging to the Republic will take place according to the conditions prescribed for the sale of national furniture."[8] There was great protest against this measure, and many colorful stories describe the bravery of organists attempting to save their instruments from the hands of angry crowds by bursting into Revolutionary hymns.[9] The outcry against the law's extension to organs caused the Convention to reconsider, and the measure was later revoked on 13 Messidor (1 July).[10]

Despite the insecurity of rapidly changing governments, important developments for the history of music in France occurred in the aftermath of the Terror: the Directory (1795–99), a period of musical liberation, is remembered for its patriotic balls and the creation of the Conservatoire de Musique.[11] Moreover, the important concerts of the Rue de Cléry began in 1799. These were renowned throughout Europe for the interpretation of symphonic music, especially the works of Haydn. Opera flourished in the years preceding Napoleon's 1807 decree which effectively reduced the number of theaters in Paris: the Opéra mounted both new works and revivals of older works (including those of Gluck and Rousseau) while the Opéra-Comique—formed from the union in 1801 of two companies—produced works of Spontini, Méhul, and others. In 1802 Bonaparte restored the Royal Chapel of the Tuileries and reintroduced music to the Church. (This was especially significant for organists, many of whom were able to reassume their lost positions.) In 1803 the Prix de Rome was created to encourage the work of talented composers; in 1805 the Concert Spirituel, which had ceased in 1791, recommenced in various Parisian concert halls.[12] Throughout this period, the State busily commissioned musical works for its many celebrations and public manifestations. While before 1793 Revolutionary music was volunteered and not commissioned, from 1793 to 1800 there was a continuous stream of State requests for music,[13] and, indeed, many "fecund and durable" musical developments took place, especially between the years 1795 and 1805.[14] Yet, the overwhelming concern for restructuring institutions and fulfilling official needs not only refocused artistic energies but undermined the creative output of musicians. As for organists, they began to direct their efforts to saving endangered instruments and finding niches for performance within the new order.

Claude-Bénigne Balbastre (1727–1799) offers one of several cases of an *ancien régime* organist surviving the Revolution. This internationally acclaimed virtuoso drew capacity crowds to Saint-Roch at Christmas in the days of Louis XVI.[15] He held several positions at court: he became organist to Monsieur, the King's brother (who later restored the monarchy under the name Louis XVIII); he was employed as organist to the Royal Chapel; and he taught harpsichord to Marie Antoinette. But with the overthrow of the French monarchy Balbastre lost his positions and lived in poverty until his death. His variations on the *Marseillaise, Marche des marseillois et l'air Ça ira arrangés pour le forte-piano*, date from 1792, the year in which the patriotic song itself first appeared: the widely circulated account of a performance by Balbastre of this piece on the organ of the deconsecrated Notre-Dame is now considered doubtful.[16]

Like Balbastre, Jean-Jacques Beauvarlet-Charpentier (1734–1794) lost his appointments as organist in the aftermath of the Revolution. His death may have been caused by the trauma of the closing of the churches in 1793 and the suppression of the organs over which he had presided at the Royal Abbey of Saint-Victor and at the church of Saint-Paul.[17] His son Jacques-Marie (1766–1834) survived the turmoil with an office job and position as organist for the Theophilanthropists at the Temple of the Renaissance. Under the Consulate, this temple was restored to its former function as Saint-Germain-l'Auxerrois. Jacques-Marie held other important posts as organist in Paris, wrote an organ method, and composed many keyboard pieces, the titles of which document his skill in adapting his art to the quick succession of political regimes in France.[18] Although he is said to have espoused republican ideals in 1793, his *Bataille d'Austerlitz* glorifies the military exploits of Napoleon as Emperor; the *Six Magnificats* for organ are dedicated to the newly restored clergy of the Empire. During the Restoration, he composed the music for *Le God save the King des Français* and he published several masses containing a *Prière pour le roi*.[19]

Armand-Louis Couperin's death in 1789 had nothing to do with the turbulent political events of that year: he was killed in a traffic accident five months before the storming of the Bastille. His son and successor at Saint-Gervais, Pierre-Louis, died later in the same year, apparently from grief at the loss of his father.[20] Another son, Gervais-François (1759–1826), took over the posts left by his father's and brother's deaths, and like Beauvarlet-Charpentier *fils*, skillfully managed to accommodate himself to the different regimes coming into power.[21] In 1793 he played patriotic airs with Nicolas Séjan on two small box organs on either side of the stage for the reopening of the Opéra. In 1799 he played dinner music on the enormous instrument at Saint-Sulpice, rededicated as the Temple of Victory, while below, Napoleon dined with the leaders of the Directory.[22] Gervais-François adroitly maintained his favor with the ruling power during the Restoration; his last opus is a piano work entitled *Louis XVIII ou le retour de bonheur en France* (ca. 1816).

Guillaume Lasceux (1740–1831), another Revolutionary-era organist of note, held the position at Saint-Étienne-du-Mont from 1774. Although he lost his patronage and several positions as organist because of the Revolution, he did manage to support himself by playing for the services of the Theophilan-thropists at Saint-Étienne-du-Mont (then known as the Temple of Filial Piety) in the 1790s.[23] This church was restored to Roman Catholic worship in 1803 (by the Concordat of 1801), whereupon Lasceux resumed his former duties until he retired in 1819. Lasceux's works have little in common with the powerful Revolutionary currents that dominated Paris: he published a *Nouvelle Suite de pièces d'orgue* (1810), he completed a collection of twelve fugues, and he also assembled two important volumes titled *Essai théorique et pratique sur l'art de l'orgue* (1809) and *Annuaire de l'organiste* (1819). The *Essai théorique et pratique*, left in manuscript, brings together in one volume information about the organ and its construction, advice on devising registrations for organ pieces, and compositions for the organ, including a *Symphonie concertante* and a *Judex crederis esse venturus* (a verset for the Te Deum). Lasceux articulated his pedagogical aim in the preface to the *Essai théorique et pratique*, where he stated that the volume would provide a useful instruction for music students drawn by their "taste" and their "spirit" to the organ.[24] The *Annuaire de l'organiste*, a "work useful to those who intend to play the organ," contains masses, hymns, and Magnificats, as well as a Te Deum.

Of the organists who lived through the Revolution, Nicolas Séjan (1745–1819) seems to have been the most successful, and he was one of the most highly esteemed. Already famous before 1789, he was reported to have improvised a Te Deum at the tender age of 14![25] He held important posts such as Saint-Séverin, Saint-Sulpice, the Royal Chapel, and Notre-Dame, and he became the first organ professor at the École Royale de Chant, before the Revolution deprived him of all his positions.[26] Nevertheless, Séjan was able to help save Parisian organs during the Terror and to reinstate the salaries of musicians who had previously worked for the Church. He was appointed professor at the newly-founded Conservatoire in 1795, and he held the position as professor of organ there from 1798.[27] In 1806 he was appointed organist at Saint-Louis-des-Invalides and Saint-Sulpice. When the monarchy was restored in 1814, he returned to the Royal Chapel and was given the Légion d'Honneur by Louis XVIII.[28] Choron expresses admiration for Séjan in his *Dictionnaire* of 1810, considering him to be the only great organist to remain after "the disastrous times when there was no longer hope that the art of the organ could be useful."[29]

One of the first French composers to write specifically for the piano, Séjan is justly considered to be one of the creators of the French piano school.[30] (Indeed, more is known today about his work in relation to the piano than to the organ.) The expressive capabilities of the new instrument were highly prized and greatly contributed to its popularity:

> The forte-piano is the most generally cultivated of all musical instruments. It has obtained preference over the harpsichord because it expresses its sounds to the degree of force or softness that is desired, and it can imitate all of the nuances of the other instruments, which one would seek in vain on the instrument [harpsichord] it replaced.[31]

After the Revolution, organists like Séjan took advantage of the growing interest in the piano, and this shift of allegiance deflected attention away from organ music.

What kind of music were these Revolutionary-era organists performing? What were the origins of this music? How did it stand in relation to the heritage of music that predated the 1790s, and how did it respond to the pressures of the Revolution? The intermingling of an established musical culture and an emerging Revolutionary one in France has been well documented: for example, a 1792 production of the comic opera Le Déserteur by Monsigny was heralded by an orchestral rendition of Ça ira.[32] Organists, too, under certain circumstances found methods of promoting an explicitly Revolutionary culture: for example, the organist Nicolas-Jean Méreaux and his son Jean-Nicolas participated in open-air festivities, playing patriotic melodies on organs mounted on platforms to accompany the passing parades.[33] But imaginative—even curious—usages of the various Revolutionary texts and tunes account for only a part of the history of music in France during these years. Organists, to be sure, also cultivated aspects of their established art—fugues, noëls, and Te Deums—that cast them in a more conservative role.[34]

In the last decades of the eighteenth century organists returned to the fugue as a significant genre of organ music. That fugal writing previously had been highly cultivated in France is beyond question: especially in the half century from 1660 to 1710, French organist-composers produced an impressive repertoire of fugues. Fugues were prominent in François Roberday's collection, *Fugues, et Caprices, à quatre parties*, a cycle of five fugues on essentially the same subject was published by Jean-Henri D'Anglebert, and fugues formed an important part of collections by François Couperin and Nicolas de Grigny (the latter's nine fugues include examples of five-voice polyphony). This rich repertoire even included such specialties as Jacques Boyvin's *Fugue chromatique* and *Fugue grave*, and Lambert Chaumont's *Fugue gaye* and *Fugue légère*. In the middle decades of the eighteenth century, dominated by *galant* ideals,

7

fugues were not cultivated with comparable enthusiasm. If Jean-François Dandrieu's fugue on an ascending chromatic subject, for example, illustrates mastery of four-voice counterpoint, on the other hand, a two-voice Fugue in D Minor by Balbastre (which, significantly, is not drawn from a *Livre d'orgue*) resembles in almost no respect the contrapuntal examples discussed above.[35] Michel Corrette, although he did demonstrate mastery of imitative texture in several pieces (for example, in *musettes*), apparently composed very few fugues.

With composers born after 1730 the fugue received increased attention. Both Lasceux and Jean-Jacques Beauvarlet-Charpentier assembled collections of fugues (Lasceux's *Douze Fugues* and Beauvarlet-Charpentier's *Six Fugues*).[36] The Fugue in G Minor of Beauvarlet-Charpentier displays one of the lengthy, meandering subjects which attained a certain notoriety among later critics (see Example 1).[37] The subject of his sixth fugue, in D Minor, admittedly eight measures long, has greater cogency (see Example 2).[38] Lasceux's Fugue in E Minor, a three-voice composition, explores a rather craggy subject (see Example 3), and a Fugue in D Minor of Lasceux displays an unusually restrained subject presented chiefly in the top and bottom voices of the three-voice counterpoint (see Example 4).[39] Séjan's Fugue in G Minor is a grand work of 122 measures which demonstrates stretto techniques and concludes with the subject transformed into a broad chordal version.[40]

Twentieth-century critical commentary from André Pirro to Brigitte François-Sappey, concerned with the identification of perceived stylistic weaknesses from this repertoire understood to have been produced in a

Example 1. J.-J. Beauvarlet-Charpentier, *Fugue en sol mineur*, mm. 1–19, as it appears in *Les Maîtres français de l'orgue*

Example 2. J.-J. Beauvarlet-Charpentier, Fugue in D Minor, mm. 1–8, from *Six Fugues pour l'orgue ou le clavecin*

Example 3. Lasceux, *Fugue en mi mineur*, mm. 1–11, as it appears in *Les Maîtres français de l'orgue*

Example 4. Lasceux, *Fugue*, mm. 1–10, as it appears in *Les Maîtres français de l'orgue*

period of disarray, may obscure an important point. Organists around 1800 preserved and cultivated the fugal practice and produced a number—and a variety—of substantial fugues in these dramatic and volatile decades. Moreover, the genre itself was drawing the attention of other musicians as well. Fugues were held up for study by pianists: the Adam method, *Méthode de piano* (1809), included among a repertoire of fugues two fugues from Bach's *Das wohltemperirte Clavier* with fingering supplied.[41] And contrapuntal writing, along with fugues, was included for study in *Principes élémentaires de musique* (ca. 1800), compiled by Gossec and others, and printed under the auspices of the Conservatoire.[42] Thus, the organists born after 1730 who were active in the Revolutionary period played a key role in the efforts to preserve this example of the high art of the pre-Revolutionary past.

The organists who worked both under the *ancien régime* and in the Revolutionary era were noted less for their fugues than for two different genres that attracted the attention of both the public and the critics: the variation set— most notably variations on noëls—and improvisations inspired by the Te Deum. The tradition of organ noëls, as it began in the seventeenth century, had both secular and sacred origins. The noëls which were the subjects for variation techniques were, in fact, popular tunes from various regions of France. At the same time, these variation sets on folkish tunes became established as a vital part of the *Messe de minuit*. The noëls, rich with associative meaning, have been considered by many critics as picturesque or evocative music.[43] Organists who composed variations on noëls in the last decades of the eighteenth century had compositional connections to trace to earlier eighteenth-century organist-composers (including Pierre Dandrieu, Louis-Claude Daquin, and Michel Corrette) if not to Nicolas Lebègue and Nicolas Gigault.

The earliest noëls, after all, stand at considerable distance from the well-known compositions of Daquin and Balbastre. *Puer nobis nascitur* beautifully illustrates the restrained grace of Lebègue's noëls: the composer arranges a continuous unfolding of four broad statements of the tune in a work characterized by a crescendo produced in four stages.[44] Variations one and two are chordal in texture, variation three employs continuous flowing eighth-note motives (occurring in alternate hands), and variation four returns to the chordal presentation, now, for the most part, heard an octave higher.

The first half of the eighteenth century was of critical importance in the historical development of the organ noël. The works of Pierre Dandrieu (whose noëls probably date from before 1720) demonstrate how the early eighteenth-century noël was defined.[45] With Dandrieu the noël expanded significantly as new techniques of variation came into usage. In *Laissez paitre vos bestes*,[46] a grand 243–measure composition, Dandrieu examines the tune first in a variation built around flowing eighth-note motives in the top, tune-bearing voice, next in a trio-textured section, then in a two-voiced section,

10

followed by a *Duo en diminution*, next as a *Grand Jeu* section alternating the Grand-Orgue and Positif, and finally as a *Dialogue* employing Grand-Orgue, Positif, and "Eco." In *Quand le sauveur Jesus-Christ fut né de Marie* he explores many of the techniques already described, including in this composition a variation titled "En viele," a rustic evocation of the tune heard against a drone.

Michel Corrette demonstrates an equally impressive array of compositional techniques in his *Nouveau Livre de noëls*.[47] In the restrained *Vous qui désirez sans fin*, Corrette composes in a style not unsympathetic to that of Lebègue, and he includes after the presentation of the tune, a *Double*, a *Duo*, a *Trio*, and a final variation based on lively sixteenth-note patterns. In *Musette: A Minuit fut fait un reveil* Corrette composes with a drone, in this instance exploring imitative texture in two treble parts heard above the immovable C. *Noël suisse* includes traces of harpsichord technique, notable especially in the running octaves in the concluding variation.

In the last thirty years of the century French composers continued to cultivate the art of noël writing. The celebrated Balbastre arranged the noëls within his *Livre de noëls* in suites which could, as indicated in the score, be played on organ or harpsichord.[48] *Joseph est bien marié* explores an array of variation techniques—including a variation in a contrasting major mode—within a spare, chiefly two-voiced, composition that does, along with many other of the composer's noëls, rely at times on the Alberti bass. Finally, Jean-Jacques Beauvarlet-Charpentier held up the noël for new consideration in his works. Several noëls "en tambourin" (a later counterpart to the drone noël of Pierre Dandrieu), the *Noël pour un élevation (Pour l'amour de Marie)* which includes written-out expressive embellishments of the tune, the *Noël dans le gout de la simphonie concertante (Ou s'en vont ces gais bergers)*, the *Noël en grand choeur (Votre Bonté grand Dieu)*, and a *Noël suisse (Il est un petit l'ange)* bearing the subtitle "en fugue" all illustrate different aspects of his noël writing.[49]

Twentieth-century commentary on noëls from the period under examination has at times dismissed the repertoire: Gilles Cantagrel and Harry Halbreich, for example, citing *Votre Bonté grand Dieu*, found Beauvarlet-Charpentier's work objectionable on the basis of stylistic traits, aesthetic values, and poverty of imagination. But, even if it can be argued that stylistic elements found in *Votre Bonté grand Dieu* can be closely compared to those of Balbastre's celebrated variations on the *Marseillaise*, it may also be argued that pieces by Beauvarlet-Charpentier such as *Pour l'amour de Marie* and *Il est un petit l'ange* represent late eighteenth-century retrospective essays on the tradition of the noël—essays that unquestionably draw on some established organ-related genres and styles. And, in the case of Lasceux, the noël took on different guises. In *Quoy ma voisine es tu fachée* Lasceux deftly incorporates within the noël's harpsichord-generated textures some passages that recall the

11

earlier organ noël (for example, the "Echo" passages in the first variation). In *Noël lorrain* he displays perhaps less connection to the development of the noël tradition from Pierre Dandrieu through Balbastre, adopting a nostalgic, even "classicistic" view of the noël as, above all, a folk tune presented on the organ.[50]

Just as organ composers after the Revolution continued to foster the established genre of the noël variations, so they also maintained the tradition of improvising settings of the Te Deum, making full use of the instrument to achieve dramatic effects. Eighteenth-century critical accounts document that Daquin's improvisations on the Te Deum were extraordinarily memorable: in particular, the 1762 improvisation was widely noted.[51] Recalling a Te Deum at Saint-Paul, a critic wrote: "More sublime than ever, Daquin thundered in the *Judex crederis*, instilling listeners' hearts with impressions so vivid and so profound that everyone paled and shivered."[52] A decade after his death, Daquin's art—his improvised art—still set standards for some critics.

> All has changed at the moment I write this. Ariettes and sarabandes are played during the elevation of the Host and the chalice; and for the Te Deum and Vespers, hunting pieces, minuets, romances and rigaudons. Where is that admirable Daquin, who thrilled me so many times? He died in 1772, and the organ with him.[53]

What were the significant issues surrounding the genesis of the Te Deum tradition, and what was its fate in the Revolutionary period?

A distinguishing feature of the Te Deum, and of the many pieces that follow not only in this tradition but also in that of the storm fantasies, is the use of special wind and thunder sound effects. Jean-Jacques Beauvarlet-Charpentier commented: "Since this piece must depict the disorder of nature, one may begin by imitating the winds, employing all the foundations."[54] And at the conclusion he advocates the use of "thunder," "prolonged as desired, to mimic the confusion of the universe." Michel Corrette, in comments included in his 1787 *Pièces pour l'orgue dans un genre nouveau*, explains how to achieve special sound effects useful in the Te Deum. In discussing the *Grand Jeu avec le tonnerre*, Corrette explains:

> Thunder is produced by placing a plank on the last octave of the pedals—the Trompette and the Bombarde having been drawn—which the foot pushes as desired. As a conclusion, to imitate the passing of thunder, one strikes with the elbow the last keys of the manual.[55]

Corrette's advice to play the thunder in this way indicates that performers enjoyed a certain freedom in works such as these in the late eighteenth century. At the same time, the question of how—and how extensively—these picturesque effects were actually combined with the more conventional musical sounds within an essentially improvised art is not easily answered. But in the case of Corrette's published pieces, at least, the thunder sound effect clearly served as an embellishment to an apparently autonomous composition. In the score Corrette adds the serrated line ("tonnerre") seven times in the first section (mm. 1–42) of this binary movement and ten times in the second section (mm. 43–90). Thus, Corrette's use of the thunder effect in his collection compares in many ways with the usage devised by Daquin for birdsong: a report from the 1780s by Mercier indicates that Daquin, in the midnight mass, "succeeded in bringing in a birdsong without upsetting the phrase structure."[56]

Lasceux not only preserved the art of the Te Deum throughout the tumultuous Revolutionary years, he provided a written account of the turn-of-the-century practice, prompting Norbert Dufourcq to name him the "theoretician" of this art.[57] Lasceux included a *Judex crederis* in his *Essai théorique et pratique* (1809), and a revised version of the work in his *Annuaire de l'organiste* (1819). In his prose introduction to the 1809 version of the *Judex crederis*, Lasceux provides information about the production of such a piece (using organ and voices), and about the practices of Armand-Louis Couperin and of Séjan.[58] Lasceux provides here, and in the course of the musical text, a valuable account of the shaping of this episodic fantasy, encompassing rustic dances, interrupting thunder, a "Trompette du Jugement dernier," a march (for the arrival, in the 1819 version, of the Judge), and a "Chœur des élus" (considerably transformed in the 1819 version). In the *Essai théorique et pratique* Lasceux explains in some detail matters of execution, including the use of the Écho division and Voix humaine for the "dances and amusements of humans," and the use of arm and hand to produce "une espèce d'ondulation acoustique" ("a kind of acoustical undulation").[59]

The *Judex crederis* as described by Lasceux, then, took the form of an extended fantasy, whose musical sections (often contrasting) followed a scenario drawn from the text of the Te Deum, the presentation of which involved special sound effects (including thunder) that could be produced at the organ. The disruption and special effects were clearly of great importance to the work as a whole—"a frightful noise proclaims the falling of the stars and the annihilation of the creation"—in keeping with the gravity to be portrayed ("the dreadful catastrophe of the final day").[60] But the Lasceux fantasy as a musical entity, in formal terms, involved an opening statement (or statements), a contrast, and a concluding statement, which stood as a resolution of the conflict introduced ("but the whole concludes cheerfully with a chorus of the chosen").[61] Lasceux, in these versions of the *Judex crederis*, in his prose and his music, left an invaluable account of a turn-of-the-century dramatic fantasy for organ that had emerged as a genre forty years earlier.

The elements that made up the *Judex crederis* of Lasceux, including sound effects, as well as the episodic structure, could also be found in the secular battle pieces that were composed in the latter part of the eighteenth century. Primarily associated with the harpsichord or fortepiano, these pieces were certainly not unknown to organists. Charles Broche at Rouen, by Dufourcq's account, performed a *Bataille à grands chœurs*, and Michel Corrette left instructions on how to perform such pieces for the harpsichord (for example, *Giboulées de Mars*) on the organ: he counsels the use of the *Grand Jeu* for *La Prise de Jéricho*.[62] The title page of Jacques-Marie Beauvarlet-Charpentier's *Victoire de l'armée d'Italie, ou bataille de Montenotte*, published in 1796, announces that the work is intended for use on the fortepiano or organ. The *Victoire de l'armée* spins out a musical essay whose broad outlines compare in many ways with those of the *Judex crederis* (and, incidentally, with those of the later storm fantasias of the nineteenth century): opening patriotic strains (including references to the *Marseillaise* and to the *Chant du départ*), engagement with the enemy ("disorder"), followed by "chants de victoire." Because such compositions were not only battle pieces, but historically specific compositions as well, listeners were invited to imagine—or recall—the battle in question (the *Bataille d'Austerlitz* of Jacques-Marie Beauvarlet-Charpentier bore the subtitle: "Pièce militaire et historique"). Such pieces partook of the French Revolutionary landscape, to be sure. And yet even works such as these had antecedents in pre-Revolutionary France. Battle pieces had been cultivated by Corrette in earlier decades, especially in the *Combat naval*, which employs sound clusters as a special effect. Yves Jaffres writes: "Ten years before the Revolution the *Combat naval* of Corrette opened the way to a musical genre whose future not even he could have suspected."[63]

In the Revolutionary era organists found themselves at different times performing patriotic tunes in the shadow of the noël and battle pieces in the shadow of the Te Deum, demonstrating the ablity to return readily to the earlier genres as the political climate of France changed. All the while they also cultivated some of the seemingly discredited high art forms such as the fugue. Organists who weathered those extraordinarily tumultuous years succeeded in carrying forward some of the traditions and practices that were well established in France before the Revolution and left compositions which, if often more notable for historical than for aesthetic reasons, preserved a highly specialized, even esoteric musical culture for following generations. Indeed, it is difficult to imagine the fugues, the noëls, and the *Judex crederis* of a composer such as Alexandre-Pierre-François Boëly without the culture organists managed to preserve in these Revolutionary years.

NOTES

[1] Jean Mongrédien, *La Musique en France des lumières au romantisme (1789–1830)* (Paris: Flammarion, 1986), 7.

[2] Bernd Scherers, *Studien zur Orgelmusik der Schüler César Francks* (Regensburg: Gustav Bosse, 1984), 8.

[3] John Paxton, *Companion to the French Revolution* (New York: Facts on File, 1988), 186.

[4] Cited in Adelheid Coy, *Die Musik der Französischen Revolution: Zur Funktionsbestimmung von Lied und Hymne* (Munich-Salzburg: E. Katzbichler, 1978), 40.

[5] Cited in Constant Pierre, *Les Hymnes et Chansons de la révolution* (Paris: Imprimerie Nationale, 1904), 2–3.

[6] François Sabatier, "Les Orgues en France pendant la révolution (1789–1802)," *L'Orgue*, no. 143 (1972): 77. See also François Sabatier, "Musique et Vandalisme: le destin de l'orgue en France entre 1788 et 1795," in *Le Tambour et La Harpe*, ed. Jean-Rémy Julien and Jean Mongrédien (Paris: Du May, 1991), 149–56, for a discussion of the Commission temporaire des arts (established in December of 1793) and of its role in preserving French organs.

[7] Sabatier, "Les Orgues en France," 78.

[8] Ibid., 79.

[9] A local tradition reports that the organ of Saint-Maximin-La-Sainte-Baume was saved from destruction and the sale of its tin because the organist played the *Marseillaise* when Paul Barras (member of the National Convention and later one of the five members of the Directory) emerged from the sacristy (Le P. Marie-Réginald A. Arbus, *Une Merveille d'art provençal, le grand-orgue de la Basilique de Saint-Maximin-la-Ste.-Baume* [Aix-en-Provence: De Makaire, 1956], 117; cited in Scherers, *Studien zur Orgelmusik*, 19).

[10] The reversal of this decision, brought about by public pressure, is not surprising, given the political instability of the period. During the fifteen years after 1789 France was ruled by no fewer than five regimes. The Legislative Assembly that had taken control immediately following the Revolution was replaced by the National Convention, which deposed Robespierre on 9 Thermidor Year II (27 July 1794). This was succeeded by the Directory, whose constitution of 22 August 1795 vested the executive authority in five directors assisted by two Councils. Bonaparte's coup d'état established the Consulate on 9 November 1799; he became Consul for life in 1802, and declared himself "emperor of the French" in 1804.

[11] Danièle Pistone, *La Musique en France: de la révolution à 1900* (Paris: Champion, 1979), 14, 34. For recent discussions of music at the time of the Revolution, see *Music and the French Revolution*, ed. Malcolm Boyd (Cambridge: Cambridge University Press, 1992); Ralph P. Locke, "Paris: Centre of Intellectual Ferment," in *Music and Society: The Early Romantic Era, between Revolutions: 1789 and 1848*, ed. Alexander Ringer (Englewood Cliffs: Prentice Hall, 1991), 32–83; and Adélaïde de Place, *La Vie musicale en France au temps de la révolution* (Paris: Arthème Fayard, 1989).

[12] Mongrédien, *La Musique en France*, 8; Pistone, *La Musique en France*, 57. See also Daniel Heartz, "The Concert Spirituel in the Tuileries Palace," *Early Music* 21 (1993), 240–48, for a brief description of the Tuileries palace in the Revolutionary era (see especially illustrations 6–8).

[13] *The New Grove Dictionary of Music and Musicians*, s.v. Revolutionary Hymn.

[14] Mongrédien, *La Musique en France*, 8.

[15] Charles Burney, eager to meet Balbastre, listened to him play the organ at Saint-Roch and the harpsichord at his home in Paris (Charles Burney, *The Present State of Music in France and Italy* [1771; reprint as *An Eighteenth-Century Musical Tour in France and Italy*, ed. Percy Scholes, 2 vols. (London: Oxford University Press, 1959), 1:23–24]). Biographical information about Balbastre can be found in Alexandre É. Choron and François J. M. Fayolle, *Dictionnaire historique des musiciens, artistes et amateurs*, 2 vols. (Paris: Valode, 1810–1811), 1:46.

[16] Nicolas Gorenstein has recently evaluated this account (Nicolas Gorenstein, *L'Orgue postclassique français: du Concert Spirituel à Cavaillé-Coll* [Paris: Chanvrelin, 1993], 46). Some

organists in France did, by most reports, help save endangered instruments in their churches by playing the *Marseillaise* or some other popular patriotic tune on these organs (see Sabatier, "Musique et Vandalisme," 54, and also Frédéric Robert, "Les Organistes face à La Marseillaise," *L'Orgue*, no. 209 [1989]: 2).

[17] Choron and Fayolle, *Dictionnaire historique*, 1:132.

[18] Ibid.

[19] Georges Servières, *Documents inédits sur les organistes français des XVIIe et XVIIIe siècles* (Paris: Au Bureau d'édition de la Schola Cantorum, 1922), 22–23.

[20] Pierre Hardouin, "Quelques Documents relatifs aux Couperin," *Revue de musicologie* 37 (1955): 18, 20.

[21] Choron and Fayolle, *Dictionnaire historique*, 1:162.

[22] Charles Bouvet, *Les Couperin, organistes de l'église Saint-Gervais* (Paris: Delagrave, 1919), 174.

[23] Servières, *Documents inédits*, 31.

[24] Guillaume Lasceux, avant-propos to *Essai théorique et pratique sur l'art de l'orgue* (Bibliothèque Nationale, MS 2249); cited in Norbert Dufourcq, "L'Orgue français dans la première moitié du XIXe siècle," *L'Orgue*, no. 194 (1985): 10.

[25] Choron and Fayolle, *Dictionnaire historique*, 2:310.

[26] Servières, *Documents inédits*, 39.

[27] Constant Pierre, *Le Conservatoire National de musique et de déclamation* (Paris: Imprimerie Nationale, 1900), 581. See also Norbert Dufourcq, "L'Enseignement de l'orgue au Conservatoire National avant la nomination de César Franck (1872)," *L'Orgue*, no. 144 (1972): 121–25. For a recent and informative summary of Séjan's career, see Jean-Luc Perrot, "Les Titulaires du grand-orgue Clicquot: Nicolas Séjan," in *Le Grand-Orgue de Saint-Sulpice et ses organistes*, ed. Kurt Lueders, *La Flûte harmonique*, numéro spécial 59/60 (1991): 31–37.

[28] Georges Favre, "Les Créateurs de l'école française de piano: Nicolas Séjan," *Revue de musicologie* 20 (1936): 71–72.

[29] Choron and Fayolle, *Dictionnaire historique*, 2:310.

[30] Favre, "Les Créateurs: Nicolas Séjan," 70.

[31] Jean-Louis Adam, *Méthode de piano du Conservatoire* (Paris: L. Marchand, 1804); cited in Mongrédien, *La Musique en France*, 294.

[32] De Place, *La Vie musicale en France*, 28.

[33] Servières, *Documents inédits*, 33.

[34] Emmet Kennedy argues that the culture of the Revolution was in no small measure indebted to the legacy of past generations, holding up for examination monuments, libraries, and collections of art in the Louvre (*A Cultural History of the French Revolution* [New Haven: Yale University Press, 1989], 231).

[35] The Fugue is found in Claude-Bénigne Balbastre, *Pièces de clavecin, d'orgue, de fortepiano*, ed. Alan Curtis (Paris: Heugel, 1974), 1–3.

[36] See Guillaume Lasceux's *Douze Fugues pour l'orgue* (Bibliothèque Nationale, MS 2250) and Jean-Jacques Beauvarlet-Charpentier's *Six Fugues pour l'orgue ou le clavecin*, op. 6 (Paris: Le Duc, [ca. 1784]) and *Six Fugues pour l'orgue*, from his *Journal d'orgue à l'usage des pariosses et communautés religieuses* (Paris: Le Duc, [1784–1785]).

[37] The piece may be found in *Les Maîtres français de l'orgue aux XVIIème et XVIIIème siècles*, ed. Félix Raugel, 2 vols. (Paris: Éditions musicales de la Schola Cantorum, 1949), 2:82–84, which also includes the Fugue in G Minor. See also the subject of the Fugue in D Major, reprinted in David Fuller, "Zenith and Nadir: the Organ Versus its Music in Late 18th Century France," in *L'Orgue à notre époque* (Montréal: McGill University, 1982), 128.

[38] Beauvarlet-Charpentier, *Six Fugues pour l'orgue ou le clavecin*, 12.

[39] The Fugue in E Minor is found in *Les Maîtres français*, 2:89–90. The Fugue in D Minor was printed in *Les Maîtres français*, 1:93–94.

[40] Séjan's fugue was included in *Les Maîtres français*, 2:85–88.

[41] Adélaïde de Place, *Le Piano-forte à Paris entre 1760 et 1822* (Paris: Aux Amateurs de livres, 1986), 65. See the section of Adam's *Méthode de piano* entitled "Fugues de plusieurs auteurs."

[42] Henri Vanhulst, "La Musique du passé et la création du Conservatoire de Paris: sa présence dans les premières méthodes," *Revue belge de musicologie* 26–27 (1972–73): 55.

[43] See Norbert Dufourcq, "Nicolas Lebègue: un précurseur?," in *Noëls variés de Nicolas*

Lebègue 1631–1702, ed. Norbert Dufourcq (Paris: Éditions musicales de la Schola Cantorum, 1952).

[44] The registrational scheme calls for mm. 1–16 on the Positif, mm. 17–41 on the Grand-Orgue, mm. 41–64 on the *Petit Jeu*, and mm. 65–88 on the *Grand Jeu*.

[45] For a discussion of the noëls of Pierre and Jean-François Dandrieu, see Gwilym Beechey, "The Organ Music of Jean-François Dandrieu (1682–1738)," *The American Organist* 24 (January 1990): 67–70. See also Norbert Dufourcq's preface to Pierre Dandrieu, *Livre de noëls variés pour orgue*, ed. Roger Hugon (Paris: Heugel, 1979).

[46] In some cases the spelling of the noël titles follows that given in the sources.

[47] For an up-to-date edition of these pieces, see Michel Corrette, *Nouveau Livre de noëls*, ed. Gwilym Beechey (Madison: A-R Editions, 1974).

[48] For a widely available edition of these noels, see Claude Balbastre, *Noels: Christmas Music for the Organ* (Melville, N.Y.: Belwin Mills, n.d.).

[49] Jean-Jacques Beauvarlet-Charpentier, *Douze Noëls variés pour l'orgue, avec un carillon des morts*, op. 13 (n.d.; reprint as *Noëls & Magnificats pour l'orgue*, ed. Giuseppe Scarpat, vol. 21 of Biblioteca classica dell'organista [Brescia: Paideia, 1984]).

[50] Lasceux's *Noël lorrain* was published in *Les Maîtres français*, 2:91–92.

[51] André Pirro, "L'Art des organistes," in *Physiologie vocale et auditive, technique vocale et instrumentale (voix—instruments à réservoir d'air)*, part 2, vol. 2 of *Encyclopédie de la musique et dictionnaire du Conservatoire*, ed. Albert Lavignac and Lionel de la Laurencie, (Paris: Delagrave, 1925), 1349.

[52] This widely quoted statement (attributed to Louis Sébastien Mercier, *Tableau de Paris*, 12 vols. [Amsterdam, 1782], 2:80–81), was printed in Pirro, "L'Art des organistes," 1349.

[53] This statement (from Mercier, *Tableau de Paris*, 2:78) was printed in Pirro, "L'Art des organistes," 1362.

[54] Pirro discusses this piece with reference to a copy housed at that time at the Bibliothèque de l'Université de Paris, "Fonds Guilmant" ("L'Art des organistes," 1363–64).

[55] Michel Corrette, *Pièces pour l'orgue dans un genre nouveau* (Paris, 1787), 16–17. Pirro discusses this method of creating thunder at the organ with reference to Corrette's instructions ("L'Art des organistes, 1363).

[56] Pirro, "L'Art des organistes," 1349.

[57] Norbert Dufourcq, *La Musique d'orgue française de Jehan Titelouze à Jehan Alain* (Paris: Floury, 1949), 121.

[58] Lasceux, *Essai théorique et pratique*, 37. For a recent publication of excerpts from Lasceux's Te Deum, see *De Louis Couperin à Guillaume Lasceux: douze œuvres françaises pour orgue publiées pour la première fois*, ed. Jean-Paul Lécot (Geneva: Slatkine, 1986).

[59] Lasceux, *Essai théorique et pratique*, 39.

[60] Pirro, "L'Art des organistes," 1364.

[61] Ibid.

[62] Pirro, in "L'Art des organistes," 1362–63, discusses Corrette's instructions. See Dufourcq, *La Musique d'orgue française*, 123, for the account of Broche's performance.

[63] Yves Jaffres, "Michel Corrette et la révolution française," in *Le Tambour et La Harpe*, ed. Jean-Rémy Julien and Jean Mongrédien (Paris: Du May, 1991), 271.

Organ Music in the Mass of the Parisian Rite to 1850 with Emphasis on the Contributions of Boëly

BENJAMIN VAN WYE

The unique liturgico-musical uses that flourished within the French Church during the eighteenth and early nineteenth centuries constitute one of the most fascinating chapters in the history of France's independence from Rome in ecclesiastical matters. Gallicanism—as this autonomy was known—stood central among the policies of Louis XIV, whose position regarding the Church was codified in a series of articles formulated by the University of Paris theological faculty in the 1660s, granting the King temporal rule over the Church of France and declaring her customs inviolable, even by the Pope. These *articles gallicans* were adopted by the Assembly of the Clergy in 1682 and remained in effect during the next 150 years.[1] Under them French bishops exercised exclusive control over the liturgy within their jurisdictions. Certain of the bishops remained faithful to Rome's monument of liturgical uniformity, the Pian missal and breviary published respectively in 1568 and 1570. Other bishops created between 1667 and 1840 the new diocesan liturgies that have come to be known as "Neo-Gallican."[2]

Valuable details about Neo-Gallican Rites are found scattered among a French cleric's descriptions of services at major French churches during the first decade of the eighteenth century. One regrets, however, that this travel diary, published in 1718 as *Voyages liturgiques de France*,[3] rarely mentions Neo-Gallican liturgical music, which at that time was admittedly in its incipient stage. Even in its fully developed form the distinctive repertoire of music adapted, improvised, and composed for the new French liturgies between the middle of the eighteenth century and the middle of the nineteenth has suffered neglect from contemporary and more recent writers. An important step toward remedying the situation was taken by the editors of *The New Grove*, who included there several articles on the subject.[4] But even *The New Grove* stops short of discussing the substantial and, for its time, unique part the organ often shared with voices in the performance of Neo-

Gallican liturgical music. This essay seeks to redress to some degree that neglect by exploring the instrument's participation in the mass of the Parisian Rite, the only Neo-Gallican liturgy for which organ music has come to light. This Rite remains the most important of the numerous new liturgies created in the heyday of Gallicanism, by virtue of its widespread use and influence beyond the diocese of Paris and owing to its use at ecclesiastical institutions employing the country's foremost organists.

In the mass of the Parisian Rite the organ was permitted to alternate with voices for the Ordinary (excepting the Credo but including the *Benedicamus* and, when appropriate, the *Domine salvum*), Prose, and Alleluia, and to play during the offertory and elevation. Permission to do so is granted in the *Caeremoniale Parisiense* in its first edition of 1662, which also stipulates that certain *alternatim* versets must incorporate the chant they replace.[5] The Roman *Caeremonial Episcoporum*, issued in 1600, does not mention cantus-firmus versets but is in other respects quite similar to its French counterpart with regard to the organ. Differences between Parisian and Roman use of the organ are therefore musical rather than functional, and they concern cantus-firmus versets. But they are also largely academic, since by the late eighteenth century, when the Parisian liturgy spread to several other French dioceses, *alternatim* use of the organ was no longer common outside France.

The Neo-Gallican Rite of the Church of Paris originated with liturgical reforms initiated in the 1670s by Archbishop François de Harlay; with the Paris breviary and missal of his successor Charles de Vintmille, published respectively in 1736 and 1738, this leading diocesan Rite assumed the form it was to retain until the Ultramontane movement replaced it and other diocesan liturgies with the Roman Rite during the middle of the nineteenth century. The task of compiling chant books for the Vintmille liturgy fell to the Abbé Lebeuf, canon of Auxerre and the foremost French musicologist of the time. His Paris Antiphoner (1737) and Paris Gradual (1738) contain a repertoire of new and traditional chants that remained the foundation of successive editions, the last appearing respectively in 1829 and 1846.[6]

The traditional chants that Lebeuf retained in greatest quantity and with least alteration are those of the mass Ordinary, even though most of them differ from Roman use in form, grouping, and classification. Chants forming cycles for the six highest ranking types of feasts appear as cantus firmi in Parisian organ masses and have therefore been listed (with a Vatican equivalent for each, where one exists) in Figure 1.

Missa cunctipotens was prescribed by the Paris *Directorium chori* of 1656 to be sung "whenever the organ is played" and is virtually the only plainchant Ordinary to appear in organ masses by Louisquatorzian composers.[7] But between 1750 and 1850, *Cunctipotens* is merely one of several mass cycles used in Parisian Rite organ masses. Moreover, on high ranking feasts it was sometimes replaced by the *Messe du premier ton* by the Parisian organist

Figure 1

Plainchant Mass Ordinaries According to Parisian Use

Classification in Paris Gradual	Vatican Edition Equivalent[a]
Pour les Annuels et Solennels-Majeurs (*or* Grands Solennels)	
Kyrie, Gloria, Sanctus, and Agnus	Mass IV (*Cunctipotens*)
Pour les Solennels-Mineurs (*or* Petits Solennels)	
Kyrie and Sanctus	Mass VIII (*De Angelis*)
Gloria	Based on Kyrie and Gloria of Mass VIII
Agnus	Based on Sanctus of Mass VIII[b]
Pour les Doubles-Majeurs	
Kyrie and Agnus[c]	Mass II (*Fons bonitatis*)
Gloria	Mass IX (*Cum jubilo*)
Sanctus	Mass XVII
Pour les Doubles-Mineurs	
Kyrie and Gloria	Mass XIV (*Jesu Redemptor*)
Sanctus	Mass XI (*Orbis factor*)
Agnus	Mass XVII
Pour les Dimanches et les Semi-Doubles	
Kyrie and Gloria	Mass XI (*Orbis factor*)
Sanctus and Agnus	Mass XV (*Dominator Deus*)

---

[a] Based in part on Amédée Gastoué, *Musique et Liturgie* (Lyon: Janin frères, 1913), 205–06.

[b] See Example 2.

[c] The second invocation of the Agnus does not correspond to the version given in the Vatican edition.

Henri Dumont (1610–1684), which however the Paris Gradual does not designate for feasts of a particular classification.[8] Dumont's setting, the first of his *Cinq Messes en plein-chant* (1699) and known variously as *Messe du Dumont* or *Messe Royale*, is an early example of a kind of Neo-Gallican chant called *plainchant musical*, which blends elements of traditional chant with those of modern melody and thus contains note values of varying duration and a more tonal orientation than its Gregorian ancestors (see Plate 1).[9]

The mass repertoire with which the organ alternated in Parisian use, then, was not limited to that of the Paris Gradual (the melodies found there did not carry the legislative force attaching to the texts in its companion missal). For example, throughout the eighteenth century religious orders—especially those bound by statute to chant the liturgy themselves and to do so with considerable frequency—preferred *plainchant musical* settings over traditional plainsong ones because of the former's greater simplicity and more modern musical style.[10] Indeed, the popularity and consequent profusion of such settings during the 1700s appear to have discouraged the printing of organ masses patterned after seventeenth-century examples such as those by Guillaume-Gabriel Nivers, Nicolas de Grigny, and François Couperin, with their versets designated to alternate with (and, in the case of cantus-firmus ones, based upon) specific chants. Instead, most French liturgical organ music published in the eighteenth century follows the plan of the ritually neutral *suite*, offering free versets of contrasting character and registration, grouped in sets unified—like the *plainchant musical* masses they often alternated with—by a single tonality (*ton*).

When supplying cantus-firmus versets many organists doubtless improvised from a manuscript organbook into which relevant portions of their church's chant repertoire had been copied, often by successive incumbents. Although books of this kind had existed long before the eighteenth century, their usefulness and prevalence increased under Parisian use, with its wider variety of chants upon which organists were expected to improvise. Among the holdings of the Bibliothèque Nationale is a volume of late eighteenth-century provenance—the so-called Méreaux Organbook—that contains a complete repertoire of Parisian Rite chants for *alternatim* versets.[11] It opens with seven mass Ordinaries drawn from the Paris Gradual, including the five described in Figure 1, each of them represented by plainchants for the first and last Kyries and Christe, all nine odd-numbered verses of the Gloria, the first Sanctus, and the first Agnus. The number of plainsong-based versets suggested by these cantus firmi exceeds that established by the *Caeremoniale Parisiense* and Louisquatorzian organ masses. In fact, free versets are implied only for the second and fourth Kyries, second Sanctus, and second Agnus; and one could reasonably argue that the second Kyrie and Agnus versets were meant to be improvised on the chant of the first, with which each is always identical.

Collections like the Méreaux Organbook, in their explicit and comprehensive content, yield valuable information about ritual use of the organ at a time when the plainsong-based piece was not a favored compositional genre. Further proof of French organists' reliance upon improvisation to supply cantus-firmus versets for the Parisian chant repertoire during its more than one hundred years of existence is offered by the paucity of organ works based on its chants. Masses from that modest corpus, summarized in Figure 2, are all the work of Parisian organists—Michel Corrette, Jean-Jacques and Jacques-Marie Beauvarlet-Charpentier, Guillaume Lasceux, Alexandre-Pierre-François Boëly, Jacques-Claude-Adolphe Miné, and Alexandre-Charles Fessy—who, with the exception of Boëly, addressed themselves to performers of limited ability who played at small or perhaps provincial churches.[12] In doing so they provided brief and simple pieces not requiring pedals and drew the cantus firmi of plainchant versets from the most common liturgical use of the time, that of the Church of Paris. The Rite followed by institutions that employed these composers, however, is irrelevant since these organists would have improvised their own service music.[13]

Each of the collections listed in Figure 2 contains *alternatim* versets for mass Ordinaries from the Paris Gradual. But although their variety of cantus firmi sets Parisian Rite organ masses apart from those by Louisquatorzian composers, the feasts for which most of them were intended—*annuels, solennels,* and *doubles-majeurs*—are nearly identical to those for which ritual use of the organ had been prescribed and organists contracted during the late seventeenth and early eighteenth centuries. The *annuels* included Christmas and Easter Day, Epiphany, Ascension, Pentecost, Corpus Christi, Assumption, All Saints, and an Anniversary Feast of Dedication. Under the next heading, *solennels-majeurs*, were observed the Virgin's Purification, Annunciation, and Nativity, Saints Peter and Paul, and Saint Denis and Companions. Classified as *solennels-mineurs* were the Christmas midnight and dawn masses, Circumcision, Holy Trinity, and such major saints as Stephen, Geneviève, Joseph, John the Baptist, Louis King of France, and Michael and All Angels. The greatest number of observances belong to the category of *doubles-majeurs*, which includes the apostles and evangelists, Holy Innocents, Easter Monday and Tuesday, First Sunday after Easter (Quasimodo), Pentecost Monday and Tuesday, Visitation, Transfiguration, and Holy Cross Day. Several feasts of solemn rank were accorded the dignity of an octave, and those falling outside Advent, Christmastide, Lent, and Eastertide could therefore be celebrated again with music on the following Sunday.

Most organ masses for annual and solemn feasts listed in Figure 2 preserve the format established by Louisquatorzian composers, whereby a few plainsong-based versets are interspersed among others that are freely composed. But whereas their predecessors, conforming for the most part to the *Caeremoniale Parisiense*, had provided cantus-firmus pieces for only the initial (and, in the case of the Gloria, eleventh) verses for each of the four Ordinary chants performed *alternatim*, several composers of the Parisian Rite organ masses did so for the Gloria verses *Benedicimus* and *Glorificamus* as well. These additional plainsong-based versets appear in Lasceux's three masses for solemn feasts, Boëly's two solemn masses, and the three solemn masses of Fessy and Miné's *Guide* as well as that of Fessy's *Office complet*. Other masses of Figure 2 depart even further from their forerunners by offering complete sets of versets of which all are *plainchant en basse* settings. Although this austerity is sometimes limited to masses for feasts of double or lower classification (as in Fessy and Miné's *Guide*), it prevails almost entirely in all four of Corrette's masses. And by limiting their content exclusively to *plainchant en basse* versets in a drastically simplified form Miné's *Manuel* and Fessy's *Proprium* were doubtless trying to accommodate France's large population of church organists of modest musical skill.

Figure 2

Liturgically Designated Organ Masses for the Parisian Rite

Composer and Collection[a]	Cantus Firmus According to Rank of Feast[b]
Michel Corrette (1709–1795) *Troisième Livre d'orgue* [1756]	*solennels-majeurs, solennels-mineurs,*[c] *doubles-majeurs,* and *double-mineurs*
Jean-Jacques Beauvarlet-Charpentier (1734–1794) *Journal d'orgue à l'usage des paroisses et communautés religieuses,* 12 *livraisons* (ca. 1780)	[*annuels* and *solennels-majeurs*] (fourth *livraison*); [*annuels* and *solennels-majeurs?*] (*Messe royale de Dumont,* sixth *livraison*)

Guillaume Lasceux (1740–1831)
  Nouvelle Suite de pièces d'orgue
  (ca. 1810)   *annuels* and *solennels-majeurs*
  Annuaire de l'organiste [1819],
  Bibliothèque Nationale, MS 2248[d]   [*annuels* and *solennels-majeurs?*] (*Messe de Dumont*), *solennels-majeurs*, *solennels-mineurs*, and *doubles-majeurs* (lacks Gloria)

Jacques-Marie Beauvarlet-
Charpentier (1766–1834)
  *Trois Messes pour les grandes
  solemnités* (after 1814)   *annuels* (*Messe de Dumont*), *solennels-majeurs*, and *solennels-mineurs*

Alexandre-Pierre-François Boëly
(1785–1858)
  Versailles, Bibliothèque
  Municipale, MS 169
  (1834–1848)   [*annuels* and *solennels-majeurs*] (two settings for Kyrie and Gloria only), *solennels-majeurs* (*Messe de Dumont*), *solennels-mineurs*, *doubles-majeurs*, and *doubles-mineurs*
  Messe du jour de Noël, 1842[e]   *annuels* and *solennels-majeurs*
  *Collection des œuvres
  posthumes pour orgue
  ou piano*, ops. 35–45 (1860)   [*solennels-majeurs*] (fragments of three settings)

Jacques-Claude-Adolphe Miné
(1796–1854)
  *Manuel simplifié de
  l'organiste* (ca. 1837)   [*annuels* and *solennels-majeurs?*] (*Messe de Dumont*), *annuels* and *solennels-majeurs*, *solennels-mineurs*, *doubles-majeurs*, *doubles-mineurs*, and *dimanches et semi-doubles*[f]

Alexandre-Charles Fessy (1804–
1856) and J.-C.-A. Miné
  Le Guide de l'organiste, 12
    livraisons [1839]ᵉ

[*annuels* and *solennels-majeurs*] (*Messe
Royale de Dumont*),ᵍ *annuels* and *solennels-
majeurs*, *solennels-mineurs*, *doubles-
majeurs*, and *doubles-mineurs*

A.-C. Fessy
  Office complet de l'année (1844)ʰ

[*annuels* and *solennels-majeurs?*] (*Messe de
Dumont*), *annuels* and *solennels-majeurs*,
solennels-mineurs

  Propium de tempore (1845)ʰ

[*annuels* and *solennels-majeurs?*] (*Messe de
Dumont*), *solennels-mineurs*, *doubles-
majeurs*, *doubles-mineurs*, and
*dimanches et semi-doubles*ᶠ

ᵃ The place of publication for all printed works is Paris.

ᵇ The mass Ordinary appointed by the Paris Gradual for each classification of feast is given in Figure 1.

ᶜ Instead of providing a Gloria this setting contains a rubric directing "Le Gloria comme aux Festes solemnels."

ᵈ Although it is not known whether the *Annuaire* was intended for publication, the title page describes it as "ouvrage utile à ceux qui se destinent à toucher l'orgue."

ᵉ Boëly's Christmas Mass is preceded chronologically by a *Messe pour le tems* [*sic*] *de Noël* in Fessy and Miné's *Guide*. Based as they are on French noëls, the free versets of both organ masses—the earliest examples of their kind—suggest that organ noëls in eighteenth-century collections may have served a similar ritual function. It should also be noted that Boëly designates *Missa cunctipotens* as the cantus firmus for his Christmas Mass, while Fessy and Miné assign this function to the *Messe Royale de Dumont*.

ᶠ These two collections also contain versets for Kyries appointed by the Paris Gradual for use (with remaining chants drawn from full cycles) on Sundays in Advent, Lent, and within the octaves of feasts of *annuel* classification.

ᵍ Includes cantus-firmus versets for optional *alternatim* performance of the Credo.

ʰ These two collections also contain versets for a mass Ordinary chanted at the vigils of Easter and Pentecost.

The free versets of the Parisian organ masses continue the registrational variety of their forerunners with such classic combinations as *Fonds d'orgue, Plein Jeu, Grand Jeu, Récit de Cromorne* (or Nasard, or Voix humaine), and *Flûtes*. Yet stylistically these pieces bear but faint resemblance to their predecessors. Excepting the second Kyrie—which continues to be fugal (often quoting the plainchant in *Cunctipotens* settings)—they are shaped by the spirit and technique of contemporary harpsichord or piano music, even to the point of lacking a pedal part altogether. Indeed, throughout the period during which the Parisian Rite was in use, many organ posts in France's capital city, including those at major ecclesiastical institutions, were held by *clavecinistes* and pianists who transferred their repertoire—stylistically and probably even literally—to the organ. Thus, while noting that Armand-Louis Couperin's versets at Saint-Gervais on the eve of the church's Feast of Dedication in 1770 resembled the playing of his illustrious uncle, Charles Burney added:

> Great latitude is allowed in the performance of these interludes [versets]; nothing is too light or too grave, all styles are admitted; and though M. Couperin has the true organ touch, smooth and connected; yet he often tried, and not unsuccessfully, mere harpsichord passages, smartly articulated, and the notes detached and separated.[14]

But by the early decades of the nineteenth century an idiomatic technique of organ playing had almost entirely ceased to exist in France owing to the serious blows the Revolution had dealt institutions where the art of the organ had been demonstrated and taught to young musicians for several centuries, for the choir schools were discontinued and major churches closed under the Terror. These conditions prompted Lasceux to write his *Essai théorique et pratique sur l'art de l'orgue* of 1809, wherein he offers organ students the following advice concerning service playing:

> [The organ] controls and orders the pious concerts with which the Sacred Vaults echo; and by giving the choir a rest, permits the Religious Assembly time for meditation, while by its melodiousness and the location assigned to it in church buildings, it seems intended to raise to the Most High and to render more worthy of him the prayers his creatures address to him; neither an insignificant and ridiculous piano piece on this great instrument, nor secular style melodies can express the pious outpourings of souls that humble themselves before the Supreme Being. Everything in the Holy Place must be grand, noble, and majestic. Lastly, it is to make the Service dignified that the Chants [versets] of the Organ should be appropriate to the words that are entrusted to the piety and talent of the Organist.[15]

Throughout the first half of the century this advice appears to have gone unheeded, even by its author (as indicated at least by his own compositions), so that as late as 1856 François-Joseph Fétis could complain that:

> None of [the French organists] has had what one might call the *education of the organist*. They are acquainted with neither manual . . . nor pedal technique.

. . . All their attention is focused upon the instrument's effects, contrasting sonorities, combination of stops and manuals, and the means of satisfying sensual instincts. Nor is it this way only today: Marchand, Clérambault, Calvière, Daquin, Balbâtre, [Jean-Jacques Beauvarlet-] Charpentier, were like this. One finds distinguished organists in France only in the seventeenth century: [François] Couperin was the last.[16]

Although in agreement with much of Fétis's assessment, a Parisian organist and priest writing under the pseudonym Théodore Nisard argued that a worthy successor to the great Couperin *had* emerged in Boëly.[17] The masses by this composer itemized in Figure 2 represent a significant portion of his total output for the organ—the most voluminous *œuvre d'orgue* that had been written in France, as Dufourcq observed—and go some way toward justifying Nisard's claim, even though some would argue that they contain more craftsmanship than imagination. Figure 3 summarizes Boëly's organ masses, written in the 1830s and 40s, with reference to their sources and their location in the most recent and accessible edition, that of Norbert Dufourcq and Amédée Gastoué (to which references in the following discussion refer).[18]

Figure 3

Organ Masses of Alexandre-Pierre-François Boëly

Title and Source[a]	Cantus Firmus According to Rank of Feast[b] and Items of Mass Ordinary[c]
[Messe solennel], 1834	*annuels* and *solennels-majeurs* Kyrie (Dufourcq and Gastoué, pp. 4–9) Gloria (Dufourcq and Gastoué, pp. 10–12,[d] 14–15[e])
Messe solennel . . . extraite de plusieurs auteurs anciens, [1836[f]]	*annuels* and *solennels-majeurs* Kyrie (Dufourcq and Gastoué, p. 43)[g] Gloria (Dufourcq and Gastoué, pp. 50, 51)[h]

28

Messe No. 1, 1836? (*Œuvres posthumes*)[i]

annuels and *solennels-majeurs*
Kyrie (Dufourcq and Gastoué, pp. 22–29)
Agnus (Dufourcq and Gastoué, p. 19)
Deo gratias (Dufourcq and Gastoué, p. 20)

Messe No. 2, 1836? (*Œuvres posthumes*)[i]

annuels and *solennels-majeurs*
Kyrie (Dufourcq and Gastoué, pp. 29, 38)
Gloria (Dufourcq and Gastoué, p. 11: *Et in terra*)

Messe No. 3, 1836? (*Œuvres posthumes*)[i]

annuels and *solennels-majeurs*
Kyrie (Dufourcq and Gastoué, pp. 39–42)
Gloria (Dufourcq and Gastoué, pp. 13, 18)

Messe du jour de Noël, 1842[j]

annuels and *solennels-majeurs*
Kyrie[k]
Gloria
Sanctus
Agnus

Messe de Dumont pour les grands solennels, 1848

Messe du premier ton[l]
Kyrie (Dufourcq and Gastoué, p. 62)[m]
Gloria (Dufourcq and Gastoué, pp. 62–63)[n]
Sanctus (Dufourcq and Gastoué, p. 63)
Agnus (Dufourcq and Gastoué, p. 63)

Messe des annuels, 1848

annuels and *solennels-majeurs*
Kyrie (Dufourcq and Gastoué, p. 64)[o]
Gloria (Dufourcq and Gastoué, pp. 64–65)[n]
Sanctus (Dufourcq and Gastoué, p. 65)[p]
Agnus (Dufourcq and Gastoué, p. 65)[q]

Messe des solennels-mineurs, 1848

solennels-mineurs
Kyrie (Dufourcq and Gastoué, p. 66)[o]
Gloria (Dufourcq and Gastoué, p. 67)
Sanctus (Dufourcq and Gastoué, p. 68)
Agnus (Dufourcq and Gastoué, p. 68)

Messe des doubles-majeurs, 1848,
Versailles, Bibliothèque Municipale,
MS 192bis   *doubles-majeurs*
                                           Kyrie (Dufourcq and Gastoué, pp. 69–70)
                                           Gloria (Dufourcq and Gastoué, pp. 70–73)
                                           Sanctus (Dufourcq and Gastoué, p. 73)
                                           Agnus (Dufourcq and Gastoué, p. 74)[r]

[Messe pour les doubles-mineurs,
1848?]][s]   *doubles-mineurs*
                                           Gloria[t]
                                           Sanctus
                                           Agnus

------

[a] Unless otherwise indicated, the source is Versailles, Bibliothèque Municipale, MS 169.

[b] See Figure 1 for identification of mass Ordinary chants that correspond to individual classifications of feasts.

[c] Numbers in parentheses refer to pages in A. P. F. Boëly, *Pièces d'orgue pour le service liturgique*, ed. Norbert Dufourcq and Amédée Gastoué, vol. 2 of *Œuvres complètes pour orgue* (1958; reprint as *Liturgical Service for the Organ*, in *Kalmus Organ Series* [Melville, N. Y., Belwin Mills, n.d.]).

[d] In its original version this Mass does not include the additional *Et in terra pax* versets (A and B) that appear in Dufourcq and Gastoué, pp. 10–11.

[e] As it appears in MS 169 this Mass only includes versets for Kyrie and Gloria (the latter lacking its last three). Dufourcq and Gastoué supply additional versets from other sources.

[f] Date proposed by Dufourcq and Gastoué.

[g] The remaining versets are by Kirnberger (*Kyrie 3*), Padre Martini (*Christe*), J. S. Bach (*Kyrie 4*), and Handel (*Dernier Kyrie*). Dufourcq and Gastoué, pp. 43–49, replace these with versets from *Œuvres posthumes* (see note i below).

[h] The remaining versets are by Handel (*Glorificamus te* and *Domine Deus, Rex coelestis*), F. Couperin (*Domine Deus, Agnus Dei*), L. Couperin (*Quoniam tu solus*), and J. S. Bach (*Tu solus Altissimus*).

[i] *Collection des œuvres posthumes pour l'orgue* (Paris, 1860).

[j] The complete title reads: *Messe du jour de Noël pour l'orgue, composée sur des airs populaires anciens dits noëls et suivant les tons du chant des grand solennels à l'usage de Paris, Œuvre 11* (Paris, 1842; reprint, ed. Ewald Kooiman, vol. 16 of *Incognita Organo* [Hilversum, Holland: Harmonia, 1981]).

[k] In the original edition the *Christe* verset is mis-labeled "2e. KYRIE," an error repeated by Kooiman in the 1981 edition.

[l] See note 7 above.

[m] Followed in MS 169 by an itemization of the four remaining versets (the second designated "fugue"), which Boëly would presumably have supplied from another source.

[n] In MS 169 the *Et in terra pax* verset is followed by an itemization of the next four versets, and the *Qui tollis* by a note that specifies the final three.

[o] Followed in MS 169 by an itemization of the four remaining versets.

[p] Followed in MS 169 by the notation "2[nd Sanctus] fonds."

[q] Followed in MS 169 by the notation "2 dernier Agnus."

[r] Followed in MS 192bis by the notation "on répète le même au dernier Agnus."

[s] Owing perhaps to its relatively low classification, this setting is unique among Boëly's masses in consisting simply of the liturgical melody in the soprano and underneath it a note-against-note figured bass.

[t] The opening pages of this mass—which presumably included versets for Kyrie and *Et in terra pax*—are missing from MS 169.

30

Whether or not one shares Nisard's high opinion of Boëly, he was in one sense quite uncontestably a successor to Couperin, albeit a distant one, by his appointment as deputy and interim organist at Saint-Gervais in the 1830s. Indeed, it was doubtless for the Parisian parish's splendid Clicquot organ—one that had been presided over by members of the Couperin family in unbroken succession from 1685 to 1825—that Boëly composed the earliest of his masses. Intended for feasts of the highest rank, these sets of free and cantus-firmus versets for use with *Missa cunctipotens* reveal the composer's knowledge and appreciation of the *Messe solennelle* left by his famous predecessor.[19] The well-known Fugue on the Kyrie from that work provided Boëly with a model for the analogous verset of his posthumously published *Messe No. 3 en ut mineur*. And in the *Messe No. 1* of the same collection he may have been paying Couperin further hommage by setting the *Christe eleison* as a *Tierce en taille* (Dufourcq and Gastoué, pp. 24–25), a genre ignored by the other composers of Figure 2, probably because of its obbligato pedal part. Other free versets in Boëly's masses of the 1830s show the composer creating idiomatic organ works from stylistic elements of Baroque harpsichord music (Dufourcq and Gastoué, pp. 4–5, 7–8, 26–27, and 40–41) and classic piano literature (pp. 8–9, 12, 14–15, 16–18, 22–23, 28–29, 42, and 59).

Further evidence of Boëly's ability to recapture for French liturgical organ music the integrity it had enjoyed during the late seventeenth century may be found in the cantus-firmus versets from these masses of the 1830s. His handling of that genre is best appreciated when set against examples by other composers listed in Figure 2: the *plainchant en basse* verset of Parisian Rite organ masses, save those of Boëly, corresponds to its Louisquatorzian counterpart in little more than registration and layout (the liturgical melody assigned to the bass voice and sounded on a pedal or manual reed registration against upper voices played on a *Plein Jeu*).

By sounding a *plainchant en basse* verset from its position at the rear or side of the nave the French church organ faithfully echoed the low-pitched, slow, and rhythmically monotonous chant bellowed from the lectern in the chancel by a "choir" that typically consisted of two or four deep male voices doubled by a serpent, ophicleide, or double bass. Furthermore, the aimlessly meandering counterpoint above a cantus firmus in the pedal-less versets of Corrette, Lasceux, and Fessy are nothing more than instrumental counterparts of the two-voice polyphony that choir singers—using a technique known as *chant sur le livre*—improvised over deep-voice intontations of the introit, alleluia, offertory, and communion chants at celebrations of the Parisian mass in major churches.[20] During the 1840s this improvised polyphony was replaced by composed settings (called "fauxbourdon" or "contre point") in four parts with cantus firmus in the tenor or by unison singing of plainsong at a comfortable pitch and accompanied by a choir organ. Nonetheless, the debased *plainchant en basse* style continued in vogue until the 1850s.[21]

None of Boëly's immediate predecessors or contemporaries was able to capture the Lullian gravity and majesty that characterizes so many late seventeenth-century cantus-firmus versets. If Jean-Jacques Beauvarlet-Charpentier retains the full and active texture of Couperin and de Grigny over long pedal notes, he shows none of those earlier composers' inventiveness and inspiration; Jacques-Marie Beauvarlet-Charpentier and Miné employ a cantus of shorter note values with minimal movement above it, clumsily harmonizing each note of a rhythmically lifeless chant with a triad or seventh chord, often in inversions (see Example 1). Perhaps it was this last kind of verset that had seemed "dull and heavy" to Burney in 1770 and "barbarous" to Ludwig Spohr in 1821.[22] Boëly's *plainchant en basse* versets, on the other hand, are fashioned after the harmonically and texturally rich *Plein Jeu* style of Couperin and de Grigny (Dufourcq and Gastoué, pp. 4, 10, 11, 15, and 19).

That this revival of the classical French style of plainchant verset was unusual for the time is indicated by an admiring account of Boëly's service playing published in 1856 (but certainly written at least a decade earlier). It likely reflects Boëly's practice during the years he held his most important organ post, at Saint-Germain-l'Auxerrois from 1840 to 1851:

> When M. Boëly gives out the intonation of a plainsong he places the melody in the bass as do all his colleagues, but faithful to sound traditions, he avoids playing above that melody the monotonous successions of sixths [inverted chords] which tire the most robust ear. Under his fingers the chant serves as a foundation for simple but magnificent combinations of fugal counterpoint.[23]

It was perhaps to accommodate the quite different style of plainchant verset cultivated by his colleagues that Boëly left a few of the usual versets to be

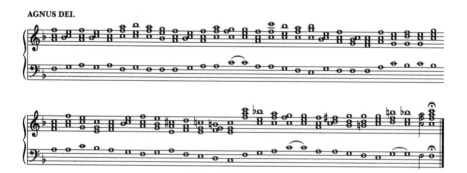

Example 1. J.-M. Beauvarlet-Charpentier, Agnus Dei verset from *Trois Messes pour les grandes solemnités*

Plate 1
Dumont, *Messe du premier ton* (Kyrie, Gloria, Sanctus, and Agnus Dei) as it appears in *Graduel de Paris* (1846 edition)

improvised by the performer in the *Messe du jour de Noël* of 1842, the only one of his organ masses to have been published during his lifetime: a *messe en noëls* (which provides noël-based versets for the traditional *alternatim* sections of the Parisian organ mass), it nonetheless gives only the appropriate excerpts of *Missa cunctipotens*, notated in unmeasured whole notes, for several of the movements.

During Boëly's tenure at Saint-Germain-l'Auxerrois, and in various collections from the 1840s, he sought new ways to revivify the traditional cantus firmus verset, making it compatible with the more melodic treatment of plainsong by the choir. In doing so he took J. S. Bach's chorale harmonizations as a model, placing the chants of the Paris Gradual in the treble and giving them a rhythmic shape and harmonization remarkably similar to Bach's treatment of Lutheran hymn tunes. Under the collective designation *Versets d'orgue en plain chant à 4 parties* Boëly set the first four ordinary cycles listed in Figure 1 in chorale style, offering five versets for each of the first three cycles and a complete set of fifteen for the fourth. In the original manuscript these four settings, dated 1848, are immediately preceded by a *Messe des doubles-mineurs*, which probably originated around the same time. In this mass the liturgical melody again appears in the soprano but is accompanied note-against-note by only a bass voice with occasional figures, the latter suggesting that when performing these versets Boëly improvised inner voices, thereby making them resemble the complete four-part settings that follow them.

Whether it was his departure from the French service playing norms of his undistinguished contemporaries or his adoption of those of his distinguished predecessors that caused Boëly to go largely unappreciated in his day is not entirely clear. Extinction of the Parisian Rite after the middle of the 1800s must have discouraged publication of his liturgical organ works, based as they are on that liturgy's unique musical uses. At the time of their composition and, presumably, performance at Saint-Germain-l'Auxerrois, Boëly's versets "dans le style de Bach" found no imitators. Indeed, these most innovative of his compositions for the Parisian mass went unnoticed until the close of the nineteenth century, when Alexandre Guilmant found in them inspiration and models for his attempt to create a repertoire of liturgical organ music based on the chants of the restored Roman Rite.

I would like to thank Craig Cramer and David Hyde Pierce for their assistance in locating materials for this essay.

NOTES

[1] See Aimé-Georges Martimort, *Le Gallicanisme* (Paris: Presses universitaires de France, 1973), 79–103.

[2] See Henri Leclercq, "Liturgies néo-gallicanes," in *Dictionnaire d'archéologie chrétienne et de liturgie,* ed. Fernand Cabrol and Henri Leclercq, 15 vols. (Paris: Letouzey et Ané, 1930), 9:1636–1729.

[3] Le Sieur de Moléon [Jean Baptiste Le Brun des Marettes], *Voyages liturgiques de France* (1718; reprint, Westmead, England: Gregg International, 1969).

[4] *The New Grove Dictionary of Music and Musicians,* s.v. Plainchant, IX; Plainchant musical; and Neo-Gallican chant.

[5] Chapter VI, "De organista et organis," appears in Norbert Dufourcq, *Miscellanea,* vol. 5 of *Le Livre de l'orgue français* (Paris: A. & J. Picard, 1982), 48–50. (This chapter does not appear in successive editions of the Parisian Ceremonial.)

[6] Concerning nineteenth-century chant books, see Amédée Gastoué, *Musique et Liturgie* (Lyon: Janin frères, 1913).

[7] *Directorium chori seu ceremoniale sanctae et metropolitanae ecclesiae ad diocesis Parisiensis* (Paris, 1656), 170.

[8] Versets for Dumont's Mass by J.-M. Beauvarlet-Charpentier and Boëly are designated respectively for feasts of *annuel* and *solennel-majeur* classification (see Figure 2). Even when lacking such designation, a Dumont setting is always placed first in sets of organ masses grouped according to level of feast.

[9] Dumont's Mass as printed in the Paris Gradual appears after the traditional plainchant cycles, whose modality and rhythmic equality it has been made to resemble by the removal of its leading-tone accidentals and mensuralist notation.

[10] Henri Quittard, *Henry Du Mont* (Paris: Société du Mercure de France, 1906), 178. See also Amédée Gastoué, *Les Messes Royales de Henry Du Mont* (Paris: Société d'éditions du chant grégorien, n.d.), 2.

[11] Cons. L. 16958. Formerly owned by the pianist Jean-Amédée Méreaux (1802–1875), the volume must have been used (and compiled?) by his grandfather Nicolas-Jean (1745–1797) after becoming organist at Saint-Sauveur, Paris, in 1769. (That parish's feast of title—the Transfiguration—is acccorded a rank of the highest level, *annuel,* and an exceptionally complete set of propers in the organbook.)

[12] Corrette served at the Église du Temple and later at the Église des Grands Jésuites. Like several other eighteenth-century Parisian organists, Jean-Jacques Beauvarlet-Charpentier held several posts at once: at the Royal Abbey of Saint-Victor as well as at Saint-Paul, Saint-Éloi des Orfèvres, and Notre-Dame. His son Jacques-Marie succeeded him at Saint-Paul before the Revolution and, after public worship was restored in 1802, held posts successively at Saint-Germain-l'Auxerrois, Saint-Germain-des-Prés, Saint-Eustache, Saint-Paul-Saint-Louis, and the Chapelle des Missions Étrangères. Lasceux's principal post was Saint-Étienne-du-Mont, where he served from 1769 until 1819, holding several additional posts in the last decades of the *ancien régime.* The three remaining composers of organ masses for the Parisian Rite worked in post-Revolutionary Paris: Miné at Saint-Roch, Fessy at Église de l'Assomption, and Boëly at Saint-Germain-l'Auxerrois.

[13] Norbert Dufourcq, in his edition of Michel Corrette's *Troisième Livre d'orgue* (Paris: Bornemann, 1984), augments the composer's title, *Messe solennel majeur,* with an editorial *à l'usage Romain et Parisien,* emphasizing in his preface (vol. 1, n. 7) that the Roman Rite was used at the Église du Temple during Corrette's sixty-year tenure there.

[14] Charles Burney, *The Present State of Music in France and Italy* (1771; reprint as *An Eighteenth-Century Musical Tour of France and Italy,* ed. Percy Scholes, 2 vols. [London: Oxford University Press, 1959], 1:26–27).

[15] Bibliothèque Nationale, MS 2249, p. 6. The suggestion that versets should mirror the text

they replace is stated more fully on pp. 3–4 of the *Essai:* "[*alternatim*] pieces . . . should, as much as possible, contain the feeling of the words and express them in imitation of the chants that they replace."

[16] François-Joseph Fétis, "L'Orgue mondaine et la musique érotique à l'église," *Revue et Gazette musicale* 23 (1856): 106.

[17] Théodore Nisard [Théodule Elzéar Xavier Normand], "L'Orgue mondaine et la musique érotique à l'église," *Revue de musique ancienne et moderne* [1] (1856): 217.

[18] A. P. F. Boëly, *Pièces d'orgue pour le service liturgique,* ed. Norbert Dufourcq and Amédée Gastoué, vol. 2 of *Œuvres complètes pour orgue* (1958; reprint as *Liturgical Service for the Organ,* in *Kalmus Organ Series* [Melville, N.Y.: Belwin Mills, n.d.]).

[19] Amédée Gastoué, "Notes complémentaires sur une copie de la 'Messe Solennelle' de Couperin," *Revue de musicologie* 13 (1929): 118–19.

[20] Stéphen Morelot, "Du vandalisme musical dans les églises," *Revue de la musique religieuse, populaire et classique* I (1845): 132–34. The title page of Corrette's *Troisième Livre d'orgue* designates as "le Fleurti" the two-part counterpoint that appears above the cantus firmus in its plainchant versets (see Abbé Jean Prim, "Chant sur le Livre in French Churches in the 18th Century," *Journal of the American Musicological Society* 14 [1961]: 39).

[21] Félix Clément, *Histoire générale de la musique religieuse depuis ses origines jusqu'à nos jours* (Paris: Adrien Le Clere, 1861), 356.

[22] Burney, *The Present State of Music,* 1:15. Ludwig Spohr, *Autobiography* (1860–1861; anon. English translation, 1865; reprint as *Louis Spohr's Autobiography* [New York: Da Capo, 1969], 124).

[23] Joseph d'Ortigue, *Dictionnaire liturgique, historique et théoretique de plainchant et de musique d'église au moyen âge et dans les temps modernes* (1854; reprint, New York: Da Capo, 1971), col. 78.

Boëly's *Quatorze Préludes sur des cantiques de Denizot*, op. 15, and the Creation of a French "Christmas" *Orgelbüchlein*

CRAIG CRAMER

Alexandre-Pierre-François Boëly (1785–1858) was one of the most important and influential composers for the organ between the French Revolution—the effective end of the French Classical period—and César Franck. Boëly, who was trained as a pianist, came to the organ late in his life. In 1834 at the age of forty-nine, he was named provisional organist at Saint-Gervais, the church of the Couperins. It was during his four-year tenure in this post that he appears to have composed his first organ pieces. Although he had published many pieces for the piano and several sets of ensemble music earlier in his career, he began to devote serious attention to the publication of works for the organ only after he had won the post of *organiste titulaire* at the prestigious Royal Parish of Saint-Germain-l'Auxerrois. Between his appointment in 1840 and his dismissal in 1851, all but one of his six collections of organ pieces that appeared during his lifetime were published:[1]

1842	Opus 9	*Quatre Offertoires*
1842	Opus 10	*Recueil contenant quatorze morceaux*
1842	Opus 11	*Messe du jour de Noël*
1842	Opus 12	*Vingt-quatre Pièces*
1847	Opus 15	*Quatorze Préludes sur des cantiques de Denizot*
1856	Opus 18	*Douze Pièces*

The *Quatorze Préludes ou pièces d'orgue avec pédale obligée composés sur des cantiques de Denizot (du 16e siècle)*, op. 15, written in 1846, is the last organ collection that Boëly published during his tenure as a Parisian church organist;[2] it remains his best known and for Brigitte François-Sappey, his biographer, "the most perfect and the most original."[3] The collection contains settings of fourteen *cantiques* (see Figure 1). The *cantique* melodies, by an anonymous composer, and the first verse of each of Denizot's texts are printed in the first edition under the following heading, "The 14 *Cantiques* of

Figure 1

The *Quatorze Préludes sur des cantiques de Denizot*[a]

1. *Seigneur Dieu ouvre la porte* (8 mm.; 3/4; à 4; F major)
2. *D'où vient qu'en cette nuitée* (41 mm.; ₵; à 4; E-flat major)
3. *Chantez mes vers ce jour* (15 mm.; C, later 3/4; à 5; G minor)
4. *Esprits divins* (21 mm.; C; à 5; G major)
5. *Réveillez-vous pastoureaux* (10 mm.; 3/4; à 4; D minor)
6. *Quel étonnement vient saisir mon âme* (11 mm.; 3/4; à 4; E-flat major)
7. *Ici je ne bâtis pas* (7 mm.; C; à 4; C major)
8. *Sus, sus qu'on se réveille* (20 mm.: 3/4; à 4; D minor)
9. *Le vermeil du Soleil* (17 mm.; ₵; à 4; F major)
10. *Lyre ce n'est pas en ce chant* (23 mm.; C; à 5; D minor)
11. *Voici la première entrée* (16 mm.; C; à 4; G minor)
12. *Muses sœurs de la peinture* (8 mm.; 3/4; à 3; G minor)
13. *Sus bergers en campagne* (17 mm.; C; à 4; D minor)
14. *Mon âme dormez-vous?* (8 mm.; C; à 4; G minor)

---

[a] The spelling of the *cantique* titles follows that given in Boëly's collection.

Denizot as they were noted [printed] in 1552,"[4] and a footnote refers the reader to a copy of that sixteenth-century source in the Bibliothèque Municipale in Versailles, Boëly's native city.[5] Nicolas Denizot (1515–1559), a poet and author of two collections of *cantiques* and one collection of noëls, was possibly the first poet to use the word *cantique* as the title of a religious song in the vernacular (*cantique*, or canticle, having previously been used for Biblical verse from the New Testament, such as the Magnificat or the Nunc dimittis). According to Amédée Gastoué, the term in the mid-sixteenth century designated "a poetic form with regular strophes, in the manner of a chanson, but more dignified."[6] The subject matter of these poems deals with the events leading up to the birth of Christ and with the first Christmas.

While Boëly's first four collections of organ music, published within three years of his appointment to Saint-Germain-l'Auxerrois, contain for the most part liturgical versets and other items intended for the mass, he took a somewhat different path with the composition of his next collection, the *Quatorze Préludes*. Less obviously tied to the liturgy than the plainsong versets and other *alternatim* pieces for mass and vesper hymns, offertories, and the like which constitute a significant portion of his organ works, the

Quatorze Préludes are clearly religious in intent but stand outside the obvious categories of liturgical organ music. François-Sappey classified these works as "paraliturgical," a category of works neither intended for a specific liturgical function (such as the versets of the *Messe des annuels* of 1848) on the one hand, nor devoid of any likely liturgical connection at all (for example, Boëly's well-known Fantasy and Fugue in B-flat Major) on the other.[7] François-Sappey suggests that the scope of paraliturgical organ music is so broad—encompassing works as varied as the *Messe du jour de Noël*, op. 11, the *Judex crederis* from the Te Deum and the *Offertoire pour le jour de Pâques* from op. 38, and the two *Choralvorspiele* on German chorales, as well as works such as the *Quatorze Préludes*—that the term obscures as much as illuminates the character and functional intent of those pieces. While the *Messe du jour de Noël* unquestionably reflects actual liturgical practice, the liturgical role, if any, of the *Quatorze Préludes* remains unclear.

Boëly and Bach

Boëly's *Quatorze Préludes* received an unusually lengthy review in the September 1847 issue of *Revue de la musique religieuse, populaire et classique*, a publication founded and edited by Jean-Louis-Félix Danjou (1812–1866), organist at Notre-Dame and founder/director of the organbuilding firm of Daublaine et Callinet in Paris. Danjou, a very influential figure in Parisian church music circles, clung to the conservative, even reactionary, tradition which espoused learned contrapuntal writing and pieces based on a cantus firmus. Danjou never missed an opportunity to praise Boëly, whose taste was likewise old-fashioned, and his latest work, and this visibility in the French press played no small part in the popularity of the *Quatorze Préludes*. Whether or not Danjou actually wrote the review of op. 15 is uncertain (the reviews in this journal were often unsigned), but the suggestion that Boëly's collection not only shows the influence of J. S. Bach but bears comparison and, indeed, stands as an equal to Bach's works probably reflects Danjou's opinion:

> We announce with yet more satisfaction the next publication of a new work by M Boëly, organist of Saint-Germain-l'Auxerrois. This work for organ, which is likely to offer interest even to amateurs who do not play this instrument, consists of a collection of French *cantiques* composed around the middle of the sixteenth century by one Denisot d'Alcincoïs. M Boëly wanted to make of these old religious songs what Sebastian Bach and all the great German organists made of the Lutheran chorales, that is to say to surround them in a rich accompaniment with obbligato pedal. We have heard this work in its entirety, and, at this performance, we felt proud to see these French melodies brought to light full of suavity with an art equal to that of the old German masters which we have not equaled until now in compositions for the organ.[8]

Indeed, a wide variety of sources reports that Boëly was an admirer—even a student—of the style of J. S. Bach. The memoires of the eminent violinist, Eugène Sauzay, with whom Boëly, a fine violist, played in a string quartet, relate that:

> On Sundays, Boëly relaxed by tuning his pianos, setting his clock, . . . [and when] everything was in order, he seated himself at his pedal piano, his snuffbox at his side, and played either some Bach chorales in three parts, or a complete book of his own etudes.[9]

Upon Boëly's death, Paul Scudo drew attention to Boëly's devotion to Bach:

> The art of music, particularly sacred music, has just suffered a painful loss with the death of M Boëly, a serious and honest musician and an organist with a severe style, who had kept the tradition of the school of Sebastian Bach intact. . . . Boëly, who studied piano with Mme de Montgeroult, familiarized himself very early with the works of the old masters such as Frescobaldi, Couperin, Handel, and especially Sebastian Bach, the god whose intelligence he adored. With a tenacious and somewhat bizarre character, he had resisted all of the innovations which were produced in sacred music for half a century. Devoted completely and almost exclusively to the worship of Bach, whose portrait alone adorned the unfurnished walls of his poor dwelling, Boëly was an organist with a learned style, dominated by the dialectic procedures of fugue and imitation. This is not the moment to question if M Boëly had not slightly exaggerated the application of excellent principles, and if the resistance which he brought to the modifications demanded by the taste of the new generations were always quite reasonable. Living in solitude and deeply involved in sacredness, I tell you, in his artistic mission, in his faith and in the ideal which formed him into a classical organist, M Boëly has remained immovable.[10]

Boëly, then, served as an exponent in France of the incipient international revival of Bach's music.[11] An outgrowth of nineteenth-century fascination with historicism, the Bach revival encompassed the scholarly activities of those attempting to make known Bach's works, through both performance and publication, as well as the many tributes to Bach in the form of compositions which mimic his style or employ the "B-A-C-H" motive. The impetus of the movement came from Germany. While to a lesser extent Vienna and London also played a part, Paris, then the artistic and intellectual center of Europe, took an even smaller role.[12] That Boëly drew attention to Bach in relative isolation does not make his efforts any less significant.

Boëly also helped to lead the Bach revival in France as a performer: soon after his appointment to Saint-Germain-l'Auxerrois he had the organ there outfitted with a German-style pedalboard and several new stops, which enabled him to play more "authentic" renditions of German Baroque organ works in general, and Bach in particular.[13] His fascination with Bach's organ works around this time is not surprising in light of his new ability to play their wonderful independent pedal parts, no longer hampered by the typical French pedal division—still reflecting French Classical practice—which was able to play only a cantus firmus on a reed stop or a slow-moving accompaniment likely on an 8' Flûte. And not surprisingly, it was Boëly who first wrote for this new type of French organ with an expanded pedal division; his first such effort was in fact the *Quatorze Préludes*.[14]

Indeed, the first mention of Boëly's use of Bach's chorale preludes as a compositional model in op. 15 appears in the 1847 review: "M Boëly wanted to make of these old religious songs what Sebastian Bach . . . made of the Lutheran chorales, that is to say to surround them in a rich accompaniment with obbligato pedal." Forty years after the composer's death, Camille Saint-Saëns, in his preface to a new edition of the *Quatorze Préludes*, stressed anew Boëly's allegiance to Bach, bringing into the discussion Bach's compositional methods:

> An impeccable writer of music and a theorist of the first rank, Boëly had that bizarre originality of trying to live in the past. He endeavored to write in the style of Scarlatti and J. S. Bach, who excited his greatest admiration.
>
> An artist imbued with such a system must not count on the approbation of his contemporaries; he cannot draw attention until later, when the question [of its use] is no longer so topical. That is why the time has come to appreciate the works of this very talented and conscientious musician.
>
> He applied to Gregorian melodies, often with success, the methods by which Sebastian Bach made the best use of German chorales; the result has been a large number of pieces which adapt themselves perfectly to the Catholic liturgy. One is pleased to encounter no error of taste, inadequate writing, or echo of the secular style which would be out of character with the austerity of the church.
>
> His best pieces belong to the old style. Some are simply masterpieces, such as the one in B minor, op. 43, no. 13 (*Toccata*) from his posthumous works; but his finest work, that which places him in the ranks of the greatest musicians, is the little collection of noëls of the sixteenth century, op. 15, harmonized for organ.
>
> By merit of having discovered and brought to light these admirable songs in a lapidary and finished style, J. S. Bach's pupil has equaled his model.
>
> This book of noëls should be part of the repertory of all organists. They combine with the simplicity indispensable to songs of the Nativity a loftiness, a perfection of style that reminds one of the illuminations of missals, of statuettes in cathedrals. It is simply a masterpiece.[15]

The Quatorze Préludes *and the* Orgelbüchlein

A great variety of specifically Bachian traits can be observed in op. 15, especially when the *Préludes* are placed alongside Bach's *Orgelbüchlein*: because the individual pieces of both collections share the same general size and scope, the *Préludes* and the *Orgelbüchlein* invite comparison.[16] Striking internal evidence links these two collections and includes indications for use of the instrument (the presence or absence of pedal parts and the related question of the layout of the score on two or three staves, as well as registration), musical style (questions of cantus-firmus treatment, motives, texture, and aspects of form including the use of canon in addition to sheer size), and finally miscellaneous topics such as tempo markings.

For the first time in his organ collections, Boëly notated the majority of the pieces on three staves rather than two.[17] Three of the pieces call for the use of the pedal division, but were notated on two staves: *D'où vient qu'en cette nuitée*, *Chantez mes vers ce jour*, and *Voici la première entrée*. Only two pieces of the fourteen are marked "manualement" and have no pedal indicated: *Sus, sus qu'on se réveille* and *Muses sœurs de la peinture*. These details about the use of the pedal are worth noting because Boëly pointed out (in large, bold type) on the title page that these pieces were "avec pédale obligée," his first collection to make such a claim. This in itself calls to mind a similar remark on the title page of Bach's *Orgelbüchlein*:

> Little Organ Book in which a beginner at the organ is given instruction in developing a chorale in many diverse ways, and at the same time in acquiring facility in the study of the pedal since in the chorales contained therein the pedal is treated as wholly obbligato.[18]

Of the three pieces notated on two staves that call for the use of the pedal, only for *Voici la première entrée* does a plausible reason emerge for the use of two, as opposed to three, staves. This piece exists in a manuscript version which does not call for the pedal, nor stipulates "à deux claviers," as in the printed version.[19] At some point before the printed version appeared, Boëly presumably confronted the problem of the large stretches in the left-hand part, which suggest the use of the pedal, even though he originally seems to have intended the piece for manuals alone. (The reason for his disposition of the piece on two manuals, the only such case in the collection, remains a mystery.) The two other *Préludes* printed on two staves again present unique situations. Boëly most frequently notated his organ fugues on two rather than three staves, and *D'où vient qu'en cette nuitée*, which contains passages of strictly fugal writing, follows this practice notwithstanding the independent pedal line. In *Chantez mes vers ce jour*, the pedal is used for a canon at the octave with the soprano; while Boëly may have thought that the canon would be heard more distinctly if one of its voices was played in the pedal rather than with the left hand on the manuals, that in itself does not explain his reluctance to score the pedal on a separate line. Interestingly, this last *Prélude* contains what is, for Boëly, an unusual example of a pedal trill; this Bachian effect calls to mind the *Orgelbüchlein* setting of *In dir ist Freude*, BWV 615.[20]

In neither collection does the composer indicate many suggestions for registrations. The *Orgelbüchlein* includes only one specific registration— "Man. Princip. 8 F; Ped. Tromp. 8 F" in *Gott durch deine Güte*, BWV 600— although Bach frequently directed a piece to be played "à 2 Clav. e Pedale."

Boëly, perhaps following Bach's lead, indicated registrations in only two preludes, one specific, the other general. *Ici je ne bâtis pas* calls for "Pédale de Trompette ou de Clairon une 8a plus bas." Even though this was one of the standard registrations of the French Classical composers, the similarity to Bach's *Orgelbüchlein* registration is perhaps not a coincidence since Boëly would not likely have employed a French Classical registration when intent on writing for a German style pedalboard. The other registration indication, *Organo pleno*, appears in *Mon âme dormez-vous?* Though Bach did not use this term in the *Orgelbüchlein*, it appears frequently in the larger chorale settings and the free works.[21] "Full organ" has been interpreted differently in various countries, and what Boëly may have understood it to mean is uncertain; he usually designated large combinations either by *Grands Jeux* (with reed stops) or by *Grand Chœur* (probably without reeds, perhaps the nineteenth-century equivalent of the French Classical *Plein Jeu*).[22] While his use of the term in the *Quatorze Préludes* seems to constitute yet another Bachian touch, paradoxically a more notable aspect of op. 15 which suggests his imitation of Bach's practices is the near total absence of registration indications, a striking change from his usual approach: every piece in ops. 10 and 11, for example, carries very specific registration instructions.

As in the *Orgelbüchlein*, the pieces in op. 15 are all reasonably brief, chiefly because not only do the *cantique* melodies resemble in size Lutheran chorales, but for the most part a single statement of the cantus firmus determines the length of the settings in both collections. The shortest of the *Préludes*, *Ici je ne bâtis pas*, contains seven measures, and the longest, *D'où vient qu'en cette nuitée*, forty-one, while the shortest piece in the *Orgelbüchlein*, *Komm, Gott Schöpfer, Heiliger Geist*, BWV 631, is eight measures, and the longest, *In dir ist Freude*, BWV 615, sixty-three. In both collections, the cantus firmus is most frequently played once in the soprano voice, unornamented. Disregarding canonic entrances, Bach placed the cantus firmus in a voice other than the soprano only once, in the alto in *Christum wir sollen loben schon*, BWV 611; Boëly put the cantus firmus in each of the other three voices one time each: in the alto in *Réveillez-vous pastoureaux*, in the tenor in *Ici je ne bâtis pas*, and in the bass in *Mon âme dormez-vous?*. Finally, there is one fugal piece in each collection in which phrases of the melody migrate through all of the voices: *In dir ist Freude*, BWV 615, and *D'où vient qu'en cette nuitée*.

The accompanying motives in both collections are often derived directly from the cantus firmus and treated imitatively throughout the piece.[23] This technique is obvious in *D'où vient qu'en cette nuitée* and *Chantez mes vers ce jour*, and so rigorously applied in *Réveillez-vous pastoureaux*—the motive appears in its original or slightly altered form in every beat of the piece, migrates to all four voices (including the bass in the pedal), and on two occasions is heard in parallel tenths (between the soprano and the tenor)—as to suggest comparison with Bach's *Mit Fried' und Freud' ich fahr' dahin*, BWV

Example 1a. Boëly, *Réveillez-vous pastoureaux*, mm. 1–4

Example 1b. J. S. Bach, *Mit Fried' und Freud' ich fahr' dahin*, BWV 616, mm. 1–3

Example 2a. Boëly, *Sus bergers en campagne*, mm. 1–3

Example 2b. J. S. Bach, *Wir danken dir, Herr Jesu Christ*, BWV 623, mm. 1–4

Example 3a. Boëly, *Lyre ce n'est pas en ce chant*, mm. 10–13

Example 3b. J. S. Bach, *Christe, du Lamm Gottes*, BWV 619, mm. 1–5

616 (see Example 1). Bach's integration of not one but two pervasive motives, memorable in several *Orgelbüchlein* pieces, is also explored by Boëly in *Sus bergers en campagne*: the cantus firmus in the soprano hovers above a complex accompaniment with a cellular motive in the alto and tenor and a contrasting motive in the pedal. Indeed, in this, the most Bach-like of all the *Préludes*, the pedal motive resembles that of *Wir danken dir, Herr Jesu Christ*, BWV 623, (see Example 2) while the overall effect of motivic saturation calls to mind *Herr Christ, der ein'ge Gottes-Sohn*, BWV 601, both from the *Orgelbüchlein*. Boëly also enriches several of the *Préludes* with canonic passagework; that in the five-voiced *Lyre ce n'est pas en ce chant*, for example, seems reminiscent of a five-voiced chorale prelude in the *Orgelbüchlein*, *Christe, du Lamm Gottes*, BWV 619 (see Example 3). If the motivic play in the last of the *Préludes*, *Mon âme dormez-vous?*, evokes Bach, the motive itself, a pervasively dotted one, is in this case likely a gesture not toward Bach but rather toward French Classical practice, in which a movement in the French overture style often closed an organ suite.[24] Boëly, who was certainly at least as familiar with the organ music of pre-Revolutionary France as he was with that of Bach, seems to have attempted with this gesture to maintain a balance in op. 15 between French and German elements.

Similarities between Boëly's *Préludes* and Bach's *Orgelbüchlein* can also be found in several other shared traits and procedures. Neither composer, for example, used introductions or codas, preferring instead a very compact format in which the first note of the cantus firmus begins the work and the last note concludes it. Moreover, Boëly followed Bach's practice—indeed, one of which Bach was very fond—when in *Sus bergers en campagne* he recalled the opening motive in its original form in the last measure. In addition, like the *Orgelbüchlein*, the *Préludes* provide very few tempo markings; perhaps in op. 15 Boëly purposefully followed older practice which assumed a *tempo ordinario* and required only those tempo markings that were needed to negate it.

In view of the probability that Bach's *Orgelbüchlein* served as a point of departure for the *Quatorze Préludes*, reasons for Boëly's choice to set melodies from an obscure sixteenth-century collection become clearer. Of his alternatives, popular noëls might well have been seen as less elevated than German chorales, especially as set by Bach; chants of the Parisian Rite for the most part lacked the clear phraseology and tonal orientation needed to approximate Bach's musical style; and German chorales themselves would likely have seemed inappropriate precisely because they would have lacked any possibility for popular appeal. (Nonetheless, Boëly did compose two chorale preludes on German tunes, including *Bin ich gleich von dir gewichen* in 1847, the year after the composition of op. 15, and these two projects may well be in some way related.[25]) Denizot's *cantiques*, on the other hand, possessed a form parallel to that of the typical chorale tunes set in the *Orgelbüchlein*, and they were, like German chorales, linked to sacred yet vernacular texts. Perhaps equally important, they must have had an aura of historicism, of obscurity and esotericism, which likely appealed to Boëly (and would have delighted critics such as Danjou). Moreover, Boëly did not hesitate to change important aspects of the old melodies to suit his purposes, and these purposes seem very much like remaking them to resemble Bach's chorales. For example, while Boëly cast all but the last half of just one of the original *cantiques* in cut time, he transforms five of them in their entirety to triple time, mirroring the mix of duple and triple meters in the *Orgelbüchlein*.[26] Neither did Boëly hesitate to alter the melodic line itself, including making it more tonal.[27] The forms of the *cantiques*, too, are often expanded by repeating various sections, a practice which not only takes these pieces farther from the world of their original texts, but makes them more like Bach's chorale melodies.[28] (That similar changes had been made to German chorales between the time of Luther and that of Bach may well not have been known to Boëly.)

That Boëly in op. 15 attempted to show how French composers working with their own musical heritage could obtain results similar to those Bach drew from his chorales, as the *Revue de la musique religieuse, populaire et classique* so boldly suggested, is indisputable; that he looked specifically to Bach's *Orgelbüchlein* for instruction seems more than likely. With Denizot's *cantiques* as his "chorales," Boëly created one of the most notable homages to Bach by a French composer of the nineteenth century.

NOTES

[1] Some 114 organ works by Boëly are found in the posthumous opus numbers 35–45 which were originally published by Richault; several of these editions were later republished by Costallat. In addition, there are about fifty pieces left unpublished during Boëly's lifetime that were not included in the posthumous publications. Most of the manuscripts currently belong to the Bibliothèque Municipale in Versailles.

[2] The six autograph manuscripts of op. 15 bear dates from October and November 1846. Curiously, Amédée Gastoué reported that "the manuscripts are dated 1847" (Amédée Gastoué, "A Great French Organist, Alexandre Boëly, and His Works," *The Musical Quarterly* 30 [1944]: 343). In the same article, Gastoué gave the date of the first edition as 1849, which is surprising considering that the actual date, 1847, is found on one of the two title pages. (In the copy of op. 15 at the Bibliothèque Nationale, the second title page, which comes immediately before the first piece, has "1849" stamped at the bottom, presumably the library's date of accession.) The *Quatorze Préludes* have been reprinted as *Album of Noëls: 14 Preludes or Pieces Composed on Denizot's Carols (16th Century)*, in *Kalmus Organ Series* (Melville, N.Y.: Belwin Mills, n.d.); three of the pieces (*Seigneur Dieu ouvre la porte, Le vermeil du Soleil,* and *Lyre ce n'est pas en ce chant*) appear in *Masters of the 18th and early 19th Centuries: Handel, Mozart, etc.*, ed. Joseph Bonnet, vol. 3 of *Historical Organ-Recitals* (New York: G. Schirmer, 1918), 64–67.

[3] Brigitte François-Sappey, *Alexandre P. F. Boëly 1785–1858: ses ancêtres, sa vie, son œuvre, son temps* (Paris: Aux Amateurs de livres, 1989), 463.

[4] The year is wrong; it should be 1553. The melodies and their texts occupy two facing pages between the two title pages of the first edition.

[5] "See the book entitled *Cantiques du premier advenement de Jesu-Christ. Par le Conte d'Alsinois.* Printed in Paris in 1553 by L. Vve Maurice de L. Porte. One can find an example of this book in the Bibliothèque Municipale in the city of Versailles under the mark and number E392C." Here the date is given correctly. This collection is now found under the number Fonds Gouget 99. The "Conte d'Alsinois" is "the pseudonym and anagram of the author" (Amédée Gastoué, *Le Cantique populaire en France* [Lyon: Janin frères, 1924], 244).

[6] Gastoué, *Le Cantique populaire*, 157. (Regarding Denizot's works, see p. 244.)

[7] François-Sappey, *Alexandre P. F. Boëly*, 443–77.

[8] *Revue de la musique religieuse, populaire et classique* 3 (1847): 320. Such reviews appeared under the heading of "Nouvelles diverses" in every issue. François-Sappey suggests as possible authors of this review J. B. Laurens and Stéphen Morelot as well as Danjou (*Alexandre P. F. Boëly*, 504, n. 233).

[9] Brigitte François-Sappey, "La Vie musicale à Paris à travers *Les Memoires* d'Eugène Sauzay (1809–1901)," *Revue de musicologie* 60 (1974): 178.

[10] Paul Scudo, *Revue des deux mondes* 34 (1859): 752.

[11] See *The New Grove Dictionary of Music and Musicians*, s.v. Bach Revival, and Friedrich Blume, *Two Centuries of Bach: An Account of Changing Taste*, trans. Stanley Godman (London: Oxford University Press, 1950).

[12] For a brief discussion of French interest in Bach's organ music in the nineteenth century, see Norbert Dufourcq, "La Pénétration en France de l'œuvre d'orgue de J.-S. Bach et sa registration étudiée comparativement à l'évolution de la facture d'orgue," *La Revue musicale* 13 (1932): 363–75.

[13] See Craig J. Cramer, "The Published Organ Works of A. P. F. Boëly (1785–1858)" (D.M.A. diss., Eastman School of Music, 1983), ch. 9, for details of these changes in the organ at Saint-German-l'Auxerrois. François-Sappey also gives an account of this episode in *Alexandre P. F. Boëly*, 383–89.

[14] Boëly was also one of five Parisian organists who joined Adolf Hesse in 1844 as inaugural performers on the new Saint-Eustache organ which featured a pedalboard in the German style.

The organ was built by Daublaine et Callinet under the direction of Danjou. (See Fenner Douglass, *Cavaillé-Coll and the Musicians*, 2 vols. [Raleigh: Sunbury, 1980], 1:36).

[15] Camille Saint-Saëns, preface to *Recueil de noëls pour orgue* by A. P. F. Boëly, ed. Herbert A. Fricker (Paris: Costallat, n.d.).

[16] While the *Orgelbüchlein* is not specifically listed in the catalogue of Boëly's library, he did own several volumes of Bach's music (*Six Sonates et pastorale et compositions pour l'orgue*; *Compositions pour l'orgue, 10 pièces*; *Musique d'orgue*; *Compositions pour l'orgue ou piano à pédale*; and *Passacaglia pour orgue ou piano*); he also had access to a remarkable amount of other eighteenth-century music including chorale preludes by several German organists, such as Walther, whose influence François-Sappey has demonstrated (*Alexandre P. F. Boëly*, 453–55). The *Orgelbüchlein* was presumably also one of the items to which he had access.

[17] Previous examples of Boëly's use of a three-stave layout for organ music include: op. 10, nos. 3 and 12; the *Offertoire* and Agnus Dei of op. 11; and op. 12, nos. 2, 6, 8, and 10.

[18] *The Bach Reader*, ed. Hans T. David and Arthur Mendel (New York: W. W. Norton, 1966), 75.

[19] *Voici la première entrée* is the only one of the *Préludes* for which a manuscript version has come to light.

[20] François-Sappey has noted this relationship (*Alexandre P. F. Boëly*, 470).

[21] For example, *Kyrie, Gott Heiliger Geist*, BWV 671; *Wir glauben all' an einen Gott*, BWV 680; *Komm, Heiliger Geist, Herre Gott*, BWV 651; *Nun komm, der Heiden Heiland*, BWV 661; *Komm, Gott, Schöpfer, Heiliger Geist*, BWV 667; and the Prelude in E-flat Major, BWV 552.

[22] For examples of *Grands Jeux* registrations in Boëly's work, see op. 10, no. 1, and the *Rentrée* and *Offertoire* of op. 11.

[23] For a discussion of this point regarding the *Orgelbüchlein*, see Alexander Brinkman, "Johann Sebastian Bach's *Orgelbüchlein*: A Computer-Assisted Study of the Melodic Influence of the Cantus Firmus on the Contrapuntal Voices" (Ph.D. diss., University of Rochester, 1978).

[24] Usually the French Classical composers presented an entire French overture; here Boëly composed only the opening section of such an overture.

[25] Found in Versailles, Bibliothèque Municipale, MS 170. Both of these curious works are included in: A. P. F. Boëly, *Œuvres complètes pour orgue*, ed. Norbert Dufourcq and Brigitte François-Sappey, vol. 3 (Paris: Bornemann, 1985), 44–47; *Bin ich gleich von dir gewichen* can also be found in: *A. P. Fr. Boëly & Fr. Benoist*, ed. Willem van Twillert, vol. 3 of *Organisten uit de 18e en 19e Eeuw* (Amersfoort: J. C. Willemsen, 1984), 20–21.

[26] The *cantiques* as they appear in the original edition of op. 15 are given in François-Sappey, *Alexandre P. F. Boëly*, 468–69.

[27] For example, Boëly made several alterations in the melody of *Esprits divins*: he changed m. 12, beat 3 from the original f-sharp'' to g''; he raised the leading tone from c'' to c-sharp'' in m. 13; and he doubled the value of the penultimate note in m. 20 so that the final note falls on the downbeat of the last measure. (Apparently Boëly was pleased with the transcribed melody because he wrote "bonne notation" at the top of the page of this sketch.)

[28] For example, the *cantique* melody in *Sus bergers en campagne* is through-composed (*abcd*) but Boëly made the piece a binary form (*ababcdcd*); moreover, although his piece is entirely in common time, the original *cantique* melody changes from duple to triple meter at *c*. *Sus, sus qu'on se réveille* is handled in the same way, while in *Muses sœurs de la peinture*, originally a bar-form (*aab*), the last phrase is repeated to create another binary form.

Lemmens, His *École d'orgue,*
and Nineteenth-Century Organ Methods

WILLIAM J. PETERSON

"Not one of those who heard Lemmens could forget the clarity, the power, the grandeur of his playing," Widor wrote in 1927.[1] Indeed, Jaak Nikolaas (Jacques-Nicolas) Lemmens's name has never dropped from view since his epochal concert appearances in mid-nineteenth-century Paris. Lemmens's achievement was inseparable from a style that struck listeners as uncompromising and serious, and that style was exhibited in the repertoire he played and in his manner—the external manifestation of a prodigious technique— that he adopted for his musical statements. Writing a review of Lemmens's 1850 concert at the Panthémont in Paris, Henri Blanchard observed that the Belgian artist's "style sévère" did not exclude grace, and it did not exclude the more modern melodic and harmonic refinements either. Lemmens expressed ideas, Blanchard wrote, with a style that combined "purity, elegance, and clarity."[2] Lemmens's style, we read in the 1881 obituary in the *Journal de Bruxelles,* was characterized by "elevation of thought."[3] But it was not only Lemmens's playing of the organ that Widor and others remembered fifty to sixty years after the Panthémont concert, it was his teaching of organ that secured, it seems, for Lemmens a notable place in history. Lemmens's celebrated method of organ playing, the *École d'orgue* of 1862, served both Charles-Marie Widor and Alexandre Guilmant. Guilmant, in the course of a famous article on organ playing, referred many times to Lemmens's method, both to his compositions and to his exercises.[4] Indeed, Lemmens's role as a teacher entered a new phase after 1900: two editions of the *École d'orgue* were printed in Paris around 1920.[5]

The name Lemmens unquestionably had significance not only for former students who were active around 1900 (Widor and Guilmant included), but for many critics as well. Around the time of the revised editions of Lemmens's *École d'orgue,* the American organist Edward Shippen Barnes claimed that Lemmens had made a weighty contribution to the art of organ music in France.

Now as to modern French organ music, I feel that some of the works of Lemmens and Boëly contained germs of the coming greatness. Lemmens's three sonatas are smooth and attractive music, and with his work begins the very considerable use of Gregorian melodies as a foundation for composition, and nothing has proved more productive and fruitful of worthy music.[6]

What compositions of Lemmens were known to American organists in the early decades of the new century? Barnes pointed to the Sonatas. In a 1913 article designed to introduce organists to worthy (and often overlooked) Christmas repertoire, Harvey Gaul included among a long list of recommended pieces Lemmens's *Hosannah!*[7] Guilmant played several compositions by Lemmens, including the Grand Fantasia in E Minor ("The Storm"), in his 1904 performances at the St. Louis World's Fair.[8] And Joseph Bonnet, in a series of New York recitals titled "The Story of Organ Music from the Early Composers to the Present Time," presented in the Hotel Astor Ball Room in 1917, included Lemmens's Prelude in E-flat Major.[9] In England, the critic Harvey Grace wrote (around 1920) of three great figures who helped form the French "organ school," which were the composers Franck, Saint-Saëns, and Lemmens (he stresses Lemmens's role and contribution as a teacher).[10]

In 1850 Lemmens was a provocative figure in the French organ scene. His style, which was often labeled in his own day as the "style sévère," stood in contrast to that of Louis-James-Alfred Lefébure-Wély in Paris, who was certainly one of the most popular—and powerful—figures in the organ world. While Lefébure-Wély's improvisational style (specializing in storm scenes) held great importance in the history of organ music at mid century, Lemmens's "style sévère" depended on his own performance of J. S. Bach's works (preludes and fugues), on other serious repertoire (Mendelssohn's works), and on the composing of works which themselves incorporated "elevated forms" such as the fugue, and at times incorporated chant themes. That Lemmens's artistic credo, as well as his conception of organ technique, owed much to the German organ art one could scarcely dismiss. Indeed, Lemmens with his rather systematic technique struck some observers as exemplifying "mezzo tedesco" leanings. Thus, "Lemmens" in one sense stands for a set of standards and ideals which defined themselves in the years between 1830 and 1870.

The organ music of J. S. Bach, to which Lemmens was introduced chiefly by François-Joseph Fétis (Director of the Brussels Conservatory, and an historian) and Adolf Hesse of Breslau, is of pivotal importance in this historical sketch. In fact it was, to judge by Lemmens's career, not only the organ music of J. S. Bach, but the use of a quasi-Bachian contrapuntal and elevated style by such composers as Mendelssohn, that pointed a direction to nineteenth-century artists: one of the options that Lemmens the composer chose on occasion was the venerable contrapuntal style, and that helped to define

Lemmens's relation to the history of organ music and to his contemporaries. (From this perspective, Lefébure-Wély's popular style is the less self-conscious, even in one sense the more "authentic" style of the 1850s and 1860s.) At the same time the cultivation of "early music" was part of the nineteenth century, and Fétis's "historical concerts" provide an example from Lemmens's own country. The history of the nineteenth-century rediscovery of early organ music has still to be written, and yet examples of notable performances— Alphonse Mailly's performance in Brussels on a Merklin organ not only of a Handel concerto but of a ricercar of Buus, Guilmant's performance of a toccata by Sweelinck on the Cavaillé-Coll organ in Amsterdam, to select examples only from the Low Countries—are not difficult to locate.[11] Indeed, the cultivation of "early music" by such figures as Alexandre-Pierre-François Boëly, Widor, and Guilmant in Paris, with special emphasis placed on the music of J. S. Bach, is of great importance in the broad history of organ music, and is of critical importance in organ music from about the 1870s to the 1920s.

Within that broad history, the line of post-Bach technique that includes Lemmens (chiefly through his *Nouveau Journal d'orgue* and *École d'orgue*), and which led to later nineteenth-century reviews and to the republication (in the 1920s) of the *École d'orgue*, will be examined here in light of the nineteenth-century French (and Belgian) traditions of organ playing as a contribution to the broader understanding of organ playing since 1750.

The Career of Jaak Nikolaas Lemmens (1823–1881)

Lemmens's term as professor of organ at the Brussels Conservatory, which began in 1849, is without question central to his career and achievement. If, as the 1881 obituary notice in the *Journal de Bruxelles* states, "This illustrious master has unquestionably shed brilliant light on the Belgian school, and his name will shine in the history of our century," it is nonetheless true that the late twentieth-century organist knows Lemmens chiefly as an important figure behind the French organ school.[12] By all accounts a spirit of reform in organ playing was manifested in Lemmens's teaching, and in particular in the two pedagogical works he published, the *Nouveau Journal d'orgue* of 1850–1851 and the *École d'orgue* of 1862. This reform and Lemmens's career itself have, not surprisingly, inspired commentary from many writers. Yet most accounts of Lemmens's career are short (no definitive biography has been published) and most owe a great deal to a nineteenth-century biographical notice written by Fétis, Lemmens's famed mentor. Thus, Fétis's power as an historian and biographer—his biographical notice on Lemmens appeared in his now famous *Biographie universelle des musiciens*—still influences the twentieth-century view of Lemmens in many ways. For example, recent accounts by

Patrick Peire and Bernard Huys, like Fétis, provide almost no information about Lemmens's time in England, a period that includes most of the years between 1857 and 1878.[13] Even a schematic outline of his life would need to take into account the following career stages:

1. Youth and Conservatory training 1839–1847 (including study with Girschner, Fétis, and Hesse)
2. Professorial years at the Brussels Conservatory (1849–1857)
3. Professorial years divided between Belgium and England (1857–1869)
4. Years in England (1869–1878)
5. Last years in Belgium (1878–1881)

1.

Lemmens acquired his professional training between 1839 and 1847, during which he spent several years at the Brussels Conservatory. (He had taken his earliest organ training with his father and with an organist in Diest, a town not far from his native village, Zoerle-Parwijs, near Antwerp.) The Conservatory training included work on the piano, on the organ with Christian F. J. Girschner, and counterpoint and fugue with Fétis. Lemmens won first prize in piano (1842), second prize in composition (1844), and first prizes in organ and composition (1845).

About Girschner (1794–1860), Lemmens's organ teacher, all too little is known. In his early career in Berlin, he had written a book on music instruction and edited the journal *Berliner Musikalische Zeitung*, which included his reviews of organ music, and in which he published a review of Hesse's organ works and organ method. In 1841 Girschner went to Brussels where he remained until 1848. There he served as organist for the Temple Protestant (Temple du Musée), and was named, by Fétis, professor of organ at the Conservatory in 1841. As professor, Girschner endeavored, according to H. V. Couwenbergh, to teach the organ according to the principles of J. S. Bach.[14] Girschner was also a composer, and his mass, performed at Ghent in the late 1840s, received a favorable notice.[15]

The final stage in Lemmens's organ training was a term of study with the famed organist Adolf Hesse in Breslau in Silesia. By all accounts Fétis had a hand in the design of this endeavor. In the *Biographie universelle* Fétis states that he, Fétis, procured from the Ministry a stipend to enable young Lemmens to study under Hesse "the traditions of the art of Johann Sebastian Bach." (The Ministry document, dated 7 July 1846, awarded Lemmens 750 francs to permit him to "complete his musical studies . . . in Silesia.")[16] Although Fétis states that Lemmens studied with Hesse for a year, the bulk of extant documentary material suggests that Lemmens may well have spent only about three months in Breslau. (Lemmens's study with Hesse is discussed below.)

After his return to the Brussels Conservatory, Lemmens won the second prize in the Belgian Prix de Rome competition for his composition *Le Roi Lear* (1847), he published *Dix Improvisations pour orgue dans le style sévère et chantant* for organ, and he perhaps heard his cantata *Le Roi Lear* in public performance. Fétis undoubtedly had high hopes for Lemmens's career, and by December 1848 Fétis was writing to Lemmens about the resignation of Girschner as organ professor and about the probable salary to be paid Lemmens as Girschner's successor.[17] In April 1849 Lemmens received his appointment as professor of organ at the Brussels Conservatory. Fétis, in a formal notice sent from the Director's office, expressed the hope that Belgian students would learn the great traditions of Bach and Handel.[18]

2.

In his early professorial years (1849–1857) Lemmens pursued three types of activity in chiefly two cities, Brussels and Paris. First, he began to establish himself as a professor of organ in Brussels. Because the Conservatory had only a small De Volder organ (installed 1834–1836), Lemmens taught organ at the Église des Augustins. At the end of the 1849–1850 academic year the organ students played their examination ("concours") at that church, and Lemmens himself played on that occasion works of Mendelssohn. In 1850–1851 Lemmens published his *Nouveau Journal d'orgue*, and the Brussels and Paris Conservatories adopted this method of organ playing in 1852.[19]

Secondly, Lemmens played concerts in Paris where he became acquainted, thanks to Fétis, with the eminent organ builder Aristide Cavaillé-Coll.[20] In his first Paris appearance Lemmens performed his own compositions and Bach fugues on the Cavaillé-Coll organ at the Temple Protestant de Panthémont in 1850. Lemmens played a celebrated concert on the new Cavaillé-Coll organ at Saint-Vincent-de-Paul in 1852, and he participated in the inaugural concert on the Ducroquet organ at Saint-Eustache in 1854. Correspondence between Lemmens and Cavaillé-Coll reveals that Lemmens wanted the Brussels Conservatory to acquire an "orgue modèle" built by Cavaillé-Coll, and Lemmens mischievously invited Cavaillé-Coll to start a rumor that Lemmens might be hired in Paris to help convince authorities in Brussels of the importance of this need.[21]

Finally, Lemmens appeared rather frequently as a pianist: he performed works of Bach, Handel, Mozart, Beethoven, Weber, and Chopin in Brussels and Paris on the piano and the pedal piano. In 1853 Lemmens wrote to Cavaillé-Coll requesting that scores for Beethoven piano concertos, and piano works of Handel, Haydn, and Chopin be sent.[22] In 1855 and 1856 Lemmens shared the concert stage with Helen Sherrington, a singer who had been studying at the Brussels Conservatory. They were soon married (1857), and they continued to collaborate professionally for decades. Lemmens himself made the suggestion, Helen Lemmens-Sherrington recalled in an interview published in 1899, that she consider advancing her career not in Belgium but across the channel in England.[23]

3.

Lemmens and his wife spent the years 1857–1869 chiefly in England, where both were pursuing careers, one as a keyboard player and one as a singer. If Lemmens spent little time in Belgium, he remained nevertheless professor of organ at the Brussels Conservatory. Early in this period (1856–1858), Lemmens was on leave, and he was also on leave for at least the last four years (1864–1869). While he was apparently in Brussels (and not on leave), in the early 60s, he published the *École d'orgue* (1862). Two of his most notable students, Guilmant and Widor (both from France), studied with him during this period. As a performer, Lemmens played concerts on the piano and grand harmonium, and he played the new four-manual Merklin-Schütze organ at the Brussels Palais Ducal for a celebratory concert in 1866.[24] Among the organ concerts he gave outside Belgium was one at Rouen Cathedral in 1860: the program included a concerto by Handel, a Prelude and Fugue in D Minor by J. S. Bach, and Lemmens's own *Hosannah!*.[25] Lemmens's frequent leaves of absence from the Conservatory and his even more frequent requests for leaves led him steadily in one direction: he sent Fétis a letter of resignation in 1867 which was not, in fact, accepted by the Ministry.[26] Josef Tilborghs (1830–1910), who had supervised the organ students in Lemmens's absence, hoped to succeed him as professor of organ.[27] When Lemmens formally severed ties with the Conservatory in 1869, Alphonse Mailly (1833–1918) was named professor of organ.[28]

During these years Lemmens made some concert appearances in England. In addition, he worked on the composition of *L'Organiste catholique* (not completed), and he brought out *Four Organ Pieces in the Free Style* (London, 1866). But the central professional activity in this period may well have been playing the harmonium. Many a reviewer wrote admiringly of Lemmens's expert performance on the harmonium. In fact, his harmonium playing is the one aspect of his professional life, it seems, that won exclusively favorable reviews. Lemmens's reforming spirit may well have informed his work on the harmonium, for he was about to play that instrument, declared a notice in 1866, in "a completely new style."[29] Lemmens appeared in public on the harmonium in Paris, Dundee, and various cities in England. In Paris he played such an instrument at the Cavaillé-Coll shop in 1864. In 1867 he announced a series of concerts on a Mustel harmonium in England.[30] Then, in 1868, back in Paris, he played another Mustel harmonium at Pleyel,

Wolff. In this period Lemmens wrote to Cavaillé-Coll not only about an organ for himself but also about the manufacture of harmoniums.[31] Furthermore, Lemmens probably taught the harmonium as well, for *Le Guide musical* of Brussels reported that Lemmens had been listed as professor of harmonium at the Academy of London in both 1866 and 1867.[32] Thus, in the years 1857–1869, if Lemmens on the one hand appeared to be solidifying his position as professor of organ in Brussels with the publication of the *École d'orgue*, he was on leave year after year, and he was devoting himself increasingly to the harmonium.

4.

During the years 1869 to 1878 Lemmens, now free from his ties to Brussels, composed important works while residing in England. He published *Trois Sonates* for organ, which remains some of his most important work, and he composed pieces destined for the collection titled *L'Organiste catholique*. In addition, Lemmens continued to work on a method of accompanying plainchant. In this regard he wrote to Cavaillé-Coll requesting a copy of Fétis's *Histoire générale de la musique* to aid him in his study of plainchant.[33] In other correspondence with Cavaillé-Coll during this period Lemmens gave favorable comments on certain features of English organs, and he mentioned again the "orgue modèle."[34]

In this same period Lemmens also presented significant concerts. As an independent performer he appeared in Paris, first in 1874 when he played piano at the Cavaillé-Coll shop, and again in 1878 when he presented a demonstration, widely discussed, of plainchant presumably using a harmonium. Plainchant, as presented by Lemmens, became "music, and often sublime music," declared one critic in 1878.[35] The team of Lemmens and Lemmens-Sherrington toured with works of Mendelssohn. (Helen Lemmens-Sherrington was a leading singer in the 1870s, especially in oratorio repertoire in England.[36]) In September of 1878 the Lemmens team jointly presented a concert at the Trocadéro: on the Cavaillé-Coll organ there he performed his own compositions including the *Sonate pontificale*, Fanfare, *Hosannah!*, and the Grand Fantasia in E Minor ("The Storm").[37]

5.

In that same year Lemmens returned to Belgium where he remained until his death at age 58 in 1881. In this period he concentrated above all on church-related musical projects. When Lemmens made his way from Rome to Belgium in 1878, he returned to a familiar location where much, of course, had changed. The tenure of Fétis and Lemmens was a part of the past. In the new stage of the history of the Brussels Conservatory François-Auguste Gevaert held the position of Director and Mailly that of professor of organ. Mailly, who was also organist at the important Église des Carmes, played concerts in the 1870s in Brussels, Amsterdam, London, and Paris.[38] And of course, he played on the inaugural concert on the new Cavaillé-Coll organ at the Brussels Conservatory in 1880.[39]

In this period—less than three years—spent in Belgium, Lemmens carried out several important projects with far-reaching consequences. In 1879 he opened the École de musique religieuse (now known as the Lemmensinstituut) in Mechelen to train clergy, organists, and choirmasters for their work in Belgium. The curriculum included courses in: religion, liturgy, and the Latin Church; plainchant; organ and piano; harmony; counterpoint and fugue; and the composition of sacred music (vocal and instrumental).[40] Lemmens held a convocation in 1880 in Mechelen to lay the foundation for a Société Saint-Grégoire. At the end of his life he was still engaged in the composition of pieces to be included in *L'Organiste catholique*, a volume that never reached its final form. Both the *Œuvres inédites* (which did include some of the pieces destined for *L'Organiste catholique*) and the book *Du chant grégorien* (prepared for publication by Joseph Duclos) appeared posthumously in print. An obituary notice published in *The Musical Times* included the following words:

> His career amongst us is too well-known for recapitulation. Enough that, not long before his death, he returned to his native land, which, though almost naturalised in England, he had never ceased to love.[41]

The author of the obituary notice in the *Journal de Bruxelles* pointed to Lemmens's method of organ playing and his compositions as especially noteworthy. "Lemmens is the author of a celebrated organ method and of magisterial compositions . . . which will soon place him among first rank masters of our school; his reputation is universal."[42]

Lemmens and Fétis

Without question François-Joseph Fétis was the most important figure with whom Lemmens was associated in his formative years in Belgium. Widely known throughout Western Europe, Fétis was one of the greatest historians of the nineteenth century, and the founding Director of the Brussels Conservatory which he guided for over thirty years, from 1833 to his retirement in 1871. Having himself played the organ at an early age, he maintained a long-standing interest in the organ, and he was eager to see the development of an organ school in Belgium. Although as Director of the Conservatory he worked with three different professors of organ (Girschner, Lemmens, and Mailly), he regarded Lemmens as the founder of the Belgian organ school. According to his own report, he judged the young Lemmens to have the signs of extraordinary ability, and he took an active interest in Lemmens's training. In his 1867 account he wrote that he had obtained the scholarship for Lemmens from the Minister of the Interior to aid in the establishment of a Belgian organ school.[43] The views and projects of Fétis on the state of organ playing and organ building, curiously enough, have not been the subject of a scholarly study.

In 1829, before Fétis moved from Paris to Brussels, he published his most detailed outline of a plan for training organists as a notice in the *La Revue musicale*.[44] This was just one of many statements published by Fétis on this topic. Far from content with the prevailing practice of French (and after his move to Brussels, Belgian) organists, and mindful of the work done by German organists, Fétis published in 1833 a review by Jean-Louis-Félix Danjou of Johann Gottlieb Werner's organ method as translated into French. Fétis had a lively interest in the German organ world, and he himself made a French translation of Werner's chapter on the use of the pedal.[45]

The 1829 notice announced a four-part treatise, *Le Parfait Organiste ou traité complet de l'art de jouer de l'orgue*. Unfortunately, the work as a whole may not, in fact, be studied today: not only was it never published, but part four alone survives, and that in but a single copy. Nevertheless, in part one Fétis planned to include a brief discussion on the notation of plainchant, an account of the construction of the organ, and a statement about the proper use of manuals, pedals, and stops. In part two he planned to address the use of the organ to accompany plainchant, and to provide thereafter an anthology of offertories, fugues, elevation pieces, and noëls. In part three he planned to address the use of the organ in Protestant churches, to provide a new method of accompanying chorales and making preludes, and to supplement this discussion with chorale-based compositions and fugues.

Part four, which is housed in the Bibliothèque Royale in Brussels, is a 190-page anthology containing representative works from Italian, French, and German composers of the sixteenth to the eighteenth centuries. This anthology provided the organist with an introduction to the "style of celebrated organists of all epochs and of all schools." Fétis took care to include many fugues in the collection (indeed, he represents Handel by two fugues), and many other free organ works, as well. Strikingly enough, the J. S. Bach works are both cantus-firmus pieces, including a trio on *Allein Gott in der Höh sei Ehr*. By no means did Fétis slight the seventeenth century, for he devoted about half the volume to works by composers including Frescobaldi, Scheidt, Froberger, Reincken, Buxtehude, Lebègue, and others. Fétis's rich bibliography contains works about the history of the organ and about organ building, an eight-page list of collections of organ compositions, and a list of twenty-two organ methods from 1608 to 1825. Fétis, the historian and critic, stands behind every aspect of the design of *Le Parfait Organiste*.

If we have little information from Fétis on technical matters because parts two and three are not extant, still Fétis did publish organ music some of which includes informative prefaces. In that of his *Vêpres et Saluts*, he describes the stops of the organ, and gives some recommendations on their use.[46] After providing some typical instructions ("The plein-jeu is played in full harmony, legato ["en jeu lié"], and without lifting the hands at the keyboard"), he discusses the accompaniment of plainchant supplemented by illustrations of "good" and "bad" techniques. After instruction on the psalms, he provides hymns, Magnificats, and antiphons in an approved technique. In the matter of keyboard technique, Fétis was greatly interested in the art of finger substitution, and he associated this technique with J. S. Bach. In his article on J. S. Bach in the *Biographie universelle*, Fétis explained that the complexities of organ and harpsichord works written in three, four, or five parts, "obliged [Bach] to invent a particular fingering, which was long known in Germany as the *Bach fingering*, but which one can designate in a more meaningful manner as *finger substitution* ."[47] In Belgium, it was Lemmens, according to Fétis, who introduced the art of finger substitution.[48]

Fétis's views on organ playing and organ building are best known today from occasionally fiery statements printed in the 1850s. In the 1856 essay, "L'Orgue mondaine et la musique érotique à l'église," ("Worldly Organs and Erotic Music in Church"), he argued vehemently against the Lefébure-Wély style and aesthetic.[49] He also published several reports on organ building. As editor of the *Revue musicale de la Belgique* he published an article on the new Cavaillé-Coll organ at Saint-Denis in Paris, various articles written by Danjou, and a review by Danjou of Rinck's *École d'orgue*.[50] Fétis, whose name appears on several official reports on new organs in Belgium, saw the installation of a De Volder organ (1834–1836) in the Brussels Conservatory shortly after his arrival.[51] And he took a lively interest in the installation of a Dreymann organ at the Temple du Musée, where he was *maître de chapelle* "du Roi." Striking in the number of 8' stops and in the absence of mutation and mixture stops, this two-manual organ departed in many ways from Dreymann's other work.[52] The major installation during his period at the Brussels Conservatory was a new four-manual fifty-four-rank Merklin-Schütze organ at the Palais Ducal in 1866, to be of use to the Conservatory. The pedal division had unquestionably been designed to fill the gap left by so many pedal-poor Belgian organs: the fourteen stops on the pedal division included one 32', two 16' stops, and extended to a 2' Montre.[53] If Fétis printed flattering references to Cavaillé-Coll's work of the 1840s (for example, Saint-Denis and La Madeleine), he later turned his attention to the Belgian firm of Merklin, claiming that Merklin had responded constructively to his lament about the state of organ building.[54]

Thus, Fétis's multi-faceted interest in the art of the organ had a great influence on the formation of the Belgian organ school in the nineteenth century. He held up as models for Belgian organ builders the best organs he knew, and he had some responsibility for the installation of organs in Brussels. His historical approach to the organ embraced the study of the instrument itself and the practical matters essential to the functioning Roman Catholic organist. He assembled an anthology of great works drawn from the rich history of organ music for the edification and training of the organist. And he procured for Lemmens the means of completing his training—in the great Bach tradition—with no less a figure than Hesse of Breslau.

Lemmens and Hesse

If behind Lemmens stood on the one hand Fétis, advocate of reform in both organ playing and organ building and spokesman for the Roman Catholic organist, on the other hand stood Adolf Hesse, representative of the "Bach tradition." Hesse, widely known throughout Europe, was greatly respected by Fétis. An accomplished organ virtuoso, composer, teacher, and author of a pedal method, Hesse could trace his connection to J. S. Bach through two lines, one through Friedrich Wilhelm Berner of Breslau and one through Johann Christian Heinrich Rinck.[55] Both German and French writers and critics greatly admired Hesse's prodigious pedal technique. Rinck wrote that Hesse "played the organ with great dexterity, and in particular he handled the pedal in a way that earned him esteem and even astonishment."[56] With a keen interest in organ design, Hesse commented in 1853 on the pedal divisions of the organs he visited in Austria, Italy, France, and England.[57] His demonstration of a masterful pedal technique and his publications stood in stark contrast to the contemporary neglect of pedal technique.

The most detailed record of what kind of instruction Hesse provided organ students is unquestionably the treatise on playing the pedal: his *Kleine Pedalschule* provides a thorough explanation of the mastery of pedal technique, the very technique that Lemmens surely encountered in 1846.[58] The aim of the method, he explains in the preface, is to enable the student to acquire a "clean" and "smooth" technique ("ein sauberes, glattes Spiel des Pedals").[59] Hesse advocates a quiet carriage at the organ, and he stresses the advantages to be gained from restrained motion at the keyboards and pedal. He begins his recommendation for diatonic and arpeggiated pedal passages by explaining the "first" practice in which the player uses alternate toes. After explaining how one foot may cross over the other foot (in passages executed by the toes alone), he provides exercises in which the student could perfect such a technique. Then Hesse explains the "second" method in which the player employs the heel and toe of the same foot, and he supplements the explanation with exercises. Hesse includes some scales such as C major played exclusively by the alternate toe method and some scales such as E-flat major in which both the first and second methods work together. Indeed, in his E-flat scale four of the fifteen notes are played by the heel (see Example 1). In the graded exercises he uses a combination of the two pedal techniques: in passages built on arpeggiated figures he employs at times the alternate toe technique and at times a technique chiefly indebted to the toe-heel method.

Several important points emerge from a study of Hesse's mid-nineteenth-century pedal method. First, the "clean" and "smooth" connection of pedal notes could be taught with reference to both the alternating toe method as well as the toe-heel method. Second, the normative method of pedaling appears to be one which relies on the toe-heel system, yet one in which passages occasionally can best be executed with the alternating toe method. In some sense, then, the point of departure for the student wishing to acquire a clean and smooth playing of pedal passages is the venerable alternating toe method.

If the link between Lemmens and Hesse has never been in doubt, the nature of the link and the amount of influence Hesse had on Lemmens has recently again been the subject of spirited debate. Fétis's claim, that Lemmens studied a year with Hesse and that Hesse wrote a letter stating that he (Hesse) had no more to teach the accomplished Belgian, has been repeated for well over one hundred years.[60] The first part of that claim, regarding the period of study, is most likely incorrect. About the second part of the claim there is grave doubt.

The steps leading to Hesse's denial in 1852 of this famous claim by Fétis are in need of clarification. In 1851 Fétis wrote a review of Lemmens's *Nouveau Journal d'orgue* in which he mentioned such a letter received (via Lemmens) from Hesse.[61] Part of Fétis's review was quoted in a long series of anonymous articles printed in the Brussels journal *Le Diapason* which, in sum, amounted to an unfavorable critique of Lemmens's compositions and his work. This series of articles, as translated into German and printed in the 1852 *Neue Zeitschrift für Musik*, attracted Hesse's attention. Hesse thereupon wrote a response, "Kleine Zeitung," in 1852, declaring that Lemmens arrived in autumn 1846 and remained there that winter, that Lemmens had lessons at the Hauptkirche St. Bernhardin, and that Lemmens departed precipitously ("ohne mir Adieu zu sagen").[62] Hesse disputed Fétis's claim that he, Hesse, had stated that he had no more to teach Lemmens. Furthermore, he declared that Lemmens's accomplishments, whatever they were, had little to do with training taken in Breslau. Indeed, there is further evidence to suggest that Lemmens's term in Breslau ended before Christmas of 1846. A brief hand-written statement bearing the signature "Hesse" states that Lemmens studied diligently (organ and composition), that he composed a fugue for organ, and that Lemmens's knowledge ("Kenntnisse") equipped him to become professor of organ playing at the Conservatory. This document, now housed in a private archive in Brussels, bears the date 16 December 1846.[63]

Doubt about Hesse's influence has certainly not come to an end. Fétis's view that Hesse guided Lemmens in the Bach tradition has been echoed recently by Hans Jürgen Seyfried (1965), who argued that Lemmens's concept of legato and his pedal technique (and matters of articulation) paid tribute to Hesse.[64] But even more recently, Christian Ahrens (1981), relying chiefly on Hesse's "Kleine Zeitung," argued that Hesse really had no great influence on Lemmens.[65] Yet Lemmens's study with Hesse surely did influence the young Belgian's career in at least its early stage. Lemmens's own pedal technique, much admired by his contemporaries, certainly resembled the model of Hesse. Moreover, Hesse's taste in music and his approach to concert programming—perhaps even his approach to composition—likely appealed to the young Belgian, and they influenced later nineteenth-century programming as well. Hesse played concert programs that included works by Bach, by Hesse, and works by other composers on tours that brought him to many European cities including Paris.[66] He surely provided Lemmens, at least in the early part of his professorial career, with a striking example of the accomplished virtuoso organist.

Lemmens and His Organ Methods

From the *Nouveau Journal d'orgue* to the *École d'orgue*

If Lemmens's achievement—embracing the organ method, the organ compositions, the teaching, the sacred music projects—stood out in the history of nineteenth-century sacred music, it was Lemmens's style of organ playing that seemed so compelling to Guilmant and Widor. Of the large number methods produced in the nineteenth-century, few have become as well-known as Lemmens's *École d'orgue*. Lemmens's method, displaying connections to both the Franco-Belgian school (through Fétis) and to the German post-Bach tradition (through Hesse), as published in its definitive form in 1862, even today commands attention. What kinds of instruction did Lemmens provide in his organ method? In what ways did the *École d'orgue* depend on principles explored first in the *Nouveau Journal d'orgue*?

Lemmens's *Nouveau Journal d'orgue à l'usage des organistes du culte catholique* (1850–1851), which appeared shortly after his initial appointment at the Brussels Conservatory, provided instruction designed for the Roman Catholic church organist. (Another Belgian organ "Journal" from around 1850, the *Journal d'orgue ou manuel de l'organiste* by the Antwerp organist Henskens, has, in contrast to Lemmens's seminal work, virtually disappeared from view.[67]) To many observers the emphasis on instruction specifically for the Roman Catholic organist in the *Nouveau Journal* (and also in the later *École d'orgue*) was significant. A short review of the *Nouveau Journal* published in 1856 had much praise for the *prières*, communions, and the *Laudate Dominum Omnes Gentes*—"a truly splendid piece."[68] In 1887, Couwenbergh noted Lemmens's role as an organ teacher of several important students. "But especially his work which first appeared under the title *Journal d'orgue* and which was soon after in everybody's hands, exerted the greatest influence on the progressive movement of this art, so profoundly degraded and neglected," he wrote.[69] In his preface to the posthumous publication of Lemmens's *Du chant grégorien*, Joseph Duclos commented on Lemmens's reliance on plainchant:

> He devoted himself therefore, in the first years of his professorial term, to the study of plain-chant, and he wrote then, for the use of his students, accompaniments to common pieces of the liturgical repertory. These harmonizations appeared in the first year of his *Nouveau Journal d'orgue*.[70]

But the stress Lemmens placed on the Roman Catholic aspect of the *Nouveau Journal* was but one part of what secured for Lemmens's method its significance in the history of organ methods. Within the *Nouveau Journal* itself, Lemmens included much else by way of instruction in organ playing: it brought together exercises, short instructional pieces (manual pieces and trios involving pedal), modulation models, pieces for use in the mass, and other major voluntaries which could be used in concerts.

At the outset Lemmens clearly had in mind a continuing project, and he published the *Nouveau Journal* in installments which totaled twelve *livraisons* (booklets) in the first year and six *livraisons* in the second year.[71] While Lemmens took exclusive responsibility for the pedagogical principles and exercises in the method, he announced in the preface his intention to incorporate works of young composers in the following issues. Thus, the *Nouveau Journal* could serve as an ongoing communication between the Brussels professor of organ and the subscribers, and Lemmens did in fact publish one work by Tilborghs within the second year (1851).

The twelve *livraisons* that make up the first year of the *Nouveau Journal d'orgue* set forth the principles of Lemmens's organ method relative to manual technique and pedal technique, they contain several didactic pieces and other pieces for organ, and they set forth the principles of accompanying plainchant coupled with mass settings. In the first and second *livraisons* Lemmens provides an explanatory note on manual technique, twenty-four exercises, six miscellaneous pieces, a *Fugue sur la Lauda Sion*, and twenty-five preludes. The third *livraison*, titled *Six Prières*, contains eight pieces for manual alone. *Livraisons* four through six contain mass settings ("In Duplicibus et Solemnis Diebus" and "In Festis Duplicibus") and motets. In the seventh *livraison* Lemmens presents an explanatory note on the accompaniment of plainchant, examples, and three pieces (two *sorties* and one *prélude*). The eighth *livraison*, "École de la pédale," contains instruction on the use of the pedal, scales for the pedal, exercises for pedal alone, and six *Petits Trios très faciles*. The remainder of the first year of the *Nouveau Journal* (*livraisons* nine through twelve) consists of organ pieces, forty-eight modulation models, and some motets. The organ pieces—thirteen works ranging from practical communions and preludes to the imposing *Scherzo symphonique concertant*—form a repertoire for manual and pedal that allows the organist to put into practice the principles espoused by Lemmens.

The second year of the *Nouveau Journal* (six *livraisons*) contains didactic works (two canons), modulation models, preludes, *sorties*, *prières*, and an *Introduction et Fugue* (with indications for pedaling included), as well as the Animato by Tilborghs. Thus, the second year included some thirty pieces by Lemmens most of which could serve the Roman Catholic organist in search of voluntaries. Fétis stated, in his article on Lemmens in the *Biographie universelle*, that the *Nouveau Journal* was the fruit of Lemmens's teaching experience.[72] Within the 222 pages of the first and second years, Lemmens included among the preludes, trios, prayers, and miscellaneous organ works around eighty original compositions covering some 140 pages.

The *École d'orgue basée sur le plain-chant romain*, published by Lemmens in 1862, was unquestionably designed for the Roman Catholic organist, and it rested on first principles initially set forth in the *Nouveau Journal d'orgue* of 1850–1851. In the *École d'orgue* Lemmens, in fact, preserved much of the material initally published in 1850–1851, and the general design of the treatise compares readily with the overall format of the first two years of the *Nouveau Journal*. Within the first section of the *École d'orgue* Lemmens reproduces much of the material found within the first three *livraisons* of the first year of the *Nouveau Journal*: about half of the exercises for manual found in the *École d'orgue* comes directly from the *Nouveau Journal*.

Lemmens divided his *École d'orgue* into two parts. Part one contains instruction on manual technique with accompanying exercises, preludes, seven miscellaneous organ pieces, ten *prières*, and the thirteen organ pieces for manual alone (drawn from seven different *livraisons* of the first and second years of the *Nouveau Journal*). Part two begins with a pedal method. This instruction on the use of the pedal with accompanying exercises, scales, octave exercises and *Petits Trios* reproduces virtually everything found in the eighth issue of the *Nouveau Journal*. The second part continues with two canons (from the *Nouveau Journal*) together with a repertoire of twenty-six organ pieces, nineteen of which first appeared in the *Nouveau Journal*, drawn from both 1850 and 1851 (see Figure 1).

The set of *Prières* in part one of the *École d'orgue* draws on both the collection of *Prières* found in the *Nouveau Journal* (third *livraison*, first year), and on miscellaneous *Prières* within the *Nouveau Journal*. The tenth *Prière* has

Figure 1

Lemmens's *École d'orgue* (1862)

Page	Contents
	Part 1 (pp. 1–67)
5	Exercises (manual)
8	Six Pieces (with fingering supplied)
12	Twenty Short Pieces
19	Seven Pieces
30	Modulations
35	*Dix Prières*
50	Thirteen Pieces
	Part 2 (pp. 68–192)
68	"École de la pédale" (exercises for pedal)
76	*Petits Trios très faciles* (six trios)
79	Two Canons
80	Twenty-six Pieces
	Trio
	Prélude funèbre
	Communion
	Communion
	Hymnus. Creator alme siderum
	Magnificat anima mea dominum
	Prière
	Communion
	Quatuor
	Prelude
	Sortie
	Offertoire
	Laudate Dominum Omnes Gentes
	Fugue
	Lauda Sion
	Introduction et Fugue
	Prelude
	Ite Missa Est
	Scherzo symphonique concertant
	Hosannah!
	Marche triomphale
	Andante avec variations
	Prelude [in E-flat Major]
	Fanfare
	Cantabile
	Final

Figure 2

Comparison of the *Prières* of 1850–1851 and 1862

Nouveau Journal d'orgue (1850–1851)		*École d'orgue* (1862)	
Year/ *Livraison* Number/ Page		Page	
1/III/29	Animato	35	No. 1 Animato
1/III/30	Animato	36	No. 2 Animato
1/III/32	Andante	38	No. 3 Andante
1/III/34	Andante	40	No. 4 Andante
1/III/35	Grâve	41	No. 5 Grave
1/III/37	Cantabile	43	No. 6 Cantabile
1/II/24	*Prière*	44	No. 17 Andante
1/XII/139	*Prière* Andante religioso	46	No. 8 Andante religioso
2/IV/41	*Prière* Andante religioso	47	No. 9 Andantino religioso
		48	No. 10 Grave

no counterpart in the earlier publication: it appears only in the *École d'orgue* (see Figure 2).

The twenty-six pieces which conclude part two of the *École d'orgue* are on the one hand pieces which could be used in church (communions, preludes, *sorties*, and an occasional cantus-firmus piece such as *Creator alme siderum*), and on the other hand longer and more ambitious compositions such as *Introduction et Fugue, Scherzo symphonique concertant, Hosannah!*, and *Andante avec variations*. Some of the pieces which had first appeared in the *Nouveau Journal* bear the signs of recomposition as published in the *École d'orgue* (*Lauda Sion*, for example). The last six compositions, which have no counterpart in the *Nouveau Journal*, include some of the works by which Lemmens is known in the latter part of the twentieth century (such as the five-part Prelude in E-flat Major and the Fanfare).

Lemmens's *École d'orgue* of 1862, then, consisted of two types of instruction. First, it provided a detailed method for learning manual and pedal technique, which included prose explanation and graded exercises supplemented by short instructional pieces. Second, it provided a collection of works composed for organ, one repertoire for manual alone and one repertoire for manual and pedal, which could be used in the Roman Catholic service and some of which could be used in concert. If the *École d'orgue* was indeed designed for the Roman Catholic organist—and was "based on the Roman plainchant"—it nevertheless carried no instruction in the accompaniment of plainchant: the *École d'orgue* did not include any material from the fourth through the seventh *livraisons* (first year) of the *Nouveau Journal*. But, to be sure, the use of the organ in the mass, in effect a third type of instruction within the *Nouveau Journal*, did not cease to interest Lemmens. The projects carried out in the latter part of his career, work on the accompaniment of plainchant, work on *L'Organiste catholique*, and work on *Du chant grégorien*, provide ample evidence of such an engagement. With the publication of the *École d'orgue*, however, Lemmens made it clear that he considered the accompaniment of plainchant—certainly an important method to be learned by the Roman Catholic organist and one vehemently advocated by Fétis—as separate from his "organ school."

Two aspects of Lemmens's organ playing and organ method, the manual technique and the pedal technique, seemed especially striking to nineteenth-century observers. Fétis, for example, in his *Biographie universelle* account of Lemmens's achievement, called attention to the art of finger substitution and the resulting "jeu lié du clavier" (legato), and to the use of the pedal as well. Indeed, taking for granted a pianistic technique, Lemmens based the instruction within both the *Nouveau Journal* and the *École d'orgue* on the cultivation of legato playing on the manuals, and on the cultivation of a highly developed pedal technique (through exercises, trios, and compositions for manual and pedal). Lemmens, who played the piano, the organ, and the harmonium, placed great emphasis on the development of a legato technique, and he very likely drew on his own experience as an organ teacher when he revised the instruction for the 1862 edition: although the explanatory note of 1862 is not markedly different from that published in 1850, the exercises have been reworked (about half of the exercise material printed in 1862 comes directly from the *Nouveau Journal*). In the 1850 *Nouveau Journal* Lemmens explains the elements that combine to form the "style lié" (legato style). When he explains the execution in the "style lié" of a chromatic scale by the thumb alone, he writes that the thumb imitates the movement of one foot while executing a pedal chromatic scale using heel and toe.[73] If such a connection of a black key and an adjacent white key is comparatively simple, Lemmens states, great dexterity is required to achieve the same effect on two adjacent white keys. In the *École d'orgue* Lemmens explains that in a "glissando" one finger glides from the first to the second note "without the finger ceasing for an instant to be depressed on one of the two."[74] Lemmens as pedagogue unquestionably laid stress on the development of the "style lié," and on the use of finger substitution to achieve the desired close connection between notes, and he found techniques to guide the development of a legato style in students who, it is probably fair to suppose, possessed less a precise than an approximate legato.

While Lemmens's modern "pedal school" ("École de la pédale") surely reflected his own prodigious technique and the experience he had had on organs in Breslau and perhaps elsewhere in Germany, it probably presumed a pedal division that had little relation to extant Belgian instruments around 1850. In the *Nouveau Journal* Lemmens remarks that his pedal method can momentarily serve but few Belgian organists who play, for the most part, on instruments that lack an independent pedal.[75] In Belgium there was great variance in pedal compass. If, on the one hand, the De Volder organ installed at the Brussels Conservatory in 1834–1836 had no independent pedal (rather a "pédale accrochée"), the Merklin organ built for the use of the Conservatory in 1866 had a thirty-note pedalboard.[76] Noting the failure of Belgian organ builders and organists to devote attention to the pedal, Lemmens recommends twenty-five (preferably twenty-seven) keys in his 1850–1851 remarks, and twenty-seven (preferably thirty) in the 1862 *École d'orgue*.[77]

The pedal technique of organists in Belgium was, in Lemmens's view, ready for reform, and he established in the 1850 *Nouveau Journal* a system of instruction that served his purpose. In preparing the "École de la pédale" for the *École d'orgue* Lemmens made only minor changes to the 1850 explanatory remarks, and he reproduced all of the pedal exercises in order (through the *Petits Trios très faciles*). In the explanatory remarks he describes, despairingly, the organist who plays the pedal with only the left foot, and maintains that proper pedal playing requires both feet. The left-footed organist, Lemmens argues, whose left foot is obliged to move from one place to another, cannot achieve a smooth connection of notes ("liaison du jeu") and cannot play rapid passages. Lemmens begins his training in pedal technique with a page of exercises in which the player may gain practice in the alternate toe technique: he provides only motives involving large intervals and no diatonic passages (see Example 2). Proceeding immediately to pedal scales, he specifies from the beginning a personalized toe-heel method, and he provides thorough guidance in the development of this technique: a comparison of Hesse's E-flat major scale with that of Lemmens shows that Hesse employs the heel four times and Lemmens employs the heel nine times (see Examples 1 and 3). After chromatic exercises he supplies trios and compositions involving pedal parts.

Two features of Lemmens's pedal school stand out. First, he relies chiefly on the toe-heel method, and he employs this toe-heel method in all exercises that depend on diatonic patterns. The alternate-toe technique (the first technique in Hesse's *Kleine Pedalschule*), then, cannot be understood as the point of departure in Lemmens's work. Second, Lemmens's toe-heel method aims to achieve a smooth connection of notes. To facilitate such a smooth connection of notes in difficult pedal passages, Lemmens recommends the use of two kinds of substitution—first one that employs both feet, and second, one that employs the toe and heel of one foot.[78] When Lemmens cautions the student

Example 1. Hesse, *Kleine Pedalschule*, p. 4

Example 2. Lemmens, *École d'orgue*, p. 69

Example 3. Lemmens, *École d'orgue*, p. 70

that the playing of three successive black keys with one foot is "very difficult" he implies that a smooth connection of three adjacent black keys is difficult to achieve.

Editions of the *École d'orgue*

If the fundamental principles of Lemmens's organ method were first published in the *Nouveau Journal d'orgue*, the *École d'orgue* is the classic statement as published by Lemmens. The *École d'orgue*, of continuing interest to performers and scholars, has been in print and available from time to time for more than a hundred years. A copy of what appears to be the first edition located in the Bibliothèque Nationale carries the line "Bruxelles, le ier août 1862." The method was issued in a new edition probably soon after its initial publication: another copy of the *École d'orgue* in the Bibliothèque Nationale bears on its title page the words "Nouvelle Édition," and a handwritten inscription in the volume indicates that it was in use by its owner in 1866.[79] (The "Avertissement" in the new edition does not carry the line "Bruxelles, le ier août 1862").[80] Minor corrections have been made in the "Nouvelle Édition": for example, the piece which follows *Prière No. 6* is "No. 7" and not "No. 17" as in the earlier print. The "Nouvelle Édition" print, then, is the post-1862 edition that most closely resembles the original 1862 print: the "Nouvelle Édition" is really a corrected first print. All of the later editions— supervised not by Lemmens but by others—include more substantial revisions.

An edition by William T. Best, published as *Organ-School* under the auspices of Schott in London, provides a careful and responsible translation of the method.[81] The table of contents of the Best edition matches that of the 1862, and his translations of Lemmens's notes are of special interest. For example, his comment (accompanying example eight in part one) helps shed light on how nineteenth-century English organists discussed legato playing:

> Sometimes, in order to play the inner parts smoothly, it is indispensable to 'glide' with the same finger from key to key, a matter which must be effected promptly so that the continuation of sound is unbroken.[82]

In his edition, Best occasionally adds some words of instruction, dynamics markings, and registration indications. He also revises some printing formats, substituting three-stave format for two-stave models (Postlude, p. 100; Magnificat, p. 90; *Lauda Sion, Salvatorem*, p. 118).

Best's edition, however, includes some divergences from the 1862 print. He occasionally omits indications such as the pedal markings in the Introduction and Fugue in C Minor (p. 123), the note at the end of *Creator alme siderum* (p. 88), and the rall. at the final cadence in the first section of *Hosannah!* (p.

145). Rarely he does add slur markings (as in the Funeral-Prelude on p. 82), and *ten.* markings on certain chords in some pieces. He revises the printing format in the Funeral-Prelude (p. 82) and in *Hosannah!* (p. 145), and prints out the closing sections in lieu of the *da capo* format found in the 1862 edition. In *Ite missa est* (p. 128) he transfers a handful of pedal notes to the octave above their 1862 placement.

A few of Lemmens's pieces in the *École d'orgue* appeared in other versions or were printed elsewhere (besides the *Nouveau Journal*), and Best occasionally relied on those sources for his edition. For example, in *Hosannah!* he prints a note—"This important chord is only to be met with in the Paris edition of the Offertoire" (p. 151)—to accompany the inserted D-seventh chord which does follow the text as printed in *La Maîtrise*. And in the Fanfare he prints the rousing *forte* ending found not in the 1862 print but in the harmonium version. Thus, Best provided a carefully prepared new edition in English translation of Lemmens's organ method.[83]

The 1920 Durand edition of Lemmens's *École d'orgue*, carried out by Eugène Gigout, retains the same general format published in the 1862 (and preserved by Best). Part one consists of manual exercises and manual pieces, *prières* and a repertoire of manual pieces. Part two contains the pedal exercises, trios, canons, and a repertoire of pieces for manual and pedal. If Gigout leaves intact the manual and pedal exercises, he shifts the dimensions of the

Figure 3

Comparison of the 1862 and 1920 Editions
of Lemmens's *École d'orgue*

1862 Edition	1920 Edition (Gigout, ed.)
Manual exercises	Manual exercises
27 Short Pieces	16 Short Pieces
10 *Prières*	6 *Prières*
13 Pieces (manual)	8 Pieces (manual)
Pedal exercises	Pedal exercises
26 Pieces (for manual/pedal)	20 Pieces (for manual/pedal)
Total: 75 Pieces	Total: 50 Pieces

various repertories within the *École d'orgue* and reduces by one third the repertoire that had appeared in the 1862 print (see Figure 3). Thus, the 192-page *École d'orgue* of 1862 became, in Gigout's hands, a revised 128-page treatise. For example, the *Dix Prières* of the 1862 edition were reduced to a set of six in the 1920 edition (see Figure 4). Within the repertoire of twenty pieces for manual and pedal included in part two of the 1920 edition, the number retained from the first edition is, in fact, eighteen: Gigout inserted in the repertoire two pieces from other sources (the *Adoration* on p. 84 and the *Fuga. Fanfare* on p. 85 are both from the *Trois Sonates*). Omitted by Gigout in 1920 from the table of contents of the 1862 edition were the *Communion* (p. 86), *Risoluto* (p. 93), *Prélude* (p. 100), *Sortie* (p. 101), *Offertoire* (p. 104), *Prélude* (p. 129), *Marche triomphale* (p. 154), and *Andante avec variations* (p. 160). Thus, of the total of fifty pieces published in the Durand edition, only forty-eight had appeared in the 1862 *École d'orgue*.

The Hamelle edition of the 1920s, *École d'orgue & d'harmonium basée sur le plain-chant romain*, by "Lemmens-Widor," includes a preface by Charles-Marie Widor. In this edition (copyright 1924), Widor reprinted (to judge from part one) all of the material which had appeared in the 1862 print. Thus, in part one (63 pages), Widor provided an edition of the *École d'orgue* which

Figure 4

Comparison of the *Prières* in the 1862 and 1920 Editions
of Lemmens's *École d'orgue*

1862 Edition	1920 Edition (Gigout, ed.)
Dix Prières	*Six Prières*
No. 1 Animato	No. 1 Animato
No. 2 Animato	No. 4 Animato
No. 3 Andante	No. 2 Andante
No. 4 Andante	——
No. 5 Grave	——
No. 6 Cantabile	——
No. 17 Andante	No. 3 Andante
No. 8 Andante religioso	No. 5 Andante religioso
No. 9 Andantino religioso	No. 6 Andantino religioso
No. 10 Grave	——

includes all of the *10 Prières* of 1862 and concludes with all thirteen pieces for manual alone that appeared in the first edition.[84]

* * *

Nineteenth-Century Organ Methods and Organ Teaching

However much Lemmens's *École d'orgue* has been acknowledged as a milestone in the history of organ playing in the nineteenth century, it remains important to ask *how* Lemmens's method fits into that history. The Lemmens case, after all, is a singular one. Because of his 1850 and 1852 performances in Paris and because of his *Nouveau Journal d'orgue* and *École d'orgue*, Lemmens was around mid century an unusually provocative figure. And yet, Lemmens's interest in organ teaching—and certainly in the promotion of J. S. Bach—was but one part of his career pursued from 1849 to 1881 in Belgium, to some degree in France, and in England. In Belgium, after the appointment of Mailly as professor of organ at the Brussels Conservatory, Lemmens's influence declined. (Indeed, Mailly did not, it seems, promote Lemmens as the founder of the Belgian organ school: in 1875 Mailly announced that the inaugural concert on the new Schyven organ at the Conservatory would celebrate the founding of the Brussels organ class in 1841 by Girschner.[85]) Between 1850 and 1890 France produced other organ methods, including comprehensive organ treatises such as those published by Clément Loret and Félix Clément, which remain less well-known today than Lemmens's treatise. Lemmens's influence, actively advanced by Guilmant and Widor after Lemmens's death, was significant but not omnipresent in France. To what extent were the Lemmens-influenced *ideals* of the "French organ school" Lemmens-specific? To what extent were Lemmensian methods adapted, adjusted, or transformed by Guilmant and Widor, not to mention later figures such as Marcel Dupré? What kind of role does Lemmens's *École d'orgue* actually play within the history of organ playing in France?

A full inquiry of just the technical aspects of organ performance would include examination of manual technique (questions of legato playing, of staccato, of detached connections), of pedal technique, of strategies for teaching by means of two-voice, three-voice, and four-voice didactic exercises and compositions, of the accompaniment of plainchant, and of the design of didactic anthologies. Such a project is beyond the scope of this study; this article addresses only selected aspects of manual and pedal technique within the tradition of organ methods in France (and to some degree in Belgium) between 1800 and 1910. While that tradition is Franco-Belgian, it is dependent in significant ways on German models. Indeed, Lemmens stood at the crossroads in his own formative years. From a small town near Antwerp,

Lemmens undertook studies in Brussels with Fétis, who had worked in Paris, with Girschner, who had come to Brussels from Berlin, and with Hesse in Breslau. There were German elements in Lemmens's own training (and the influence of Bach was significant), and there were German influences in the French tradition as it developed within the first half of the nineteenth century. Nevertheless, this study does restrict itself to the Franco-Belgian tradition and to the German sources *it* found helpful: it is concerned with the German lessons the French elected to take, not with the entire post-Bach tradition as a whole. (Consequently, the works of Werner and Rinck, translated into French, remain within the focus while the rich contributions of Türk, C. P. E. Bach, and others remain just beyond this focus.) Thus, the study includes the generation of Fétis and Hesse, and other teachers whose work was drawn into the Franco-Belgian arena, of the figures active at mid century (Fessy, Lemmens, Loret, Niedermeyer, Schmitt), and of those active in the last third of the century. This century-long tradition, with important German elements in its early stage, oriented to the Roman Catholic tradition, also stands behind the "French organ school" that dominated the organ world in the early decades of the twentieth century.

1800–1840

The new directions which could be found in the 1850s and 1860s were slow to establish themselves for the process of rebuilding a tradition, ravaged by the Revolution, depended on the reinstatement of the Church's historic role, on the establishment of a professorship of organ at the Conservatoire, the striking contribution of a maverick named Boëly, and, of course, the achievement of the organ builder Cavaillé-Coll whose career got underway in the 1840s. At the same time critics explored their dissatisfaction with the state of organ playing in France within several journals in the early decades of the nineteenth century: Fétis, as historian and critic, demonstrated great energy in developing this theme. In the early decades of the century, French critics looked to Germany: Danjou declared that the German organ school allowed only the "style lié." (He added that if the French organists were too far removed from this style, the Germans were too devoted to it.[86]) The dissatisfaction of critics of French organ playing led to the importation of organ methods from those who had been energetically supervising their design, the Germans. Thus, organ methods by Johann Gottlob Werner and Johann Christian Heinrich Rinck were translated into French and published for organists in France, Jean-Paul Martini published a method which depended in many ways on that of Justin Heinrich Knecht, and Jacques-Claude-Adolphe Miné published in 1835 a *Manuel simplifiée* with "Leçons de Kegel" attached to it.[87]

That the close connection of notes was a matter that required careful explanation (often with reference to the coordination of finger motion and sound) in the period ca. 1800–1840 can scarcely be questioned: Knecht, Werner, and Rinck all address the issue. Both the Rinck and Werner methods were known in France, Alexandre Choron having directed the French translation and publication of both the Rinck and Werner methods for the use of students in the Institution Royale de Musique Classique et Religieuse in Paris.[88] Danjou reviewed the French translation of the Rinck method in *La Revue et Gazette musicale* in September 1833, and he later published a review of Johann Georg Herzog's *Der Praktische Organist* in 1846.[89]

The Werner *Orgelschule* (printed in Germany between 1805 and 1824), recommended by Rinck, praised by Choron, and included by Fétis in his annotated list of organ methods, will serve as an example. In his discussion of manual technique as translated in the *Méthode élémentaire*, Werner stresses the fact that on the organ (as opposed to other keyboard instruments) the tone lasts only as long as the key remains depressed:

> It is thus necessary to be careful: 1) to give to each note its just duration, and 2) to introduce neither space nor overlap in the passage from one note to another note, that is to say to take care that there be neither interruption nor simultaneity between tones that ought to succeed one another, the former producing a choppy playing, the latter cacophony: two defects between which it is necessary to know how to hold to a true middle course.[90]

In his *Orgelschule* Werner warns the organist to avoid playing two adjacent keys with the same finger because it would result in an undesired separation of tones. In the same source he discusses finger substitution, with one musical example (a series of three-voice chords to be played by the right hand) as an illustration of a technique which, according to his note, is often useful in the playing of chorales (see Example 4).[91]

Werner, like Rinck, presents detailed explanations of the proper method of connecting notes in the pedal. In both the *Orgelschule* and the *Méthode élémentaire* Werner reminds the player that to play well requires the use of both feet. In the *Méthode élémentaire*, the author states:

> To play the pedals well, that is to say, on the one hand, to connect the tones, and on the other to give to the performance all the speed of which it is

Example 4. Werner, *Orgelschule*, p. 8

Example 5. Werner, *Orgelschule*, p. 12

capable, it is necessary to employ the two feet, and as much as is possible to employ them alternately.[92]

In the more detailed *Orgelschule* Werner took to task the organist who relied chiefly on the left foot, reserving the right foot only for notes seldom needed:

> With this mistaken method of playing the pedal, one must jump here and there always with one foot (especially the left foot), and the tones cannot be properly connected, as they should be; . . . and rapid tempos, which are certainly played on the pedal, are unimaginable.[93]

In Werner's exercises employing diatonic ascending and descending passages he indicates by signs the method of passing one foot in front of or behind the other. Werner teaches the student how to play not only diatonic scale-like passages but the chromatic scale as well with alternating toes. After presenting exercises in this method, Werner then presents as a second method the toe-heel practice. Expecting complaints, Werner warns that the second method is less accommodating and less convenient than the other method.[94] Werner suggests, finally, that the student make use of both methods in the playing of the pedal. In the portion preceding the introduction of the second method he presents some special cases (using alternate toes), shows *when* two successive toes (of the same foot) should be used in a diatonic passage, and shows also an example in which the right foot jumps a third (see Example 5).[95] (Also, he explains how to employ toe substitution.) Werner devotes more space to the explanation of the toe-toe technique than he does to the toe-heel technique, and clearly it is the alternating toe technique which serves as the point of departure.

Rinck in the *L'École pratique d'orgue* (the Choron translation) and Martini in the *École d'orgue* both teach the alternating toe method as the first method to be mastered, and the toe-heel method as the second.[96] Rinck provides in his exercises practice of the chromatic scale with first the toe-toe then the toe-heel method. He gives an illustration in which he counsels, in effect, using both methods within a passage.[97] Martini, who begins with a short sampling of toe-toe scale exercises, states that the toe-heel method is preferable, and that a third method, a combination of the two methods, "is the most convenient."[98] Martini explains that there are two rules about the use of the second method: to avoid the heel on sharps, and to avoid using the toe to jump from one key to another. In this regard, Martini provides a special explanation in a double pedal exercise to permit the organist to glide from B flat down to A with the left toe (this clearly is an exceptional practice). Both Rinck and Martini provide exercises to train the organist in playing thirds, chords, trills, and double pedal.

The comments above on manual technique confirm the fact that the German treatises put to use by the French between 1800 and 1840 assign sovereign importance to the legato connection of notes. Despite the fact that much ink has been spilled on the question of "legato" from the time of J. S. Bach to 1840, and that many considerations make it perilous to generalize, it is fair to say that scholars have described a determined attempt in keyboard music (and beyond keyboard music) around 1800 and onward to explore new dimensions of legato. Although a complex issue, there is widespread agreement that the late eighteenth-century theorists' description of the "normal" connection of notes (one that is not indicated in the music, and one that results in a connection that is neither staccato nor slurred) was a more detached connection than the one sought by Werner, Rinck, and Martini.[99]

As for pedal technique, the point of departure in the methods of Werner, Rinck, and Martini (and also that of Kegel published by Miné in 1835) is the alternating toe technique.[100] Moreover, the alternating toe technique was the point of departure for Hesse in the *Kleine Pedalschule*, and was described as well by theorists before 1800. Thus, the pedal methods of Werner, Rinck, and Martini (whose pedal method is more extensive than that of his model, Knecht, published 1795), brought to the French organists full comprehensive instruction in pedal technique, instruction that synthesized German pedal technique of the post-Bach tradition.[101]

1840–1870

Between 1840 and 1870 many treatises were published in France by French organists representing a diversity of approaches, from Schmitt's conservative, elaborate explanation of pedal technique (indebted to German methods) to Loret's detailed instruction on the legato style. In this period institutional training became even more established, with François Benoist teaching, as he had since 1819, a great many organists at the Conservatoire, and with Loret teaching at the new École Niedermeyer.[102] Organ playing was vigorously alive in Paris and Cavaillé-Coll installed many new instruments at notable Paris churches (La Madeleine, Saint-Vincent-de-Paul, Sainte-Clotilde, Notre-Dame, Saint-Sulpice, and others). The installation of new instruments brought opportunities for inaugural concerts in the churches, and while many organists made contributions to these concerts, Lefébure-Wély established a reputation as one of the most celebrated of the Parisian organists. Also in this period the harmonium became an instrument of consequence, and methods of playing began to appear (including those by J. L. Battmann and Lefébure-Wély).[103] Publications of organ music were abundant, and there was great diversity within the organ repertoire heard in these middle decades, from the wildly popular improvisations by Lefébure-Wély (often depicting some calamity, such as a storm or flood), to the compositions in the "style sévère" by Lemmens and others, and the occasional performance of works by J. S. Bach.

Georges Schmitt, while he does not address the topical questions about manual technique in his treatise *Nouveau Manuel complet* of 1855, does provide detailed instruction on pedal technique indebted to the German methods discussed earlier.[104] With the alternating toe technique serving as a point of departure, Schmitt explains how to pass one foot behind (and in front of) the other foot. As a second method Schmitt presents the toe-heel technique, and he counsels that the second method will prove less effective for diatonic passages and more advantageous for chromatic passages. After an explanation of a third technique—the use of the right side and left side of one foot—he suggests that the best method would combine all the techniques as circumstances permit. In Schmitt's practical instruction he advocates the alternating toe method (with the use of scales and passages which, inciden-tally, call for one toe to play adjacent keys). Schmitt then provides exercises to perfect the toe-heel method with diatonic and chromatic scales, and intro-duces the technique of left foot/right foot subsitition on one pedal key. After exercises that call for a double pedal technique, he presents excerpts from organ works of J. S. Bach, Rinck, Brixi, Hesse, Schmitt, and others. In a separate publication, *Le Musée de l'organiste* (1852), Schmitt designed an anthology of organ works composed by himself and by contemporaries, as well as by composers from the eighteenth century (F. Couperin, Handel).[105]

Alexandre-Charles Fessy, in *Manuel d'orgue à l'usage des églises catholiques* (1845?), displays an historian's perspective, leaving no doubt that he consi-dered the organ of his time the culmination of improvements made through-out history:[106]

> In the following centuries, important improvements were introduced, and organ building made rapid progress until our own days, in which the most complete perfection made the ORGAN the largest, the most beautiful, and the most noble of instruments.[107]

In manual technique Fessy instructs the keyboard player how to play legato ("très lié"), and also provides instruction on how to play in a detached manner.[108] In his instruction on pedal technique Fessy takes an historical view, for he ties differences in pedal technique to differences in pedalboards. He hails the contemporary French builders who provide pedalboards on which the organist can execute passages almost as complex as those played by the left hand.[109] He explains that the old pedalboards permitted only the use of the toe (and even with this technique one could not truly play rapid passages), and that in the worst case the organist used only the left foot. The new pedalboards, Fessy continues, permit the use of both feet and one can play legato by using alternately the heel and the toe of the foot.[110] (Fessy does not, however, acknowledge the alternating toe technique as used in diatonic passages.) Near the end of the treatise Fessy provides a prelude which demands a double-pedal technique and other preludes (using three-staff format) which call for "pédale obligée."

Clément Loret had studied with Lemmens, and he published his first didactic works in the same decade Lemmens published the *Nouveau Journal d'orgue,* and before Lemmens published the *École d'orgue.* His "Exercice journalier" of 1858–1859, published in *La Maîtrise,* included a preface by Louis Niedermeyer, the head of the École Niedermeyer established in Paris in 1853. In that preface, Niedermeyer stressed the necessity of holding down each key as required

> because, in the legato style ["style lié"]—the true style of the instrument and that, with short and rare exceptions, is the only one employed—the least interruption in the tones produces the most unpleasant effect . . .[111]

In the "Exercice journalier" Loret presents an exhaustive series of exercises designed to train the organist in the use of finger substitution and the legato style.[112] The first part begins with an explanatory introduction to a set of thirty exercises. (From the beginning the student practices finger substitution in first one-voice, then two- and three-voice textures.) In the second part, Loret presents short pieces with fingering to achieve legato connection by means of finger substitution. Later Loret introduces the notion of "détaché" with exercises in which each hand controls two voices one of which is legato and the other détaché. Within this section Loret uses individually beamed notes to indicate a connection that is "détaché" (for example, 4-4-4-4 on ascending notes F-G-A-B in the right hand). Without specifying the length of the notes connected through détaché style, he does counsel that it is necessary to observe the length of the notes and the rests, "and to have care not to leave the finger too long" on the notes followed by rests.[113] Following the explanation of detached playing, Loret supplies a musical example from a fugue by J. S. Bach in which he indicates the detached notes with staccato dots.

In a letter to Lemmens, Loret remarked that the instruction in his "Exercice journalier" in pedal technique (especially in the practice of substitution) was indebted not only to Lemmens but also to methods of Schneider, Werner, Knecht, "Martini:Choron," and Miné.[114] He begins his pedal instruction with major and minor scales which call for a toe-heel technique. (Incidentally, he provides no explanatory introduction therewith, except a note to define the symbols used in the scales to indicate heel and toe and right foot and left foot.[115]) In his method one foot commands a stretch of scale degrees up to six notes. He supplies exercises designed to show how the heel and toe of one

Example 6. J. S. Bach, Prelude and Fugue in E Minor, BWV 533, mm. 12–15, as edited by Louis Niedermeyer

foot can play the interval of a third. He employs alternating toes in exercises based on intervals such as the octave, the fourth, and the third (but not in any diatonic passage).

In a revealing example of mid-nineteenth-century editorial practice, Niedermeyer annotated J. S. Bach's Prelude and Fugue in E Minor, BWV 533, for publication in *La Maîtrise*. For a passage that could easily be played by the alternating toe technique, he suggests that the heel and toe technique could produce a legato "jeu lié" (see Example 6).[116]

Loret and Niedermeyer unquestionably pointed the way in their work in Paris to the mid-nineteenth-century legato technique that Lemmens advocated in his *Nouveau Journal d'orgue* and *École d'orgue*. Loret in his "Exercice journalier" and Niedermeyer in his editorial markings appear to have championed the extreme legato style that Lemmens taught in Brussels. Within this period in which conservative and progressive tendencies co-existed, important teaching traditions were established which had far-reaching influence.

1870–1890

Around 1870, two leading organists took center stage as professors of organ in distinguished conservatories in Belgium and France. In 1869, Alphonse Mailly succeeded Lemmens to become professor of organ at the Brussels Conservatory, and in 1872, César Franck succeeded Benoist as professor of organ at the Conservatoire in Paris. Unlike Mailly, Franck, by virtue of his compositions for organ, was a central figure in the second half of the century: his contribution to the organ art from 1860 to 1890 was, by any account, one of the most important. Yet Franck left distressingly little in the way of conventional documents relating to the teaching of organ technique. During the same years, other notable organists played a role in the history of French organ playing, and some of these far less prominent figures, namely Loret and Clément, did publish treatises. Before considering Franck, a word about their work is in order.

Clément Loret, who published his "Exercice journalier" under the auspices of *La Maîtrise* (1858–1859), also published a larger treatise, *Cours d'orgue*

(Méthode complète d'orgue).[117] Loret's treatise consists of four parts: 1) exercises and etudes; 2) pedal exercises and etudes; 3) practical knowledge about the organ; and 4) improvisation and the accompaniment of chant. Joseph Kreps lists the date of publication for the *Méthode complète d'orgue* as 1880, and extant copies suggest that there were several printings of the treatise.[118] Two copies of the treatise are housed in the Bibliothèque Nationale. The first, Vm.8.R.184, includes parts one and two, and the second, CR.73, includes parts one through four. Parts three and four, unlike one and two, include larger compositions by the author (in much the same way as Lemmens's *École d'orgue*). Comparison of parts one and two in these two sources suggests that Loret made editorial additions to CR.73. Indeed, CR.73 is marked "15e. Édition," and is thus a reprint with some changes.

Loret begins the manual instruction not with an explanatory introduction but with diatonic exercises accompanied by the instruction to play with a "good legato without allowing the finger to drag on the key."[119] He does not, then, begin with exercises illustrating finger substitution, as he had done in 1858–1859. (The first exercise and the first étude contain no instances of finger substitution at all.) He then instructs the student in legato playing in which the soprano moves at a faster rate than does the alto (all in one hand) with a caution to hold the fingers down throughout the duration of the notes. In subsequent exercises he does provide thorough instruction in various techniques using finger substitution, in which one hand plays two-voice and three-voice chords. In CR.73 he adds ties of common tones in successive chords, ties which did not appear in Vm.8.R.184. The tenth étude provides a rich example of the close connection of notes his legato style entailed, marked "toujours bien lié" (see Example 7).

In the *Cours d'orgue*, Loret chose a point of departure for pedal technique that was different from the one adopted in 1858–1859. In his explanatory introduction (there had been none in 1858–1859), he states that "the pedal notes are played alternately with the right and left foot, or with the toe and heel of one single foot" and he provides as the first example a rocking-motive passage, using heel and toe of one foot (with the instruction "Liez bien").[120]

Example 7. Loret, *10me Étude*, mm. 1–2, from *Cours d'orgue*

When he employs an alternating toe technique he does so only in passages built on octaves or other large intervals. (He does provide one exercise in which alternating toes play an arpeggiated passage.) He also instructs the student in the practice of substituting toes on one pedal key. And he even provides an explanatory note to help the student turn the feet correctly to achieve heel and toe of alternating feet on successive notes. In CR.73 he adds some pedal indications not found in Vm.8.R.184, and changes others. If some revisions appear to be corrections, others reflect new strategies in the use of heels and toes: for example, he revised several pedalings so that they are less reliant on one foot proceeding with heel and toe and more reliant on the two feet working together. The études include striking examples of imaginative pedal writing: the eleventh étude, a three-voice canon, calls for the pedal to be played on the 8' Violoncelle, and the nineteenth étude, for double pedal, employing a prodigious technique, calls for *Fonds de 8 p.*. (A further instance of an 8' pedal line occurs in the *Trio pour trois claviers* in part three.) Loret in the second half of the nineteenth century unquestionably promoted the most demanding of pedal techniques in his didactic works and compositions, and he provided some of the most detailed instruction on legato style by means of finger substitution.

Félix Clément (1822–1888), in his *Méthode d'orgue* of 1873, published a treatise of a different sort: he provided a comprehensive method of playing combined with information on organ building, an introduction to counterpoint and harmony, a study of the accompaniment of plainchant, and an anthology of pieces by other composers (including Rinck, Benoist, and Guilmant).[121] Regarding manual technique, Clément offers a comment on legato in relation to the motion of fingers on the keys:

> One should press the fingers without brusqueness, but in a lively manner, and decisively, without any hesitation, and with equal force; to make all the notes distinctly heard, do not allow the key to rise except at the moment when the note which follows is depressed.[122]

After several exercises designed to promote finger independence, equality, and strength, Clément provides a detailed instruction in finger substitution to facilitate the close connection of notes.[123]

Clément's pedal studies begin with the toe-heel method, and he explains the practice of substitution (heel and toe of one foot) on a pedal key which occurs when the left foot executes a chromatic scale from low C to middle C, and he relates this practice to the finger substitution used on the manuals. Unlike Loret, Clément does provide one example of alternating toe technique used in a diatonic passage, an ascending and descending C-major scale using left and right toes. He also illustrates the use of alternating feet in exercises involving octaves and wide intervals. Strikingly enough, Clément also provides a chromatic scale executed by alternating toes. Later, he suggests another method of playing the chromatic scale in which the left foot plays the lower half (heel and toe) and the right foot the upper half of the pedalboard. Like so many previous authors he includes passages using double pedal technique at the end of his instruction.[124] In his avoidance of the term "jeu lié," in his instruction designed to make fingers equal, and in his reference to the toe-toe pedaling technique of the past, Clément provides a striking and somewhat unusual treatise on organ playing in the last three decades of the century.

Despite statements and recollections of his students and others, Franck's own technique—not to mention his own teaching—remains somewhat in the shadows. Anything but a treatise writer, he left little documentary evidence about his methods, and some post-1890 accounts present more problems than explanations. Adolphe Marty, a student of Franck, has been credited with a famous observation, "We have no idea of the freedom with which Franck played his own pieces." This provocative statement suggests that Franck embraced a dynamic notion of interpretation: different ways of performing his music (different tempi, different registrations, different rhythmic manipulations) could all qualify as authoritative or authentic, in short, as the music. And thereby one of the twentieth century's most cherished notions—that one particular way to perform a work can be considered the most authentic—has perhaps little relevance to the case of Franck.[125] In another often repeated statement, Marcel Dupré wrote that Franck played "as one played in France in his time: approximate legato, approximate observance of durations."[126] But if the statement clearly suggests that Franck's notion of "legato" was less rigorous than absolute, and if this was a trait of the nineteenth century ("in his time"), then Dupré appears to be implying that his own legato is the standard. The notion of tying common tones in successive chords, advocated so strenuously by Widor since before the turn of the century, and later by Dupré, may not in fact have been a feature of Franck's own technique. If it was a feature, and if Franck performed differently on different occasions, it may not have been systematically observed by Franck himself.[127] It is not clear how these questions can at present be resolved.

Franck's own training as an organist included two separate stages, his experience as a student at the Conservatoire just before 1840 and further self-guided study around 1860. In some ways, it was the later period which was decisive for Franck's career. From 1858 he worked with a pédalier, and at Sainte-Clotilde beginning in 1859 he played an organ with a pedalboard that was larger than the ones he had earlier played. Thus, at this time he developed a pedal technique that he surely had not acquired in his earlier training, allowing him to conceive and perform pedal passages of great virtuosity such as those found in his *Grande Pièce symphonique*.[128]

Much has been written about Franck's emphasis, during his years as professor of organ, on improvisation, for in retrospect, Franck's tenure seemed remarkable to many for its lack of emphasis on technique. Louis Vierne's often quoted remark, "Performance ["L'exécution"] interested him little," and Henri Büsser's remark, "To tell the truth, technical instruction was rather neglected, especially the study of the pedal," suggest that Franck did not demonstrate a pedagogical mission that compared with those of Widor and Guilmant which found favor in the 1890s and beyond.[129]

What, then, can be said about Franck's methods of playing the organ? In manual technique he left but few bits of evidence. The *Choral* No. 1 in E Major contains an example of his fingering which illustrates the use of thumb glissando.[130] And he indicated at least once the use of 5–4–5 in the right hand in an ascending diatonic passage. Moreover, in the Braille scores that he prepared a few years before his death he illustrated the use of finger substitution to ensure legato within Bach works.[131] As for pedal technique, he left few indications, and those were chiefly in the works of Alkan (his own edition) and of Bach (as found in the Braille scores). In the ascending pedal scales of Alkan, Franck uses a mixed toe-heel technique in which each foot plays two (or at most three) notes in sequence.[132] In the Braille scores, Franck pedals repeated-note motives with either heel and toe, or with alternating toes.[133] In the subject of the D-Major Fugue (at the end of the work) he uses a toe-heel solution, mixing alternating toe technique with toe-heel technique.[134] And a rare example in his own music, the heel-toe rocking third (A-F#) motive in the *Pièce héroïque* is not easy to interpret: the pedaling can be understood to indicate a legato effect, yet it could just as well be made into a detached figure since it brings out a timpani-like motive.[135] The evidence, fragmentary as it stands, does not suggest that Franck was a proponent of systematic training in the matter of technique, as understood to include manual and pedal exercises.[136]

1890–1911

Within the broad history of organ teaching at the Paris Conservatoire, the years 1819–1872 (Benoist) and 1872–1890 (Franck) had, in some respects, several elements in common; a decisive turn, however, occurred in 1890 with the appointment of Charles-Marie Widor. Widor brought with him a new philosophy and a new methodology which certainly proved disruptive to organists who had been studying previously with Franck. Vierne reported a comment attributed to Widor that has been quoted many times: "In France, one neglects far too much performance to the gain of improvisation: this is more than a mistake, this is nonsense."[137] Widor stressed that a well-developed technique was a prerequisite for the execution of works by J. S. Bach, and he considered those works of paramount importance in the study of the organ. Rowland Dunham reported (referring to conversations with Henri Libert) that Widor did change the prevailing style of Bach playing—and away from the "flexibility" and "rubato" that Franck had used.[138] With Widor's appointment the Conservatoire entered a twenty-year period in which organ instruction, by Widor from 1890 to 1896 and by Guilmant from 1896 to his death in 1911, was guided by two great figures in the Parisian organ scene who had both studied with Lemmens early in their careers. Moreover, both Widor and Guilmant held Lemmens and his teaching in high regard, and both were devoted to the organ music of J. S. Bach.

Widor studied with Lemmens in Brussels in 1863: Widor's father and Cavaillé-Coll arranged for the young Widor to go to Brussels where he in fact studied not only with Lemmens but with Fétis as well. Adolphe Boschot reported that Widor's typical day in Brussels began with a lesson with Fétis, that he practiced organ in the morning and afternoon, and that he would then play an important composition by heart for Lemmens (the two categories of such works mentioned by Boschot are preludes and organ chorales of J. S. Bach).[139] Finally, in the evening Widor worked on counterpoint. Moreover, Widor was also introduced to the music of Hesse, which he performed, and Widor reported that Fétis spoke often in those Brussels lessons of Rinck. Widor, who in this way learned the tradition embraced by Lemmens and Fétis,[140] on at least one occasion later in his life referred to Belgium as his "artistic home."[141]

Widor's views on the art of organ playing combined ideas from Lemmens, from Hesse no doubt via Lemmens, and ideas about Bach, with a firm advocacy of the modern Cavaillé-Coll organ of his own time. He echoed Hesse in his frequently articulated recommendation that, in gauging tempos for Bach's music, one should start with the smallest note value, playing it rapidly and making it at the same time perceptible to the listener.[142] Yet, certainly no antiquarian, he felt fortunate to be living in the age of Cavaillé-Coll: he wrote that while the art of playing the organ had remained the same since Bach's day, instruments had greatly improved.[143]

If Widor did not systematize his views in a treatise, he did leave many written remarks about manual and pedal technique. Clearly, Widor considered J. S. Bach the model for organists of his own day. In the preface to André Pirro's *L'Orgue de Jean-Sébastien Bach*, Widor described Bach at the organ:

> He played, the body slightly forward, immobile, with an admirable rhythm, an absolute polyphonic ensemble, a marvelous clarity, not fast, master of himself and, so to speak, of time, giving the idea of an incomparable grandeur.[144]

In his comments about pedal technique he made precise recommendations: he advised that the foot should attack the key from a position close to the surface, without any noise, and with the toe "one or two centimeters from the black keys."[145] A notable feature of his playing, A. M. Henderson observed, was his use of heel and toe. Widor, according to this report, advocated the use of the heels as often as the toes, and recommended not only beginning a passage but also playing short notes with heels.[146] Widor stressed the desirability of absolute vertical alignment of the constituent parts of a musical texture, and that the alignment depended on careful coordination of the hands and the feet.[147] In keyboard playing, he advocated a principle of articulation in which the articulated note loses half its value, and, in addition, he counseled that "détaché" playing should be executed with the finger as close as possible to the keys.[148]

An element of Widor's teaching "method" which warrants particular emphasis is his notion of rhythmic vitality. This issue, which concerns the just tempo, was of great importance in his teaching, and certainly developed from his earlier study with Lemmens. "What is rhythm?" he asked in the preface to André Pirro's book on Bach. "The constant demonstration of will ["volonté"] or periodic return of the strong beat."[149] Widor recalled a lesson in Brussels in which Lemmens mentioned "volonté": Widor had apparently performed a work in such a way as to confirm for Lemmens that "speed" is the false ideal of the youthful virtuoso. Having completed the piece, and believing that he had succeeded, he received instead an admonishment from Lemmens:

> "It is nothing," he said mechanically, "without will." What did he mean by "will?" I did not dare to ask him. I finally understood: it is the art of the orator, its authority manifested by the calm, the order and just proportions of the discourse. To musicians, the will shows itself above all through rhythm.[150]

If this will grows out of the rhythmic dimension of music, it signifies at the same time something more profound. Harry Jepson, an American who studied with Widor, reported that Widor, listening to organists playing sixteenth-note passages as fast as possible, would insist that they play instead in what was said to be a more Bach-like manner, "always melodically and [with] due respect for the expressiveness of the passage."[151] Playing in this manner led to a clear and even brilliant execution: it also opened up a "broader higher ideal of the realm of organ music, as expressed in the achievement of its most important composer."

Late in his life, Widor commented on Lemmens's role in the tradition of organ playing in Paris. He wrote that Cavaillé-Coll had wished to attract Lemmens to Paris.

> It worked out otherwise. Lemmens was obliged to divide his life between England and Belgium. But his students, responsible for the tradition, had the happy fortune to be able to uphold it here at the Paris Conservatory.[152]

Widor, along with his fellow Lemmens student Guilmant, took this responsibility with great seriousness.

"Alexandre Guilmant. French organist, composer and editor." This introductory biographical summary from *The New Grove Dictionary of Music and Musicians* reduces Guilmant to just five words.[153] As an organist Guilmant played the Cavaillé-Coll instrument at La Trinité in Paris for thirty years, and as a recitalist he played an impressive number of recitals—and recital series—in Paris and many other countries including the United States. As a composer he wrote a staggering amount of music, most of it for the organ, including multi-movement sonatas, stately marches, character pieces, and many works based on plainchant. As an editor he worked on the publication of notable anthologies including the *École classique de l'orgue* and the *Archives des maîtres de l'orgue*. But the five-word summary above fails to mention his critical role as a teacher. Indeed, he was highly esteemed in this capacity: he taught organ at the Conservatoire (from 1896) and at the Schola Cantorum (which he helped found in the 1890s). And in his teaching he drew on his knowledge of past traditions, and on his own period of study with Lemmens.

If Guilmant's study in Belgium with Lemmens in the 1860s was brief, it was certainly not inconsequential: he formed an attachment to Lemmens's notions of organ playing, to some of Lemmens's works, and to the Lemmens family itself. Through the years he became known for his command of an astonishingly large repertoire, in which Lemmens's works always retained a place. In the 1870s he arranged to play Lemmens's recently published *Sonates* on a tour in England. Indeed, a letter in a private collection in Brussels reveals that he wrote to Lemmens requesting answers to questions about registration in the first two *Sonates*.[154] At his series of concerts played on the Cavaillé-Coll organ at the Trocadéro (1880), he included works by Lemmens. And in the forty programs played at the St. Louis World's Fair in 1904, he found a place in this vast survey for eight works by Lemmens, including the Grand Fantasia in E Minor ("The Storm"), the *Final* and the Fanfare (from the *École d'orgue*), and the complete *Sonate pontificale*.[155] In another letter to Lemmens (also in a private collection) he expresses delight that Lemmens—the "chef de notre école"—would be playing on the 1878 Trocadéro series. Finally, he also corresponded with Mme Lemmens in the 1880s about the posthumous publication of the *Œuvres inédites*.[156]

Guilmant's playing and his teaching, by all accounts powerful and impressive, have not been forgotten in the twentieth century. While his systematic approach never took the form of a published method, there is at least one intriguing reference to a written method, and William C. Carl (it was reported) had received a copy:

> His [Carl's] student days in Paris with Alexandre Guilmant speedily ripened into a friendship which lasted till the famous composer's death, when he gave in writing to Dr. Carl his own method of organ playing and teaching—a legacy of which he is the sole possessor.[157]

Guilmant's written "method of organ playing and teaching," if it were to appear, would surely be an important document. At the moment our knowledge of his "method" depends on two kinds of statements, first, those printed by Guilmant himself, and second, accounts written by students and sympathetic observers. He had an historian's interest in organ playing, and his library contained works pertaining to organ playing by Schmitt and Rinck.[158] Moreover, he copied out Herzog's organ method.[159] And he referred many times to Lemmens's method.

In one of his most important printed statements, the article "La Musique d'orgue: les formes, l'exécution, l'improvisation" in the *Encyclopédie de la musique et dictionnaire du Conservatoire*, Guilmant explains in great detail many aspects of proper manual technique.[160] Not surprisingly, he addresses himself to the legato connection of notes. "When there are neither slurs nor dots above the notes it is understood that one plays the piece in the 'style lié,' which is the true manner of playing the keys on the organ," he states, adding that this legato is the goal of progress in digital technique.[161] In his discussion of fingering, he provides a striking example drawn from Bach's *Orgelbüchlein*: the organ chorale *Christum wir sollen loben schon*, BWV 611. He explains that the chorale tune (in the alto voice) may be played using chiefly thumbs and the thumb glissando technique. To amplify his discussion of the use of the thumb on three successive diatonic notes, he refers to Lemmens's Andantino (*École d'orgue*), which also calls for such a technique, and he recommends to the reader Lemmens's thumb glissando exercise, as well.[162] (Incidentally, this musical example reveals that Guilmant regarded finger substitution at the sixteenth-note level to be appropriate in playing Bach's *Christum wir sollen loben schon*.) In discussing phrasing and articulation he comments on the use of "détaché/legato" to clarify accentuation in musical passages. He goes on to explain that phrasing and articulation give "life to subjects of fugues and other motives," and he brings into the discussion bowing techniques used in playing string instruments, even mentioning models to be consulted in pieces such as Bach's *Wachet auf*.[163] In a passage of compelling interest he presents musical examples of subjects with proper articulation, attributing these examples to Lemmens. And he uses Lemmens's *Laudate Dominum Omnes Gentes* (*École d'orgue*) to illustrate the proper articulation of chordal texture. Furthermore, he states that Lemmens carefully differentiated in printed scores the "notes détachées" (separately beamed) from the "notes liées" (beamed together): he holds up a passage from Lemmens's *Ite Missa Est* (*École d'orgue*) as evidence.[164] Finally, he counsels the musician to adapt the "style lié" to actual acoustical settings, and to play less strictly legato in rooms of larger dimensions. His own "style lié" made a deep impression on contemporaries.[165] Henderson, in 1937, pointed to his idiosyncratic legato style with these words:

> I still remember the profound impression his playing made upon me, and especially in the qualities of clarity and rhythm. Indeed it was quite a revelation to me, as until then I was familiar with only the very legato, rather stodgy and dull organ-playing which was so general at the time.[166]

In his discussion of pedal technique Guilmant reports that formerly an older method of pedal playing was used in which alternate toes were employed, and he supplies a musical example illustrating the execution of an A-minor pedal scale by toes alone.[167] Moreover, he refers in a footnote to the French translation of Rinck's method. With the new pedal method, that of Lemmens, he states, one can play without agitation and with a smooth connection ("bien lié"), and he recommends to the reader Lemmens's method.[168] He addresses himself to double-pedal techniques in this article (he mentions in passing a method of executing Bach's *Aus tiefer Noth*, BWV 686),[169] and he prints in *L'École classique* an entire piece (labeled there as *Prélude-Chorale, Wir glauben all' an einer Gott, Vater* by Krebs/Bach [BWV 740]) with complete markings to show how to execute two voices on the pedalboard (see Example 8).[170]

From the wealth of written accounts of Guilmant's teaching made by his students, a very few will have to suffice. First, many observers commented on the "clarity" of his style, and they related that "clarity" to his masterful handling of the rhythmic and metric vitality of the music. Henderson stated:

> In the class constant insistence was made on the need for clarity, for articulation, for commas or breathmarks, and accuracy not only of notes but also in the value of rests, so that the time-value of the bar would not be disturbed.[171]

Carl commented on the "magnificent underlying pulsation, the steady rhythmic beat, which was always evident."[172] Second, Guilmant apparently related musical playing to singing. Carl reported that he advised: "Never play a note that does not sing, and when you compose, make each of the inner parts sing as well as the soprano."[173] (Marshall Bidwell reports that Widor and Libert depended on singing in their teaching as well:

> Both Widor and his worthy colleague, Henri Libert . . . were always singing the melodies, and this seems to be a favorite hobby of French musicians. The value of this is quite obvious, in that a phrase, whether in a Bach fugue or anything else, is pretty apt to be musical if it is sung.[174])

Finally, in Guilmant's *Encyclopédie* article on organ playing, he stressed that the goal of playing was "un jeu parfaitement lié et chantant sur l'orgue."[175]

Example 8. Krebs/Bach, *Prélude-Choral, Wir glauben all'an einer Gott, Vater*, BWV 740, mm. 7–10, as edited by Guilmant

Harvey Gaul, in remarks about the achievement of Guilmant's student Joseph Bonnet, explained what Bonnet stood to gain from the Lemmens-Guilmant school:

> His style is that of the Lemmens-Guilmant school—cleanliness and vigor, mastered legato and staccato, and above all exact note-values. If there is one thing that the French organist, like the French philosopher, believes in, it is clarity.[176]

Guilmant accepted his inheritance of a systematic method from Lemmens and he accepted the centrality of Bach with great seriousness. Acknowledging that Boëly had championed Bach—with but limited success—in France earlier in the century, Guilmant gave credit to Lemmens with this statement:

> But M. Jacques Lemmens, from whom I had the honor of receiving instruction, was more fortunate. His efforts to introduce the best style of organ music in France began in 1852. His playing of Bach was a complete revelation to French organists, and formed the foundation of a more serious style of playing and composition.[177]

Taking a broad, historical view of organ playing and organ repertoire, Guilmant made mighty contributions in the very categories established by Lemmens and Fétis. Guilmant taught a great many students and he reportedly said, "If I can leave behind me a correct style and method of organ playing, it is all I ask for."[178] He championed Bach, he created a repertoire based on plainchant, and he published two kinds of anthologies: in the tradition of Lemmens, one drawn from his own works, and in the tradition of Fétis, one drawn from the history of organ music.

Research for this article was made possible by a Fulbright grant and by research grants from Pomona College. The staffs of the Lemmensinstituut of Leuven, Belgium, the Bibliothèque Royale Albert Ier/Koninklijke Bibliotheek Albert I of Brussels, the Conservatoire Royal de Musique of Brussels, the Bibliothèque Nationale, and the British Library, London, all provided helpful assistance. The Clerfaÿt family of Brussels generously allowed access to its archives. I gratefully acknowledge the assistance kindly offered by Jean Ferrard and the late Hubert Schoonbroodt. Orpha Ochse graciously allowed me access to her collection of materials concerning French and Belgian organ music. Finally, I am indebted to Jan Van Landeghem and Fabian Lochner for the valuable help they provided in the early stages of this project.

NOTES

[1] Charles-Marie Widor, "La Classe d'orgue du Conservatoire de Paris . . . et Jacques Lemmens," *Musica sacra* 34 (1927): 166.

[2] Henri Blanchard, *La Revue et Gazette musicale* 33 (1850): 274.

[3] "Arts, sciences, et lettres," *Journal de Bruxelles*, 1 February 1881.

[4] Alexandre Guilmant, "La Musique d'orgue: les formes, l'exécution, l'improvisation," in *Physiologie vocale et auditive, technique vocale et instrumentale (voix—instruments à réservoir d'air)*, part 2, vol. 2 of *Encyclopédie de la musique et dictionnaire du Conservatoire*, ed. Albert Lavignac and Lionel de la Laurencie (Paris: Delagrave, 1926), 1125–80.

[5] J. Lemmens, *École d'orgue*, ed. Eugène Gigout (Paris: Durand, 1920); and J. Lemmens, *École d'orgue & harmonium basée sur le plain-chant romain*, ed. Charles-Marie Widor (Paris: Hamelle, 1924).

[6] Edward Shippen Barnes, "An Organ Student in France: An Informal Talk," *The Diapason* 12 (July 1921): 21. (Barnes's statement suggests a lack of familiarity with the large body of liturgical organ music based on chant composed in France in the nineteenth century.)

[7] Harvey B. Gaul, "Department for Organists," *The Etude* 31 (1913): 900.

[8] On Guilmant's 1904 concerts in the United States see *The Forty Programs Rendered by M. Alexandre Guilmant at Festival Hall, World's Fair, St. Louis* (1904; reprint, Richmond, Va.: The Organ Historical Society, 1985).

[9] *The Story of Organ Music from the Early Composers to the Present Time* (New York: G. Schirmer, 1917). This booklet details five recitals given by Bonnet between 12 November and 10 December 1917.

[10] Harvey Grace, "Modern French Organ Music," *The Musical Times* 58 (1917): 19.

[11] Mailly's performance is noted in *Annuaire du Conservatoire Royal de Musique de Bruxelles* 1 (1877): 114. On Guilmant's appearance in Amsterdam, see C. M. Philbert, *L'Orgue du Palais de l'Industrie d'Amsterdam* (Amsterdam: Binger Frères, 1876), 160.

[12] "Arts, sciences, et lettres."

[13] François-Joseph Fétis, *Biographie universelle des musiciens et bibliographie générale de la musique*, s.v. Lemmens; Bernard Huys, "Lemmens," *Biographie Nationale* (Brussels: Émile Bruylant, 1976), 39:col. 616–21; *The New Grove Dictionary of Music and Musicians*, s.v. Jaak Nikolaas Lemmens.

[14] H. V. Couwenbergh, *L'Orgue ancien et moderne* (Lier: Joseph van In, 1887), 76.

[15] E. G. J. Grégoir, *Galerie biographique des artistes musiciens belges du XVIIIe et du XIXe siècle* (Brussels: Schott, 1882), 82. For further information on Girschner, see Fétis, *Biographie universelle*, s.v. Girschner, and Couwenberg, *L'Orgue ancien et moderne*, 76.

[16] The document, dated 7 July 1846, issued from the Ministère de l'intérieur, is now housed in the Clerfaÿt archives.

[17] Letter from Fétis to Lemmens, dated 2 December 1848, now in the Clerfaÿt archives.

[18] Letter from Fétis to Lemmens, dated 30 April 1848, now in the Clerfaÿt archives.

[19] Letters from Fétis to Lemmens, dated 26 January 1850 and 11 December 1852, now in the Clerfaÿt archives; letter from Daniel-François-Esprit Auber, Director of the Paris Conservatoire, to Lemmens, dated 8 April 1852, now in the Clerfaÿt archives.

[20] For a fuller discussion see Fenner Douglass, *Cavaillé-Coll and the Musicians*, 2 vols. (Raleigh: Sunbury, 1980), 1:71–82. Also see Georges L. J. Alexis, "Aristide Cavaillé-Coll et ses amis belges," *Mélanges Ernest Closson* (Brussels: Société belge de musicologie, 1948), 32–34.

[21] Letter from Lemmens to Cavaillé-Coll, dated 23 January, published in Alexis, "Aristide Cavaillé-Coll," 37.

[22] Ibid., 38.

[23] See "Madame Lemmens Sherrington," *The Musical Herald*, 1 July 1899, pp. 195–97, a copy of which is now housed in the Clerfaÿt archives.

[24] *François-Joseph Fétis et la vie musicale de son temps 1784–1871* (Brussels: Bibliothèque Royale Albert 1er, 1972), 89.

[25] *La Revue et Gazette musicale* 27 (1860): 90–91. A review of the concert written by Amédée Méreaux (originally published in *Le Journal de Rouen*) appeared in *La Maîtrise* 3 (March 1860): 175–76.

[26] Letters from Fétis to Lemmens, 14 June 1867, and 29 December 1867, now housed in the Clerfaÿt archives.

[27] Letter from Tilborghs to Lemmens, dated 20 March 1867, now in the Clerfaÿt archives.

[28] Tilborghs is listed as "Prof. (*ad interim.*)" for the "concours" of 1869 in *Le Guide musical* 15 (5 and 12 August 1869). On Tilborghs, see Grégoir, *Galerie biographique*, 173. On Mailly, see also Fétis, *Biographie universelle*, s.v. Mailly.

[29] "Angleterre," *Le Guide musical* 12 (22 November 1866).

[30] See *Le Guide musical* 13 (14 March 1867).

[31] See letter from Lemmens to Cavaillé-Coll, dated 2 December 1865, in "A propos du cinquantenaire de la mort de Cavaillé-Coll 1879 [sic]–1949, Lemmens et Cavaillé-Coll (publication de lettres)," *L'Orgue*, no. 64 (1952): 88.

[32] *Le Guide musical* 12 (6 September 1866); *Le Guide musical* 13 (19 September 1867).

[33] "A propos du cinquantenaire de la mort de Cavaillé-Coll 1879 [sic]–1949, Lemmens et Cavaillé-Coll (publication de lettres)," *L'Orgue*, no. 65 (1952): 112.

[34] Letter from Lemmens to Cavaillé-Coll, dated 17 November 1876, printed in Alexis, "Aristide Cavaillé-Coll," 39.

[35] L. A. Bourgault-Ducoudray, "Un Nouveau Système pour l'accompagnement du plain-chant," *La Revue et Gazette musicale* 45 (1878): 57–58.

[36] *The New Grove Dictionary of Music and Musicians*, s.v. Helen Lemmens-Sherrington. Also a teacher of singing, Helen Lemmens-Sherrington published *Six Vocal Studies in the Form of Waltzes* (London: Duncan Davison, n.d.). After her return to Belgium she was appointed professor of singing in 1881 at the Brussels Conservatory. She later taught singing at the Royal Academy of Music in London in the 1890s ("Necrologie," *Le Ménestrel* 42 [1906]: 156).

[37] *La Revue et Gazette musicale* 45 (1878): 305–06. Rollin Smith's article in this volume gives the program of Lemmens's concert at the Trocadéro.

[38] Rollin Smith's article in this volume gives details about Mailly's concert at the Trocadéro in Paris in 1878.

[39] See Ph. J. van Tiggelen, "Le Grand Orgue Cavaillé-Coll du Conservatoire Royal de Musique de Bruxelles (1880)," in *Communications de l'archives centrales de l'orgue* (Brussels: Archives centrales de l'orgue, 1983), 17.

[40] Joseph Duclos, "Essai sur la vie et les travaux de l'auteur," in Jacques-Nicolas Lemmens, *Du chant grégorien, sa mélodie, son rythme, son harmonisation*, ed. Joseph Duclos (Ghent: Annoot-Braeckman, 1886), xxxv.

[41] "Jacques Nicolas Lemmens," *The Musical Times* 22 (1881): 138.

[42] "Arts, sciences, et lettres." Some selected studies (including short notices) that deal specifically with Lemmens's life include, besides the 1881 mention in *The Musical Times*, the following: "The Late Chevalier Lemmens," *The Monthly Musical Record* 9 (1881): 68; Couwenberg, *L'Orgue ancien et moderne*, 327–28; Douglass, *Cavaillé-Coll and the Musicians*, 1:71–82; Fétis, *Biographie universelle*, s.v. Lemmens; Grégoir, *Galerie biographique*, 123–24; Huys, "Lemmens," 39:col. 616–21; Joseph Kreps, "Bach et l'orgue catholique: Lemmens à l'école de Fétis," *Musica sacra* 53 (1952): 72–96; Lowell Lacey, "Jaak-Nicolaas Lemmens (1823–1881) jeugd en opleiding," *Adem* 1 (1979): 27–35; Duclos, "Essai sur la vie," vii–xlix; Flor Peeters, "Jaak Lemmens, Orgelcomponist en pedagoog," *Gamma* 25 (1973): 197–98; Patrick Peire's "Jaak Nikolaas Lemmens" in *The New Grove Dictionary of Music and Musicians*; and Carol Weitner, "Jacques Nicolas Lemmens: Organist, Pedagogue, Composer" (DMA diss., University of Rochester, 1991). Journals which contain important information about Lemmens's life include *Le Diapason* (*Revue musicale de Bruxelles*), *Le Guide musical*, and *La Revue et Gazette musicale*. For a guide to materials about Lemmens and the Brussels Conservatory (including materials concerning Helen Lemmens-Sherrington at the Brussels Conservatory) now housed in the Archives générales du royaume in Brussels, consult Emile Vandewonde, *Inventaris van het fonds koninklijk muziekconservatoriam te Brussel 1832–34, 1876–1931* (Brussels: Archives générales du royaume, 1980).

[43] Fétis, *Biographie universelle*, s.v. Lemmens.

[44] Fétis's notice appears in *La Revue musicale* 6 (1829): 357–59. Important commentaries on Fétis's treatise (on both the design and the extant portion) include Kreps, "Bach et l'orgue

catholique," 72–96, and Robert Wangermée, *François-Joseph Fétis, musicologue et compositeur, contribution à l'étude du goût musical du XIXe siècle* (Brussels: Académie Royale de Belgique classe des beaux-arts mémoires, 1951): 85–89. Part four of Fétis's treatise (the extant portion) is now housed in the Bibliothèque Royale in Brussels (Fonds Fétis 2072).

[45] Fétis's autograph manuscript copy of Werner's chapter, titled "Trad. par lui-même d'un chapitre de la *Orgelschule* de J. G. Werner, 1824," is now housed in the Bibliothèque Royale in Brussels (MS 54).

[46] François-Joseph Fétis, *Vêpres et Saluts du dimanche pour l'orgue* (Paris: Canaux, [1843]), 2. See also the preface to his *Six Messes faciles pour l'orgue* (Paris: Lemoine, [1840]), which is similar but not identical to the former preface.

[47] Fétis, *Biographie universelle*, s.v. Bach. "Bach . . . eut aussi le talent d'enseigner, avec une incontestable supériorité, la composition et l'art de jouer du clavecin et de l'orgue. La nature compliquée des ouvrages pour ceux deux instruments, toujours écrits à trois, quatre ou cinq parties, l'avait obligé à inventer un doigter particulier, qui fut connu longtemps en Allemagne sous le nom de *doigter de Bach*, mais qu'on peut désigner d'une manière plus significative par le nom de *doigter de substitution*, . . . "I am indebted to Orpha Ochse who drew my attention to Fétis's comments on finger substitution in the German organ tradition.

[48] Fétis, *Biographie universelle*, s.v. Lemmens.

[49] François-Joseph Fétis, "L'Orgue mondaine et la musique érotique à l'église," *La Revue et Gazette musicale* 23 (1856): 105–06. For a recent assessment of the concert by Lefébure-Wély and of Fétis's critical account, see Jean-Pierre Félix, "Autour de l'inauguration par Lefébure-Wély, de l'orgue Cavaillé-Coll de l'église St-Nicolas à Gand en 1856," *L'Organiste* 25 (1993): 15–36.

[50] François-Joseph Fétis, "Construction d'un orgue dans l'église de Saint-Denis," *Gazette musicale de la Belgique* 1 (1833): 158–59; Jean-Louis-Félix Danjou, "Méthode élémentaire pour l'orgue," *Gazette musicale de la Belgique* 1 (1833): 57–58.

[51] On De Volder see Couwenberg, *L'Orgue ancien et moderne*, 82–89; Ernest Closson, *La Facture des instruments de musique en Belgique* (Brussels: Huy, 1935), 19; and Antoine Fauconnier, "Werk van de Orgelmakers De Volder," *De Mixtuur* 18 (1976): 370–80. The specification of the Conservatoire organ (1835–1836) appears in Fauconnier's article (p. 373).

[52] The specification of the Dreymann organ at the Temple du Musée (I=16.8.8.8.4.2.Cornett Bass.Cornett Discant, II=8.8.8.4.2.8, Pedal=16.8.16.) is detailed in *L'Orgue Dreymann (1846) de Notre-Dame aux Riches Claires* (Brussels: Sauvegarde des instruments de musique à clavier, 1985), 20–21.

[53] François-Joseph Fétis, *Rapport adressé à M. Le Ministère de l'intérieur, sur le grand orgue construit pour le Conservatoire Royal de Musique, dans le palais de la rue Ducale* (Brussels: Delatombe, 1866).

[54] François-Joseph Fétis, *Sur l'état actuel de la facture des orgues en Belgique, comparé à sa situation des orgues en Allemagne, en France, et en Angleterre* (Brussels: Académie Royale de Belgique, 1850); and François-Joseph Fétis, *Sur les progrès de la facture des orgues en Belgique, dans les dernières années* (Brussels: Académie Royale de Belgique, 1856).

[55] For a discussion of Hesse's link to J. S. Bach, see Hans Jürgen Seyfried, *Adolph Friedrich Hesse als Orgelvirtuose und Orgelkomponist* (Regensburg: Bosse, 1965), 15.

[56] Rinck included this comment in a paragraph found at the end of a review published in *Caecilia* 10 (1829): 42–45. In the concluding sentence of that paragraph Rinck paid Hesse great tribute: "so wird er gewiss ein sehr ausgezeichneter Künstler, der unserm Vaterland Ehre machen wird." A portion of this paragraph appears in Seyfried, *Adolph Friedrich Hesse*, 15.

[57] Adolf Hesse, "Einiges über Orgeln, deren Einrichtung und Behandlung in Oesterreich, Italien, Frankreich und England," *Neue Zeitschrift für Musik* 39 (1853): 53–56.

[58] Adolf Hesse, *Kleine Pedalschule* ([1831]; reprint in *Adolph Hesse's Ausgewählte Orgelcompositionen in 40 Lieferungen*, vol. 14 [Leipzig: n.p., n.d.]).

[59] Hesse, *Kleine Pedalschule*, 1.

[60] Fétis, *Biographie universelle*, s.v. Lemmens.

[61] François-Joseph Fétis, "Revue critique/*Nouveau Journal d'orgue à l'usage des organistes du culte catholique, publié par M. Lemmens, professeur d'orgue au Conservatoire Royal de Musique de Bruxelles*," *La Revue et Gazette musicale* 18 (1851): 29–30.

[62] "Monsieur Fétis," *Le Diapason* 2 (20 February 1851): 1–2; 2 (6 March 1851): 9–10; 2 (20

March 1851): 19–21; 2 (3 April 1851): 31–32; "Encore M. Lemmens!," *Le Diapason* 2 (15 May 1851): 55; C. Gollmick, "Herr Fétis," *Neue Zeitschrift für Musik* 36 (1852): 16–17; 36 (1852): 31–32; 36 (1852): 44–45; 36 (1852): 51–53; Adolf Hesse, "Kleine Zeitung," *Neue Zeitschrift für Musik* 36 (1852): 163.

[63] Document housed in the Clerfaÿt archives. "Herr Lemmens, ein sehr talentvoller Tonkünstler, ist seit dem Monate September bei mir gewesen, und hat meinen Unterricht im Orgelspiele und der Komposition [——] für dieses Instrument genossen. Herr Lemmens war in dieser Zeit so fleissig, dass er mehrere der schwersten und grössten Orgel-Kompositionen jetzt mit Ruhe und der wahren Auffassung vorträgt, auch hat er eine Fuge für dieses Instrument unter meiner Leitung komponiert, die von seiner tüchtigen Bildung in der ernsten Musik Zeugniss giebt. Seine Kenntnisse befähigen ihn Professor des Orgelspiels am Konservatorium zu werden." See also Lacey, "Jaak-Nicolaas Lemmens," 27–35, and Ewald Kooiman, "Jacques Lemmens, Charles-Marie Widor und die französische 'Bach-Tradition' (I)," *Ars Organi* 37 (1989): 198–206, and "Jacques Lemmens, Charles-Marie Widor und die französische 'Bach-Tradition' (II)," *Ars Organi* 38 (1990): 3–14. Although very few comments about the Breslau study by Lemmens himself have come to light, one is particularly striking. In a letter to his parents Lemmens wrote disparagingly about Hesse as a pianist, and revealed that, as a student in Breslau, he played the organ for three to four hours a day and furthermore, that Hesse had found his playing excessively "fast." An excerpt from this letter—a copy of which was owned by the late Lowell Lacey—appears in the revised edition of Sandra Soderlund, *Organ Technique: An Historical Approach* (Chapel Hill: Hinshaw, 1986), 161.

[64] Seyfried, *Adolph Friedrich Hesse*, 42.

[65] Christian Ahrens, "Deutscher Einfluss auf die französische Orgelmusik der Romantik?," *Die Musikforschung* 34 (1981): 311–12; see also Kooiman, "Jacques Lemmens, Charles-Marie Widor und die französische 'Bach-Tradition' (I)," 198–206; finally, for provocative conclusions about Lemmens, Hesse, and Fétis, see Josef Burg, "Les Organistes français du XIXe siècle et la tradition de J. S. Bach," *L'Orgue*, no. 223 (1992): 1–27.

[66] A concert reportedly played by Hesse in Paris contained a Fugue in E Minor of J. S. Bach as well as a Fantasie, Trio, Introduction and Fugue, and God Save the Queen, all by Hesse (Seyfried, *Adolph Friedrich Hesse*, 33).

[67] J. E. Henskens, *Journal d'orgue ou manuel de l'organiste/Recueil de pièces pour l'orgue des meilleurs maîtres, anciens et modernes, applicables aux différentes parties de l'office divin* (Antwerp: Chez l'auteur, 1850–1854).

[68] See review published in the *Bulletin de la Revue de musique ancienne et moderne*, no. 2 (February 1856): 27–28 (the *Bulletin de la Revue de musique ancienne et moderne* has been reprinted [Scarsdale, N.Y.: Annemarie Schnase, 1968]).

[69] Couwenberg, *L'Orgue ancien et moderne*, 76.

[70] Duclos, "Essai sur la vie," xxviii.

[71] It was, in fact, the first two years of the *Nouveau Journal d'orgue* that served as the foundation of the *École d'orgue*. Fétis, in his article on Lemmens in *Biographie universelle*, stated that the third year consisted of a simple mass for three voices.

[72] Fétis, *Biographie universelle*, s.v. Lemmens.

[73] J. Lemmens, *Nouveau Journal d'orgue à l'usage des organistes du culte catholique*, first year, vol. 1 (Brussels: Vanderauwera, 1850–1851).

[74] J. Lemmens, *École d'orgue basée sur le plain-chant romain* (Brussels: Chez l'auteur, 1862), vii. "On entend par glisser, lier deux notes du même doigt, en glissant de l'une sur l'autre, sans que le doigt cesse un instant d'être appuyé sur l'une d'elles."

[75] Lemmens, *Nouveau Journal*, 1:1:91. "Notre école de la pédale qui est la plus complète qui ait paru, ne pourra servir pour le moment qu'à peu d'organistes belges, attendu que leurs instruments bâtards qui ne méritent pas le nom d'orgues, n'ont en général ni pédale séparée ni même un deuxième clavier."

[76] See Fauconnier, "Werk van de Orgelmakers De Volder," 373, and Fétis, *Rapport adressé à M. le Ministre de l'intérieur.*

[77] Lemmens, *Nouveau Journal*, 1:8:91; Lemmens, *École d'orgue*, 68.

[78] Lemmens, *Nouveau Journal*, 1:8:96.

[79] This volume, in the Bibliothèque Nationale, bears the number Vm.8.R.120A.

[80] The volume, in the Bibliothèque Nationale, bears the number Vm.8.R.120.

[81] J. Lemmens, *Organ School . . . New Edition*, ed. W. T. Best (London: Schott, n.d.). It bears the following on its title page:
Organ-School
Part 1. Exercises to acquire the Organ touch. Short Preludes. Exercises in Modulation. Ten Prayers. Short Pieces for Church use: the whole chiefly without the Pedals.
Part 2. Exercises for the Pedals. Short and Easy trios. Collection of Pieces in Various Styles, for Church and Concert purposes.
By J. Lemmens/New Edition/The English Translation, Fingering, and the Adaptation to English Organs throughout/by W. T. Best
A copy of this edition is in the British Library (h.2715.a.1–2).

[82] Lemmens, *Organ School*, 2.

[83] Although the Best edition housed in the British Library does not bear a printed date, a cataloguer has suggested 1884.

[84] Only part 1 has been examined.

[85] *Le Guide musical* 21 (12 and 19 August 1875). In his professorial role at the Brussels Conservatory, Mailly maintained an historical perspective with regard to organ teaching. Some years after the 1875 tribute to Girschner, at the "concert jubilaire donné à l'occasion du 50e anniversaire de la fondation du Conservatoire" (1882), Mailly included two works composed by Lemmens—*Prière, en fa* and the *Scherzo symphonique*—in a program which carried a notice about Lemmens's tenure at the Conservatory (defined as "1849 à 1869"). See *Annuaire du Conservatoire Royal de Musique de Bruxelles* 7 (1883): 127.

[86] Jean-Louis-Félix Danjou, "Souvenirs de voyage: Allemagne," *Revue de la musique religieuse, populaire et classique* 1 (1845): 151–52.

[87] For recent discussions of organ methods by Werner and Rinck, see Ewald Kooiman, "De 'Orgelschule' van Johann Gottlob Werner (1777–1822)," *Het Orgel* 87 (1991): 121–28, and also "Rinck's Theoretisch-practische Anleitung zum Orgelspielen," *Het Orgel* 88 (1992): 1–19. For a recent discussion of Knecht's organ method see Wolfram Syré, "Justin Heinrich Knecht: 'Vollständige Orgelschule für Anfänger und Geübtere' 1795–1798—eine wichtige Quelle zum Orgelspiel in der zweiten Hälfte des 18. Jahrhunderts (I)," *Ars Organi* 35 (1987): 84–90, and its conclusion (35 [1987]: 147–53).

[88] Johann Gottlob Werner, *Orgelschule, oder Anleitung zum Orgelspielen und zur richtigen Kenntnis und Behandlung des Orgelwerks* (Mainz: Schott, 1824); Johann Gottlieb Werner, *Méthode élémentaire pour l'orgue très facile et préparatoire à L'École d'orgue de Rinck* (Paris: Richault, n.d.); Johann Christian Heinrich Rinck, *Praktische Orgelschule von Christian Heinrich Rinck* (Bonn & Cöln: Simrock, n.d.); Johann Christian Heinrich Rinck, *L'École pratique d'orgue, méthode transcendante formée de la réunion de plusieurs recueils offrant une série graduée de pièces de tout genre propres à l'étude de cet instrument, par M. Ch. H. Rink. Traduite de l'Allemand, par M. A. Choron* (Paris: Richault, n.d.); Johann Christian Heinrich Rinck, *Les Trois Premiers Mois de l'organiste pour servir d'introduction à l'école pratique d'orgue*, op. 121 (Paris: Richault, n.d.).

[89] Jean-Louis-Félix Danjou, [review of *Méthode élémentaire pour l'orgue très facile et préparatoire à L'École d'orgue de Mr. Ch. H. Rinck. Traduite de l'Allemand, par Mr. Hellert*], *La Revue et Gazette musicale* 7 (1833): 265–66; Jean-Louis-Félix Danjou, [review of *Méthode élémentaire pour l'orgue très facile et préparatoire à L'École d'orgue de Mr. Ch. H. Rinck. Traduite de l'Allemand, par Mr. Hellert*], *Gazette musicale de la Belgique* 1 (1833): 57–58; Jean-Louis-Félix Danjou, "Revue critique: Der Praktische Organist (L'Organiste pratique), von Herzog," *Revue de la musique religieuse, populaire et classique* 2 (1846): 250–56. Danjou also published an article on organ playing in Germany ("Souvenirs de voyage: Allemagne," *Revue de la musique religieuse, populaire et classique* 1 [1845]: 146–55), as well as a lengthy biography of Rinck (*Revue de la musique religieuse, populaire et classique* 2 [1846]: 275–84 and 320–32).

[90] Werner, *Méthode élémentaire*, 2. "Il faut donc avoir soin 1o) de donner à chaque note sa juste durée, en tenant le doigt sur la touche précisément autant de tems que l'indique la valeur de la note, 2o) de n'introduire ni de vide, ne de cumul, dans le passage d'une note à l'autre, c'est-à-dire de faire ensorte qu'il n'y ait ni interruption, ni simultanéité entre les sons qui doivent se succèder, la première produisant un jeu hâché, et la seconde une cacaphone: deux défauts entre lesquels il faut savoir tenir un juste milieu."

[91] Werner, *Orgelschule*, 8. "Angehende Orgelspieler müssen sich bei mehrstimmigen Griffen, besonders beim Choralspielen, gewöhnen, die Töne genau verbunden, nicht abgesetzt und

getrennt, anzugeben. Das stille Wechseln der Finger auf einer Taste wird oft mit Vortheil angewendet werden können."
[92] Werner, *Méthode élémentaire*, 30. "Pour bien toucher les pédales, c'est-à-dire, d'une part, pour lier les sons, de l'autre pour donner à l'exécution toute la rapidité dont elle est susceptible, il faut employer les deux pieds et autant que possible les employer alternativement: . . ."
[93] Werner, *Orgelschule*, 11. "Viele ungeübte Orgelspieler bedienen sich für das pedal meistenheils des linken Fusses, und treten mit dem rechten nur die letztern oder höhern Töne, die sie selten brauchen. Bei dieser schlechten Methode, das Pedal zu spielen, muss man immer mit einem Fusse, besonders mit dem linken, hin und her springen, und die Töne können durchaus nicht gehörig zusammenhängend, wie es sein sollte, vorgetragen werden, und an geschwindere Gänge, die auf dem Pedal wohl auch zu spielen sind, ist gar nicht zu denken." Fétis, translating into French this chapter on the use of the pedal, wrote that dependence on the incorrect method makes it impossible to "put between the notes the connection ['liaison'] that ought to unite them, . . ." (Fétis, manuscript translation of Werner chapter in Brussels, Bibliothèque Royale, MS 54.)
[94] Werner, *Méthode élémentaire*, 32.
[95] Werner, *Orgelschule*, 12.
[96] Jean-Paul Martini, *École d'orgue, résumée d'après les ouvrages des plus célèbres organistes d'Allemagne* (Paris: Imbault, n.d.).
[97] Rinck, *L'École pratique*, 43, exercise 55.
[98] Martini, *École d'orgue*, 39.
[99] See Daniel Raessler, "Change in Keyboard Touch around 1800: From Non-Legato to Legato," *Early Keyboard Journal* 1 (1982–1983): 25–39, and "Türk, Touch and Slurring: Finding a Rationale," *Early Music* 17 (1989): 55–59.
[100] Jacques-Claude-Adolphe Miné, *Manuel simplifié de l'organiste ou nouvelle méthode pour exécuter sur l'orgue tous les offices de l'année selon les rituels parisien et romain . . .; suivi des leçons d'orgue de Kegel* (Paris: Roret, 1835).
[101] Knecht's treatise, *Vollständige Orgelschule für Anfänger und Geübtere*, was published in Leipzig in the 1790s. For a discussion of Knecht's *Vollständige Orgelschule*, see Syré's "Justin Heinrich Knecht," *Ars Organi* 35 (1987): 84–90 and 147–53. The pedal techniques described in the treatises published in France might well be examined against the background of German instructive comments between the time of J. S. Bach and 1800. Johann Christian Kittel, whose relation to J. S. Bach is unquestioned, described in 1803 first the use of both feet (alternating toe technique), second the use of heel and toe of the same foot, and third a comprehensive technique. And yet it remains a fact that Johann Samuel Petri described the employment of the left foot in the lower octave and the right foot in the upper octave as *one* technique in use in 1767. For a discussion of Kittel and Petri, see Ewald Kooiman, "Pedaalapplikatuur: Kittel, Tuerk, Petri en Bach," *Het Orgel* 76 (1980): 393–402. Kooiman wisely questions Kittel's description of the second technique as the "older" of the two. See also Josef Burg, "Johann Christian Kittel (1732–1809), un grand pédagogue de l'orgue, maillon important dans le tradition de Jean-Sébastien Bach," *L'Orgue*, no. 228 (1993): 1–12.
[102] On Benoist, see Norbert Dufourcq, "L'Enseignement de l'orgue au Conservatoire National avant la nomination de César Franck (1872)," *L'Orgue*, no. 144 (1972): 121–25.
[103] J. L. Battmann, *Méthode d'orgue harmonium*, op. 78 (Paris: H. Lemoine, n.d.); and Louis-James-Alfred Lefébure-Wély, *Méthode théorique et pratique pour le poïkilorgue*, op. 9 (Paris: Canaux, n.d.).
[104] Georges Schmitt, *Nouveau Manuel complet de l'organiste* (Paris: Roret, 1855); ch. 7, 59–60, and ch. 19, 1–8.
[105] Georges Schmitt, *Le Musée de l'organiste* (Paris: Richault, 1852).
[106] Alexandre-Charles Fessy, *Manuel d'orgue à l'usage des églises catholiques* (Paris: Troupenas, ca. 1845).
[107] Fessy, *Manuel d'orgue*, 3.
[108] Fessy, *Manuel d'orgue*, 32 and 34.
[109] Fessy, *Manuel d'orgue*, 30. ". . . aujourd'hui les facteurs ont suivi l'usage adopté par leurs confrères d'Allemagne et d'Angleterre, et ce système est excellent, puisqu'un habile organiste peut avec les pieds exécuter des passages presque aussi difficiles qu'il le ferait avec la main gauche."
[110] Fessy, *Manuel d'orgue*, 31.

[111] Louis Niedermeyer, avant-propos to "Exercice journalier [1]" by Clément Loret, *La Maîtrise* 2 (1858–1859). ". . . car, dans le style lié,—le véritable style de l'instrument, et qui, à de courtes et rares exceptions près, est le seul employé,—la moindre interruption dans les sons produit le plus mauvais effet: . . ." On Niedermeyer, see "Louis Niedermeyer," *Illustration musicale (1863–1864)* (Paris: Repos, 1863–1864), col. 11–52.

[112] See especially the exercises in Loret, "Exercice journalier [1]," 2–12.

[113] Loret, "Exercise journalier [1]," 13. "[I]l faut observer la valeur des notes et des silences, et avoir soin de ne pas laisser trop longtemps le doigt sur les croches suivies d'un soupir."

[114] Letter from Loret to Lemmens, dated 31 August 1858, now in the Clerfaÿt archives.

[115] Loret, "Exercice journalier [3]," 16.

[116] Johann Sebastian Bach, "Prélude et Fugue en mi mineur," ed. Louis Niedermeyer, *La Maîtrise* 1, musical supplement, no. 1 (1857–1858): 4.

[117] Clément Loret, *Cours d'orgue*, 4 parts (Paris: Loret fils et H. Freytag, n.d.). This treatise has not been adequately studied as a late nineteenth-century source: for example, Rudolph Kremer, in his article on Loret, does not discuss it (Rudolph Kremer, "Clément Loret, A Pioneer of the 19th-Century French Organ Revival," *Early Keyboard Journal* 4 [1985–1986]: 43–50).

[118] *Die Musik in Geschichte und Gegenwart*, s.v. Loret. In addition, information in part 3 of the treatise, concerning organs in France to the year 1878, suggests that the treatise was drafted around 1880.

[119] Loret, *Cours d'orgue*, 1:1. "Bien lié sans laisser trainer le doigt sur la touche."

[120] Loret, *Cours d'orgue*, 2:1.

[121] Félix Clément, *Méthode d'orgue et d'accompagnement* (Paris: Hachette, 1873). Incidentally, Clément's treatise, published in 1873 and reprinted in 1894, included a composition by "L. Lemmens" which Huys classifies as a work by J. N. Lemmens (see Huys, "Lemmens," col. 616–21).

[122] Clément, *Méthode d'orgue*, 18. "On doit appuyer les doigts sans brusquerie, mais vivement, avec décision, sans hésitation aucune, avec une égale force; faire entendre distinctement toutes les notes, ne laisser remonter la touche qu'au moment où la note qui suit est abaissée."

[123] Clément, *Méthode d'orgue*, 45. "Pour lier les sons sur l'orgue de telle manière qu'il n'y ait aucune solution de continuité entre eux, pour garder les notes tenues et exécuter les doubles valeurs, sans interrompre le dessin de chaque partie, on a recours au *doigté par substitution*, . . ."

[124] Clément, *Méthode d'orgue*, 53.

[125] Marie-Louise Jaquet, "L'Œuvre d'orgue de César Franck et notre temps," *L'Orgue*, no. 167 (1978): 6. "Nous n'avons aucune idée de la liberté avec laquelle Franck interprétait ses propres œuvres."

[126] Dupré's comment, "comme on jouait en France à son époque: legato approximatif, observance approximative des durées," is quoted in François Sabatier, *César Franck et l'orgue* (Paris: Presses universitaires de France, 1982), 14.

[127] Daniel Roth's article in this volume also discusses Franck and common tones.

[128] See Rollin Smith, *Toward an Authentic Interpretation of the Organ Works of César Franck*, Juilliard Performance Guides, no. 1 (New York: Pendragon, 1983), 15–17, for an account of the 1864 performance.

[129] Jaquet, "L'Œuvre d'orgue de César Franck," 14; Ewald Kooiman, "César Franck als orgelleraar," *Het Orgel* 77 (1981): 160.

[130] See Smith, *Toward an Authentic Interpretation*, 28.

[131] Marie-Louise Jaquet-Langlais, "Une Curiosité: l'œuvre d'orgue de Jean-Sébastien Bach doigtée par César Franck," *L'Orgue*, no. 207 (1988): 5. See also Karen Hastings, "New Franck Fingerings Brought to Light," *The American Organist* 24 (December, 1990), 92–101, for a thorough discussion of Franck's fingerings and pedalings in the Braille edition of Bach's organ works, and for observations on Franck's legato in his own organ works.

[132] See Smith, *Toward an Authentic Interpretation*, 32–33.

[133] Jaquet-Langlais, "Une Curiosité," 4.

[134] Ibid., 3.

[135] See Smith, *Toward an Authentic Interpretation*, 32–33.

[136] Whether the pedal method of Franck's student, Adolphe Marty, sheds light on Franck's own ideas about pedaling is far from clear. In his method, *L'Art de la pédale du grand orgue* (Paris: Mackar & Noël, [1891]), dedicated to Franck, Marty relies on a toe-heel technique in

which one foot may execute an entire region of the pedalboard (up to seven successive notes in a scale passage). He also introduces glissando techniques and substitution, in the latter case the heel of one foot yielding to toe of other foot in one instance, and a substitution involving the heel and toe of just one foot in another instance (see p. 21). Like Loret in the *Cours d'orgue*, Marty illustrates the use of the alternate toe technique by means of exercises using intervals such as the third and fourth. He closes the method with the introduction of double pedal technique, and he provides as his final example a prelude for four voices on the pedal (see p. 39).

[137] Kooiman, "César Franck als orgelleraar," 161.

[138] Rowland W. Dunham, "From Yesterday/No.2: Franck, Libert, Widor," *The American Organist* 37 (1954): 402–03.

[139] Adolphe Boschot, "Notice sur la vie et les œuvres de M. Charles-Marie Widor Secrétaire Perpétuel" (Paris: Firmin-Didot, 1937), 5.

[140] Charles-Marie Widor, preface to *L'Orgue de Jean-Sébastien Bach* by André Pirro (Paris: Fischbacher, 1895), xiv.

[141] John Scott Whiteley discusses a letter dated 21 March 1935 in the possession of Jacques Jongen ("Jongen and his Organ Music," *The Musical Times* 124 [1983]: 189).

[142] Widor, "La classe d'orgue," 166. "Les mouvements de BACH?—disait Hesse—Prenez le groupe des moindre valeurs, le trait le plus rapide, rendez-le perceptible à l'auditeur; il vous donnera le vrai mouvement."

[143] Widor, preface to *L'Orgue de Jean-Sébastien Bach* by Pirro, xx.

[144] Ibid., xvii. "Il jouait, le corps un peu penché en avant, immobile, avec un rythme admirable, un ensemble polyphonique absolu, une merveilleuse clarté, pas vite, maître de lui-même pour ainsi dire du temps, donnant l'idée d'une incomparable grandeur."

[145] Ibid., xxxi. "Le pied ne doit point attaquer la pédale perpendiculairement, mais bien d'arrière en avant, d'aussi près que possible, en patinant un peu, sans bruit, la pointe à un ou deux centimètres des touches noires."

[146] A. M. Henderson, "Widor and His Organ Class," *The Musical Times* 78 (1937): 343.

[147] Widor, preface to *L'Orgue de Jean-Sébastien Bach* by Pirro, xxiii. "A l'orgue, comme à l'orchestre, tout doit pouvoir se réaliser exactement: l'ensemble des pieds et des mains est rigouresusement nécessaire, soit qu'on attaque, soit qu'on quitte le clavier."

[148] Ibid., xxvi-xxvii.

[149] Ibid., xxviii-xxix.

[150] Charles-Marie Widor, "L'Orgue moderne," *Les Nouvelles musicales* 1 (March 1934): 6. "'C'est nul,' disait-il, mécanique, 'sans volonté.' Qu'entendait-il par 'volonté?' Je n'osais le lui demander. Je finis par comprendre: c'est l'art de l'orateur, son autorité qui s'impose par le calme, l'ordre et les justes proportions du discours. Chez nous musiciens, la volonté se manifeste avant tout par le rythme."

[151] Bruce T. Simonds, "The Organ Department at Yale," *The American Organist* 1 (1918): 26.

[152] Widor, "L'Orgue moderne," 6. "Il en fut autrement. Lemmens dut partager sa vie entre l'Angleterre et la Belgique. Mais ses élèves, responsables de la tradition, eurent l'heureuse fortune de pouvoir la défendre ici même, au Conservatoire de Paris, . . ."

[153] *The New Grove Dictionary of Music and Musicians*, s.v. Félix-Alexandre Guilmant.

[154] Letter from Guilmant to Lemmens, dated 12 October 1876, now housed in the Clerfaÿt archives.

[155] *The Forty Programs Rendered by M. Alexandre Guilmant.*

[156] Letters from Guilmant to Lemmens, dated 2 April 1878, and to Mme Lemmens, dated 12 June 1885, and 20 May 1887, now housed in the Clerfaÿt archives.

[157] Harold Vincent Milligan, "Guilmant School Commencement," *The American Organist* 1 (1918): 359.

[158] Guilmant's library is now housed at the Institut de musicologie de l'Université de Paris.

[159] Guilmant's manuscript copy of Herzog's *L'Organiste pratique* is now housed at the Bibliothèque Nationale (Cons. L. 11884).

[160] Guilmant, "La Musique d'orgue," 1125–80.

[161] Ibid., 1157.

[162] Ibid., 1153–54.

[163] Ibid., 1155.

[164] Ibid., 1157.

[165] Ibid.

[166] A. M. Henderson, "Memories of Some Distinguished French Organists," *The Musical Times* 18 (1937): 976.

[167] Guilmant, "La Musique d'orgue," 1159.

[168] Ibid.

[169] Ibid., 1160.

[170] Alexandre Guilmant, *L'École classique de l'orgue morceaux d'auteurs célèbres/publiés et annotés par Alexandre Guilmant*, 2 vols. (Paris: Durand, 1901), 2:#23.

[171] Henderson, "Memories," 978.

[172] William C. Carl, "Some Reminiscences of Alexandre Guilmant," *The Diapason* 15 (May 1924): 6.

[173] William C. Carl, "Alexandre Guilmant, Noted Figure Viewed 25 Years After Death," *The Diapason* 27 (June 1936): 4.

[174] Marshall Bidwell, "Organ Music in Paris Cathedrals/III. Widor and St. Sulpice," *The American Organist* 5 (1922): 422–24.

[175] Guilmant, "La Musique d'orgue," 1157.

[176] Harvey B. Gaul, "Bonnet—Bossi—Karg-Elert: Three Aperçus," *The Musical Quarterly* 4 (1918): 357.

[177] Alexandre Guilmant, "Organ Music and Organ-Playing" (1898; reprint in *The Organ Music of Alexandre Guilmant*, ed. Wayne Leupold, 12 vols. [Melville, N.Y.: Belwin-Mills, 1984–1993], 1:xxvii).

[178] William C. Carl, "Guilmant's Contribution to Organ Music and Organ-Playing," (1912; reprint in *The Organ Music of Alexandre Guilmant*, ed. Wayne Leupold, 12 vols. [Melville, N.Y.: Belwin-Mills, 1984–1993], 1:xxx).

Franck:
The Texts

Paris, Bibliothèque Nationale, MS 8707:
A New Source for Franck's Registrational Practices and Its Implications for the Published Registrations of His Organ Works

JESSE E. ESCHBACH

A remarkable series of manuscripts by César Franck, hitherto unassessed, came to light some ten years ago when Robert Bates and this author prepared the Forberg edition of the Franck Fantasy in C Major. The Bibliothèque Nationale houses a series of manuscript pages under the call number Cons⌐ Ms 8707 and identified as "César Franck. Copies de Sujets d'Improvisation par la classe d'Orgue." Of and by themselves, such contents shed light on the activities and standards of Franck's organ class at the Conservatoire during his tenure there from 1872 to 1890. Examination of MS 8707, however, quickly suggests that the cataloguer's identification is at best a half truth. Although several manuscript leaves are indeed marked "Examen" or "Examen du 15 Juin" and followed by thematic material to be treated in improvisation, the remaining contents are two additional essentially independent items. The first, and subsequent topic for investigation in this paper, consists of two bifolios both entirely filled with quotations from plainsong, borrowed material from other composers, and original themes clearly composed by Franck; in many cases, registrations are given adjacent to these themes, and in a number of examples, the registrations are sufficiently detailed to permit positive identification of the Sainte-Clotilde organ designed and built by Aristide Cavaillé-Coll during the years 1853 to 1859, the instrument to which Franck was appointed titular organist in 1859. The second item is a set of fourteen sheets in small format containing themes from celebrated works by Beethoven, Schubert, Mendelssohn, Méhul, Chopin, Rossini, Meyerbeer, and Haydn. These loose pages, which clearly at one point were folded in half, call to mind Gabriel Pierné's report that Franck kept on his person a small notebook with themes from the leading composers of the eighteenth and nineteenth centuries for use as the source of melodic material for improvisations at Sainte-Clotilde, and this material in all likelihood formed a portion of Franck's once-bound notebook.[1] Although each of the three independent sources found in MS 8707 provides valuable data on Franck's daily musical responsibilities, it is the set of registered themes outlined above which provides clues to the musical content of the liturgies celebrated at Sainte-Clotilde and, more importantly, the manner in which Franck handled his legendary Cavaillé-Coll during services.

An Inventory of the Second Section of MS 8707

The first bifolio of the second section of MS 8707, identified in the hand of a cataloguer as "1" (one of a total of thirty-seven "pièces" in MS 8707, not page "1") is completely filled with themes, themes with skeletal harmonizations, or simply an identification of a liturgical item followed by registrations. On the top three staves of the front page of this first bifolio is an original theme of which only the first three measures are supplied with a bass line. This "incipit," as it were, was apparently sufficient to cue the organist how to proceed. The registration appears in Figure 1a. Underneath and to the left is a series of five registrations, unlabeled (see Figure 1b). To the right side are three registrations labeled "Kyrie" (see Figure 1c). Underneath, still on page

Figure 1

Registration and Other Indications on the First Bifolio of MS 8707

a)

R: Octavin, Hautbois
P: Viole de Gambe, bourdon 16
GO: Bourdon

b)

1. gd chœur
2. Hautb. recit, bourdon 16 pos
3. 8 Pieds
4. V^x Celestes
5. fonts [*sic*] et basson à la ped.

c)

1. Plein Jeu
3. Clairon Recit et Bourdon 16 pos
5. Jeux d'anches récit. Solo sur ped bien large avec 32 p$^{ds.}$

104

d)

1. Imposition Plein-Jeu 7. 16 pieds
3. Cromore [*sic*] 9. (Flutes)
5. Voix Humaine + Bourdon 16 11. Grand Chœur

e)

Voix Celestes et Montres au Gd Orgue

f)

Voix Humaine et Bourdon de 16

g)

G^d Choeur

h)

3 Agnus 16 pieds

i)

1. Eleven measures of soprano and bass, registered "Cromorne."

j)

2. Six measures in D minor, registered "Hautbois et Octavin."

k)

3. Nine measures in D-flat major, soprano and bass completed, registered "16 p^{ds.}"
4. Eight measures identified as "Marche," soprano and bass only, not registered.

l)

1. Eight measures in D minor, soprano and bass, registered "Tous les fonts" [*sic*].

m)

2. Eight measures in C major, soprano and bass with alto and tenor present in most measures, registered "8 pieds: motif en mineur avec le Cromorne."
3. Sixteen measures identified as "March," bass line only with soprano supplied at end, no registrations.
4. Chromatic chord progression in D minor involving sequence, no registrations.

one, are six registrations marked "Magnificat" (see Figure 1d). Page two of the first bifolio contains three separate phrases. The first, a passage in F-sharp minor, shows an unidentified soprano and bass with occasional harmonies sketched (see Figure 1e). A second phrase is identified as "Communion" (see Figure 1f). The function of the third phrase is not specified (see Figure 1g). In the middle of this page, with no incipit supplied, Franck writes a registration (see Figure 1h). Page three contains four separate phrases (see Figures 1i, j, and k). Like page three, page four contains four unrelated phrases (see Figures 1l and m).

The second bifolio containing sketches for liturgical improvisations is similar to the first in all respects: reasonably detailed registrations for liturgical items on the front, followed by "incipits" with abbreviated registrations on the other three pages. (The number "7," not in the hand of Franck, identifies this manuscript as the seventh item in MS 8707.) Franck's notations on the front can be divided into seven items:

1. Eight measures of melody in G minor.
2. To the right of item one are three registrations marked "Kyrie" (see Figure 2a).
3. Underneath the Kyrie are three consecutively numbered registrations (see Figure 2b).

Other registrations are found:

4. in the lower left-hand corner (see Figure 2c),
5. to the right of item four (see Figure 2d),
6. to the right of item five (see Figure 2e),
7. and underneath item six (see Figure 2f).

The reverse side also contains various markings (see Figure 2g). The third page contains various items (see Figures 2h and i). Page four was probably intended for some Requiem mass (see Figures 2j and k). Evaluation of these liturgical registrations offers insight into Franck's quest for color and sonority

Figure 2

Registration and Other Indications on the Second Bifolio of MS 8707

a)

Kyrie
1. 8 Pieds
2. R. Clairon
   P. bourdon 8 acc^t d'8ves du R.
   GO. bourdon 16

3. R. 8 pieds
  P. Bourdon 16 v^b 2. gambe 8
  GO. fl 8 Bourdon 8

b)

1. Grand Chœur
2. Hautb. recit bourdon 16 pos
3. 16 pieds

c)

R. Clairon
P. Bourdon 8
GO Bourdon 16
Ped fl 8 et 16
accoupl. des Claviers

d)

R. les 8 pieds
P. Bourdon 16
GO. Prestant Octave
Ped. Octave 8^{ves} du Recit
Chant aux Pédales

e)

Magnificat
1. imposition pl. jeu
3. Cromorne
5. Voix Humaine et Bourdon 16
7. 8 Pieds et solo de péd avec teneur de récit
9. Violons
11. G^d Chœur

f)

R Octavin, Hautb
P Viole de Gambe, Bourdon 16
GO tous les fonds sauf la montre 16 et le Prestant

g)

1. Eight measures of soprano and bass in E major in 6/8 meter, marked "Elevation Voix Celestes et Humaines."
2. Staves three to ten show additional short, two-voice sketches. None are registered.

h)

1. Eight measures of a four-voice texture, occasional omission of the inner voices, marked "Andante 8 pieds."

i)

2. Eight measures of C major in 6/8 meter, "Flute" designated over the G clef and "echo" stipulated in measure two.

3. Additional two-voice "incipts," all unregistered.

j)

1. First theme from the second movement of Beethoven's Symphony No. 3 ("Eroica") notated by Franck.

k)

2. Fourteen measures in B minor, essentially soprano and bass throughout, registered "16 pieds et Voix Humaine."

3. "Sortie Funèbre," no registration.

at his renowned Sainte-Clotilde Cavaillé-Coll. Of no lesser interest in a broader sense are references to the role of the organ in nineteenth-century Parisian liturgies, especially the use of *alternatim* practice.

Significance of the MS 8707 Registrations

In the nineteenth century, the *Plenum* or *Grand-Plein Jeu* of the French Classical period is scarcely ever encountered (after Alexandre-Pierre-François Boëly, it can be viewed as exceptional). It was common practice, however, to combine mixtures with chorus reeds and foundations for the *Grand Chœur*. In the published organ works of Franck, the use of the Plein jeu stop is never specified in spite of its frequent placement on the Grand-Orgue divisions of moderate to large size and on many Positif divisions in French organs of the middle and late nineteenth century. Franck, who had two mixture stops available at Sainte-Clotilde (one on the Grand-Orgue, and a second, pre-sumedly non-repeating, on the Positif), undoubtedly followed the nineteenth-century practice of drawing the mixtures in tutti passages. Yet until MS 8707, there was no evidence whatsoever to suggest that he even knew the Classical *Plein Jeu* registration or its traditional liturgical use, let alone employed it in his playing. The registrations sketched in this source show that Franck was keenly aware of the older tradition ("*Imposition* Plein Jeu") and in keeping with it, often began his versets with the *Plenum*, a practice which traces its roots in specified French registrations to at least Guillaume-Gabriel Nivers and probably as far back as the medieval Blockwerk organ in the case of improvised versets.

Solo registrations in the Franck organ works most frequently require the Récit Hautbois or the Récit Trompette and Hautbois combined, supported by several 8' foundations. Figures 1a, j, and 2f demonstrate a modification of this timbre: the combination of the Récit Hautbois 8' and the Octavin 2'. The Octavin, invariably harmonic and at 2' pitch, was reputedly invented by Cavaillé-Coll at the beginning of his career, although in fact the concept of overblowing pipes had long been understood and practiced especially in Germany. Unlike many American builders who continue to treat this register as a (Swell) 2' Principal, the French have invariably imparted a bright, telling flute sonority to this stop. With the Hautbois, together these gapped 8' and 2' pitches yield an extraordinarily piquant, colorful timbre, a solo effect unique in Franck's treatment of the organ.

The Récit Clairon 4', usually reserved for "*Grand Chœur* Récit" combinations, is put to some very unexpected uses in MS 8707. In Figure 2c, it is coupled to 16' and 8' Bourdons from the other manuals; these three pitches, 16', 8', and 4', of which the 4' is a bright reed, easily create one of the most singular effects ever concocted by a nineteenth-century French organist (yet one anticipated by Franck in the scherzo of the *Grande Pièce symphonique* where the Récit Clairon is combined with the quieter Hautbois and 8' foundation stops of its own manual plus the 16' and 8' Bourdons and Flûtes of the Positif). Figure 2a indicates the use of the Récit Clairon in the 8' range: it would appear that Franck detected sufficient timbral differences between the Récit Trompette 8' and the Clairon 4' to make the suboctave couplings desirable.

A phrase sketched by Franck in Figure 2g is registered "Voix Célestes et Humaines," another combination which appears to be a bold step in Franck's quest for color. Such a registration, while plausible on almost all nineteenth-century French organs, is not mentioned by any other of the chief composers of the day with the exception of Alexandre Guilmant.[2] Charles Tournemire, Franck's student and successor at Sainte-Clotilde, not only championed this sonority (particularly with the addition of the foundation stops from the Récit as well as the Tremulant) in many of his organ works but also promoted its use throughout his *Précis d'exécution, de registration, et d'improvisation à l'orgue.*[3] It now seems likely, based on MS 8707, that Tournemire learned the essential feature of this effect—the combination of the Voix céleste with the Voix humaine—from Franck, if not from Guilmant, rather than pioneering it himself.

Despite earlier reports to the contrary, it is now certain that the Positif division at Sainte-Clotilde contained a Cromorne 8'. As with many other French organs, it was the only solo reed on the division. The particular qualities of a nineteenth-century French Cromorne can be discerned best in comparison with the Clarinette stop, which to some degree superseded the Cromorne by the end of the century. This is especially true when the comparison can be made on the same nineteenth-century instrument. On the Cavaillé-Coll organs at Saint-Étienne in Caen (1884) and Saint-Ouen in Rouen (1890), as well as in other instances, there is a marked contrast between a Positif

Cromorne and a Récit Clarinette: the Clarinette is smoother, rounder, more orchestral in nature while the Cromorne—to be sure no longer that of Dom Bédos—is less suave and still lends a certain "crispness" and bite to the overall timbre. Cavaillé-Coll instruments possessing both a Cromorne and Clarinette invariably date, however, from the last period of his career (ca. 1880–1899), which must be borne in mind when comparisons between them and earlier instruments are made. How Cavaillé-Coll scaled and voiced Cromornes in his early (ca. 1830–ca. 1858) and middle (ca. 1858–ca. 1879) periods is a topic not yet fully investigated. In the case of Sainte-Clotilde various rebuildings of the instrument now make it impossible to be certain of its original timbre. Tournemire reports that Franck eschewed his Cromorne because it was big and not behind swell shades. On the basis of his published work, this indeed appears plausible since only in the *Grande Pièce symphonique* does Franck require a Cromorne. Yet based on Figures 1d, i, m, and 2e, it is clear that Franck exhibited no prejudice against this stop either in his improvised versets or in his free improvisations.

Another stop highlighted in the present source is the Positif Bourdon 16'. Those who know the velvety, limpid Bourdon stops of eighteenth- and nineteenth-century France will not be surprised that Franck finds frequent use for this stop. While Jean Fellot characterizes Cavaillé-Coll's Bourdons as dark and colorless because allegedly they were not treated *à cheminée* in the treble as in earlier generations, examination of numerous instruments demonstrates quite the contrary: Cavaillé-Coll continued the older practice of Bourdon construction and frequently employed chimney pipes in the higher ranges of both his 16' and 8' Bourdons and the Sainte-Clotilde Grand-Orgue and Positif Bourdons were probably no exception.[4] It is unclear in MS 8707, however, if Franck accompanied his Récit reeds on the Positif Bourdon 16', or coupled Récit to Positif and played the stops together with both hands on the Positif. Tournemire provides a relevant clue in his book on Franck: "He frequently used the manuals II+III, and with the Bourdon 16' from II, the *octave grave* III/II, the foundations 8', Hautbois 8', and Trompette harmonique from III as well as the Swell box, obtained *grand Récit* effects."[5] Moreover, in the *Précis d'exécution*, Tournemire often refers to coupling Récit stops to the Positif 16' Bourdon, probably in order to enhance overall sonority and impart more *Gravität* to the 8' stops of the Récit division. All this suggests that Franck frequently coupled his Récit and Positif divisions together to obtain 16' pitch, unavailable on the vast majority of Récit divisions of the middle nineteenth century, for effects not unlike those found in his Fantasy in C Major (Adagio) and *Pastorale*. Given the abbreviated style of notating registrations in the present source and the evidence relating to Franck's *grand Récit* effects, these Bourdon 16' registrations strongly suggest the use of couplers between Récit and Positif.

Regarding the scoring of solo lines, MS 8707 contradicts as much as it reflects Franck's practices as demonstrated in his published organ works. His predilection for solos on the Récit Hautbois or Trompette-Hautbois combination is well known (from memorable passages of his Cantabile; Fantasy in C Major; Prelude, Fugue, and Variation; and *Chorals* Nos. 1 and 3), yet nowhere in the present source is solo material given to the Récit Trompette. Use of the Hautbois as a solo stop is restricted as well (and when it is mentioned, the Positif Bourdon 16' is invariably present). More in keeping with Franck's published registrational practices is his avoidance of Flûte harmonique solos. Unlike Charles-Marie Widor, who composed some of his finest music for these sensuous stops, Franck tends to minimize their use in this role.

Another registration rarely encountered in Franck is the traditional Récit Viole de gambe and Voix céleste combination, ubiquitous throughout other French organ music of the same period. Indeed, the *Grande Pièce symphonique* is the only example in the Franck *œuvre* to require this sound. In the present source, the Voix céleste is listed specifically in Figures 1b and e, and implied in Figure 2e (the Magnificat registration), where Franck writes "Violons," probably a generic expression for strings from all divisions to be coupled together, thereby including the two undulating stops, the Récit Voix céleste and the Positif Unda maris. The effect must have been similar to that at the beginning of Widor's Adagio from the Sixth Symphony, aphoristically marked "Gambes." Elsewhere in MS 8707, the Positif Viole de gambe and Bourdon 16' appear to be used together as an accompanimental foil, again without precedent in the published Franck works.

Finally, perhaps most unusual is the registration indicated in Figure 2d. Wholly unlike any use of the organ ever conceived by the composer in his published works, Franck combines all of the 4' principals from the Grand-Orgue and Pédale divisions and solos out a melody (*chant*), possibly a cantus firmus, accompanied by the Récit foundation stops coupled at the suboctave to the Positif Bourdon 16'.[6] Did Franck also employ the unison *Récit sur Positif* coupler? This would likely be the case inasmuch as the composer did not list either the *Anches Grand-Orgue* or *Tirasse Grand-Orgue*, both of which are indispensable for his registration to sound. In any case, Figure 2d demonstrates one of the most imaginative uses yet encountered of a nineteenth-century organ, perhaps the most creative registration left by Franck. It may testify to more than a passing interest in older German practices and certainly ranks with the registrations of Guilmant in its ingenuity.

Seen through his published organ works, Franck's style of registration shows a number of patterns distinctly favored by the composer: solos on the Récit Hautbois or Hautbois-Trompette combined with supporting foundations (the Trompette combination is most frequently accompanied by the Positif Flûte and Bourdon); intimate passages on the Récit Voix humaine; broader sounds on foundations 8' or 16' and 8' from all divisions, coupled together on the Grand-Orgue to which Franck simply adds the *Jeux de combinaison*, division by division, in order to effect a crescendo to the *Grand Chœur*. Other sonorities, more rarely encountered, may be viewed as atypical of the composer. One of the chief lessons of MS 8707 is that this composer possessed a much broader, more comprehensive sense of color as well as the ability to manifest that color with creative registrations than might otherwise be concluded on the basis of his published organ works. Indeed, the recurring *Plein Jeu* registrations and attention to unusual combinations such as the 4' Principal registration appear atypical of nineteenth-century French organ composers in general, and may well imply that distinct, contrasting styles of registration existed for published concert works on the one hand and liturgical use on the other.

Yet another reason may be postulated as to why these registrations contrast so sharply with those in the composed works: those in MS 8707 were conceived especially for the Sainte-Clotilde Cavaillé-Coll while those of the twelve pieces— the *Six Pièces*, the *Trois Pièces*, and the *Trois Chorals*—to a large extent, indeed, a greater extent than is generally believed, reflect Franck's image of the "orgue-type" of this time and place as much if not more so than the Sainte-Clotilde organ itself. That the MS 8707 registrations are uniquely associated with Sainte-Clotilde is easier to demonstrate than the degree to which the registrations of the twelve pieces are not. Franck held only three appointments during his life where he was responsible for playing the liturgy, and the "detail" registrations, for liturgical use, in MS 8707 such as Prestant and Octave on the Grand-Orgue, Bourdon 16' on the Positif, Octave in the Pédale (usually dubbed Flûte on other Cavaillé-Coll organs), and Basson 16' in the Pédale (Figure 1b) clearly point to the Sainte-Clotilde instrument. (Neither the organs of Notre-Dame-de-Lorette nor Saint-Jean-Saint-François du Marais, his previous positions, had these resources available).[7] That the twelve pieces were registered narrowly and exclusively for the Sainte-Clotilde organ—part of the organist's credo since the time of Louis Vierne and Tournemire—deserves reassessment, for not one of these pieces is compromised on the majority of moderate to large three-manual instruments constructed by Cavaillé-Coll in his middle and last periods. Indeed, the *Final* requires foundations and reeds 16', 8', and 4' on the Récit, yet that 16' pitch was not available on the Sainte-Clotilde Récit during Franck's lifetime. Likewise, the *Trois Pièces*, premiered by Franck at the Trocadéro in 1878, would probably be more effective if performed on instruments with a *grand Récit* than on the Sainte-Clotilde *petit Récit* of just ten stops.[8] Each of the three pieces makes use of a large-scale crescendo intended to be achieved by opening the Swell box rather than by adding stops. Given the imposing specification of the Trocadéro Récit with its reed battery of 16', 8', and 4', Cornet V, Carillon mixture I-III, and rich 16', 8', and 4' foundation stops, such an effect must have been overwhelming, fully in keeping with the structural importance of the passages highlighted by those crescendos. Performance on a smaller Récit is significantly less effective.

Without question there are many correlations between Franck's registrations and the instrument at Sainte-Clotilde, for the majority of his pieces fit the celebrated Cavaillé-Coll "like a glove." Yet to say that is not quite the same thing as to claim, as many have, that a number of "idiosyncrasies" in Franck's treatment of the organ derive directly from his long association with that particular instrument. Indeed, a new and richer perspective on these issues can be found in the wider context that is Cavaillé-Coll's instruments from the middle of the builder's career, the general style of which was well known to Franck.

Perhaps the most frequently cited example is Franck's use of the Récit Hautbois and foundations coupled to the foundations of the Positif and Grand-Orgue. Presumedly, the three foundation stops on the Récit, when coupled to the remainder of the organ, produced only a minimal effect when the Récit box was opened or closed. Much has been made of the small size of Franck's Sainte-Clotilde Récit, especially its lack of principal tone, and this may indeed be a contributing factor in Franck's habitual use of the Hautbois in such passages. The division itself contained ten stops and may be understood as a logical outgrowth of the eighteenth-century half-compass Récit in which often only a Cornet and Trompette were found. French nineteenth-century Récits in the main "gallery" organ almost never included principal stops until the last period of Cavaillé-Coll's work when a Diapason or Principal 8' began to appear in the division. Saint-Sulpice, with its *Plenum* beginning at the 4' Prestant, was the clear exception and even Notre-Dame, with its 16' Récit division, was originally devoid of all principals. Yet Widor, who at Saint-Sulpice was restricted to the same three 8' foundation stops as Franck had on the Sainte-Clotilde Récit (Bourdon, Flûte harmonique, string), never mixed the Hautbois in the foundation chorus. Moreover, Vierne, who studied with both Franck and Widor, followed Widor's practice in his foundation registrations. Rather than a specific influence of a particular organ, then, it is quite probable that Franck may simply have preferred this particular sonority, its frequent appearance in his scores a matter of an individual composer's unique taste and style in choosing registrations.

Another so-called "unusual" combination is the Récit Trompette-Hautbois duo most frequently employed for solos. Supposedly, the Récit Trompette at Sainte-Clotilde was delicate and needed the support of the Hautbois. While the two rebuilds of the organ make the characterization of these stops with certainty impossible, on other contemporary instruments built by Cavaillé-Coll this registration is effective, far from overwhelming or undesirable. Placing the most suave, refined solo reeds in the Récit while relying on the Trompettes of the Positif and Grand-Orgue for *éclat* in the *Grand Chœur* passages were stylistic features of these organs, confirmed by the bulk of nineteenth-century registrations found in published pieces. In all likelihood Franck favored the Trompette-Hautbois registration not so much because of idiosyncrasies at Sainte-Clotilde but rather as a personal preference in a sonority which was effective on the vast majority of organs in France at the time.

Yet a third topic frequently cited to establish an exclusive relationship between Franck's registrations and the Sainte-Clotilde organ is the question of the coupling system. Franck had available in 1859 the following couplers operated by the latch-down *pédales de combinaison*:

Tirasse Grand-Orgue
Tirasse Positif
Récit sur Positif
Positif sur Grand-Orgue
Grand-Orgue Octaves Graves
Positif Octaves Graves
Récit sur Positif Octaves Graves

Again, much has been made of the fact that Franck was "deprived" of a *Tirasse Récit* at Sainte-Clotilde, and therefore when playing on the Récit, bass lines had to be doubled between left hand and pedal. Independent pedal couplers for each manual division were still quite rare in France at this time, as Rollin Smith has summarized.[9] In fact, the absence of a *Tirasse Récit* was standard, a feature Franck must have all but taken for granted during his early years at Sainte-Clotilde. Given the number of instruments where only the accumulative *Tirasse Grand-Orgue* was available, Franck may well have considered his instrument, with its *Tirasse Positif*, a "luxury" model.

Much the same may be said of the manual couplers. The systematic use of a complete set of inter-manual couplers was far from common in Cavaillé-Coll's middle period. At the time of their completion in 1862 and 1868 respectively, the five-manual organs at Saint-Sulpice and Notre-Dame allowed for coupling only to the principal manual, the Grand-Chœur. A direct coupler between the Récit and Positif did not exist, although secondary manuals could be easily coupled together through the Grand-Chœur (merely leaving the latter uncoupled from its Barker). The absence of the *Récit sur Grand-Orgue* at Sainte-Clotilde, then, was in keeping with the general style of the era which did not see the necessity of equipping an instrument with all possible inter-manual couplers.

Thus it seems clear that Franck, like so many of his organist-composer colleagues in France, wrote for a relatively standardized three-manual organ of some forty to fifty stops. Such an instrument would invariably contain foundations and reeds on all divisions, a complete *Plenum* on at least the Grand-Orgue, refined reed solo stops (including the Voix humaine) of exquisite beauty as well as the Gambe-Voix céleste pairing on the Récit, an 8' Flûte harmonique on most if not all of the manual divisions, and the 8'-4'-2' pyramid of harmonic flutes on the Récit. That the Sainte-Clotilde instrument was a good example of this kind of instrument is supported by the fact that its

1853 design is virtually identical to Cavaillé-Coll's proposal for Bayonne in 1849, as Fenner Douglass has shown.[10] Moreover, eight- to ten-stop Récit divisions from Cavaillé-Coll's middle period show that an extremely standardized design for this all-important manual was used throughout the 1850s and 1860s. Likewise, Grand-Orgue divisions display many common characteristics. A good example is the 1862–1863 Cavaillé-Coll at Saint-Bernard-de-la-Chapelle in Paris, an organ of some twenty-six stops. Fourteen of them are specified on the Grand-Orgue and form an exact replica of the principal manual at Sainte-Clotilde, stop by stop. In other words, the unique beauty of the Sainte-Clotilde Cavaillé-Coll, attested to time and time again by French organists as well as visitors from abroad before Tournemire's rebuild of 1933, must have been due not so much to its specification as to its incomparable voicing (a perfect combination of scaling and Gabriel Reinburg's voicing).[11] Franck, a friend and supporter of the genial organbuilder, understood the common threads running through Cavaillé-Coll's work and shrewdly published his registrations with them in mind.

Finally, the MS 8707 registrations provide information about Sainte-Clotilde's mysterious *Récit sur Positif Octaves Graves*, a suboctave coupler which, unlike the commonplace suboctave coupler on the Grand-Orgue, was unusual in the majority of Cavaillé-Coll's work. Throughout the years, sources on the Sainte-Clotilde organ have disagreed as to its very existence; these discrepancies have been summarized by Smith.[12] Both Figures 2a and d refer to "8ves du Récit"; Figure 2a, in which Franck writes this direction immediately after the Positif registration, is a strong indication that Sainte-Clotilde did indeed possess this suboctave coupler from the Récit to the Positif and not *Octaves Graves Récit*. Furthermore, as a rule, Cavaillé-Coll supplied *octaves graves* couplers only on Barker machine divisions. Given the small number of stops (ten) on the Sainte-Clotilde Récit, it likely played with direct mechanical action. For it to have had a Barker machine would have been quite exceptional for Cavaillé-Coll. Furnished with fourteen stops (many of which were large foundations), the Positif probably did have a Barker action, making octave coupling from the Récit feasible.[13]

Thus MS 8707 provides precious evidence—available for the first time—concerning Franck's experiments in selecting unique, colorful registrations specifically tailored to his Sainte-Clotilde Cavaillé-Coll, the majority of which are not to be found in his published organ works. Furthermore, this source attests to the use of *alternatim* practices at Sainte-Clotilde and to the continuation in the nineteenth century of its typical opening *Plein Jeu* registration. Moreover, it shows that Franck, as *titulaire* of the *grand-orgue*, improvised on plainsong. Finally, MS 8707 offers new evidence toward establishing the authentic nineteenth-century specification for an organ now twice rebuilt and as such lost as a primary source in the study of Franck's organ music.

NOTES

[1] Pierre de Lapommeraye, "César Franck intime. Une conversation avec M. Gabriel Pierné," *Le Ménestrel* 84 (1922): 484–86. Quoted in Léon Vallas, *César Franck*, trans. Hubert Foss (London: George G. Harrap, 1951), 226, and Rollin Smith, *Toward an Authentic Interpretation of the Organ Works of César Franck*, Juilliard Performance Guides, no. 1 (New York: Pendragon, 1983), 159–60. The existence of this notebook is also reported by Paul Poujard (see Amédée Gastoué, "César Franck et Paul Poujard, à propos d'un thème de folklore, le 'Chant de la Creuse'," *Revue de musicologie* 21 [1937]: 37).

[2] The article in this volume by Edward Zimmerman and Lawrence Archbold refers to this sonority in the organ music of Guilmant. *Ed.*

[3] Charles Tournemire, *Précis d'exécution, de registration, et d'improvisation à l'orgue* (Paris: Max Eschig, 1936); see in particular p. 91.

[4] Jean Fellot, "Chronologie de l'œuvre de Cavaillé-Coll," in *Orgues historiques*, no. 11 (Paris: Harmonie du monde, 1965).

[5] Charles Tournemire, *César Franck*, Les Grands Musiciens par les maîtres d'aujourd'hui, no. 5 (Paris: Delagrave, 1931), 54.

[6] The pedal stop called Octave 4' was probably no principal, but rather a large-scale Flûte 4' in keeping with not only other Cavaillé-Coll instruments throughout the century, but also long-standing French tradition.

[7] Marie-Louise Jaquet-Langlais's article in this volume discusses in detail Franck's instruments and their relationship to his organ music. *Ed.*

[8] The traditional view of the registrations found in the *Trois Pièces*—that they, too, reflect Sainte-Clotilde—is given in Marie-Louise Jaquet, "L'Œuvre d'orgue de César Franck et notre temps," *L'Orgue*, no. 167 (1978): 30. (The discovery of early versions of the *Trois Pièces*, however, has led the way to a revised assessment, presented by her in this volume. Rollin Smith's article in this volume provides details about the premiere of the *Trois Pièces*. *Ed.*)

[9] Smith, *Toward an Authentic Interpretation*, 71.

[10] Fenner Douglass, *Cavaillé-Coll and the Musicians*, 2 vols. (Raleigh: Sunbury, 1980), 1:114–22.

[11] Smith has summarized these reports in *Toward an Authentic Interpretation*, 75. None other than Cavaillé-Coll himself recognized this instrument's exceptional beauty when he wrote to Widor on 8 June 1891, "We have just completed the overhaul or rather the restoration of the Sainte-Clotilde organ which we built thirty years ago. The priest has given me an appointment for Wednesday the 10th at one o'clock at the church for the 'organ proofing' by Pierné and Rousseau. I thought that you will wish to attend this little test if you are free. I've also asked Gigout to join us. I would be quite glad that you could try this organ which is one of the best instruments we have built." Quoted in Claude Noisette de Crauzat, *Cavaillé-Coll* (Paris: La Flûte de Pan, 1984), 45.

This letter is important for at least two reasons. Concerning the issue at hand, it confirms the builder's own assessment that indeed Sainte-Clotilde was a most successful instrument. Secondly, the work completed by the original builder in 1891 was apparently more far-reaching that often thought. Called a restoration by Cavaillé-Coll, it may have important ramifications for the understanding of Tournemire's compositions, as well as his *Cinq Improvisations* recorded there in the early 1930s.

[12] Smith, *Toward an Authentic Interpretation*, 70–72.

[13] Additional evidence is provided by Jean Gallois (*Franck* [Paris: Seuil, 1966], 69) in a photograph of the 1859 Cavaillé-Coll console, as it appeared in Flor Peeters's residence, showing the *pédales de combinaison* (all visible except two hidden by the bench); they read: *Tirasse Grand-Orgue, Tirasse Positif, (Tirasse Récit), Anches Pédale, (Octaves Grand-Orgue), Octaves Positif, Octaves R/P, Anches Grand-Orgue, Anches Positif, Anches Récit, Positif sur Grand-Orgue, Récit*

sur Positif, Trémolo (Récit), *Expression Récit.* In their article concerning these pedals, Hans Brink and Paul Peeters, after examining the action remaining inside the 1859 console, conclude that only the *Tirasse Récit* was added to the organ, replacing the original *Effet d'Orage* pedal; according to their investigation, the *Récit sur Positif Octaves Graves* as it now stands in the console is original ("Het Orgel van César Franck in de Ste. Clotilde: 'Continuing Story' of prijsvraag voor organisten?" *Het Orgel* 79 [1983]: 35).

From Manuscript to Publication: Franck's *Choral* No. 1

KAREN HASTINGS-DEANS

An autograph manuscript of César Franck's *Choral* No. 1 in E Major, the first work in the set of *Trois Chorals* composed in 1890, is located in The Pierpont Morgan Library.[1] Judging from the date, "Le 7 Aout 1890," this manuscript is the original, which Franck wrote at Nemours. The manuscript, which is unsigned, bears the surprising dedication, "à ma chere Eleve/ et petite amie/ Mlle Clotilde Bréal." (The work is dedicated to Eugène Gigout, the noted organist of Saint-Augustin, in its first and subsequent editions.) This manuscript is apparently the only extant autograph of the E-Major *Choral*; however, the first published edition—which was issued by Durand shortly after Franck's death late in 1890—was almost undoubtedly made from another source.[2] Many rhythms and pitches are different in the two versions; in the manuscript, no dynamics are included, and no information is given concerning registration except for a few manual changes. In contrast, the manuscript used to prepare the first publication of the *Choral* in B Minor, the second of the *Trois Chorals*, contains many dynamics and registrations (some of them rewritten in an editor's hand).[3] Franck's notation is much more legible in this latter manuscript than in the autograph of the First *Choral*. The "8ª bassa?" marking in mm. 157–58 is perhaps the most convincing evidence that this autograph is not Franck's final version of the First *Choral*. (This passage is written an octave lower in the publication.) Although many factors point to the conclusion that this autograph is not the final manuscript, the great similarity between the publication and the autograph accords this manuscript greater status than that of a draft.

General Characteristics of the Manuscript and of Franck's Notation

The manuscript measures thirty-seven by twenty-seven centimeters. Franck employed four fascicles of staff paper for this manuscript. Each of the booklets has four sides (front, back, and two middle pages).[4] The score comprises fourteen pages of music, two of which are labeled "11." The first page 11 (third fascicle, inside right) contains one crossed-out measure plus one pedal note. Curiously, the notes are identical to those which begin the second page 11 (fourth fascicle, front page), except for the rhythm of the isolated pedal note, which is a quarter note on the first page and a dotted half note on the second. This rhythmic difference could be the reason for Franck's having rejected the first page 11, although the manuscript contains several examples of quarter notes which were changed to dotted or regular half notes, including one in the pedal part in the fifth measure of the complete page 11. There seems to be no satisfactory explanation as to why Franck abandoned the original page. Furthermore, the second page 11 is sometimes more diffi-cult to read because portions of its first four measures were written twice.

Actually, many passages in the manuscript were notated twice. Even from a photocopy, it is always possible to tell which notes are the intended ones, for they are definitely darker. However, even when looking at the manuscript in person, it is often impossible to determine whether Franck made an effort to erase the lighter notes or merely wrote over them. In thirty-six measures, the lighter notes duplicate the darker notes, making one wonder why they were rewritten. This duplication is especially baffling because the final, darker versions are also written in pencil and none too tidily. Some of the lighter notes occur as much as two beats in advance of the darker duplicates.

Other sets of lighter notes have different pitches and rhythms from their darker counterparts and constitute early versions of these passages. Emory Fanning, in his commentary to the Second *Choral* facsimile, has observed that "Franck often drafted the intended harmony in large note values and added non-harmonic material later to provide unity, interest and movement."[5] This practice of Franck's may account for some of the early versions in the manuscript of the E-Major *Choral*.

The First *Choral* seems to have been hurriedly notated, perhaps because the composer's ideas flowed rapidly and he was anxious to record them as quickly as possible and move onward. Many dots and ties and even an occasional clef change were apparently forgotten. Numerous accidentals were omitted. These characteristics help provide evidence that the manuscript of the First *Choral* was not a fair copy. When an entire measure was to be silent in a particular part, Franck often neglected to notate the whole rest. Likewise, rests of smaller duration were sometimes omitted. It is often difficult to determine whether a note head is on a line or space. When two or more notes share a stem, the stem often touches only one of the notes. Some of the sixteenth notes have quarter-note stems in the opposite direction, as if, before adding the beams, the composer had changed his mind about which direction to put the stems and had forgotten or not bothered to erase the original stems. Most probably, Franck made a neater copy later.

At the beginning of a new line or page, Franck generally did not repeat the clefs or key signature unless they had just changed. In the autograph of the Second *Choral*, the clefs and key signature are usually indicated at the beginning of each new page, whether or not they represent a recent change. With rare exceptions, Franck placed all stems to the right of the notes in the manuscripts of both *Chorals*. Franck's distinctive natural signs resemble the letter "S." Obviously, this type of natural sign is quicker to write than the traditional symbol since it can be drawn with a single stroke, yet Franck did employ the more usual shape on occasion.

Almost all of the manuscript is in pencil, but some fifty musical symbols, most of them accidentals, are in ink. The ink portions of the manuscript were most likely added at a later time, presumably by Franck himself. Ink additions were probably made on at least three different occasions, using black ink during one sitting (as in mm. 38 and 116), using brown ink at another time, perhaps with a thinner nib (as in mm. 53, 54, 63, 74, and 255), and, a third time, employing a pen capable of providing at least four shades of ink in quick succession (black, brown, blackish, and brownish, as evidenced in the triplet of m. 232). Far more important than Franck's pen collection is the fact that not one of the ink figures is contradicted by Durand's text.[6] Most of the ink figures are cautionary accidentals, or constitute corrections of various sorts, or reflect a change in thought, representing a first step in Franck's revision process. The hundreds of conflicts between the edition and the pencil portions of the manuscript will be discussed and tabulated below.

Omitted Accidentals

Although the composer evidently discovered that he had omitted some accidentals, and added them later in ink, he seemingly overlooked many other accidentals which appear in the first edition. These are listed in Figure 1. Although many accidentals were omitted in the manuscript, a number of extra, cautionary accidentals were included. Some of these do not appear in the first edition. Also, that edition contains some cautionary accidentals not found in Franck's manuscript. Differences between the sources as to the presence or absence of these technically unnecessary accidentals will not be listed or discussed further since they in no way alter the music. These many differences do, however, provide additional evidence that the first published edition was not prepared from this manuscript.

Other Differences in Pitch

On the third beat of m. 28, the manuscript assigns a natural to the soprano d" while the first edition does not. (Interestingly, the modern Durand edition,

Figure 1

Omitted Accidentals: Accidentals Which Are Present in the First Edition but Not in the Manuscript

Measure No., Beat No.	Voice Part	Manuscript Lacks the Edition's	Probable Correct Source; Comments
22, b. 2	bass[a]	♮ on first C	ed.; original MS note was apparently C♯ (or B♯?)
22, b. 3	bass	♮ on D	ed.
23, b. 3	alto 1	♮ on D	ed.; 2 D ♮'s b. 1; forms sequence with m. 25
24, b. 3	alto 2	♭ on B	ed.
24, b. 3	tenor (1)	♮ on G(?)	ed.; there is a rather unclear, superfluous ♭ on the baritone E
25, b. 1	bass	♮ on G	ed.; not tied over in MS
25, b. 2	baritone	♭ on E	ed.
25, b. 3	bass	♭ on E	ed.
29, b. 3	alto 2	♭ on E	ed.; bass E♭, b. 1; see alto 2's E♭ m. 30, b. 1
32, b. 2	soprano	♭ on B	ed.; MS has unnecessary ♮ sign instead
32, b. 3	alto 1	♭ on A	ed.
51, b. 2	tenor	♮ on D	ed.; soprano D♮
67, b. 3	bass	♮ on first B	ed.
73, b. 1	soprano	♮ on D	ed.
73, b. 2	alto	♮ on G	ed.
74, b. 1	alto 1	♮ on G	ed.
74, b. 1	alto 2	♮ on D	ed.
75, b. 1	soprano	♮ on tied-over D	ed.[b]

Measure No., Beat No.	Voice Part	Manuscript Lacks the Edition's	Probable Correct Source; Comments
75, b. 1	alto	♮on tied-over G	ed.; in the MS, the ♮ is missing at both ends of the tie
76, b. 3	soprano and alto	♮on D(?)	ed.; either the ♮ and the upward stem are combined or one is missing
79, b. 3	soprano	♮on first D	ed.
85, b. 3	bass	♮on G	ed.; G♮'s b. 1 and 2, tenor
91, b. 2	tenor (1)	♮on D	ed.; same omission in m. 51
103, b. 2	alto 1	♮on D	ed.; like m. 62
111	baritone	♭on B	ed.; dominant 7th chord like the transposition in m. 120
133, b. 2	middle or lower	♮on C or A	ed.; matches m. 129
153, b. 3	alto 2	♮ on F	ed.
155, b. 3	alto 1	♮on A	the MS's ♮ on C might be for the A instead, although it is placed very high; ed. has ♮'s on both
155, b. 3	bass	♭on E	ed.(?); MS has unnecessary ♮ instead
157, b. 3	alto 1	♭on E	
158, b. 1 1/2	soprano	♭on B	missing because the chord on b. 1 originally included this pitch, not the B♭ an octave lower
158, b. 2 1/2	soprano	♭ on G	missing because the chord on b. 1 originally included this pitch, not the G♭ an octave lower
160, b. 3	bass	♯on C	ed.

Measure No., Beat No.	Voice Part	Manuscript Lacks the Edition's	Probable Correct Source; Comments
166, b. 1	bass	♭ on tied-over B	ed.
167, b. 1	alto 2	♭ on B	ed.; in MS, a crossed-out B appears on middle staff (tenor 1)
169, b. 1	pedal	♭ on A	ed.; doubles bass; faint tie from m. 168 to m. 169 is visible
170, b. 3	soprano	♭ on E	
170, b. 3	alto	♮ on C	ed.; see later transpositions, for example, m. 182, 194
178, b. 3	soprano	♭ on A	ed.
186, b. 2	bass	♭ on A	ed., like m. 174
190, b. 2	bass	♭ on first E	ed.; like m. 178
194, b. 3	alto	♭ on G	ed.
194, b. 3	tenor	♭ on A	ed.
195, b. 3	tenor	♭ on A	ed.
205, b. 3	pedal	♯ on C	ed.; mm. 205–06, pedal part imitates mm. 204–05, soprano part, which has C♯
206, b. 2	soprano	♯ on C	
207, b. 2	soprano	♯ on C	
211, b. 1	soprano	♮ on tied-over F	ed.
226, b. 2	alto	♯ on C	
228, b. 2	alto 2	♮ on G	ed.
253, b. 3	bass	♮ on E	ed.

ᵃ In this table and throughout this article, the term "bass" is only used for manual notes; "bass" refers to the lowest note on the second staff (unless there are four-note chords on this staff, in which case "bass 2" means the lowest note and "baritone" the note just above). "Tenor" (or "tenor 1") refers to the highest note on the second staff. Similarly, "soprano" (or "soprano 1") denotes the highest voice on the top staff, and "alto" (or "alto 2") the lowest voice part on this staff.

ᵇ On this same beat, the tied-over tenor D has a natural sign in the manuscript and the modern Durand edition, but not in the first edition. D natural was certainly Franck's intent.

which, while labeled "Édition originale," contains many departures from the first edition, also gives d'' natural.) In this case, the reading given in the manuscript is most likely correct. However, most differences between the manuscript and the first edition resolve in favor of the edition. Figure 2 illustrates the other note differences between the manuscript and the first edition which cannot be attributed to the omission of an accidental in the manuscript.

It is instructive to compare the manuscript with the first edition, even though the exact relationship between these two sources cannot be determined. Some of the differences in pitch can probably be attributed either to misprinting from the intermediate source or to recopying incorrectly from this manuscript. For instance, in m. 196, the e' in the manuscript is most likely correct, for it is in accordance with the figure introduced in m. 126 (which Franck derived from the *con fantasia* motive in m. 112). In the manuscript, the e' in question is placed so high that it also resembles f sharp'. In m. 248, when one uses the manuscript's b sharp' for the alto's second note, mm. 248 through 250 (beat 2) become an exact sequential repetition of mm. 245–47 (beat 2).

The reasons for other differences are less clear. In m. 187, the manuscript may be correct, for the inclusion of the fifth of the chord is consistent with m. 175, to which m. 187 corresponds. (The passage in mm. 183–88 is a transposition of mm. 171–76 with the right- and left-hand roles reversed.) Also, the autograph's b flat provides a resolution for the a natural in the left hand's middle voice. There is, however, a rhythmic inconsistency: the b flat in m. 187 is an eighth note while the corresponding note on the downbeat of m. 175 (the g' in the first alto) is a sixteenth.

In m. 225, the autograph's c sharp''' seems more suitable than Durand's c natural''', but either reading is possible within the chromatic, dissonant context. If Franck meant to have a c natural''', he may have intended to include a cautionary natural sign because of the clash with the alto's c sharp'', and it is at least possible that he wrote a sharp accidentally.

It is curious that neither the autograph nor the Durand editions (old or new) show an a natural' for the third beat of m. 232. If played as written, the dramatic chord which begins the triumphant final statement of the chorale theme will be a B-major seventh chord instead of the more logical dominant seventh. The modern "Édition originale" lacks one note that is found in both the manuscript and the first edition: a quarter note d' in the alto voice on the third beat of m. 167.

The first edition gives a small alternative note in mm. 180 and 192, but the manuscript only provides an alternate reading in m. 192. In that measure, the large reach between f'' and d flat' is not a problem because both hands are on the same manual. When the f'' (the preferred note) occurs, the same pitch is already sounding in another voice. Consequently, the longer f'' which began

Figure 2

Pitch Differences Which Cannot Be Ascribed to the Omission of an Accidental in the Manuscript

Manuscript[a]	First Edition	Comments
		MS text is probably an early version.[b]
		MS text is probably an early version.
		MS text is probably an early version.
		MS version is probably a mistake or an early version.
		MS text is probably an early version.

126

Manuscript[a]	First Edition	Comments

MS text is clearly an early version. In m. 157, b. 3, there is only one flat for the right hand, but it may be for the E rather than for the G.

Differences in m. 186: edition is probably correct; m. 187: MS may be correct (see the discussion).

MS is probably correct; see the discussion.

M. 224: MS is probably an early version; m. 225: the tenor's B is articulated only in the MS version; soprano C ♯ vs. C ♮ : see the discussion.

MS may be correct; see the discussion.

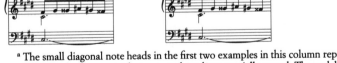

[a] The small diagonal note heads in the first two examples in this column represent notes which are visible in the manuscript but seem to have been partially erased. The pedal doubling found in m. 16 continues in m. 17, but is written more lightly. The pedal line is abandoned altogether in m. 18. Phrase marks are omitted from this table (MS and edition).

[b] The differences between the two versions of mm. 16, 21, 23, 153, 157-58, and 224 seem to preclude the possibility that this manuscript was used to prepare the edition. Durand must have used another, later manuscript which has since been lost.

a sixteenth note before should be rearticulated almost immediately (after a thirty-second note, according to Marcel Dupré[7]), altering the chorale melody. The alternate note, f', is an effective solution, because it can sustain the sixteenth-note motion without modifying the chorale melody. Furthermore, the first four notes of the phrase initiated by this alternate note will have a familiar contour because of the similarity to the beginning of the motif featured in mm. 112–13, 121–22, 125, 126–27, 130–31, 171–72, 175–76, 183–84, 187–88, 196 (shown in Figure 2), 197, and 201–02.

In contrast, the d''' in m. 180 does not have another note of the same pitch conflicting with it, and the only potential reason for the alternate note is the stretch between this soprano d''' and the alto b flat', a stretch complicated by the fact that the hands are playing on different manuals. This major tenth, although problematic for many organists, could easily have been negotiated by Franck, who could reach a twelfth comfortably with one hand.[8] Even an organist with small hands could probably play the b flat' by reaching up with the left hand from the Grand-Orgue to the Positif, thus freeing the right hand for the high d'''. It seems as if the inclusion of an alternate note, d''', was really not necessary, which makes Franck's omission of it in the manuscript particularly significant.

Rhythmic Differences

Figure 3 enumerates the many rhythmic discrepancies between the manuscript and the first edition. Many of these differences display a common factor: the manuscript versions are less legato. The manuscript contains many fewer ties than the edition and sometimes uses two repeated notes in places where the edition shows a longer single note (for example, mm. 9 and 38). After examining the huge list of rhythmic differences and noticing the trend toward a less legato style in the manuscript, it is tempting to speculate that an editor might have tampered with Franck's intent. This is, however, unlikely. (The first edition of the Second *Choral* is faithful in almost every detail to the manuscript from which it was made; even if a different editor prepared the First *Choral* for publication, the Durand firm would certainly not have permitted rhythmic changes, and it truly seems impossible that such a great number of misprints could have occurred in a single composition.) A more likely explanation would take note of the fact that the First *Choral* was composed at the piano, where repeated notes would have helped sustain a fuller harmony. Franck may have decided to tie many of these repeated notes after having played the *Choral* on the organ of Sainte-Clotilde.

Moreover, a full comparison of the available portions of the pencil and ink manuscripts of the Second *Choral* is revealing, and resembles the comparison between the manuscript of the First *Choral* and the first edition of that work.[9]

Figure 3

Rhythmic Differences Between the Manuscript and the First Edition

Measure No., (Beat No.)	Voice Part	Manuscript	First Edition (Durand)	Probable Correct Source; Comments
1–2	alto 1	E's not tied	E's tied	
4, (b. 3)	soprano	♫ (♩♩ ?)	♫	
4, (b. 3)	alto	♫	♫	
5, (b. 3)	soprano	♫ (♩♩ ?)	♫	looks like ♫ in MS
5, (b. 3)	alto	♫	♫	
6, (b. 3)	soprano	♫ (♫ ?)	♫	looks like ♫ in MS
6, (b. 3)	alto	♫	♫	
7–8	tenor	G's not tied	G's tied	ed.; ♮ not repeated
9	tenor	♩ ♩	♩.	
9–10	alto	♩ ♩ ∣ ♩	♩. ∣ ♩	
10	tenor	♩. ♫♫	♩. ♩ ♪	
11	alto	♩ ♩	♩.	
11	tenor	♩ ♩	♩.	
12	tenor	♩. ♪♩	♩. ♩ ♪	
15	bass	♩.	♩	MS; like modern "Édition originale"
16–17	tenor (1)	♩ ♩ ∣ ♩	♩. ∣ ♩	
18–19	bass/ baritone	D's not tied	D's tied	
23	alto 1	D's not tied	D's tied	
24	alto 1	♩ ♩ (?)	♩.	♩ might possibly be a dot (but see m. 26)
24–25	bass	G's not tied	G's tied	♮ not repeated in MS, m. 25 (but see Example 1 and related discussion)

Measure No., (Beat No.)	Voice Part	Manuscript	First Edition (Durand)	Probable Correct Source; Comments
26	alto 1	♩♩	♩.	
35–36	tenor	F♯'s not tied	F♯'s tied	
38	tenor	♩♩	♩.	
38–39	alto	G♯'s not tied	G♯'s tied	
40	tenor	♩♩	♩. ♩	sound the same; MS more logical
40–41	alto	F's not tied	F's tied	
41–42	alto	F♯'s not tied	F♯'s tied	
42–43	alto	G's not tied	G's tied	
43	tenor	♩	♩.	ed.; original, erased rhythm in MS ♩♩
48	tenor	♩. ♩|	♩♩|	ed.
48	bass	♩. ♩┤	♩. |	intended MS rhythm probably ♩♩
55–56	bass	G♯'s not tied	G♯'s tied	
58	bass	♩♩	♩♩	ed.
62	alto 1	D's not tied	D's tied	
63	alto (1–2)	♩♩♩	♩♩♩	MS rhythm sounds like ♩♩♩
63	tenor	♩♩♩	♩♩	first note in MS ♩ and ♩ combined
63–64	alto	D♯'s not tied	D♯'s tied	
63–64	tenor	A's not tied	A's tied	
64	all	♩♩|	♩♩𝄾|	ed.
65	bass	♩♩ (or ♩. ♩)	♩.	
65–66	bass	E's not tied	E's tied	
71	tenor (1)	G's not tied	G's tied	
71	baritone	C's not tied	C's tied	
71–72	soprano	E's tied	E's not tied	
72–73	tenor 1/ soprano	D[♮]'s not tied	D♮'s tied	
73	alto 1	♪♩♩ (or ♪♩)	♪𝄾 ♩♩	intended MS sound seems to be ♪𝄾♩ or ♪𝄾♩♩
74	alto (1)	♩♩♩	♩♩♩	
79	bass	♫♩♬	♫♩♬	ed.

Measure No., (Beat No.)	Voice Part	Manuscript	First Edition (Durand)	Probable Correct Source; Comments
79–80	alto	F ♯'s tied	F ♯'s not tied	MS, (which matches the modern Durand "Édition originale" ed.
86	soprano	♫♫♩_	♩♫♫ ♩	ed.
86	pedal	♩ (♩. ??)	♩.	ed.
89	soprano	♪♫ ♫♫♩	♪♫ ♫♫♩♪♪	
92	soprano	♪♫ ♫♫♩	♪♫ ♫♫♩♪♪	
97	bass	♩	♩.	ed.
99	bass	♩♩	♩♩	MS (see pedal part)
104	alto (1–2)	♩♩♩	♩♩♩	
110	bass/ baritone	_ ♩ o	♩ ♩	
118	soprano	♩ ♫♩ |	♩ ♫♩. |	ed.
119–20	tenor 1	B's not tied	B's tied	
129	pedal	³₄ ♩♪♪	³₄ ♪♪♪♪	
130, (b. 1)	bass	♩	♪	
133	pedal	♩♪♪	♪♪♪♪	
138, (b. 1)	tenor 1	♪♪	♪♪♪	
145	soprano	C ♯'s not tied	C ♯'s tied	
147–50	pedal	♩.♩♩.♩ ♩.♩♩. |	♩♩♪|♩♩♪| ♩♩♪|♩♩♪|	
156	alto	♩♪♩♩	♪♪♩♩	ed.
156–59	pedal	♩.♩♩.♩ ♩.♩♩. |	♩♩♪|♩♩♪| ♩♩♪|♩♩♪|	
158	soprano (1)	♪♩♩♩	♪♩♩♪	ed.
158	bass	♪♩♩	♪♪♩♩	ed.
161–62	pedal	D ♯'s not tied	D ♯'s tied	
167–[69]	pedal	♩♩|♩♩♩|♩♩♩| Péd. ad lib	♩♩|♩♩♩|♩♩♩|	ed.
170	pedal	♩	♩.	ed.
170–71	pedal	G's not tied	G's tied	
172–73	pedal	G's not tied	G's tied	
173	pedal	♩	♩.	ed.
173–74	pedal	G's not tied	G's tied	

Measure No., (Beat No.)	Voice Part	Manuscript	First Edition (Durand)	Probable Correct Source; Comments
176, (b. 2–3)	soprano	E♭'s not tied	E♭'s tied	
184–85	pedal	B♭'s not tied	B♭'s tied	
185	soprano	♩♩	♩.♩	ed.
186	pedal	♩♪♪♩	♩♪♪♩	MS; like m. 174
188, (b. 2–3)	tenor	G♭'s not tied	G♭'s tied	see m. 176 in figure (consistent within each source)
193	pedal	♩	♩ 𝄾	
195	bass	♫♫♩	𝄾 ♫♫♩	ed.
203–04	tenor	F♯'s not tied	F♯'s tied	
208–09	alto	F♯'s not tied	F♯'s tied	
212	tenor/bass	♪♪𝄾 ♫	♪♪𝄾 ♫	ed.
214–15	pedal	B's not tied	B's tied	
215	alto	♩♩♩	♪♪♩♩	
215 (b. 1)	tenor	♩	♪♪	
215	bass	♩♩♩	♪♪♩♩	
221, (b. 1)	soprano	♩	♪♪	
221, (b. 1)	bass	♩	♪♪	
226–27	pedal	B's not tied	B's tied	
229–30	alto	E's not tied	E's tied	
232	pedal	♩♩♩	♩♩♪♪	
243, b. 1–2	alto	B's not tied	B's tied	first note in MS is actually a ♩, ♩ and dot combined
243	tenor	G♯'s not tied	G♯'s tied	ed.; lower octave of melody
243–44	soprano	G♯'s not tied	G♯'s tied	
244	alto 1	E's not tied	E's tied	
244	alto 2	B's not tied	B's tied	
246	alto	♩. ♩	♩ ♩	ed.; see m. 249
246	bass	♩	♩.	ed.; see m. 249
246–47	pedal	B's tied	B's not tied	MS; see mm. 249–50
249	pedal	♩♩	♩.♩	ed.
257–58	pedal	E's not tied	E's tied	
258–59	pedal	E's not tied	E's tied	

The practice of including fewer ties in a first draft than in a later copy of the same work was evidently normal for Franck. When comparing the pencil and ink autographs of mm. 250–73 and 285–88 of the Second *Choral*, one finds six differences in ties within these twenty-eight measures alone. Yet, a comparison of the final manuscript of this *Choral* with the first edition reveals only six differences with respect to ties in the entire 288 measures.

There are two additional rhythmic inconsistencies between the manuscript and the first edition of the First *Choral* (which cause a difference in sound but are difficult to describe effectively in a figure). In m. 22, the tenor a in the manuscript is sustained as the alto performs a triplet composed of the notes d', b, and c natural', while in the publication, on the other hand, the alto d' is sustained and the triplet occurs in the tenor part with the pitches a, b, and c natural'. In m. 26, the first alto's rhythm is written very clearly in the autograph and undoubtedly represents an early version rather than a mistake (see Example 1). Moreover, in the edition, mm. 25 (beat 3) to 27 (beat 3) are an exact transposition of mm. 23 (beat 3) to 25 (beat 3). Likewise, in the

Example 1a. Franck, *Choral* No. 1, mm. 23–27, as it appears in the manuscript

Example 1b. Franck, *Choral* No. 1, mm. 23–27, as it appears in the edition

manuscript, the rhythm of m. 26 was probably intended to match that of m. 24 in the same source, which would suggest that the rhythms of the lower three voices in m. 26 should be as follows: first tenor, half/quarter; second tenor, half/quarter; bass, dotted half. The manuscript's untied bass notes in mm. 24–25 and 26–27 may represent an early version of these passages. When tying a note across a bar line in this manuscript, Franck more often than not would repeat an accidental if it were not in the key signature of the second measure; therefore, no definitive conclusion about ties can be drawn from the absence of a natural sign for the bass's g at the beginning of m. 25 or from the presence of the unnecessary sharp for the d' on the first beat of m. 27.

Fermatas, Tempo Indications, and Dynamics

Details relating to interpretation also differ widely between the manuscript and the first edition. Four of the five fermatas in Durand's first and subsequent editions also occur in this manuscript: in mm. 55 (second beat), 111, 120, and 259 (the final measure). Durand shows an additional fermata in m. 105, above the rests on beat 3.

No initial tempo is given in the autograph; the first edition has the marking Moderato. Measure 106 in the manuscript is labeled Largo; the edition reads Maestoso. Durand used Largo for the similar section which begins in m. 115; the manuscript has no tempo marking for this section. The second and final tempo-related indication found in the autograph is the Molto rall- at the end of m. 124 and the beginning of m. 125. It is written somewhat later in the manuscript (after the fourth sixteenth note of beat 3) than in the first edition (after the third sixteenth of beat 3). Neither source has an a Tempo after this Molto rallentando, but in the autograph, the curved dash following the Molto rall- ends shortly after the beginning of the second beat of m. 125. The Durand edition contains numerous tempo indications which do not appear in the manuscript. Also missing in the manuscript are the publication's markings which encourage the use of tempo rubato: *cantabile, sempre cantabile,* and *con fantasia.*

As mentioned before, the manuscript of the First *Choral* contains no dynamic indications whatsoever. The edition, however, has numerous dynamic markings.

Manual Indications

Above the third beat of m. 80, there is a large, clear "R"—presumably an abbreviation for "Récit." Franck probably intended this manual indication to affect only the top voice (as in Durand's version). In the manuscript, the upper voice receives its own staff one beat later. Two symbols which resemble "GO" (or "Gt" for that matter) were placed above the upper staff at the end of m. 64; since the two symbols also resemble "64," it seems likely that they represent the measure count—the first measure number thus far, placed over the measure which concludes the exposition of the seven initial periods of thematic material. (The next measure number, 105, just before the Largo, also occurs at the end of a major section.) As further evidence, the Durand registration does not involve the Grand-Orgue at all.

On the first beat of mm. 151, 160, and 182, Franck wrote the first of the four sixteenth notes separately, with its own flag, and connected the last three with a beam. The use of this notation to indicate phrasing would have been superfluous because the first two sixteenths are repeated notes and would be separated automatically. The composer was probably envisioning changing manuals at these points. Each time in the publication, there is indeed a manual change between flag and beam.

Franck employed four staves at once for mm. 129–34 (see Plate 1[10]). He probably used this arrangement to clarify that the uppermost line (the main melody) should be played on a separate manual, although the right hand sometimes moves to the other manual to assist the left hand with the accompaniment's interludes. Franck actually marked "m.d." ("main droite") in m. 129 above the second staff, where the top staff's rest begins. The curved line at the beginning of m. 130 presumably cancels this "m.d.," indicating that the left hand should perform both middle staves.

Phrasing

The manuscript contains many fewer phrase marks than the original edition. Most of the phrasings found in the autograph are matched by Durand: mm. 19–20, soprano; 23–25, soprano; 36–38, soprano; 79, third beat, tenor; 147–48, soprano and alto; 148–49, soprano and bass; 149–50, soprano; 150–51, soprano; 157–58, bass; 158–59, soprano; 159–60, soprano; 167, second alto to first tenor; and 159–60, bass.[11]

One of the phrase marks found in the manuscript begins in the penultimate measure of page 1 and extends beyond the barline of the last measure, but does not resume on page 2. This phrase begins on the third beat of m. 25, as in the Durand editions. Franck probably intended the phrasing to match that of the preceding soprano phrase (mm. 23–25), for mm. 25–27 constitute a sequential repetition of mm. 23–25, in all voices (see Example 1). The phrase, then, would end with the second note of the new page (m. 27, second beat, as in Durand). Any other end point would spoil the perfection of the sequence.

Somewhat similar problems can be found in the following passages. In mm. 156–57 (pp. 7–8 in the manuscript), the second half of the phrase mark is also

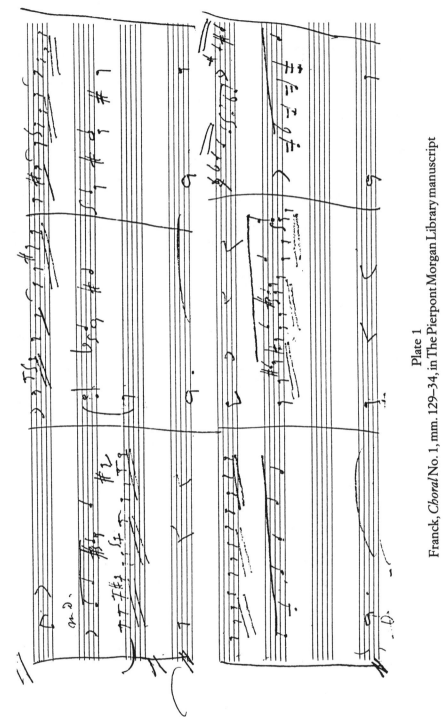

Plate 1

Franck, *Choral* No. 1, mm. 129–34, in The Pierpont Morgan Library manuscript

Example 2a. Franck, *Choral* No. 1, mm. 36-40, phrasing as it appears in the manuscript

Example 2b. Franck, *Choral* No. 1, mm. 36-40, phrasing as it appears in the edition[a]

[a] The modern Durand edition has a dot on the tenor's first note in m. 40, but the 1891 edition and the manuscript do not.

missing, but, because the first note of m. 157 is followed by a rest, there is only one potential ending point, which is the same as Durand's. In addition, although the soprano lines in mm. 36–38 and 38–40 are sequential, the manuscript's phrasing of them is inconsistent (see Example 2). The edition remains uniform in its phrasing of the soprano part (but not of the bass part). Yet one more discrepancy in phrasing is found in mm. 149–50. In the edition, a slur connects the first tenor's note on beat two with the next two alto notes. The same phrasing is used in the similar passage in mm. 158–59. In the manuscript, the slur begins in the same place as in the edition but links only two notes instead of three. No tenor-to-alto phrase mark is found in the analogous mm. 158–59. It is possible that Franck did not intend the slur in m. 149 to indicate phrasing but only used it to show that the voice line which began on the second staff is continued on the upper staff. The first note of this melodic line was evidently placed on the middle staff to indicate that it should be played with the left hand (unless one's right hand can span a twelfth, as Franck's could).

Summary

The manuscript of the First *Choral* dated 7 August 1890 can be taken to be the original autograph of this composition. It was surely not, however, the manuscript from which the first edition was made, and there must have been a later autograph, which has since been lost. These conclusions are based upon the great number of differences between the 7 August manuscript and Durand's first edition, and also upon the fact that this manuscript includes no editorial marks to show where the lines were to end in the publication. (Such marks are present in the last manuscript of the Second *Choral* and in the autograph of the *Grande Pièce symphonique*.)

Even though the autograph of the First *Choral* is not a fair copy, familiarity with this source is of benefit to present-day organists. Several of the manuscript's notes provide plausible—even preferable—alternatives to Durand's text.[12] The autograph also gives some insight into Franck's compositional process. Perhaps some day the lost manuscript will reappear and provide us with additional information concerning César Franck's *Choral* No. 1.[13]

NOTES

[1] César Franck, "Choral N° I." The Pierpont Morgan Library [Lehman collection], New York City. The author would like to thank The Pierpont Morgan Library for permission to include musical examples from this manuscript.

[2] Marie-Louise Jaquet-Langlais's article in this volume gives the date of this publication as 1891, while that by Daniel Roth suggests a date of 1891 or 1892. *Ed.*

[3] *Chorale No. 2 in B Minor for organ: Fascimile of the Autograph Manuscript by César Franck* (1981). An introduction and annotations are provided by Emory Fanning; see pp. [ii-iv] of Fanning's commentary for information about the editor's recopying of registrations.

[4] In the upper left-hand corner of the front page of each fascicle, the following is embossed: LARD-ESNAULT/*Paris*/25, RUE FEYDEAU.

[5] Emory Fanning, "Chorale II: César Franck: The Autograph Manuscript," in *Chorale No. 2 in B Minor for organ: Fascimile of the Autograph Manuscript by César Franck* (1981), [ii].

[6] All of the symbols written in ink match Durand's text, except for the clef at the beginning of m. 123 (which is not necessary in the edition because the clef does not change until m. 124) and an unnecessary, cautionary flat in m. 173.

[7] Marcel Dupré, *Méthode d'orgue* (Paris: Leduc, 1927), 65.

[8] Norbert Dufourcq, *La Musique d'orgue française de Jehan Titelouze à Jehan Alain* (Paris: Floury, 1949), 151; cited by Rollin Smith, *Toward an Authentic Interpretation of the Organ Works of César Franck*, Juilliard Performance Guides, no. 1 (New York: Pendragon, 1983), 35, n. 68.

[9] In Emory Fanning's facsimile of the ink autograph of the Second *Choral*, he included (on the back of the title page) a reduced copy of the pencil draft of mm. 250–88. Of these thirty-nine measures, only twenty-eight are complete (mm. 250–73 and 285–88). For mm. 274–84, Franck wished to repeat mm. 115–25 and, as a shorthand notation, he wrote out the top voice only for the first five beats, closing m. 275 with "a characteristic doodle" (Fanning commentary, p. [ii]) and a long stretch of empty staff lines.

[10] Franck indicated the key signature of E minor and the 3/4 meter three measures before the excerpt begins. The lower octave of the pedal part in mm. 132–33 is apparently the original version. An attempt to erase it clearly was made. The first edition and the modern Durand edition show an extra eighth-note e' on the downbeat of m. 129, on the same staff as the c' (played on the Positif, whereas the other e' is assigned to the Récit). The extra e' begins a phrase mark which leads to the f sharp' in the soprano and ends on the first beat of the next measure with the c'' on the second staff.

[11] This phrase concludes with the first note of m. 160 (not with the last note of m. 159, as in the "Édition originale").

[12] Consider especially e' instead of f sharp' in m. 196, beat 3, second sixteenth note; c sharp''' instead of c natural''' in m. 225; and b sharp' in place of b natural' in m. 248.

[13] A microfilm of the first Durand edition can be purchased from the New York Public Library, Reprographics Services, Fifth Avenue at 42nd Street, New York, N.Y. 10018. For a comparison of the first Durand edition and the modern Durand "Édition originale" of the First *Choral* see David Craighead and Antone [*sic*] Godding, "A Comparison of the 1959 Durand and Kalmus Editions of Franck's Organ Works with the Original Printing," *The American Organist* 19 (April 1985): 56–58.

Franck:
Issues in Performance

The Organ Works of Franck:
A Survey of Editorial and Performance Problems

MARIE-LOUISE JAQUET-LANGLAIS

In the 1950s the revival of Baroque instruments and repertoire caused France to turn away from the organs of Aristide Cavaillé-Coll and the music written for these instruments. The small minority of organists who remained faithful to this repertoire thus found themselves isolated; and yet, outside of France, Romantic and symphonic organ music did not decline so noticeably. Especially in the United States, organists continued to perform works of Franck, Widor, and Vierne. Since the mid 1970s, however, France has seen a resurgence of interest in the organs and organ repertoire of the nineteenth century.

Twenty years ago, our chief concern was the preservation of Classical organs; during those same years it was fashionable to replace the harmonic stops typical of the Romantic period with mutations and mixtures. In more recent years, an inventory of Cavaillé-Coll's instruments has been made by the Ministry of Culture, an association for the preservation of his organs has been founded, and numerous books and articles have been written on his work. There has also been a renewed interest in the repertoire written for this type of instrument, in particular, the music of César Franck. Thus it is now possible both to respect the Baroque repertoire—placed in the context of appropriate instruments—and appreciate the music of Franck—through the organs of Cavaillé-Coll—with the same concern for authenticity.

Dozens of notable studies from the last one hundred years have already examined Franck's organ works, so there is no need to reopen the subject from an analytical point of view. Even so, certain discoveries made in the last fifteen years, even if they fail to resolve all the mysteries surrounding Franck's works, throw new light on some controversial points: in particular, questions regarding manuscripts, editions, and instruments. In this context, our understanding of some enduring problems of interpretation may be meaningfully reevaluated.

Manuscripts

Many of the surviving manuscripts of Franck's organ works were given to the Bibliothèque du Conservatoire in Paris in 1947 by Franck's granddaughter, Mme Thérèse Chopy-Franck. These sources were subsequently transferred to the Bibliothèque Nationale, where they can be found today.[1] This collection includes manuscripts of the *Pastorale*, the *Prière*, several versions of the Fantasy in C Major, the Piece in E-flat Major, and the Piece in A Major:[2]

> *Pastorale*, op. 18 (Cons. MS 8562). Autograph manuscript used for engraving, unsigned, dated 19 September 1863. Eight pages of music. Dedicated to M Aristide Cavaillé-Coll. The original registration indications have been visibly erased and replaced in Franck's own hand.[3] The opus number was added (as an afterthought?) in different ink.
>
> *Prière*, op. 20 (Cons. MS 8563). Autograph manuscript used for engraving, unsigned, no date. Ten pages of music. Dedicated to M Benoist. The original registration indications have been visibly erased and replaced in Franck's own hand.[4] The opus number is in the same ink as the rest of the indications.
>
> *Fantaisie*, op. 16 (Cons. MS 8564/1 and 8564/3). The first folder contains a manuscript of twenty-two pages, of which pages 3 (final section) to 15 are crossed out. Franck kept only the initial Poco lento in C Major for engraving. Pages 16 to 22 contain another work, the Andantino in G Minor. Unsigned, no date. The original registration indications are crossed out, yet they coexist with the indications given later in the engraved version.
>
> A second folder entitled Quasi lento (Cons. MS 8564/2) contains a manuscript of twelve pages. The first four pages are crossed out; the following pages are the continuation of the first three pages from the first folder. Manuscript used for engraving, signed, dated October 1863.
>
> A variant manuscript of the Allegretto cantando in F Minor (Rés. F 1418) was found inserted between pages 4 and 5 of the Fantasy in C Major in the Maeyens-Couvreur edition. Unsigned, no date. Seven pages of music. No registration indications at the beginning.
>
> *Pièce* (Cons. MS 8571). Signed, dated 29 October 1846. Fourteen pages of music.[5]
>
> [*Pièce*] (Cons. MS 8620/1). Unsigned, dated 19 May 1854. Ten pages of music.[6]

This important gift is but a portion of the manuscripts for Franck's organ works. Certain other manuscripts that have reappeared over the last twenty years not only increased our understanding of Franck's organ music; they have given rise to the hope that more manuscripts will appear in the future. The manuscripts that have recently come to light, given in their order of their reappearance, are as follows:

> *Grande Pièce symphonique*, op. 17 (property of the Stiftelsen Musikkulturens Främjande, Stockholm, MS 880212). Autograph manuscript used for engraving, signed, dated 16 September 1863. Twenty-seven pages of music. Dedicated to M Ch. V. Alkan. The original registration indications at the beginning of the work have been visibly erased and replaced in Franck's own hand. The opus number was added in different ink.

Choral no 1 (property of The Pierpont Morgan Library, New York).[7] Autograph manuscript, unsigned, dated 7 August 1890. Thirteen pages of music. Dedicated to Mlle Clotilde Bréal.[8] No registration indications. (The manuscript was acquired by Alfred Cortot, sold after his death in 1962 to Robert Owen Lehman, and given to The Pierpont Morgan Library in 1972.)

Choral no 2 (in the collection of Emory Fanning, Middlebury, Vermont).[9] Autograph manuscript used for engraving. Seventeen pages of music. No dedication. Registration indications are not in Franck's hand; original registrations erased. (Sold by Sotheby's of London on 27 November 1980 to Fanning.)

Sketches of the end of *Choral* No. 1 and of the entire *Choral* No. 3 (in the collection of Emory Fanning, Middlebury, Vermont). Autograph manuscript in pencil, unsigned, dated 30 September (1890?). Eleven pages of music. No registration indications. (Acquired by Fanning at the Sotheby auction in 1980.)

Trois Pièces (property of the Bibliothèque Nationale, MS 20151).[10] Autograph manuscript containing the versions of the *Trois Pièces* Franck performed for the inauguration of the Trocadéro organ in 1878. (Acquired by the Bibliothèque Nationale in 1984.) Specifically:

Fantaisie Idylle. Signed, dated 10 September 1878. Fourteen pages of music. No dedication. Registration indications for the Trocadéro organ.[11]

(Untitled work, tempo marking Cantabile.) Unsigned, dated 17 September 1878. Six pages of music. No dedication. Registration indications for the Trocadéro organ.

Pièce héroïque. Signed, dated 13 September 1878. Thirteen pages of music. Registration indications for the Trocadéro organ. This manuscript contains an ending different from the one Franck later published (see Plate 1).

Final, op. 21 (property of the Bibliothèque Nationale, MS 22410). Autograph manuscript used for engraving, signed, dated 18 September 1864. Nineteen pages of music. Dedicated "à son ami Monsieur Lefébure-Wély." Registration indications in Franck's own hand. The final thirty measures are crossed out and replaced by the final eighty-five measures which appear in the edition. (Acquired by the Bibliothèque Nationale at a Drouot auction on 16 December 1992.)

Questions about the location—or even survival—of other manuscripts (engraver's copies as well as sketch material) remain unanswerable at the present time. In the case of the *Six Pièces*, the manuscript that was used for the engraving of the Prelude, Fugue, and Variation has not been found, nor have any sketches of this work. Similarly, the engraver's manuscript of the *Trois Pièces* of 1878 (which included the final version of the ending of the *Pièce héroïque*) has not come to light. Also apparently lost are the engraver's manuscripts of the First and Third *Chorals* as well as early drafts, if any, of the Second and Third *Chorals* (following the model of The Pierpont Morgan Library manuscript of the First *Choral*). Representatives of the Durand publishing firm have denied that any of these manuscripts remain in their possession. Thus several important manuscripts are unaccounted for at the present time.

The extant manuscripts answer a number of interesting questions. The various manuscript versions of the Fantasy in C Major are particularly instructive, for they shed light on Franck's compositional process. In or before 1858 (the date of the edition of the Andantino in G Minor, the next piece in Cons. MS 8564/1), Franck wrote a fifteen-page piece without title, of which the last twelve measures were crossed out and of which only the first fifty-six measures were saved. This piece was composed for an unusual and as yet unidentified four-manual organ that included, in addition to the Positif and Grand-Orgue, two expressive divisions: a small Récit and a large Récit.[12] Franck revised the work in October of 1863. The revision contains twelve pages of music, of which the first four are crossed out. Eventually, the fifty-six measures of Franck's first manuscript (MS 8564/1) were placed side by side with the final eight pages of the 1863 version: the result was published in 1868 (by Maeyens-Couvreur) with the title *Fantaisie*. At some point, Franck wrote yet another version of the largest section of the work, the Allegretto cantando in F Minor, and inserted it into his copy of the published score. One might well imagine (as Jesse Eschbach and Robert Bates have proposed) that this less intimate version—so brilliant near its conclusion—was composed especially for Franck's performance during the inauguration of the monumental new Cavaillé-Coll organ at Notre-Dame on 6 March 1868.[13] (The program for that concert indicates that Franck played his own *Fantaisie en ut*.) In any case, as this interpolation was designed for the Maeyens-Couvreur edition of 1868 rather than the Durand edition of 1880, we may assume it was composed before 1880. Even if the exact dates of the versions are not certain, there can be no doubt that the Fantasy in C Major took shape over a remarkably long period.[14]

A further comparison of the extant manuscripts suggests that the order in which the *Six Pièces* appear in print is not the order in which they were composed. The second version of the Fantasy in C Major (the first piece of the collection) was completed in October 1863, shortly after the *Grande Pièce symphonique* (the second piece of the set), dated 16 September of the same year.[15] If the *Final* and the *Grand Pièce symphonique* are compared with the *Pastorale* and the Prelude, Fugue, and Variation, a difference in style cannot be denied. It seems likely that Franck composed the *Six Pièces* between 1859 and 1864, a longer period than has generally been believed. While the printed order of these pieces might in some way be a function of their keys or forms, a more coherent pattern does not emerge from their chronology. There are, to be sure, many uncertainties that might be resolved if the missing sketches and manuscripts of these works were to resurface.

The case of the *Trois Pièces* has become more fully understood since the reappearance of the manuscripts associated with Franck's performance of these works at the Trocadéro in 1878. In these manuscripts Franck registered the *Trois Pièces* (which had not, except for the *Pièce héroïque*, received their definitive titles) very precisely for the four-manual Trocadéro organ. The very different registrations which were printed in the Durand first edition reflect Franck's wise decision to revise his original conceptions in favor of a more typical instrument, one closer to his familiar organ at Sainte-Clotilde. The most striking difference between the two versions is at the end of the *Pièce héroïque*, where Franck had the good sense to replace the very *pompier* gestures of the Trocadéro version with a more somber and majestic ending.

The manuscripts of the *Trois Chorals* pose a different kind of question: who devised the registrations on the manuscript of the Second *Choral*? The registrations are not in Franck's hand nor are they in the hand of any of his students. Several features of these registrations stand out: most notably, the fact that each indication also appears in accurate English translation (the first occurrence of such translations in the works of Franck). Curiously, there are spelling errors in the indications in French (such as "anches préparés" in place of "anches préparées" and "recit" instead of "récit"). This problem is certainly not insignificant, for Franck may not have been able to provide detailed registrations for the *Trois Chorals*: they are dated 7 August, 14 September, and 30 September 1890, respectively, and he died on 8 November of the same year. Were these indications perhaps written by someone to whom Franck dictated? Could they date from after his death? Gaston Litaize (a student of Adolphe Marty, himself a student of Franck) maintained that the registrations of the Third *Choral* were not by Franck. As plausible as this idea now seems in view of the reappearance of the Second *Choral* manuscript, Litaize's claim was always vigorously denied by Jean Langlais (a student of Albert Mahaut, himself also a student of Franck).

Editions

French Editions
The Costallat Edition of the Andantino in G Minor

Because of its inferior quality, Franck never saw fit to publish his first organ work, the Piece in E-flat Major of 1846, nor did he publish the Piece in A Major of 1854. His first published work for the organ was the Andantino in G Minor, released by Constallat in 1858. In the engraved version of the Andantino, Franck omitted his initial registration indications, which had been formulated specifically for a four-manual organ (including two expressive divisions) with fifteen combination pedals.

The Original Maeyens-Couvreur and Durand Editions of the Twelve Pieces (the Six Pièces, the Trois Pièces, and the Trois Chorals)

After Franck's unsuccessful attempt to publish the *Six Pièces* with the German publisher Schuberth, he turned to a small Parisian publishing house, that of Mme Maeyens-Couvreur.[16] The resulting edition of 1868, engraved by Cointé, was extremely precise, to judge from the surviving manuscripts. The *Six Pièces* were sold both individually and as a collected set, but the price for all six together (twelve francs) was the same as that of the *Grande Pièce symphonique* by itself. (The other five sold for nine francs each, or less.)

It is difficult to determine the initial success of the *Six Pièces*: all we know is that in 1880, the new and enterprising publishing house of Durand—founded by a then-famous organist-composer, Auguste Durand—bought the firm of Maeyens-Couvreur, and with it, the rights to the *Six Pièces*. Durand promptly reissued the *Six Pièces* (plate numbers 2679 to 2684) in the same year, both as a collection and as separate numbers.[17] In 1883 the *Trois Pièces* were also issued by Durand (plate numbers 3175 to 3177), some five years after their composition. Durand published the *Trois Chorals* (plate numbers 4414 to 4416) even quicker than the *Trois Pièces*; the former first appeared in 1891, just one year after their completion.[18] At first, Durand was cautious when it came to publishing Franck's music: only twenty-five copies of the *Six Pièces* were printed in 1880. This collection, Franck's first published volume of organ music, must have made an impression: the *Trois Pièces* were released three years later in a publication run of 150! While it is clear that Franck had achieved considerable recognition as a composer by the time of his death, the first (posthumous) publication of the *Trois Chorals* included only some 300 copies. Given that very few copies were printed, it is easy to understand why early editions of the Franck organ works are so difficult to find.

Subsequent printings of the Franck organ works by Durand appeared at regular intervals (see Figure 1).[19] The varying popularity of individual pieces, made plain by Durand's statistics, might just as easily be deduced from concert programs: there has been, over the last hundred years, a marked preference for the Prelude, Fugue, and Variation, the *Pastorale*, the *Pièce héroïque*, the Cantabile, and the Third *Choral*. The Fantasy in C Major, and especially the Fantasy in A Major, along with the *Prière* and the *Final*, have been less popular.

In the 1950s, Durand abandoned the original vertical format ("à la française") in favor of an oblong format ("à l'italienne") for its edition of the Franck organ works, reorganizing the twelve pieces into four volumes of three works each.[20] These changes necessitated a new engraving of the entire *œuvre*, which unfortunately introduced many new errors into the scores, even

Figure 1

Printings of the Franck Organ Works in the Durand Edition

Work	Years	Number of Printings	Total Number of Copies	Number of Copies for the First Year	Number of Copies for the Last Year
Six Pièces (as a set)	1880–1973	33	12,100	25	1,000
Fantasy in C Major	1880–1963	14	2,800	50	500
Grande Pièce symphonique	1880–1970	19	5,000	25	1,000
Prelude, Fugue, and Variation	1880–1972	27	10,500	25	1,000
Pastorale	1880–1967	28	9,850	50	1,000
Prière	1880–1947	15	3,050	25	1,000
Final	1880–1970	18	4,925	25	1,000
Trois Pièces (as a set)	1883–1971	32	12,200	150	3,000
Fantasy in A Major	1883–1947	13	2,975	150	1,000
Cantabile	1883–1973	23	6,700	150	500
Pièce héroïque	1883–1971	28	9,700	150	1,000
Trois Chorals (as a set)	1891–1968	33	20,400	300	2,000
Choral No. 1	1891–1969	19	6,700	350	500
Choral No. 2	1891–1970	14	4,600	300	500
Choral No. 3	1891–1975	24	11,200	300	500

though the volumes still carry the title "Édition originale." The 1956 edition of the *Final*, a more or less typical example, includes several striking errors (see Example 1).

Example 1a. Franck, *Final*, m. 134, left hand, as it appears in the 1956 Durand "à l'italienne" edition

Example 1b. Franck, *Final*, m. 134, left hand, as it appears in the original Durand "à la française" edition

Example 1c. Franck, *Final*, m. 204, right hand, as it appears in the 1956 edition

Example 1d. Franck, *Final*, m. 204, right hand, as it appears in the original edition

Example 1e. Franck, *Final*, m. 240, left hand, as it appears in the 1956 edition

Example 1f. Franck, *Final*, m. 240, left hand, as it appears in the original edition

150

For the *Trois Chorals*, however, Durand published another edition in 1973 as revised and annotated by Maurice Duruflé.[21] In his preface, Duruflé makes these comments:

> Lastly, concerning the general interpretation of this music, it is certain that one must bring to it a wide-awake sensitivity, but a sensitivity the measure of which must ceaselessly be controlled. Even though it is delicate and even dangerous to give too precise indications in this realm, which remains personal, I have allowed myself without striking anything out of the original edition, to add a few notes in brackets concerning tempo, dynamics, and certain **ritenuto's, a tempos, poco animados** [*sic*], which are obviously only suggestions. They were pointed out to me by my Master Charles Tournemire, who was a pupil of Franck.[22]

It is valuable to have an edition of those works with comments by Duruflé, not only because he was well known for precision and detail, but because, as a student of Charles Tournemire, he was an important representative of the Franck tradition as understood by Tournemire. As a student of Franck, Tournemire played the *Trois Chorals* at the piano with the composer; he also wrote a book about Franck that details many of his own ideas about Franck interpretation. He did not, however, publish an edition of Franck's organ music, making Duruflé's volume all the more important.

The Bornemann Edition of the Twelve Pieces as Revised by Dupré[23]

The edition prepared by Marcel Dupré (and issued by Bornemann) has been in competition with the Durand edition ever since its appearance in 1955. To understand how and why this edition differs from the Durand edition, it is absolutely necessary to turn to the introductory preface, in which Dupré explains his editorial practice:

> The object of this Preface is not to analyze Franck's works, a study which has often been made. Introducing an edition for students, it merely deals with all that concerns the performing of those works. César Franck, who was a marvellous pianist, had very big hands and could span the widest intervals with ease. As regards the organ, he was a genius both as an improviser and composer. But as an organ virtuoso, he played... as they played in France at that time, with approximate legato and approximate observance of [note] values. It was customary too, to double the pedal basses with the left hand. It should be said however that organists had some excuse then, for they were never sure to find pedal couplers on all manuals in an organ.
>
> This lack of precision in playing led as a consequence to some notations which, owing to their equivocal meaning, puzzle the performer: excess of ties, vague dynamics, [fermatas] which mean no more than a breath, [and] useless doubling of pedal. Nevertheless, the few precise indications concerning the phrasing remain most precious to us.

César Franck was the first organ composer who marked the registration for his works. Before him, Mendelssohn alone had given a few general indications in the short Preface to his three Preludes and Fugues and to his six Sonatas. But Franck's modesty was such (and it is known he was not overwhelmed by success) that he indicated the registration of his works specially for his own organ as if he considered that no one [else] would ever play them.[24]

Dupré then gives a description of the Sainte-Clotilde organ and explains how Alexandre Guilmant (and later he himself) inherited the Franck tradition:

Guilmant, who was appointed organist of [La Trinité] in 1872, was introduced to Franck whom he highly admired, by Aristide Cavaillé-Coll. One evening, Franck played his [S]ix Pieces at the Cavaillé-Coll factory (15, avenue du Maine, Paris) for Saint-Saëns, Widor and Guilmant who were gathered there. This was related to me, first by Guilmant, then later on by Widor, and lastly by Saint-Saëns, when I visited him after my "Prix de Rome", on July 6th 1914. All three agreed about the year of their meeting, which took place in 1875.

After the publishing of the Three Pieces in 1878, Guilmant played at Cavaillé-Coll's, before Franck alone, the Nine Pieces which had been printed and which he had learned. Franck was most moved as he had never heard his pieces performed in that way. Guilmant did not fail to ask him for all possible details about their interpretation, which Franck gave him willingly while Guilmant scrupulously noted down all his indications.

During his lifetime, Franck also showed Guilmant the outlines of his three Chorales which Guilmant was thus acquainted with before their posthumous publication.

I received this tradition directly from my Master Guilmant when I studied all the works of César Franck with him in the course of the years 1907–1908, at Meudon, three years before he died. Later on, I was able to ascertain the perfect identity of this tradition with the indications I received in 1917 from Gabriel Pierné, Franck's pupil and his immediate successor at Sainte-Clotilde.
. . .
But, as a consequence of the remarks I have made above, there will be found as well [in this edition]:

1° the appropriate phrasing, i.e: all the necessary ties between notes and the exact value of each note so as to leave no ambiguity;

2° the suppression of all unnecessary ties, as well as of the [fermatas] which are replaced by commas at the necessary places;

3° the indications of registration, of manuals[,] and rational dynamics suited to modern instruments and in conformity with the tradition and esthetics of Franck;

4° the suppression of doubling of left hand and pedal, when in unison. In this case, the left hand notes are printed in smaller characters so as to respect Franck's text;

5° a different distribution of the polyphony between both hands, at certain places, in order to ensure a better legato. Needless to say that no difference ensues for the ear[,] as no change whatever is introduced in the text;

6° with the same object, the allotment to the pedal of other passages which were written for the hands, but with such wide intervals that the proper legato cannot be secured with hands of average size. In this case, pedal couplers on manual must, of course, be left "on", but pedal stops are cancelled.

These passages, thus arranged, are printed at the bottom of the page of Franck's text, which enables the student to compare them immediately;

7° a few tempos which had been omitted are indicated and a few wrong notes and accidental[s] corrected;

8° when a note which is doubled in unison, either between the hands or between the left hand and pedal[,] should not be played, it is set between brackets. If this occurs in a whole passage, the latter is printed in smaller notes so that the text such as written by Franck should be respected.

Lastly, I cannot but bear in mind that many organists only have two-manuals [sic] organs at their command. Though it is not possible to suggest here several solutions that might meet all the problems thus entailed, I will just mention that, in many cases, Choir and Great are played on Great.[25]

Dupré's preface inspires a variety of responses, some of which are favorable while others necessarily call into question his more contentious statements. Among the positive aspects of this edition are the very careful fingerings, which are well suited for small hands. Several passages originally for manuals only requiring large stretches have been rewritten for manuals coupled to a silent pedal division. Dupré's reading of these sometimes awkward passages facilitates performance while preserving the sound of Franck's original text.

Dupré's comment concerning Franck's unusually large hands is confirmed by several photographs. Norbert Dufourcq's work on the genesis of Franck's first organ pieces is equally insistent upon this fact: he remarks specifically on the length of the composer's right thumb.[26] Maurice Emmanuel (who was *maître de chapelle* at Sainte-Clotilde from 1904 to 1907, and in 1909 became professor of music history at the Conservatoire) emphasizes this point further: "the immense stretch of his hands permitted him to play the largest chords. As a result, he wrote them!"[27] Nonetheless, Emmanuel makes this startling remark: "Franck did not err when he arpeggiated large chords at the organ, in imitation of piano technique."[28] Emmanuel, who was a great admirer of Franck, can be considered a reliable witness. Did Franck, given the large size of his hands, really arpeggiate chords in his own music? Dupré makes a suggestive comment in his preface: "he played... as they played in France at that time, with approximate legato and approximate observance of [note] values." It was, after all, Charles-Marie Widor who introduced in France, following the principles of Jaak Nikolaas (Jacques-Nicolas) Lemmens, the "legato school," for which Franck, it is sometimes said, cared so little.

The supposedly "approximate" approach to matters of technique is directly contradicted, however, by the meticulous fingerings Franck included in his 1887 Braille edition of the works of J. S. Bach.[29] In this edition Franck makes systematic use of an absolute legato. Would he have conceived of a perfect legato for Bach when he rejected it for his own works? This seems illogical, raising questions for the interpretation of Franck's own music. The all-too-rare fingerings indicated in his own works are our only clue: they favor a legato touch with its full range of substitutions, finger sliding, and even over-legato effects.[30]

Dupré's remark about doubling "the pedal basses with the left hand" is well taken: the Sainte-Clotilde organ did not have a Récit to Pedal coupler. In order to mitigate that deficiency, Franck imitated the effect of such a coupler by scoring the bass line for both the left hand and pedal. The most famous example of this technique appears in the Second *Choral* in the Voix humaine sections, in which Dupré eliminates the left-hand bass line and calls for a Récit to Pedal coupler, changes which simplify performance of this section without altering the sonority. More controversial is Dupré's claim that a "lack of precision in playing led as a consequence to some notations which, owing to their equivocal meaning, puzzle the performer." He notes an "excess of ties, vague dynamics, [fermatas] which mean no more than a breath, [and] useless doubling of pedal"—a seemingly harmless catalogue of criticisms, but a sign of an enormous difference in the temperaments of the two artists: Franck, the sensitive poet who above all sought freedom from constraint, and Dupré, the musician devoted above all to order, who upheld the value of formal constraints. Convinced of the validity of his own interpretation of Franck's notational habits, Dupré added what he believed to be the appropriate phrasing and "all the necessary ties between notes and the exact value of each note so as to leave no ambiguity." He also suppressed unnecessary ties and replaced fermatas with commas. These editorial practices make the Bornemann edition fundamentally different from that of Durand. (Just one example is the beginning of the *Final*: Dupré suppressed all the fermatas in a passage where it is particularly difficult to believe, as Dupré apparently did, that they function merely to indicate the end of a phrase rather than to punctuate the declamation of Franck's solo pedal line.)

Dupré made even more sweeping changes of registration, manual disposition, and dynamics in his effort to update Franck for twentieth-century organs. Even his initial claim—that "Franck was the first organ composer who marked the registration for his works"—ignores the tradition of registration in French Classical organ music. (Many seventeenth- and eighteenth-century French composers specified the exact timbres and appropriate stop combinations in their organ music; in the nineteenth century, Alexandre-Pierre-François Boëly and Louis-James-Alfred Lefébure-Wély indicate the specific sonorities for their works in luxurious detail.[31]) Dupré's registrations themselves are often clearly at odds with Franck's original indications. The beginning of the Second *Choral* illustrates this problem. Dupré calls for Récit 8' and 4' foundations, Positif 8' soft foundations, Grand-Orgue 8' foundations, Pedal 16' and 8' Bourdons, Récit and Positif coupled to the Grand-Orgue, and Positif coupled to the Pedal. The Durand edition specifies Récit 8' foundations and Hautbois with *anches préparées* (stops pulled out but ventil not engaged), Positif 8' foundations with *anches préparées*, Grand-Orgue 16' and 8' foundations with *anches préparées*, Pedal 16' and 8' foundations with *anches préparées*, keyboards coupled with the Positif and the Grand-Orgue coupled to the Pedal. Dupré's transformation effectively erases Franck's sonority of 8' foundations plus the Hautbois of the Récit. As Tournemire reports, this particular combination of stops was an essential color in Franck's musical expression:

> At the old Sainte-Clotilde organ, . . . Franck registered in a serious yet decorative fashion. . . .
> When he wanted to project large musical ideas, he pulled [all] the foundation stops and strengthened the sound with the addition of the Récit Hautbois.[32]

Other divergences with the Durand original can also be found in Dupré's version of the Second *Choral*. In m. 17 Dupré indicates a manual change from the Positif to the Récit, followed by a return to the Positif enriched by the addition of mutations in m. 33; Franck's score has none of these indications. Dupré puts the passage at m. 49 and following on the tutti of the Récit, while Franck specifies the Grand-Orgue with both Récit and Positif reeds. (The Positif reeds at Sainte-Clotilde, equal in volume to those of the Grand-Orgue, would produce a more intense sonority than the Récit tutti of Dupré's edition.) Finally, in the characteristic passage for the Voix humaine, Dupré calls for that stop by itself; Franck asks for the Voix humaine, Tremulant, 8' Flûte, and 8' Bourdon, which together create a much richer sound. Changes—indeed, deformations—of timbre of this magnitude are legion in the Dupré edition, and will be described in more detail below.

Finally, Dupré adds various tempo indications such as Doppio lento and Largamente in the Third *Choral*. He also includes metronome markings that are taken directly from the Guilmant tradition but are not acknowledged as such. Indeed, a comparison of the first thirty measures of the Third *Choral* in the original Durand edition with that of Dupré's version provides an excellent summary of the preceding observations (see Figure 2).

Clearly, the Dupré edition cannot substitute for the original edition; it must be regarded as a secondary resource. If the value of the Durand edition is that it presents the music in its original printed form, and the value of the Duruflé edition of the *Trois Chorals* is that it presents the Franck tradition as understood by Tournemire and Duruflé, then the value of the Dupré edition is that it presents the Franck tradition as understood by Guilmant, Pierné, and Dupré.

Figure 2

Comparison of the First Thirty Measures of the *Choral* No. 3 in A Minor in the Durand and Bornemann Editions

	Durand "Édition originale"	Bornemann (Leduc) Edition revised by Marcel Dupré
Registration	Tempo indication: Quasi allegro 8' foundations and reeds on all manuals, manual couplers; Pedal 16' and 8' foundations and reeds, Grand-Orgue to Pedal	Tempo indication: Quasi allegro; quarter note = 100 8' and 4' foundations and reeds, mixtures on all manuals; Pedal 16', 8', 4' foundations and reeds, mixtures, all manual and pedal couplers
mm. 6 and 15	Largamente	Doppio lento; eighth note = 100; + all 16' manual stops
mm. 7 and 16	Fermata on the half rest	No fermata
mm. 8 and 20	No indication	Tempo 1°; quarter note = 100; – all 16' manual stops
mm. 2, 3, 9, 21, 22	Slur marks for the left hand on the octave jumps	No slur marks
m. 19	Più largamente	No indication
m. 26	+ 16' foundations; – Grand-Orgue reeds; dim.	Rit.; 8' and 4' foundations of the Grand-Orgue and Positif; Récit tutti; all couplers; Pedal 16' and 8' foundations
m. 27	Rit.	No indication
m. 28	– Positif reeds; dim.	No indications
m. 30	– 16' foundations	Cantabile; quarter note = 92; Récit 8' foundations

The Schola Cantorum Editions of the Piece in E-flat Major and Versions of the Fantasy in C Major

In 1973 Schola Cantorum Editions released two previously unavailable works: the Piece in E-flat Major of 1846 and two alternative versions of the Fantasy in C Major.[33] The Piece in E-flat Major, clearly an early work, is interesting not only because of its use of combination pedals (a recent invention in 1846) but also because it sheds light on how the young Franck wrote for the organ. Unfortunately, the two versions of the Fantasy in C Major contained in this volume result from a misreading of the manuscripts: the two primary manuscripts (Cons. MS 8564/1–3 and Rés. F 1418) are conflated. Instead of publishing two versions and one variant (Rés. F 1418), this edition presents two versions, both of which combine fragments from different sources that may not date from the same period. A more plausible reading of these sources appears in the Forberg edition of 1980 (see below).

The Musicales du Marais Edition of the Piece in A Major of 1854[34]

This work was recently discovered by Joël-Marie Fauquet among the materials given to the Conservatoire (and later transfered to the Bibliothèque Nationale) by Mme Chopy-Franck. Though it lacks a title, it bears the date 19 May 1854; this date, along with telling registration indications in the score, makes Fauquet's hypothesis that the work was composed for Franck's participation in the inauguration of the Saint-Eustache organ in 1854 very tempting indeed:

> The *Pièce* in A major for *grand orgue* by César Franck (1822–90) was never published, and never even figured in any catalogue of the composer's works. It is the only finished work by Franck written specifically for an instrument with four keyboards and pedals. He completed it on 19 May 1854, just one week before the inauguration of the *grand orgue* in the church of Saint-Eustache in Paris. For the inaugural concert it was decided just two weeks beforehand to engage the services of Lemmens, Cavallo, Bazille and Franck, which may explain why Franck was unable to compose his *Pièce* until the last moment, and makes it likely that the *Pièce* in A major is one and the same as the *Fantaisie*, as yet unidentified, that Franck performed on 26 May 1854 following on an improvisation on the four [-manual] organ restored by Ducroquet. Certainly the *Pièce*, with its five sections[,] has the free form of a fantaisie, while the style of writing, with dramatic contrasts, would show to advantage the different timbres of the new *grand orgue*. It also constitutes the missing link between the E flat piece of 1846 and the *6 Pièces d'orgue* published in 1868.[35]

Non-French Editions

The numerous editions of the twelve pieces by American, English, and German publishers reflect, for the most part, a desire to have the indications in Franck's scores available in languages other than French. These editions exhibit varying degrees of fidelity to the Durand text, ranging from the reissues of recent Durand editions by Kalmus and Dover to adaptations which are less faithful to the original. The latter group includes versions by Schirmer (edited by Barnes), Novello (edited by Grace), Marks (edited by Alphenaar), and Peters (edited by Barblan). More recently, German publishers have begun issuing scholarly editions of Franck's organ music: Forberg (edited by Eschbach and Bates) gives the manuscript versions of the Fantasy in C Major; Butz (edited by Busch) reprints the very earliest prints of the Durand edition; and Schott/Universal (edited by Kaunzinger) provides for the first time an actual critical edition of Franck's *œuvre* for organ. Of these many editions, those by Peters (as an example of a highly edited non-French edition), Forberg, Butz, and Schott/Universal deserve attention here.

The Peters Edition of the Twelve Pieces[36]

Like the others of its type, the Peters version respects Franck's basic musical text. Editorial additions and emendations, however, alter the intent of the composer in several important respects. The editor, the Swiss composer Otto Barblan, provides an exemplary German translation of Franck's indications. He may rightly be criticized, however, for adding long phrase lines that replace Franck's shorter phrase marks. Indeed, Barblan's editorial techniques tend to obscure to a considerable degree a proper understanding of these pieces. In the conclusion of the *Final*, phrasing in the coda is neither in accord with the composer's indications nor with the recollections of Franck's students. In the *Prière*, at the *très mesuré* indication (ten measures before the reexposition of the first theme), Barblan adds portato marks not found in the original. In the Allegretto cantando of the Fantasy in C Major, Barblan's staccato indications (mm. 20–23) are not authentic, and near the end of the same movement he calls repeatedly for the use of the Grand-Orgue to Pedal coupler—an indication not included in the original text. In the Second *Choral* editorial inventions include the use of a 32' Pedal stop (mm. 56–57) as well as articulation marks at the beginning of the Largamente con fantasia passage. A more complex case in the same work concerns the ending of the 1° Tempo ma un poco meno lento section: Barblan indicates a registration on two manuals and pedal with the main theme soloed out by the left hand (mm. 33–40 of the 1° Tempo section), while Franck's own indications assign the entire passage to only one manual (the Positif). In Barblan's defense, Tournemire endorsed such a plan, even though the Durand edition does not employ such a scoring.[37] Finally, at the beginning of the *Le double plus vite (Mouvement du commencement)* passage in the Third *Choral*, Barblan calls for a staccato rendition of the left-hand material. Even stranger is the left-hand phrasing that begins twenty-three measures before the end of the same work (a series of tenutos that stress the first note of each arpeggio).

Barblan's editorial additions to the twelve pieces (only a few of which have been detailed here) are not a small matter. None of these emendations is identified as such, whether or not they reflect the Tournemire tradition. Most troubling, perhaps, are the editorial phrase marks, which impede the player's ability to read the score and (at times) alter completely the sense of the music.

The Forberg Edition of the Three Versions of the Fantasy in C Major[38]

The Schola Cantorum edition of the manuscript versions of the Fantasy in C Major, as described above, inverted and mixed the pages of the three Bibliothèque Nationale manuscripts of this work. In 1980, Jesse Eschbach and Robert Bates, American musicologists and organists, prepared an edition of the three versions of the same Fantasy. The three manuscripts are given in their entirety, without rearrangement. Certainly, this is the edition to consult to gain a clear understanding of Franck's long engagement with this work: it offers a uniquely rich opportunity to view Franck's creative process as a composer.

The Butz Edition of the Twelve Pieces[39]

Hermann J. Busch has recently edited for Butz some of the very earliest prints of Franck's *Six Pièces*, *Trois Pièces*, and *Trois Chorals*. For example, the version of the *Grande Pièce symphonique* presented in this edition is clearly an earlier one than that found in the Durand version published in the late nineteenth and early twentieth centuries. The differences are small but important: in most cases, it would appear that errors in the version published by Busch were later corrected by Durand.[40] Moreover, some of the performance indications in the later Durand editions are not to be found in the Busch version.[41] Thus, this edition makes readily available some otherwise very rare research materials.

The Schott/Universal Edition of the Complete Organ Works[42]

Since the currently available Durand edition (in the oblong format) cannot quite be considered a fully reliable *urtext* edition, this new *Wiener Urtext Edition* fills a definite need. The readings, presented by Günther Kaunzinger, are based on Franck's extant manuscripts and the older, more reliable Durand printings. Following *urtext* practices, the text is not overlaid with editorial emendations. Moreover, for the first time, an edition of Franck's organ music includes genuine critical notes. Of special interest is the inclusion of the first version of the ending of the *Pièce héroïque* (as found in the Trocadéro manuscript), printed alongside the final version (as found in the Durand edition).

Instruments

The claim is often made that Franck's organ works were composed specifically for the Sainte-Clotilde Cavaillé-Coll. This assumption is potentially misleading: Franck held several different positions in Paris as a church organist before his appointment to Sainte-Clotilde, as a recitalist he played many other instruments in Paris, and, after gaining the post at Sainte-Clotilde, he was willing to present himself as a candidate for several other positions.[43]

In 1846, at the age of twenty-four, Franck was named organist-accompanist at Notre-Dame-de-Lorette, home to the first Paris instrument built by the brothers Cavaillé-Coll (between 1833 and 1838). This instrument of forty-seven stops on three manuals and pedal was approximately the same size as the 1859 Cavaillé-Coll at Sainte-Clotilde (forty-six stops similarly disposed). Their specifications were aesthetic opposites, however. The Notre-Dame-de-Lorette organ contained a large number of mutations and mixtures; a short-compass Récit (thirty-seven notes) with only two expressive stops (Hautbois and Voix humaine); no Gambe and no Voix céleste; an 8' Flûte on the Grand-Orgue that played only in the treble; and a pedal *ravalement* down to AA with only loud flutes and reeds. (Its specification in 1846, the year of Franck's appointment, appears in Figure 3.) An uncharacteristic example of the French Romantic organ tradition, this instrument was one of the last built primarily in the older, French Classical style.

It was during his time at Notre-Dame-de-Lorette that Franck composed his Piece in E-flat Major.[44] Dufourcq comments about this work:

> Franck seems to have ignored the art of registration, or not to have concerned himself with it, limiting himself to the dynamic nuances of the piano, that is,

Figure 3

Specification of the Notre-Dame-de-Lorette Organ

I. Positif (54 notes, C-f''')
Bourdon 8
Flûte 8
Prestant 4
Flûte 4
Nasard
Doublette 2
Tierce
Plein jeu V
Cornet V
Trompette
Cromorne
Hautbois
Clairon

II. Grand-Orgue (54 notes)
Montre 16
Bourdon 16 (from c)
Montre 8
Bourdon 8
Dessus de Flûte 8
Prestant 4
Flûte 4
Nasard
Quarte 2
Doublette
Grosse Fourniture IV
Petite Fourniture IV
Cymbale IV
Cornet VII
Bombarde 16
Trompette 8
Clairon 4

III. Récit (37 notes)
Bourdon 8
Flûte traversière 8
Flûte 4
Flûte octaviante 4
Flageolet 2
Cornet III
Voix humaine 8 (expressive)
Hautbois 8 (expressive)
Trompette 8
Cor anglais

Pédale (21 notes, AA-f)
Flûte ouverte 16
Flûte ouverte 8
Flûte ouverte 4
Bombarde 16
Trompette 8
Clairon 4

crescendi and diminuendi; he uses the Récit, Positif, and Grand-Orgue, coupling them with more or fewer registers... And he makes the best of the pedals supplied by the builder. A single savory detail: before the entrance of the fugue subject, the composer requires the organist to remove the two Flûtes (8' and 4') of the Récit (expressive) and to draw the Clarinette, Hautbois, and Trompette harmonique... One can imagine the harmonious combination![45]

And yet, on the first page of this work there are precise indications that already give an idea of Franck's later style. Beginning with "*Grand Chœur* and all the combination pedals engaged, except for the one sounding the octave," after eleven measures there is an indication to move to the Récit: "disengage all the ventils except for those coupling the Récit and the Positif to the Grand-Orgue." Franck is thus already concerned with different levels of sonority.

In this regard, it is necessary to note the importance of the *pédales de combinaison* (ventils). As Marie-Claire Alain reminds us:

> It should be remembered that in Cavaillé-Coll organs there are always two [chests] for each manual. One usually caters [to] the foundation stops (16', 8' and 4') and these come into action as soon as the player pulls out the [appropriate] stopknobs, which are all on one side of the console (on the left at Ste. Clotilde). On the other [chest] are grouped the upperwork, mutations and chorus reeds. These stops are to be found on the other side of the console with their names ringed in red. In order to use this part of the organ, the player has not only to pull out the stops he requires but also to depress a pedal named "Appel d'Anches" (Reeds). Hence a confusion . . . between the reeds and the "jeux de combinaison" in general.[46]

In addition to the usual pedal and manual couplers (although those for the Récit are often not present), Cavaillé-Coll's consoles also typically feature an *Introduction Grand-Orgue* and *octaves graves*. Sometimes there are ventils for stops on each manual, especially for the principals (as at Saint-Vincent-de-Paul). All of these devices helped to facilitate the organist's playing and to eliminate the need for registrants.

Toward the end of 1851, the Abbé Dancel, who had officiated at Franck's marriage at Notre-Dame-de-Lorette in 1848, became priest at Saint-Jean-Saint-François du Marais and proposed that Franck become titular organist there.[47] Franck, who was only the organist-accompanist at Notre-Dame-de-Lorette, immediately accepted Dancel's proposal. The Saint-Jean-Saint-François organ, built by Cavaillé-Coll in 1843, was of very modest proportions, with eighteen stops on two manuals and pedal. There were no 16' manual stops, the Récit had only thirty-seven notes, and in comparison to Notre-Dame-de-Lorette, the number of mutations and mixtures was miniscule. Nevertheless, with six reeds out of eighteen stops, the instrument was powerful. Above all, unlike the organ at Notre-Dame-de-Lorette, this Cavaillé-Coll instrument was built in a more orchestral style and was capable of special effects. As Franck's remarked in 1853: "My new organ? It's an orchestra!" (The specification of the organ as Franck knew it is given in Figure 4.)

Figure 4

Specification of the Saint-Jean-Saint-François du Marais Organ

I. Grand-Orgue (54 notes)
Montre 8
Bourdon 8
Salicional 8
Prestant 4
Nasard 2 2/3
Doublette 2
Plein jeu III
Trompette
Clairon

II. Récit expressif (37 notes)
Voix céleste
Flûte harmonique 8
Flûte octaviante 4
Octavin 2
Cromorne
Cor anglais
Trompette

Pédale (20 notes, C-g)
Flûte ouverte 16
Bombarde 16

This organ was certainly not the instrument reflected in Franck's first version of the Fantasy in C Major (Cons. MS 8564/1 and 3). Eschbach and Bates believe that this version of the Fantasy was designed for the Cavaillé-Coll at Carcassonne Cathedral (an instrument that was eventually modified and moved for political reasons to Luçon Cathedral).[48] Franck is said to have played this instrument in the Cavaillé-Coll factory in 1856. The association is tempting: the early version of the Fantasy in C Major may well have been created in 1856 for the Carcassone instrument. (The Andantino in G Minor, which follows this version of the Fantasy in the manuscript, might therefore be dated 1856 or 1857.) There is, alas, no firm evidence at present for this hypothesis. In particular, there is no archival substantiation for such a four-manual organ with two expressive divisions in these years. One wonders whether Franck imagined this instrument as a new source of registrational possibilities, thereby demonstrating an avant-garde position vis à vis the organ building of the time. This latter hypothesis would contradict the accepted view that Franck was indifferent to organ building, or worse, behind the times. Indeed, a new instrument was about to enter Franck's life in 1858. How involved was Franck in the design of this now-famous organ at Sainte-Clotilde?

The extant documents do not explain how the organist of Saint-Jean-Saint-François became choirmaster and then titular organist at Sainte-Clotilde. As part of the project for a new church on the Left Bank, the advisory council agreed to install a large gallery organ that would conform to current taste. Cavaillé-Coll was the obvious builder for such an instrument, and he often asked Franck (whose playing and brilliant improvisations he appreciated) to try out his instruments or to participate in their inaugural concerts. Could Cavaillé-Coll have asked the priest of the future basilica to appoint Franck as choirmaster and later as organist?[49]

Whatever the case, near the end of 1857, Franck took up his new job, first as the choirmaster in a provisionary chapel, and a short time afterwards at the church, which was dedicated on 30 November. On 19 December 1859, the official inauguration was held for the large forty-six-stop organ. The program was shared by Franck, now the titular organist, and by that great organist of fashionable society, Lefébure-Wély. The critic Adrien de LaFage noted that at the inaugural concert Franck began with a "coarsely hewn" piece (Dufourcq thought that this may have been the Piece in E-flat Major), whose "forceful style was noticed by the entire audience." He also "demonstrated the genius of Johann Sebastian Bach with the Prelude and Fugue in E Minor." To conclude, he returned to play his final piece on the *Grand Chœur.* "In his performance of this finale, one heard the ideas of a veritable master."[50] Was this the *Final* later published in the *Six Pièces?* It is perhaps significant that Franck dedicated the *Final* to Lefébure-Wély, with whom he shared the concert at Sainte-Clotilde.

One can follow each step in the history of the organ at Sainte-Clotilde, thanks to the contracts and letters of Cavaillé-Coll published in 1980 by Fenner Douglass.[51] The first contract, dated 21 January 1853, concerns an instrument of forty stops on three manuals and pedal. (This design was not a new one but a copy of that proposed by Cavaillé-Coll for the Cathedral of Bayonne in 1849.) The plan did not include certain stops that appeared later on the organ: a Voix céleste in the Récit, a 16' Bourdon in the Positif, 4' Clairons in the Positif and Récit, and a 32' stop in the Pedal. Cavaillé-Coll's progress reports (of 29 September 1857, 15 December 1857, and 12 July 1858) do not indicate that any changes were made in the original specification. Meanwhile, in August 1859, the architect of the church reported that the organ was finished. The published specification describes an instrument of forty-six stops (not the forty of the original contract) and fourteen *pédales de combinaison* (instead of the original ten).[52] It seems that between July 1858 and August 1859, the specification of the organ was enlarged to include the following: a Voix céleste and a 4' Clairon in the Récit; a 4' Clairon, an Unda maris, and a 16' Bourdon in the Positif; and a 16' Basson and a 32' Soubasse in the Pedal. The one change to the Grand-Orgue was the conflation of the original four-rank Fourniture and three-rank Cymbale into a seven-rank Plein jeu harmonique.

Was it Cavaillé-Coll or Franck who suggested these important changes which increased the price of the organ by 40% over the original contract? If Franck were to have taken a hand in the changes made to the design of the organ—could we imagine Franck disinterested in the progress of the instrument?—it would suggest that he did have precise ideas about organ building, ideas which helped to shape the Sainte-Clotilde masterpiece (see Figure 5). The organ builder responsible for the 1983 rebuilding of the organ, Jacques Barberis, has noted:

> If one takes into account that at that time Cavaillé-Coll's career was on the rise, and that he had 120 employees, nothing would have been easier for him, in a year, than to make substantial modifications to the original plan conceived for Sainte-Clotilde, since the changes made consisted for the most part of adding ranks to the chest (4' Clairons in the manuals and a 16' Basson in the pedal). He demonstrated in other circumstances, and practically at the same time (as at Saint-Sulpice), that he was capable of completely overturning a design, *without consulting anyone at all.*[53]

In the absence of any additional contracts or correspondence on the subject of the Sainte-Clotilde modifications, we cannot know whether it was Franck or Cavaillé-Coll who wanted these changes. Either hypothesis would be equally plausible.

Among the most significant features of the instrument, the Récit stands out as perhaps the most important. Located at the rear of the case, the Récit was hardly aggressive at the time of Franck; it was a relatively small, sweet-sounding division with ten stops, including a delicate Hautbois and a mild Trompette. These characteristics explain many of the idiosyncracies of Franck's Récit registrations, in particular, his frequent inclusion of the Récit Hautbois in the ensemble of 8' foundation stops. The relatively quiet Haut-bois brings to this ensemble an *indispensable* coloring: without the Hautbois, it is difficult to realize Franck's dynamic nuances; when the Hautbois is added, however, there is a very precise sensation of crescendo and diminuendo, due to the unusually sensitive expression pedal of the Récit. Adding the Hautbois to the foundations is essential in Franck's *œuvre*; its omission in the Dupré edition is thus quite incomprehensible.[54] On occasion Franck also calls for the combination of 8' foundations, Hautbois, and Trompette to accompany a solo line on the Positif Cromorne, 8' Bourdon and Flûte (as, for example, in the first Andante of the *Grande Pièce symphonique*). At Sainte-Clotilde, this registration is perfectly balanced; elsewhere, the effect can be disastrous, with the Récit overpowering the Positif.[55] To achieve a similar effect on other instruments, it may be preferable to avoid using the Hautbois and even the 8' foundations; the Trompette alone may be sufficient if its timbre clearly sounds the fundamental. (Indeed, while Franck has been criticized for adding foundation stops to solo reeds, for him to do so might well be understood as a continuation of the Classical practice of often combining the Cromorne with

Figure 5

Specification of the Sainte-Clotilde Organ

I. Grand-Orgue (54 notes, C-f''')
Montre 16
Bourdon 16
Montre 8
Flûte harmonique 8
Viole de gambe 8
Bourdon 8
Prestant 4
Octave 4
Quinte 2 2/3
Doublette 2
Plein jeu VII
Bombarde 16
Trompette 8
Clairon 4

II. Positif (54 notes)
Bourdon 16
Montre 8
Flûte harmonique 8
Bourdon 8
Viole de gambe 8
Unda maris 8
Prestant 4
Octave 4
Quinte 2 2/3
Doublette 2
Plein jeu harmonique III-VI
Trompette 8
Cromorne 8
Clairon 4

III. Récit (54 notes)
Flûte harmonique 8
Bourdon 8
Viole de gambe 8
Voix céleste 8
Basson-hautbois 8
Voix humaine 8
Flûte octaviante 4
Octavin 2
Trompette 8
Clairon 4

Pédale (27 notes, C-d')
Soubasse 32
Contrebasse 16
Flûte 8
Octave 4
Basson 16
Bombarde 16
Trompette 8
Clairon 4

(Stops in italics are controlled by the *anches* pedals.)

other stops.) Finally, the Récit had no 16' reed and no mixture, but the Voix humaine and the Voix céleste—of incomparable beauty—combined marvelously with the 32' Pedal Soubasse (an extremely light stop) to create effects of exceptional mystery and depth.

As there was no Récit to Grand-Orgue coupler on the Sainte-Clotilde instrument, one had to use both the Récit to Positif and the Positif to Grand-Orgue couplers to achieve the desired effect. Even though the original console now includes a Récit to Pedal coupler, André Marchal reports:

> When Charles Tournemire invited me to play [the Sainte-Clotilde organ] for the first time in 1912, the organ had undergone but one rebuilding since the death of Franck. At the beginning of the century Mutin added a *Tirasse Récit*, something that did not previously exist on the organ. This explains why (in passages written for Récit with Pedal) Franck doubled the Pedal with the left hand.[56]

Thus, when the score indicates Grand-Orgue coupled to Pedal, Positif coupled to Pedal, and manuals coupled, it is also necessary to add the Récit to Pedal coupler to achieve the effect Franck would have expected at Sainte-Clotilde.

As for the Positif, its location in the case is highly unusual: situated in the middle of the façade, it is framed on either side by the pipes of the Grand-Orgue. Because of this placement, the stops of this division (and in particular its reeds) are as powerful as those of the Grand-Orgue. In effect the division functions as a second Grand-Orgue. Because of this feature, organists often find it difficult to perform the works of Franck on English, German, or American instruments, where the Positif is usually smaller than the Grand-Orgue, especially with regard to the reeds.[57]

On the Grand-Orgue the exact composition of Franck's Plein jeu has been a matter of some dispute. Marie-Claire Alain believes the stop to have had five ranks; Duruflé and Tournemire claimed there were six ranks; Jean Fellot and Langlais claimed seven—a combination of the original Fourniture (four ranks) and Cymbale (three ranks). During the restoration of 1983, Barberis found seven ranks in the Plein jeu, composed according to Dom Bédos, with the Fourniture breaking back at f and f' and the Cymbale breaking back twice per octave (at c and f) from tenor c. The pipes sounding the 16' resultant, however, had been silenced; this may help explain the disagreement over the total number of ranks.

Franck's organ works never indicate the use of a cornet, mutation, or mixture with the foundations without also using the reeds. As Marie-Claire Alain explains:

> It will be noticed how misleading the labels "Foundation Stops" and "Reeds" can be, since the Hautbois and the Voix Humaine are grouped with the Foundation Stops while some of the 4' stops, the 2' stops, the quints and the mixtures are grouped with the reeds.

So, to look at the music, one would think that Franck never used mixtures, mutations or 4' stops! That is far from the truth. As was customary in that period, Franck would pull out all the stops before beginning to play. Thus, when he puts: "Add Great Reeds" he means: "Depress the pedal marked Great Reeds". This action has the effect of adding all the Great "jeux de combinaison", i.e. . . . besides the reeds, the mixture, mutations and even an Octave (4')—a second Principal which meant that a four foot stop could be added or removed without using the hands. That is why Franck almost never refers to 4' stops.[58]

An exception to this latter rule can be found in the indication at the beginning of the *Final*: foundations and reeds 16', 8', and 4' on all manuals, except the Prestant. Because Franck wanted the 8' foundations and the Récit Hautbois *without* 4' stops once the reed ventils are released, he took the 4' Prestant out of the larger sonority, since it speaks with the foundations and not with the reeds (the 4' *Octave* speaks with the reeds).

A second important registration question of this type concerns the indication at the beginning of the Third *Choral*: 8' foundations and reeds on all manuals. Many performers interpret this to mean the addition of the mixtures and mutations to the reeds, without 16' stops. Langlais, however, was certain that this registration—one feasible perhaps only at Sainte-Clotilde—should consist of the reeds without mixtures.[59]

Finally, the identity of the fourteen *pédales de combinaison* has been the subject of much controversy. A study of the original console (given by Tournemire to Flor Peeters after the instrument's 1933 rebuilding) suggests that the original instrument was configured as follows:

> *Pédale d'Orage*
> *Tirasse Grand-Orgue*
> *Tirasse Positif*
> *Anches Pédale*
> *Octaves Graves Grand-Orgue*
> *Octaves Graves Positif*
> *Octaves Graves Récit au Positif*
> *Anches Grand-Orgue*
> *Anches Positif*
> *Anches Récit*
> *Positif au Grand-Orgue*
> *Récit au Positif*
> *Tremblant Récit*
> *Expression Récit*

It may come as a surprise to note that a decade after his appointment to Sainte-Clotilde, Franck applied for other posts. His first application, in 1870, was for the position at Saint-Sulpice that had become vacant with the death of its titular organist, Lefébure-Wély.[60] The post went to Widor. We will never know what impact there may have been on Franck's organ music had he played the huge Saint-Sulpice organ for the last twenty years of his life. Would the monumental style, which can be discerned in works such as the *Final* and parts of the *Grande Pièce symphonique*, have gained prominence in his later organ music? Just a year later, Franck applied for the position of organist at La Madeleine upon the resignation of Camille Saint-Saëns. This instrument was comparable in size to that of Sainte-Clotilde, although less complete at the time (no 16' or 4' reeds on the Grand-Orgue, with the Voix céleste and Hautbois mounted on the Positif and therefore not expressive). Despite Franck's interest in the position, the post went to Théodore Dubois. Although the motivation for Franck's attempts to leave Sainte-Clotilde may have had more to do with the prestige of the posts he sought rather than with the size or design of their instruments, these two incidents over the space of two years do suggest that, ten years after his appointment at Sainte-Clotilde, Franck had not yet found the complete identification between himself and his instrument that he later seemed to enjoy.

In 1872 Franck was appointed professor of organ at the Conservatoire, succeeding his former teacher, François Benoist. From this time onward, there is no more indication that Franck wanted to change instruments. Surely he was sincere when, during these years, he said to his priest: "If you only knew how I love my organ! It is so supple to my fingers and so obedient to my thoughts!"[61]

One further experience with another Parisian organ cannot be overlooked: Franck's recital on the Trocadéro organ in 1878.[62] In the inaugural series of concerts, Franck presented a program which included the *Trois Pièces*. The surviving manuscripts give detailed registrations for this large instrument of sixty-three stops on four manuals and pedal. Interestingly, when these pieces were published by Durand in 1883, Franck significantly modified the registration indications, making the works more suitable for the Sainte-Clotilde instrument.

While it has often been said that *all* of Franck's organ works were conceived for the Sainte-Clotilde organ, there are a couple of exceptions: Franck wrote the Pieces in E-flat Major and A Major before the Sainte-Clotilde organ was built. The first and second versions of the Fantasy in C Major and the Andantino in G Minor were conceived for an as-yet-unidentified organ. As for the rest, it is clear that Franck was thinking of the Sainte-Clotilde organ when he prepared for publication the Fantasy in C Major, the *Pastorale*, and the *Grande Pièce symphonique*. And yet the *Final*, from the same collection, calls for foundation stops and reeds at 16', 8', and 4' on all the manuals, a registration which could not have been designed for Sainte-Clotilde. Perhaps in this work Franck was thinking of the gigantic organ of Saint-Sulpice, whose rebuilding was completed in 1862. The published registrations of the *Trois Pièces*—although those works were first heard at the Trocadéro (and likely composed with that organ in mind)—reflect the Sainte-Clotilde instrument far more than that of the Trocadéro.[63] Finally the first drafts of the *Trois*

Chorals show unquestionably that Franck was thinking of the organ at Sainte-Clotilde; and yet it remains impossible to say who wrote the registrations on the manuscripts.

Interpretation

"We have no idea of the freedom with which Franck played his own pieces" —so affirmed Adolphe Marty. Other recollections from Franck's students, in particular, those of Albert Mahaut, Louis Vierne, and Tournemire, corroborate this point of view. It is not surprising, therefore, that the published accounts of Franck's performance style reveal a number of disagreements. In this regard, as Marie-Claire Alain has observed: "The various surviving traditions of interpretation are so different that one is led to reflect on the fallibility of human memory."[64] A brief consideration of the various recordings and writings left by Tournemire and Langlais confirms this view. Tournemire recorded the Cantabile, the *Pastorale*, and the Third *Choral* in 1930.[65] In the following year his book on Franck appeared, in which he noted many details of interpretation—including the tempi—of Franck's twelve major organ works.[66] Yet there are some striking differences between his printed comments and his recorded performances. In the *Pastorale*, for example, he suggests a tempo of quarter note equals 58 for the beginning of the work but plays at 50; at the Allegretto, he indicates quarter note equals 100 but plays at 120. Moreover, for the fugal section (beginning at m. 81) he suggests quarter note a little slower than 100 but performs at 100.[67] Langlais recorded the *Grande Pièce symphonique* three times: in 1953, 1963, and 1975.[68] The first performance takes 24 minutes and 52 seconds; the second, 26 minutes and 12 seconds; and the third, 27 minutes and 42 seconds. The last performance, a remarkable 2 minutes and 50 seconds slower than the first, clearly proves that as Langlais became older, he played the piece more and more slowly. There are many other examples of this sort.

Even these modest examples suggest the difficulty of believing in one single tradition of Franck interpretation among French organists. In order to facilitate a survey of the works, one by one, it will be helpful to divide "the tradition" into four camps: that of Tournemire (following his book on Franck), that of Guilmant-Pierné-Dupré (epitomized in the Dupré edition), that of Mahaut-Marchal-Tournemire-Langlais (abbreviated here as the Langlais version), and finally that of Tournemire-Duruflé (following Duruflé's edition of the *Trois Chorals*). Despite the fact they are all intertwined, these interpretive positions have become traditions in their own right. For example, a comparison of the different tempi of these traditions regarding the *Trois Chorals* is quite revealing (see Figure 6). Agreement can be found in some passages (for example, the beginning of the Second *Choral*), but the differences

Figure 6

Comparison of the Tempi of the Various Traditions in the *Trois Chorals*

(q = quarter note; e = eighth note)

	Guilmant-Pierné Tradition by Marcel Dupré	Charles Tournemire (*Précis d'exécution*)	Tournemire Tradition by Maurice Duruflé	Tournemire-Marty-Mahaut Tradition by Jean Langlais (Arion records)
Choral No. 1				
Moderato	q = 56	q = 69	q = 60	q = 69
Maestoso	q = 88		q = 76	q = 63
Poco animato	e = 126		q = 80	q = 69
m. 126	q = 56		q = 60	q = 76
Poco animato	q = 72		q = 100	q = 88
Rit. (end)	q = 63		q = 72	q = 56
a Tempo (end)			q = 88	q = 56
Choral No. 2				
Maestoso	q = 76	q = 76 (approx.)	q = 76	q = 72
Largamente con fantasia	q = 84		q = 66	q = 58
1° Tempo ma un poco meno lento	q = 80		q = 88	q = 80
m. 195	q = 72		q = 76	q = 66
m. 230	q = 80		q = 92	q = 84
m. 258	q = 76		q = 80	q = 76
m. 274	q = 60		q = 58	q = 50
Choral No.3				
Quasi allegro	q = 100	q = 100	q = 108	q = 88
m. 30	q = 92		q = 92	q = 84
Adagio	e = 84	e = 76	e = 84	e = 72
a Tempo	e = 84		e = 92	e = 88
Molto slargando			e = 108	e = 88
Le double plus vite	q = 108	q = 100	q = 108	q = 88

are quite striking (as at the beginning of the First *Choral*, the Largamente con fantasia of the Second, and virtually all of the Third). Of course, one should not take metronome marks too seriously: Tournemire wrote, after all, that when playing Franck's organ works, the metronome should not be used. Nonetheless, these traditions merit study, for whether one believes the first generation of "Franckians" (Guilmant, Mahaut, Marty, Tournemire, and Vierne) or the second (Dupré, Duruflé, and Langlais), they all believed they truly represented *the* Franck tradition.

Six Pièces

At the time of their appearance in 1868, the *Six Pièces* represented a revolution in style within the history of organ music. With these works Franck developed and rejuvenated certain forms, such as the sonata (Fantasy in C Major), the prelude and fugue (Prelude, Fugue, and Variation), and the *pastorale* of the seventeenth- and eighteenth-century masters (*Pastorale*). Moreover, he tried his hand at new symphonic genres for organ with a sonata movement on two themes (*Final*), a large lied (*Prière*), and a massive cyclic composition (*Grande Pièce symphonique*).[69] Very few organists of the time were prepared to come to terms with this significant achievement.

Fantasy in C Major

Dupré registers the Poco lento with 8' foundations, while Langlais conforms to the original indication (foundations plus Hautbois) to make the dynamic nuances created by the Récit's sensitive expression pedal more perceptible. Dupré's tempo suggestion for this section is quarter note equals 76, while Langlais suggests 72, and Tournemire around 66. Later, at the *Animez beaucoup* (Dupré indicates merely Animato), Dupré and Langlais both indicate that this passage should be played portato and not staccato; moreover, Dupré removes the fermatas that occur in the original just before the next section.

For the Allegretto cantando section, Dupré indicates quarter note equals 69, while Langlais suggests 72, and Tournemire about 76. Franck's registration (Récit 8' Flûte, Bourdon, and Trompette; Positif 8' Flûte harmonique) is possible only on an organ like that of Sainte-Clotilde, where the Positif Flûte and the very soft Récit Trompette balance perfectly. In this movement Dupré's registration is precarious: his indication of the Récit Trompette against the Positif Bourdon would likely not balance well. In the Quasi lento Dupré includes a staccato indication for the manuals that is not present in the original. He indicates quarter note equals 63, while Langlais suggests 60.

The registration of the final movement, the Adagio, is the only place in the twelve pieces where Franck calls for the Voix humaine with all the 8' foundations of the Récit (Bourdon, Flûte, and Gambe), a very rare combination which exploits the mysterious sonorities of the small foundation stops of that Récit. Dupré changes this combination to the Voix humaine alone. (A better adaptation for this registration on other instruments would be the Voix humaine and a small Principal or Bourdon, or the Voix humaine, a Flûte, and a Bourdon, depending on the stops available.) For this movement, Dupré suggests eighth note equals 52 and Langlais 69. Instead of indicating a specific tempo, Tournemire claimed: "The concluding Adagio, of an infinite calm, rejects metronomical movement, thank God! It is all introspection and contemplation...."[70]

Grande Pièce symphonique

In this, the first cyclical organ symphony composed in France (a remarkable accomplishment that prepared the way for similar works by Widor, Vierne, and many others), Franck begins not with an Allegro but with an Andantino. For this Andantino serioso, Tournemire suggests quarter note equals about 69, Dupré quarter note equals 72, and Langlais 76. Dupré omits the Hautbois from the ensemble of foundation stops. Dupré and Langlais both agree that *Quasi ad libitum* implies a slower tempo (for Dupré quarter note equals 63), and both take the indication to add the 16' stops and the Récit reeds to mean that all the 16' manual stops of the organ should be added in addition to the Récit reeds. For the *Grand Chœur* of the Allegro non troppo e maestoso, Dupré and Langlais both indicate a tutti with mixtures. Langlais does not include the *octaves graves* here because Franck calls for the addition of those couplers to the *Grand Chœur* in the finale. For this Allegro, Langlais suggests half note equals 76, Tournemire around 80, and Dupré 84.

In the first Andante, all the traditions suggest quarter note equals 60, but their registrations are different: Dupré suggests Récit 8' Flûte, while Franck, registering for the unusual Sainte-Clotilde Récit, indicates foundations and reeds. Similarly, the registration of the following Allegro, very unusual in Franck's *œuvre*, seems conceived with the unique resources of Sainte-Clotilde in mind: Récit 8' Flûte and Bourdon, Hautbois, and 4' Clairon combined with Positif 16' and 8' Bourdons and 8' Flûte. The registration of the Andante reprise is also typical of Sainte-Clotilde, with a dialogue between the Voix célestes of the Récit and the Positif.[71] Dupré's tempo, the same as Tournemire's, is quarter note equals 60, as opposed to Langlais's eighth note equals 92.

The following Allegro non troppo e maestoso, which contains fragments of earlier parts of the work, leads to a finale for which Dupré suggests a tempo of quarter note equals 120, Langlais 112, and Tournemire a significantly slower 80. Tournemire, however, suggests a faster tempo of half note equals 60 at the fugal exposition, with the tempo gradually broadening in the final thirteen measures. For all three interpreters, the chords in the concluding passage must be played staccato (Dupré gives portato marks), if they are to be comprehensible in a large, reverberant acoustic space.

Prelude, Fugue, and Variation

For the opening Andantino, Langlais suggests dotted quarter note equals 58, Tournemire around 60, and Dupré 63. At the end of the Prelude, Franck indicates the addition of an 8' or 4' stop to the Pedal in order to bring out the theme, a direction which Dupré omits. For the Lento, Franck uses a registration of which he was evidently fond: Grand-Orgue 16', 8', and 4' foundations, Positif 8' and 4' foundations, and Récit 8' and 4' foundations and reeds coupled (Dupré adds to this combination the 16' foundations of the Récit). All three interpreters recommend that the tempo of the Fugue should be quarter note equals 88 and that the Variation should return to the tempo of the Prelude.[72]

Pastorale

For the Andantino, Tournemire indicates quarter note equals 58, Dupré 60, and Langlais 69. Franck's original registration strives for clarity: the right hand plays on the Récit Hautbois, 4' Flûte, and 8' Bourdon (instead of the heavier 8' Flûte). Surprisingly, Dupré indicates only Hautbois and 4' Flûte. For the Quasi allegretto, Langlais recommends quarter note equals 88. This surprisingly slow tempo is not adopted by either Tournemire or Dupré, who recommend 100 and 108, respectively. (These faster tempi are more in line with the indication Quasi allegretto.) Moreover, Langlais prefers a staccato articulation with comparatively long note lengths, in which the silence takes one-fourth of the note value; Dupré prefers, as one might expect, a half-length staccato. On the subject of this passage, Tournemire made this comment: "Generally the staccato part is played in a vertiginous tempo.... which completely destroys the equilibrium of the work."[73]

Prière

For Tournemire "the Prière is the most remarkable of the Six Pièces." He adopts a tempo for this piece in which the quarter note equals 66 (an

Andantino and not an Andante).[74] Langlais retains this tempo, while Dupré indicates that the quarter note equals 58. The indication for *Tirasses du Grand-Orgue* (Grand-Orgue to Pedal couplers) suggests that Franck was, in effect, coupling all three manuals to the Pedal. (With the Récit and Positif coupled to the Grand-Orgue, the Grand-Orgue to Pedal coupler would have automatically connected the Positif and the Récit to the Pedal, as mentioned above.)

At the *Quasi recitativo*, where extreme metric freedom is in order, Franck adds the Récit Trompette to the 8' foundations and Hautbois, a maneuver that on any other organ might well produce a questionable effect. But because the Sainte-Clotilde organ had a small Récit division encased within a tightly sealed box, Franck found it necessary to combine the Trompette with four other Récit stops. For this reason, organists should here employ the Récit foundation stops and Trompette without the Hautbois (or the Hautbois without the Trompette), as the different traditions specify. Later in the work Franck obviously failed to indicate the removal of the Récit Trompette; this is corrected by both Dupré and Langlais.

In the *a Tempo très mesuré* the composer presents an unaccompanied theme in octaves, a unique occurrence in Franck's organ works. Both Dupré and Langlais note that Franck apparently failed to include a registration change in mm. 197–98: the left-hand chords (f#-a) certainly should be played, as Dupré and Langlais suggest, on the Positif rather than on the Grand-Orgue. Near the end of the piece, Franck's final indication to remove gradually several Positif stops might best be carried out by removing first the Montre, then the Salicional, and finally the Flûte.

Final

The dedication, "To my friend, Monsieur Lefébure-Wély," is tempting: was Lefébure-Wély's brilliant, even operatic, style the reason for the work's pompous fanfare-like motive, which the composer thunderously reiterates in the opening twenty-nine-bar pedal solo? As Joël-Marie Fauquet justly observes: "Franck's purpose in writing this piece dedicated to grand effects seems to have been to beat Lefébure-Wély at his own game."[75] Tournemire begins the Allegro maestoso at quarter note equals 132, in contrast to Dupré's tempo of 112 (arriving at 132 for his Più mosso) and Langlais's tempo of 104 (and later, at the final statement, 112). Tournemire adds: "Fluctuations of movement are left to the taste of the interpreter."[76] Dupré's removal of fermatas over the rests in the pedal solo should be noted.

Trois Pièces

The Fantasy in A Major, Cantabile, and *Pièce héroïque* were completed between 10 and 17 September 1878. Franck played them on 1 October of the same year at the Trocadéro, and they were printed in 1883; the edition differs in many ways from the manuscript (see above). These occasional pieces reaffirm the symphonic idea as developed by Franck, for the pieces seem to constitute three movements of a symphony.

Fantasy in A Major

Before the work's publication, Franck replaced the original title, *Fantaisie Idylle*, with *Fantaisie*. Along with the change of title Franck made several substantive changes in registration, eliminating half of the indications of the Trocadéro version. (A few examples of those changes are given in Figure 7.) Having initially conceived a sonorous plan based on contrasts with clear oppositions of colors and divisions, Franck, in preparing the print, replaced these contrasts of colors with variations of intensity achieved entirely by means of the expressive capabilities of the Récit box. Unfortunately, the

Figure 7

Selected Comparisons of the Trocadéro Manuscript and the Durand Edition of the Fantasy in A Major

	Trocadéro Manuscript	Durand Edition
m. 9	Récit: remove reeds	Récit: *p*
m. 13	Grand-Orgue: add Récit reeds	Grand-Orgue: *f*
m. 21	Positif: remove Récit Clairon	Récit: *meno p*
m. 27	Récit: remove reeds; *pp*	Récit: remove reeds; *pp*
m. 34	Remove Grand-Orgue to Pedal coupler	No indication
m. 35	Positif: remove the Positif to Grand-Orgue coupler; add 16' stops	Positif: *p*

simplification of registration at times undercuts the sonorous equilibrium in the work. For example, the printed version of the passage beginning at m. 47, fails to specify the removal of the Grand-Orgue to Pedal coupler.[77]

Several aspects of the work are curious. In m. 44 there are parallel fifths (which, according to Saint-Saëns, provided a bad example for young composers). Another oddity is the passage beginning at m. 47: the pedal part is notated in eighth notes, yet when the "second theme" returns near the end of the piece—in the same key and in the same texture but, perhaps significantly, at a much louder dynamic level—the pedal notes are written as quarters. There is nothing mysterious about the optional pedal line which appears in the edition (but not in the Trocadéro manuscript) at the *Très largement*, mm. 206–10: the compass of the pedal at the Trocadéro was thirty notes while that of the Sainte-Clotilde organ was twenty-seven. Thus if organists have at their disposal a modern complete pedalboard, they should certainly play the version with e'.

Tournemire's beginning tempo of quarter note equals 88 is faster than Dupré's 72 and Langlais's 69. Regarding the quiet close of the work, Tournemire remarks: "The delicate end fades like a sweet, mystical thought, barely outlined."[78]

Cantabile

Similar registrational simplifications can be found in the published version of the Cantabile. The manuscript used for the Trocadéro performance mentions a Récit Tremblant, added to the 8' foundations, Hautbois, and Trompette of the same division. The Tremblant is removed at m. 51, then added again at m. 65. This sonority, producing a strange effect, was omitted from the score of the published version. Tournemire comments:

> This page—one of the most remarkable by Franck—is a simple line, with a soft contour like the shore of a lake. . . . General movement: quarter note equals 69. As for the rest... one must follow one's own intuition!"[79]

Dupré also suggests a tempo of quarter note equals 69, and Langlais 66.

Pièce héroïque

As indicated above, Franck composed a different ending—an ending which seems an improvement upon the original—for the publication of this piece (see Plate 1). There are also some pencil indications in the manuscript version that Franck did not retain in the 1883 print (for example, the *lentement* markings placed at mm. 7, 70, and 108). Despite the suppresion of these

Plate 1
Franck, ending of *Pièce héroïque* in MS 20151

nuances, one may suppose that the composer observed them when he played the piece himself.

As he had done for the other two of the *Trois Pièces*, Franck simplified the registration indications of the *Pièce héroïque* for the Durand print. Perhaps he oversimplified the indications when, in the middle of the piece, he omitted the instruction found in the manuscript to "remove the *tirasses* but leave all the stops in the pedal engaged." Without this indication the balance between the manuals and pedal is jeopardized.

The tempo suggestions of Dupré and Langlais are identical: both indicate quarter note equals 80 at the beginning, while Tournemire suggests 96. Tournemire also indicates that the central section should be played slower, an interpretation endorsed by both Dupré (quarter note equals 72) and Langlais. For the Più lento finale, the different schools agree that the pedal should be played legato while the manual chords are played in a détaché manner.

Trois Chorals

The surviving manuscripts of the *Chorals*—the first version of the First *Choral* and the fair copy used for the engraving of the Second *Choral*—are unfortunately less instructive in matters of interpretation than is the Trocadéro manuscript of the *Trois Pièces*. The manuscript of the First *Choral* includes no registration or manual indications. In the manuscript of the Second *Choral*, the registration indications (in both French and English) are not in Franck's hand. Because death prevented Franck from supervising the engraving of the *Trois Chorals*, the editor presumably reproduced the text found in the manuscript.

Lacking any new evidence about Franck's interpretative intentions, we turn to the diverse sources: Tournemire is the most trustworthy (he played these works at the piano with Franck himself); Guilmant has less authority (Franck merely showed him the sketches of the *Trois Chorals*). Nevertheless, Tournemire and his own students Duruflé and Langlais do not espouse a single set of ideas about the works. Langlais enjoyed access to additional members of Franck's circle, namely Mahaut, one of Franck's favorite students, and Marty, another blind student of Franck; in addition, Langlais also consulted with Marchal, a student of Eugène Gigout.

Perhaps everything has already been said about these last pages of Franck: the *Trois Chorals* are the end product of a slow and complex evolution. Franck revived a form that was perfected by J. S. Bach, gave it immense proportions, and yet kept his distance from his illustrious predecessor. As Franck said mischievously to his students: "You will see, the chorale is not what you think; the real chorale emerges during the course of the piece."[80]

The *Trois Chorals* were created during August and September 1890 at

Nemours, where Franck was staying with friends while recuperating from a carriage accident. He completed the Second and Third *Chorals* on 17 and 20 September, respectively. There is no doubt that these three masterpieces were composed for the Sainte-Clotilde organ. Franck knew his organ so well that he did not need to be at the instrument in order to register his score. The manuscript was at his bedside when he died on 8 November of the same year.

In light of the extant evidence, the dedications of the *Trois Chorals* are certainly posthumous: dedications are not found in the manuscripts except for the inscription (discussed above) to Mlle Bréal found at the end of the First *Choral*. Was this an actual dedication or did Franck simply write this inscription on a manuscript for one of his friends? For his part, Gigout, to whom the First *Choral* is dedicated in print, formally contested the matter. It is likely that Durand took the initiative in establishing the dedications, thereby dedicating of the Second *Choral* to himself.

Choral No. 1 in E Major

The second half of this work raises several questions. Langlais believed that the registration for the Maestoso, where Franck indicates 16' and 8' foundations and reeds on all keyboards, is only possible at Sainte-Clotilde, where the 16' and 8' stops are rich in 4' overtones: such a registration would probably be impractical on other instruments. All the traditions agree that in the second of the two Poco animato passages, the score very likely contains an error. In the first passage there is a whole note on e flat in the left hand, while in the second passage the whole note B is found not in the left hand but on full Pedal, thus rendering the manual parts inaudible. Two solutions present themselves: the B can be taken by the left hand on the Récit (if one has hands the size of Franck's!), or it can be played in the Pedal after removing the pedal couplers. The latter solution is suggested by Tournemire, Dupré, and Langlais; Duruflé scores the B in the Pedal, but with the Récit to Pedal coupler only.

The beginning of the second large variation at m. 126, for which Franck supplied no tempo marking, is marked *vivante* by Tournemire, and for Langlais it is *assez rapide*. With Dupré this second variation returns to the opening tempo of quarter note equals 56; for Duruflé it is Moderato—the same indication he gives at the opening of the work, but at quarter note equals 63 (slightly faster that the 60 he gives at the beginning). Like Duruflé and Langlais, Dupré believed the right-hand theme in B-flat minor should be on the Grand-Orgue and not on the Positif. At the end of this passage (m. 194), however, Langlais indicates that the right hand should be on the Récit, while Dupré and Duruflé both place it on the Positif.

For the *tutta forza* ending, the traditions agree that only the soprano and the pedal, the two parts with the melody, are played smoothly; the accompanying chords are detached. On this passage Tournemire comments: "the very end, in bright light."[81] Three measures before the end, Duruflé adds a rallentando and indicates that the staccato (which he begins at the a Tempo) should gradually become longer. Dupré and Langlais maintain a legato phrasing, adding a rallentando (or allargando) at the end of the penultimate bar.

Choral No. 2 in B Minor

All the traditions agree on the opening tempo: quarter note equals 76. Dupré and Langlais disagree, however, on the registration. At the right-hand passage in octaves (m. 41) all four commentators indicate that the left hand should not be legato, as opposed to the octaves of the right hand which should be very "flowing."[82] At the return of the right-hand octaves (m. 57), there are awkward crossings between the two hands—if indeed they are both supposed to be on the Grand-Orgue, as the score seems to suggest. Various alternatives have been proposed: Langlais suggests that the left hand should play on the Positif, Dupré indicates that it should play on the Récit, and Duruflé gives a distribution of the parts to facilitate playing the passage entirely on the Grand-Orgue.

At the *cantabile* (m. 65) Franck indicates the removal of the Grand-Orgue and Positif reeds, as well as the Grand-Orgue 16' stops. Dupré changes the registration to 8' foundations on all manuals, all manual and pedal couplers, and 16' and 8' Pedal foundations. While Dupré does not give a dynamic marking for this passage, Duruflé indicates *mf* while Langlais adds a *pp* at this point, since the score subsequently calls for a crescendo. In Dupré's edition the notes in the left hand that are doubled by the pedal are given as small notes (and can be omitted because of the pedal couplers). Curiously, in the following passage on the Voix humaine, instead of doubling the left hand and pedal in this manner, Dupré omits the manual scoring of the voice in question.

Langlais plays the Largamente con fantasia passage very freely. Tournemire and Langlais both take "con fantasia" to include subtle accelerandi and rallentandi with a broadening of the highest notes in the melodic line. In all the traditions, the left-hand chords are played detached.

For the passage marked 1° Tempo ma un poco meno lento, Tournemire writes: "the passage with the chorale theme *in the middle* ought to be played *on two manuals*, in spite of the immense technical difficulty inherent in the parts crossing from one manual to the other."[83] While the Peters edition adopts this solution, Duruflé, Dupré, and Langlais do not propose it.

What Tournemire calls the "ascent" begins after the passage in F-sharp minor with the progressive introduction of reeds on different manuals (m.

226). For Tournemire, this ascent, "like an uninterrupted rising of light—...
must be performed with great freedom. To interpret this metronomically
would be major heresy."[84] The Dupré edition removes all of Franck's indications to engage and release the reed ventils, replacing them with less precise
annotations such as crescendo and sempre crescendo. Especially problematic
is the removal of Franck's diminuendo indications in mm. 241–42, as well as
the shift of the right hand at m. 246 from the Grand-Orgue to the Positif
(which also decreases the dynamic level somewhat). Indeed, at m. 246 Dupré
indicates sempre crescendo. These changes significantly alter the way the
passage approaches the climax of m. 258. When the passage originally heard
on the Voix humaine returns at the end of the work, Franck included no
reference to a 32' Pedal stop; his indication reads: "Pedal: very soft stops."
The different traditions call for 32' in the Pedal, believing it to be indispensable for the ecstatic atmosphere of this passage.

Choral No. 3 in A Minor

Tournemire writes:

> The most simply treated of the three, in the sense of oscillating between A
> major and A minor.
> The beginning makes one involuntarily think of the undulating Prelude in
> A Minor [BWV 543] of J. S. Bach, chiefly in its severity of style.
> It is followed by decorative, arpeggiated chords that under the performer's
> fingers must create the idea of infinity...[85]

The considerable tempo variations for the beginning of the Third *Choral*, as
found in the various traditions, are shown in Figure 6. Langlais advocates the
slowest tempo, quarter note equals 88, and Duruflé the fastest, quarter note
equals 108. Dupré omits all the fermatas and, like Duruflé, he adds the manual
16' foundations for the Largamente passages and then removes them for the a
Tempo passages. Langlais does not endorse this practice. At m. 30 Tournemire
explains that a fermata is necessary "in order to underline clearly the entrance
of the chorale."[86] This recommendation is not mentioned by anyone else.
    Tournemire and Dupré believe that Franck omitted a tempo indication
before the second entrance of the chorale theme (mm. 53–56). Tournemire
suggests a return of the previous Largamente indication while Dupré provides
the same Doppio lento marking that appeared in m. 6 of his edition. Langlais,
however, leaves this passage in the prevailing Quasi allegro tempo. Duruflé
gives a compromise version: he proposes a tempo in which the quarter note
equals 80, halfway between his Quasi allegro (108) and his Largamente (54).
He does the same for the last arpeggio before the Adagio. Dupré and
Tournemire return to the tempo of the Largamente (in Dupré's case, his
Doppio lento) while Langlais makes a progressive rallentando.

For the Adagio, Dupré and Duruflé indicate eighth note equals 84; Tournemire gives 76, "*but with great freedom*";[87] and Langlais 76. Tournemire reports that Franck played this passage with rubato and that he would surely shudder if he heard certain literal interpretations of Tournemire's own day.[88] (Thus, already in the 1930s there are cautions against too strict a style.) Langlais emphatically insists on rubato in this Adagio, explaining that it is necessary to lengthen all of the syncopated notes in the theme. At the Molto slargando Tournemire provides an interesting detail: "the pedal octaves must be played non-legato, very much in the manner of trombonists. *Franck played it this way.*"[89] Duruflé adopts this practice; Dupré does not.

The indication *Le double plus vite (Mouvement du commencement)*, which begins the third and last large section of the work, is respected metronomically by the different traditions: all return to the tempo they indicate for the beginning of the work. When the chorale theme enters in half notes in the right hand, Tournemire, Dupré, and Duruflé all indicate that the Récit expression box must be exactly three-quarters open. The same holds true for the chorale theme found eight measures later. Regarding the climax of the work, Tournemire remarks:

> The soprano line of the chorale must soar, and to achieve this it is helpful to detach the inner voices to shorten them accordingly.
> The light becomes all the more intense.
> The final measures, "più largo"—aspire to extreme grandeur.[90]

Marchal made sense of the various traditions of Franck interpretation by assimilating them:

> In my interpretation as in my registrations, I aim above all to preserve the spirit of the indications of César Franck. Having known intimately and listened to three students of Franck—Albert Mahaut, Adolphe Marty, and Charles Tournemire—all of whose interpretations were quite different, I have all the same kept in mind a certain tradition.[91]

It seems clear that Franck's students themselves differed in their approach to their teacher's works; that the disparities multiplied in the following generations in hardly surprising. At this point, having compared the different traditions, it is appropriate to acknowledge the obvious difficulty: how can we reconcile such contradictory "traditions"?

All the sources agree on the extreme freedom taken by Franck when he played his own works; the performer must, therefore, consider the suggestions transmitted by the different traditions while seeking expressivity above all else. In light of the fingerings Franck devised for the works of Bach in the Braille scores, it is clear that his standard approach was a smooth and legato style. The same approach certainly should be taken with Franck's own works, even if there is diversity of opinion on this matter (due in part to testimony by Franck's contemporaries about an "approximate" technique). Tempi should be flexible, as Tournemire insisted. As for instruments, the player should keep in mind the peculiar characteristics of the Sainte-Clotilde organ, which, from all evidence, inspired Franck from the time of the *Six Pièces* onward.

Finally, to understand better the "Franck style," it is important to remember the man himself. Was he only, as many describe him, a mystic, beaming with generosity and goodness? It would be a great mistake to see Franck only as an ethereal being, and not as a man and an artist. When this view of Franck was expressed to the pianist Georges Mathias, he retorted: "A mystic? Ask Augusta Holmès about that!"[92] When Langlais taught the works of Franck, he always began with this provocative proclamation: "There is no point in learning Franck's music if you haven't previously endured twenty-five years of love!" Is this not the best spirit in which to consider the interpretation of Franck's organ works?

(TRANSLATED BY MATTHEW DIRST AND KIMBERLY MARSHALL)

NOTES

[1] See Wayne Leupold, "The Organ Manuscripts of César Franck," *The American Organist* 24 (December 1990): 109–11.

[2] Also included are materials relating to *L'Organiste*. (Since that collection is one of Franck's volumes of harmonium music, these manuscripts will not be taken into account in this study.)

[3] It is not clear whether the replacements are the same as those which were erased or are different ones.

[4] As with the *Pastorale*, the relationship of these registrations to those which were erased is unclear.

[5] See Norbert Dufourcq, *César Franck et la genèse des premières œuvres d'orgue*, Cahiers et mémories de l'orgue, no. 147 bis (Paris: L'Orgue, 1973).

[6] See Joël-Marie Fauquet, "L'Orgue de Ducroquet et la 'Fantaisie de Saint-Eustache' (1854)," in *César Franck*, L'Orgue: cahiers et mémoires, no. 44 (Paris: L'Orgue, 1990), 73–80.

[7] Karen Hastings-Deans's article in this volume discusses this manuscript in detail. *Ed.*

[8] Pieces in C Major and D Major from *L'Organiste* were also dedicated to Clotilde Bréal. The autograph of these pieces, dated 22 August, is also found in The Pierpont Morgan Library. (Incidentally, Clotilde Bréal was the wife of writer Romain Rolland from October 1892 to 1901.)

[9] See Emory Fanning, "Chorals II and III: Two Franck Autographs," *The American Organist* 24 (December 1990): 112–14.

[10] See François Sabatier, "Les Trois Pièces du Trocadéro," in *César Franck*, L'Orgue: cahiers et mémoires, no. 44 (Paris: L'Orgue, 1990), 26–34.

[11] Wayne Leupold has pointed out that there are also registrations for Saint-Eustache in these manuscripts. Franck is reported to have played this Fantasy in 1879 at Saint-Eustache. (Leupold, "The Organ Manuscripts of César Franck," 110.)

[12] The Positif, rather than the Grand-Orgue, was the bottom manual.

[13] Jesse Eschbach and Robert Bates, preface to *Fantaisie für die Orgel in drei Versionen* by César Franck, ed. Jesse Eschbach and Robert Bates (Bonn-Bad Godesberg: Rob. Forberg, 1980).

[14] As for the registration of the Fantasy in C Major, in the printed version Franck's indications are designed for a standard three-manual organ (whose specification irresistibly evokes that of Sainte-Clotilde).

[15] How can one not be puzzled by the words of Charles Tournemire, one of Franck's last organ students, who claimed that Franck performed the *Grande Pièce symphonique* at the inauguration of the new organ at Saint-Eustache on 26 May 1854, nearly nine years before the date on its surviving manuscript? This claim by Tournemire, not supported by other sources, appears strange, if not in error. Tournemire's account has been thrown into yet more doubt with the discovery by Joël-Marie Fauquet of Franck's Piece in A Major, which appears to have been written in 1854 for the inaugural concert at Saint-Eustache.

[16] See Franck's letter addressed to Schuberth, dated 23 August 1867, in Dufourcq, *César Franck et la genèse*, 10.

[17] The Prelude, Fugue, and Variation was published in four versions: for piano and organ or harmonium; for violin, harmonium, and piano; for two pianos; and for piano four hands.

[18] Daniel Roth's article in this volume suggests a date of 1891 or 1892 for this publication. *Ed.*

[19] This figure is incomplete, since the information used to compile it, for which the author is grateful, was supplied by Durand editions in 1975. New printings, to be sure, have occurred since that date.

[20] César Franck, *Œuvres complètes pour orgue*, 4 vols. (Paris: Durand, [1956]).

[21] César Franck, *Les Trois Chorals*, ed. Maurice Duruflé, vol. 4 of *Œuvres complètes pour orgue* (Paris: Durand, 1973). This edition (not to be confused with the "Édition originale") clearly indicates "Révision et annotations de Maurice Duruflé."

[22] Maurice Duruflé, "Note to the Performer," in César Franck, *Les Trois Chorals*, ed. Maurice Duruflé, vol. 4 of *Œuvres complètes pour orgue* (Paris: Durand, 1973).

[23] César Franck, *Œuvres pour orgue de César Franck*, ed. Marcel Dupré, 4 vols. (Paris: S. Bornemann, 1955). In 1989, the publications of Bornemann were acquired by Leduc (Paris).

[24] Marcel Dupré, preface to *Œuvres pour orgue de César Franck* by César Franck, ed. Marcel Dupré, 4 vols. (Paris: S. Bornemann, 1955), xi. (The English translation is that published in these volumes; emendations have been supplied in cases where the translation is faulty or unclear. *Ed.*)

[25] Dupré, preface to *Œuvres pour orgue* by Franck, xii. (On the same page, in his description of the Sainte-Clotilde organ, he lists a Récit to Pedal coupler which, it is now generally accepted, was added after the death of Franck.)

[26] Dufourcq, *César Franck et la genèse*, 4.

[27] Maurice Emmanuel, *César Franck* (Paris: H. Laurens, 1930), 101.

[28] Emmanuel, *César Franck*, 102.

[29] See Marie-Louise Jaquet-Langlais, "Une Curiosité: l'œuvre d'orgue de Jean-Sebastien Bach doigtée par César Franck," *L'Orgue*, no. 207 (1988): 1–6. See also Karen Hastings, "New Franck Fingerings Brought to Light," *The American Organist* 24 (December 1990): 92–101.

[30] These examples are found in the *Grande Pièce symphonique*, Allegro, m. 88; the First *Choral*, mm. 174 and 186; the Prelude, Fugue, and Variation, m. 58 of the Fugue and m. 28 of the Variation; and the *Prière*, m. 179.

[31] See, for example, Boëly's Fantasy for the verset *Judex crederis* of the Te Deum, op. 38, no. 4, where the first page reads: "on the Récit, the Hautbois; on the Grand-Orgue, the 16' Montres and Bourdons with the 8' Flûtes, without the Prestant; on the Positif, 8' Flûtes and Bourdon without the Prestant; on the Pedal, 8' and 4' stops." For a modern reprint, see *A. P. Fr. Boëly & Fr. Benoist*, ed. Willem van Twillert, vol. 3 of *Organisten uit de 18e en 19e Eeuw* (Amersfoort: J. C. Willemsen, 1984), 6–11. (In this edition the *Judex crederis* is incorrectly identified as op. 32.)

[32] Charles Tournemire, *Précis d'exécution, de registration, et d'improvisation à l'orgue* (Paris: Max Eschig, 1936), 104.

[33] César Franck, *Pièces inédites de César Franck*, ed. Norbert Dufourcq (Paris: Les Éditions musicales de la Schola Cantorum, 1973).

[34] César Franck, *Pièce pour Grand Orgue (1854)*, ed. Joël-Marie Fauquet (Paris: Musicales du Marais, 1990).

[35] Joël-Marie Fauquet, introduction to *Pièce pour Grand Orgue (1854)* by César Franck, ed. Joël-Marie Fauquet (Paris: Musicales du Marais, 1990), v. (The English translation is that published in the volume; emendations have been supplied in cases where the translation is faulty or unclear. *Ed.*)

[36] César Franck, *Orgelwerke*, ed. Otto Barblan, 4 vols. (Leipzig: Peters, 1919).

[37] Tournemire, *Précis*, 83.

[38] César Franck, *Fantaisie für die Orgel in drei Versionen*, ed. Jesse Eschbach and Robert Bates (Bonn-Bad Godesberg: Rob. Forberg, 1980).

[39] César Franck, *Six Pièces; Trois Pièces; Trois Chorals*, ed. Hermann J. Busch, 4 vols. (Sankt Augustin: Dr. J. Butz, 1988).

[40] Daniel Roth's article in this volume gives several examples. *Ed.*

[41] Daniel Roth's article in this volume discusses these early prints. *Ed.*

[42] César Franck, *Complete Works for Organ*, ed. Günther Kaunzinger, 4 vols. (Vienna: Schott/Universal, 1990).

[43] For a more complete list of the organs on which Franck performed see Rollin Smith, "César Franck and the Organ," *The American Organist* 24 (November 1990): 66–76.

[44] This despite the fact that the range of the Piece, FF to a flat''', is larger than that of the instrument, AA to f''' (see Dufourcq, *César Franck et la genèse*).

[45] Dufourcq, *César Franck et la genèse*, 12.

[46] Marie-Claire Alain, "The Organ at Sainte-Clotilde," trans. Marcus Huxley, accompanying *César Franck: Intégrale de l'œuvre pour orgue: Marie-Claire Alain aux grandes orgues Cavaillé-Coll de l'église Saint-François-de-Sales, Lyon* (Erato STU 71035/7, 1977), [vi]. (Emendations have been supplied in cases where the translation is faulty or unclear. *Ed.*)

[47] Today this church is the Orthodox cathedral Sainte-Croix.

[48] Eschbach and Bates, preface to *Fantaisie für die Orgel* by Franck.

[49] For a detailed discussion of these issues see Kurt Lueders and Ton van Eck, "Franck, Cavaillé-Coll, and the Organ of Sainte-Clotilde," *The American Organist* 24 (December 1990): 115–19.

[50] Adrien de LaFage, "Inauguration de l'orgue de Sainte-Clotilde," *La Revue et Gazette musicale* 27 (1860): 4.

[51] Fenner Douglass, *Cavaillé-Coll and the Musicians*, 2 vols. (Raleigh: Sunbury, 1980). See also Lueders and van Eck, "Franck, Cavaillé-Coll, and the Organ of Sainte-Clotilde."

[52] *La France musicale* 23 (1859): 507.

[53] Personal communication. (The 1983 restoration of the Sainte-Clotilde organ, requested by Langlais, reestablished the *octaves graves* and the Clarinette of the Positif.)

[54] Others have argued, such as Lueders and van Eck, that, given the special quality of the Hautbois of the Récit at Sainte-Clotilde, it may not always be wise to try to duplicate Franck's combination of foundations and Hautbois on other instruments. (See Lueders and van Eck, "Franck, Cavaillé-Coll, and the Organ of Sainte-Clotilde," 118.)

[55] Contrary to what was always believed, the Clarinette of the Positif is really a Cromorne. (This is confirmed by Barberis who points not only to the scale of the stop but also to the inscription on the first pipe, information gleaned during his 1983 rebuilding of the instrument.)

[56] André Marchal, "L'Instrument," accompanying *César Franck: L'Œuvre intégral pour orgue: André Marchal aux grandes orgues de l'église Saint-Eustache de Paris*, 3 vols. (Erato EDO 203–5, 1959), 2:[iii]. (These recordings have been reissued as *Franck: L'Œuvre intégral pour orgue* [Erato CD 4509–94828–2, 1994].)

[57] It is sometimes possible to remedy this lack of power with the help of a Bombarde manual.

[58] Marie-Claire Alain, "Franck's Registration," trans. Marcus Huxley, accompanying *César Franck: Intégrale de l'œuvre pour orgue: Marie-Claire Alain aux grandes orgues Cavaillé-Coll de l'église Saint-François-de-Sales, Lyon* (Erato STU 71035/7, 1977), [vi].

[59] When adapting Franck's music to different organs, the timbre of the reeds should predominate and not be overpowered by mixtures and mutations. In a description of the original state of the Sainte-Clotilde organ, Marchal (who was one of five experts consulted for the rebuilding of the organ in 1933) remarks upon the extreme mildness of the reed stops (Marchal, "L'Instrument," [iii].) Marie-Claire Alain also agrees with Marchal, stating that: "It should perhaps be pointed out that this was a characteristic of the Cavaillé-Coll organs of that period. It was only much later, and especially after the death of the master organ builder himself, that instruments made under the name of Cavaillé-Coll were given big reeds. Many early Cavaillé-Coll [organs] were revoiced and made louder in the early years of this century." (Alain, "Franck's Registration," [vi].)

[60] See Cécile and Emmanuel Cavaillé-Coll, *Aristide Cavaillé-Coll* (Paris: Fischbacher, 1929), 125–26.

[61] Quoted in Jean Gallois, *Franck* (Paris: Seuil, 1966), 68.

[62] Rollin Smith's article in this volume also discusses Franck's Trocadéro concert. *Ed.*

[63] Jesse E. Eschbach's article in this volume also discusses the relationship between Franck's organ music and the Sainte-Clotilde organ. *Ed.*

[64] Marie-Claire Alain, "A Few Problems of Interpretation," trans. Marcus Huxley, accompanying *César Franck: Intégrale de l'œuvre pour orgue: Marie-Claire Alain aux grandes orgues Cavaillé-Coll de l'église Saint-François-de-Sales, Lyon* (Erato STU 71035/7, 1977), [vi].

[65] Tournemire's recordings of Franck have been reissued on *César Franck: Pupil and Successors at Sainte-Clotilde [performed by] Charles Tournemire [and] Jean Langlais* (Opal 811, 1983).

[66] Charles Tournemire, *César Franck*, Les Grands Musiciens par les maîtres d'aujourd'hui, no. 5 (Paris: Delagrave, 1931), chs. 5 and 5*bis*.

[67] For a fuller discussion of Tournemire's recordings, see Rollin Smith, *Toward an Authentic Interpretation of the Organ Works of César Franck*, Juilliard Performance Guides, no. 1 (New York: Pendragon, 1983), ch. 7.

[68] The earliest of these recordings has been reissued on *César Franck: Pupil and Successors at Sainte-Clotilde*; the others are included in *The Complete Organ Works of César Franck by Jean Langlais at the organ of St. Clotilde-Paris* (Gregorian Institute of America 108–10, [1963]) and *César Franck à Sainte-Clotilde: Jean Langlais aux grands orgues Cavaillé-Coll de Sainte-Clotilde* (Arion ARN 336 008, 1975).

[69] For additional information see Marie-Louise Jaquet-Langlais, "Les Six Pièces," in *César Franck*, L'Orgue: cahiers et mémoires, no. 44 (Paris: L'Orgue, 1990), 4–25.

[70] Tournemire, *César Franck*, 21.

[71] The "Voix célestes" indication for the Positif must have meant the Viole de gambe plus the Unda maris at Sainte-Clotilde.

[72] In the original Maeyens-Couvreur edition as well as subsequent Durand editions of this movement, there is a puzzling indication for the 8' Bourdon of the Grand-Orgue, which is not used a single time during the rest of the piece.

[73] Tournemire, *César Franck*, 24.

[74] Ibid.

[75] Joël-Marie Fauquet, [notes], accompanying *César Franck à Sainte-Clotilde: Jean Langlais aux grandes orgues Cavaillé-Coll de Sainte-Clotilde* (Arion ARN 336 008, 1975), [vi].

[76] Tournemire, *César Franck*, 25.

[77] It is tempting to conjecture that both the change of title as well as the fact that Franck made no mention of a dedication (as he had done in the *Six Pièces*) for the *Trois Pièces* are due to personal reasons (which he did not wish to make public). It has been suggested that the title change may have been due to the influence of Mme Franck.

[78] Tournemire, *César Franck*, 25.

[79] Ibid., 25–26.

[80] François Sabatier gives this quotation as follows: "Vous verrez, le choral, ce n'est pas celui qu'on croit. Le vrai choral, il se fait au cours même de l'œuvre." (François Sabatier, *César Franck et l'orgue* [Paris: Presses universitaires de France, 1982], 87.)

[81] Tournemire, *Précis*, 82. (Elsewhere he writes "the end, in a ray of glory" [Tournemire, *César Franck*, 31].)

[82] Tournemire gives "bien 'coulées'" (Tournemire, *Précis*, 83) and "aussi chantantes que possible" (Tournemire, *César Franck*, 33).

[83] Tournemire, *Précis*, 83.

[84] Ibid.

[85] Ibid.

[86] Ibid.

[87] Ibid., 84.

[88] Ibid.

[89] Ibid.

[90] Ibid.

[91] André Marchal, "Les Registrations," accompanying *César Franck: L'Œuvre intégral pour orgue: André Marchal aux grandes orgues de l'église Saint-Eustache de Paris*, 3 vols. (Erato EDO 203–5, 1959), 1:[iv]. The tradition of Langlais rather than that of Marchal has been emphasized here because Langlais was for forty-two years organist at Sainte-Clotilde and always scrupulously respected the registrations specified by Franck.

[92] This quotation has also been attributed to Franck himself. See Nancy Theeman, "The Life and Songs of Augusta Holmès" (Ph.D. diss., University of Maryland, 1983), 120, for its various sources. (Mathias taught piano at the Conservatoire.)

Some Thoughts on the Interpretation
of the Organ Works of Franck,
on His Organ, and on the Lemmens Tradition

DANIEL ROTH

Many problems arise in the search for an authentic interpretation of César Franck's organ works. First, what about the editions? The *Six Pièces*, ops. 16–21, and the *Trois Pièces* were published during the composer's lifetime, but the *Trois Chorals* appeared only after his death. The *Six Pièces*, composed around 1860, were first published by Mme Maeyens-Couvreur in 1868 (with plate numbers 161 to 166). This firm was first taken over by J. Pegiel and subsequently by Durand et Schoenewerk. The *Six Pièces* were then given new plate numbers: 2679 to 2684. Around that time some corrections were made to the *Six Pièces*, probably under the direction of Franck, yet some scores have the corrections and others do not, even though they carry the same plate numbers.[1] In 1883 Durand et Schoenewerk published the *Trois Pièces* (with plate numbers 3175 to 3177). In 1891 or 1892 the *Trois Chorals* were published by Durand (plate numbers 4414 to 4416).[2] Afterwards, many prints of these twelve pieces have been made; while the name of the firm changed several times (A. Durand et Fils, Durand et Cie, etc.), the plate numbers remained the same.[3] Were corrections made to the *Trois Pièces* or to the *Trois Chorals*? Were additional corrections made to the *Six Pièces*? Answers are not currently available. In any event, in 1959 Durand issued a new edition in Italian format (the currently available one) with many errors and also many changes of the text.[4] At the present time the most reliable edition for the *Six Pièces* would appear to be the Durand et Schoenewerk with the corrections, for the *Trois Pièces* the Durand et Schoenewerk of 1883, and for the *Trois Chorals* the Durand of 1891–1892.

Performance Style and Interpretation

Beyond the question of editions lie the problems of the contradictory performance traditions that each claim the authority of Franck. Whom should one believe? How should one proceed to discover the truth?

Sound quality and harmony play an important role in the music of the nineteenth century; the styles of many composers are so original that they can be recognized unmistakably from the first chords. This is certainly true of Franck's music, that mysterious uniting of French and German elements (his ancestors were German), with a completely personal style of sound which surely owes something to the Cavaillé-Coll organ, above all the instrument of Sainte-Clotilde. His music needs the tone colors of these instruments to come to life. Franck's encounter with his instrument was an event of utmost significance, comparable perhaps to Chopin's engagement with the piano of his time.

Unfortunately, since 1933 the organ of Sainte-Clotilde has been altered repeatedly, to the point that it is really no longer a Cavaillé-Coll organ. This instrument, unique in the *œuvre* of its builder, ought to have been preserved as a monument to its first *titulaire*, as a witness of eminent importance; it could have provided valuable information to help solve the questions arising from Franck's registration indications. The Cavaillé-Coll organ influenced France's symphonic organ literature, and even a later composer like Olivier Messiaen. Charles-Marie Widor expressed it aptly in 1932: "Our school owes its creation—I say it without reservation—to the special, magical sound of these instruments." For music is tied to sound; sound colors allow entire works to arise. From François Couperin to the present, France's organ music tradition with its predominant melodic and harmonic character is very much tied to the color of the sound, in contrast to the German organ and its literature, which embody to a greater degree the linear, polyphonic style. With Franck's music and with his organ playing—by all accounts highly individualistic—we find ourselves in the realm of this completely self-contained world of sound. A musician concerned with authentic performance must strive to recapture this sound as accurately as possible. That demands, in addition to biographical and historical insight, above all detailed analysis of the composer's works, including form, structure, melody, harmony, and rhythm. Such investigations then permit the determination of three principal aspects of performance: touch, declamation, and registration. Let us attempt to define them.

By attack we understand not only the art of initiating the individual note, but also the manner in which notes are connected to one another to a greater or lesser degree. Here the organ offers a wide range of possibilities, from absolute legato to the most abrupt separation. Organists should accommodate themselves to the acoustic of the space, so that the tones do not blur in the reverberation and the desired articulation is clear to the listener at all times. At the same time, the performer must take pains to permit the alternation of strong and weak beats, accented and unaccented tones, the articulation, phrasing, and the overall structure of the piece to be heard. In order to emphasize a note or a chord one can, if the character of the passage permits, place a slight break before it; if however the passage should be played legato, one can play the note or the chord with a slight delay. The break or the delay, as the case may be, must however be performed with great care lest exaggeration cause the melodic line to be lost.

Attack and declamation are closely related. Maurice Ravel maintained that the notes should simply be played, recreating the text; the music would speak for itself. Others demand reading between the lines, interpreting, and still further stressing the musical punctuation by adding particular emphasis here and there by "emphatically holding out"; according to Franck's student, Charles Tournemire, who described this practice with the word "*insister*" in his writings about Franck, Franck himself advocated such interpretation. Retardation of the tempo emphasizes here a dissonance, there an expressive chord. Many interpreters base their decisions on subjective perceptions, or else on the rules of a particular school or tradition. They forget, however, that composers have very precise ideas about the interpretation of their works and that their style of declamation is a component of their sonic conception: consider Girolamo Frescobaldi, who provides advice on this matter in the forewords to his *libri*, showing that he expected a genuinely new act of creation from his interpreters.

Can we form an idea of the playing of the composer Franck? If today he occupies a place of honor in the history of music as a composer and improviser, nevertheless he had many opponents during his lifetime, and later was scarcely recognized as an organist. Widor, Franck's successor as professor of organ at the Conservatoire, gave a talk on the occasion of his first meeting with his students, as Louis Vierne reports in his memoirs: "Widor revealed himself to be properly respectful of his predecessor, but nothing more. He could not question the greatness of the composer and improviser; the organist he passed over in silence." Closer to our own time, Marcel Dupré wrote in the foreword to his edition of Franck's organ works: "He was brilliant as an improviser on the organ and also as a composer. But as an organ virtuoso he played as was usual in France at the time: only approximating a legato, and with a casual regard for note values." (By contrast, Franz Liszt heaped praise on Franck the performer and improviser.) Can Franck be interpreted without knowing something about his manner of playing and his registration? What could have given rise to the critical statements of Widor and Dupré?

Franck and the Lemmens Tradition

A sketch of the history of organ performance in France would certainly include as a first high point the *Livre d'orgue* of Nicolas de Grigny published in 1699. In the eighteenth century comes the epoch of the folk-like noëls, less polyphonically elaborate than de Grigny, but so much the more delightful to play; this extensive literature of settings of Christmas songs found particular favor with the public. During that time pedal playing was rather neglected. When around 1830 the pedal keyboard of the German type was introduced to France, Alexandre-Pierre-François Boëly wrote pieces with obbligato pedal parts which at the time was a new, still largely unnoticed development. During this time (in which, despite François Benoist's organ class at the Conservatoire, no genuine organ school existed) the young Franck became a musician. He treated the organ like a pianist, with the extremely free rubato playing of his time. A later student, Adolphe Marty, reports: "We have no idea of the freedom with which Franck played his own pieces." Tournemire also stressed again and again in his suggestions for interpretation of Franck's music how pernicious it is to play metronomically, and urged holding out important chords. Maurice Emmanuel confirms that Franck readily arpeggiated broad chords on the organ. Perhaps he also used the mannerism of a superlegato, common among pianists, as well as the technique in which the two hands do not always play perfectly together.

Around 1840, a Parisian organist, soon to be organist of La Madeleine, Louis-James-Alfred Lefébure-Wély, caused a stir with his virtuoso displays. Following the fashion of the day, he often imitated storms on his instrument, complete with thunder and lightning effects, and, as a concession to his audience, launched into tearful romances. A friend of Cavaillé-Coll, Lefébure-Wély dedicated many of the builder's instruments around mid century.

One day in the organ loft of La Madeleine, Lefébure-Wély received a young organist from Brussels, Jaak Nikolaas (Jacques-Nicolas) Lemmens, who gave as his reference his teacher, Adolf Hesse, of Breslau. Lefébure-Wély, highly impressed by his guest's playing, said: "One who plays as you do needs no references." Similar praise greeted Lemmens and his teacher when they played in Paris. At organ dedications and in concerts they fascinated the Parisian public with a completely novel manner of organ playing; bored with the "literature" described above, that public also probably heard many works of Bach that were at the time still unknown in France. The experts wondered at the unusual manner of Lemmens's playing: the virtuoso pedal technique, the absolute legato. Benoist wrote enthusiastically to Cavaillé-Coll (18 March 1852) about Lemmens's admirable performance style, the calm and the religious grandeur, the strength of the style, fitting the majesty of the house of God. Cavaillé-Coll also admired Lemmens, whom he considered the modern organist *par excellence*, and under the influence of his playing, Cavaillé-Coll's taste changed. He would happily have installed Lemmens in a prestigious Parisian post and thereby introduced the Belgian organ school into France. But since Lemmens refused, he sent two young French organists, Alexandre Guilmant and Widor, to study in Brussels. The Lemmens method, however, first entered official French organ pedagogy only in 1891, when Widor succeeded Franck at the Conservatoire. (However, it was taught in Paris considerably earlier by Clément Loret, another Lemmens student, in the private Niedermeyer School, opened in 1853.) With this official change, the tradition of Franck's performance was gradually lost, because the Lemmens method taught precise regard for the value of notes and rests and absolute legato in all voices of polyphony, based on fingerings with many silent substitutions and slides; notes of the same pitch following one another immediately in different voices (the so-called "notes communes") are likewise tied; those that initiate a separation lose half their value; finally, large slurs indicate phrasing, small ones articulation. Composers from the Lemmens tradition (such as Widor, Guilmant, Gigout, and Vierne) use many slurs to indicate articulation, but, with a few exceptions such as, for example, the main theme of the *Final* of Vierne's First Symphony, these do not indicate separation (see Example 1). Noted in this example are the following: 1) Because the F sharp is accented, the preceding A must be played an eighth note shorter. That is the way Vierne played, according to André Fleury, a student of Vierne, Gigout, and Dupré. 2) The E and the D are slurred with a slight accent on the D. When Vierne places a slur over every measure of his Toccata in B-flat Minor, he does not mean that a break should occur at the end of every slur—that would be completely unmusical. Rather, it means, as Fleury told me, that the piece is conceived to be legato throughout. But to play legato does not mean to play without accents: slight emphases must be made on certain strong beats. Furthermore, one should play with a perfect legato in a dry acoustic but with a "light" legato in a reverberant room.

Franck's education as an organist occurred *before* the introduction of the Lemmens method in France. Concerning his articulations, one may suppose that the last note of a slurred group is slightly shortened. How ponderous the left hand of the first section of the Prelude, Fugue, and Variation, op. 18, would be, played according to Lemmens, without shortening the eighth note (see Example 2). Another question: must one tie Franck's "notes communes," as Lemmens prescribes, as illustrated by the E in the following example from the Third *Choral* (see Example 3)? Such ties under many circumstances could cause the listener confusion (see Example 4). To tie the F would give the impression of a voice crossing (see Example 5). The listener's confusion is even greater when the intervals are descending. Franck, who did not play according to the Lemmens method, probably never systematically tied such "notes communes." Finally, concerning "détaché," a standardized shortening

Example 1. Vierne, *Final*, m. 2–6, from the First Symphony

Example 2. Franck, Prelude, Fugue, and Variation, m. 1

Example 3. Franck, *Choral* No. 3 in A Minor, mm. 30–32

Example 4   Example 5

of notes by half their value would be completely out of place in Franck. Rather, the separated note must be fitted to its musical context.

To return to the rules of the Lemmens tradition: even very lively tempi never exceed an Allegro moderato. Cavaillé-Coll recalled with astonishment the slow tempo of Bach's Fugue in D Major at Hesse's concert at Sainte-Clotilde. Widor once played that Fugue for Lemmens in a very lively tempo. Lemmens's comment: "It is nothing without will." Widor asked himself: "What did he mean by will?" Later he understood: "It is the art of the orator, its authority manifested by the calm, the order and just proportions of the discourse. To musicians, the will shows itself above all through rhythm." Widor also said:

> Polyphony cannot tolerate fast performance; it leaves one breathless, causes confusion, and becomes a caricature. Above all: when a too-rapid tempo does not permit the listener to perceive the changes in the musical event, the listener indeed hears, but superficially, no longer attentively.

Such a fundamental truth goes far beyond the Lemmens organ method in its significance, and becomes a guiding principle that every interpreter should constantly bring to mind.

It has often been claimed that the Lemmens tradition stems directly from Bach: Lemmens learned it from Hesse, and Hesse from students of Bach's own students. This has long been disputed, and rightly so. One has only to read the description of Bach's playing by his first biographer, Johann Nikolaus Forkel, to recognize clearly that Bach did not systematically play with an absolute legato.

It would be interesting to trace the numerous effects of the Lemmens tradition on the interpretation and composition of organ music in France, where it was fated to be carried over to the performance of the entire literature of the organ. In the nineteenth century the organist's repertoire consisted primarily of contemporary works and of Bach. As Buxtehude and Frescobaldi, for example, were rediscovered, they too were played in the same manner. Can one imagine a pianist who interpreted Bach, Schumann, Chopin, and Debussy with only one touch? With the onset of the Lemmens method in the French organ world, the individuality characteristic of Franck's organ playing disappeared. Only a few of his pupils, above all Tournemire, played Franck's music in the spirit of its creator into our own century. The interpretation of the works of Franck is a separate and unique problem.

Works conceived according to the rules of the Lemmens method sound correct only with absolute legato, with staccatos of half a note's value, and in a tempo that corresponds to the expanse of a cathedral. The rules of this tradition are among the tools of a modern organist, just as are other methods, for example those for Bach or for Franck. Now we are no longer astonished by many alterations of Franck's text found in Dupré's edition, conceived in the wake of the Lemmens tradition. We need only compare the final measures of the first part of the Third *Choral*, at the transition to the Adagio, in the original edition by Durand and in that of Dupré (published by Bornemann), or the treatment of the fermatas in the *Final*, op. 21, which Dupré interprets as breath marks, even though one of Franck's fermatas expressly bears the notation *très long*.

Franck, it can be assumed, played with remarkable freedom. We use the word "rubato" only hesitantly; it carries the reputation of a "shameful disease," or so, at least, those under the spell of neoclassicism around 1930 believed. Perhaps rubato had previously been carried too far; instead of choosing the middle way, we perpetually fall into extremes. To be sure, certain variations in tempo, a flexible yielding, were not first heard in the nineteenth century; Frescobaldi already spoke of it in the foreword to his toccatas. We must break ourselves of the habit of identifying "rubato" and "nineteenth century" with one another. We should also cease to believe that rubato is something freely improvised. Admittedly, with many performers, freedom degenerates into anarchy. We know that Franck played very freely, certainly not because of the fashion of the day, but rather to proclaim his message more effectively. His music requires such accents, needs this emphasis in order that its dramatic high points achieve their effect. Quickening and retardation in tempo rubato, pushing ahead and slowing again with the goal of accentuating the tension and relaxation of an entire phrase, can vary in length. The various cadences of a piece, according to their importance, demand various rallentandi from mere slackening to the large concluding rallentando. There are also delays of shorter duration, for instance in a beat or even a fraction of a beat, in order to highlight expressive chords or dissonances (in everything one acknowledges the importance of previous analysis). The personal style of the composer determines how far one may stray from the basic tempo. In every case, performance should accommodate itself flexibly to the course of the melody and permit the rising and falling of the phrase to come to the fore.

In the Prelude, Fugue, and Variation, op. 18, for example, the successively larger melodic intervals (a typical feature of Franck's melodic style) should not be played in tempo; the result would be mechanical and boring. Like a singer, one would slightly lengthen the upper note, the high point of the phrase (see Example 6). Another example can be found in the pedal solo from *Final*, op. 21. Here one should provide successively greater emphasis, corresponding to the larger intervals, but without accentuating the first beat of the measure; that would have a vulgar effect. On the contrary, the eighth-note upbeat would need to be slightly accented (see Example 7).

An example of a brief accentuation-rallentando can be found at the beginning of the *Pièce héroïque* (see Example 8). It is extremely important to return to the basic tempo after a rubato, so that the work maintains unity of tempo. The longer the held back or accelerated periods last, the more difficult is this return. One of the great dangers of rubato playing is that one slows down more and more at each cadence and ends by dragging. Unquestionably, tempo memory is crucial.

If one has once experienced the completeness that arises from the encounter of Franck's creations for organ with an essentially unaltered organ by Cavaillé-Coll, one could be tempted to react puritanically and to say that one should play Franck only on the organs of Cavaillé-Coll. Unfortunately, few unaltered instruments survive from that time. Franck specified registral combinations (and even the activation of couplers and prepared stops) very precisely, as a composer specifies instrumentation. (He once said: "My new organ? It's an orchestra!") It proves extremely helpful to study the instruments of the time with respect to structure, disposition, and sound, and then to attempt to come as close as possible to the original on today's instruments. This is no easy task, for many instruments of Cavaillé-Coll have lost their character through the addition of higher mixtures (it was thought that they would be better able to play Frescobaldi, Buxtehude, and Bach!). Cavaillé-

Example 6. Franck, Prelude, Fugue, and Variation, mm. 16–19

Example 7. Franck, *Final*, mm. 1–4

Example 8. Franck, *Pièce héroïque*, mm. 2–7

Coll organs, after the addition of *Orgelbewegung*, neoclassic mixtures, do not at all play Bach better, but they have surely lost important elements of their aesthetic! So writes the organ builder Georges Lhôte about the the instrument at Sainte-Clotilde:

> Organist Charles Tournemire, who had insisted so much on getting his "grand Récit"—with 16' Quintaton, Cornet décomposé and complete 16', 8' and 4' reeds—was appalled with the result. The wonderful Cavaillé-Coll stops had lost their lustre although nothing had been changed in their voicing. But the acoustical characteristics of the expression box had been modified too much and we will never again hear these stops as César Franck enjoyed them.[5]

Fortunately, there remain the well preserved Cavaillé-Coll organs of Saint-Sulpice in Paris, Saint-Étienne in Caen, and Saint-Ouen in Rouen, among others, to demonstrate *ad aures* the unique characteristics of Franck's registrations.[6]

(TRANSLATED BY DAVID GRAMIT)

NOTES

[1] Some examples of these corrections include the following. *Grande Pièce symphonique*: m. 16, soprano, d natural" in Maeyens-Couvreur (and in the autograph manuscript, Stockholm, Stiftelsen Musikkulturens Främjande, MS 880212) changed to d sharp" in the corrected Durand et Schoenewerk; m. 185, in the corrected Durand et Schoenewerk "accelerando poco a poco" appears but is absent in the Maeyens-Couvreur (and the manuscript); first Andante, m. 9, soprano, second beat, dotted-eighth and sixteenth in the Maeyens-Couvreur (and the manuscript) changed in the corrected Durand et Schoenewerk to two eighths; finale, m. 15, pedal, second half of the second beat, B in Maeyens-Couvreur (and the manuscript) changed in the corrected Durand et Schoenewerk to c double sharp. *Prière*: m. 51, left hand, d' is not tied into the next measure but a is tied twice in the Maeyens-Couvreur while in the corrected Durand et Schoenewerk d' is tied and a is tied only once; m. 212, soprano, presents a more complex situation with e sharp''' a half note and the c sharp''' on beat three double-stemmed in the manuscript while in the Maeyens-Couvreur e sharp''' is a dotted half and c sharp''' is single-stemmed yet the corrected Durand et Schoenewerk gives e sharp''' as a half note and c sharp''' as single-stemmed. *Final*: m. 181, left hand, Maeyens-Couvreur gives F natural while the corrected Durand et Schoenewerk gives F sharp.

[2] The articles in this volume by Marie-Louise Jaquet-Langlais and Karen Hastings-Deans suggest 1891 as the date of this publication. *Ed.*

[3] Sometimes the first page of a piece has the new name of the firm while the following pages retain the plate numbers preceded by D. S. (that is, Durand et Schoenewerk).

[4] For a list of errors in those scores, see David Craighead and Antone [*sic*] Godding, "A Comparison of the 1959 Durand and Kalmus Editions of Franck's Organ Works with the Original Printing," *The American Organist* 19 (April 1985): 56–58. (The plate numbers for the 1959 edition are: *Six Pièces*, 13791 and 13792; *Trois Pièces*, 13793, *Trois Chorals*, 13794.)

[5] Georges Lhôte, "Remarks on the French Organ," *ISO-Information* 1 (February 1969): 76.

[6] See the author's remarks on the "couleurs sonores" of Franck's organ music in the text accompanying his recordings of *César Franck: Douze Pièces et Pièces choisies*, 3 vols. (Motette-Ursina CD 11381, 11391, and 11401, 1991).

Widor
and His Contemporaries

"Why Should We Not Do the Same with Our Catholic Melodies?": Guilmant's *L'Organiste liturgiste*, op. 65

EDWARD ZIMMERMAN and LAWRENCE ARCHBOLD

Of all the leading French organist-composers in the last decades of the nineteenth century—César Franck, Camille Saint-Saëns, Charles-Marie Widor, Alexandre Guilmant, and Eugène Gigout—Guilmant was not only the most prolific composer of organ music, but the only composer who demonstrated a lifelong interest in writing organ works based on chant. For Amédée Gastoué, one of the leading French musicologists of the early years of the twentieth century and the first scholar to publish a genuine assessment of Guilmant's liturgical organ music, "if he was less brilliant in his compositions than Franck and Widor, he was also more liturgical."[1] Moreover, Guilmant's commitment to this genre cannot be equaled among French organist-composers of lesser rank. Yet his works of this type, of which his most important collection is *L'Organiste liturgiste*, op. 65, have not remained in the repertoire. For the most part too modest for concert use, they are now largely obsolete for their intended roles as service music, and have not enjoyed the attentions of an attempted revival as have some of the composer's eight organ sonatas. Furthermore, Guilmant, an indefatigable recitalist, did not champion them in his own concerts, if his forty programs at the St. Louis World's Fair in 1904 are any indication.[2] These programs included many of Guilmant's compositions, both large and small. While he performed many liturgical pieces—generic *prières*, *élévations*, and *offertoires*—the closest he came to playing an actual chant-based piece was the *Lamentation*, op. 45, no. 1, which concludes with a brief quotation of *Jerusalem, Jerusalem convertere ad Dominum Deum tuum* (whose appearance is justified programmatically rather than liturgically), and the *Impression grégorienne*, op. 90, which does not actually quote a chant melody at all.

To understand *L'Organiste liturgiste* one must turn rather to Guilmant the organist of La Trinité, a post he held from 1871. In that year he was called to Paris from Boulogne-sur-mer where he was born in 1837. (At La Trinité he replaced Charles-Alexis Chauvet who had died at an early age.) He held that post until 1901, when he resigned in protest over the rebuilding, carried out in his absence, of the Cavaillé-Coll organ there.[3] Like Franck at Sainte-Clotilde and Widor at Saint-Sulpice, Guilmant attracted considerable attention for his liturgical organ playing. His duties were similar to theirs, and were described by William C. Carl (founder of the Guilmant Organ School in New York) as "to play the prelude, offertory, postlude and incidental music on the grand organ during the mass. At vespers he improvised the interludes, of which there were many, besides playing the set pieces."[4] According to many reports, Guilmant took his calling as a church organist with utmost seriousness; this one from Frederic B. Stiven is typical:

> For thirty long years this greatest of organists was at his organ every Sunday, except when he was on his concert-tours; and he entered into his work with a devotion and a religious fervor that is all too rare.[5]

A. M. Henderson, more than twenty-five years after Guilmant's death, recalled many details of Guilmant's playing during a Sunday morning service during his last year at La Trinité:

> The opening prelude and interludes were improvised, in most impressive church-like style; quite as fine, I thought, as his best published work. At the Offertory, he played the lovely Allegretto from Franck's Fantasia in C, which was then new to me. His Postlude was the noble Prelude in E flat by Bach, which was ever one of Guilmant's favourites. (It opened his recitals at the World's Fair.) The whole performance impressed me deeply, and I did not forget to express my gratitude to Guilmant for his kindness inviting me to join his small company. Never before had I heard organ-playing so finished, so accurate, so alive, and above all, so musical. It is a model which has remained with me in all the intervening years.[6]

Improvisation was an integral part of Guilmant's service playing, and his powers in this art were legendary. Wallace Goodrich (who in 1917 published *The Organ in France*, a book which was undoubtedly definitive for its day and is still useful seventy years after its publication) upon Guilmant's death in 1911 expressed a preference for his improvisations on liturgical melodies:

> In the Roman Catholic Church in France artistic improvisation is not only cultivated, but is indispensable, and for many years Guilmant's improvisations have been noted. We heard examples of his power in this line in the various concerts that he gave in this country [the United States], although it must be acknowledged that the themes on which he was asked to improvise were often of a type less fitted to display his best qualities than the ecclesiastical melodies upon which it was his habit to improvise in the regular church services in Paris.[7]

In another memorial essay, Guilmant's liturgical compositions were singled out for praise by one of his students:

It must be frankly stated that Guilmant wrote too much for his abiding reputation. Some of his finer compositions are seldom played, and his harmonic and contrapuntal skill are perhaps best displayed in compositions based on plainsong and designed chiefly for use in the service of the church—in which he worshipped devoutly.[8]

An observation by André Cœuroy regarding Guilmant that:

One of his chief claims to glory is his revival of the cult of the liturgical organ by his masterly improvisations on Gregorian themes in the service (his *Versets d'Hymnes* in Op. 65 keep alive a splendid echo of these), . . . [9]

suggests that some, perhaps many, of these liturgical compositions praised by various observers in Guilmant's era were improvisations which had gained second life in *L'Organiste liturgiste*.

Guilmant summarized his views of liturgical organ music late in his career in "Du rôle de l'orgue dans les offices liturgiques," published in 1895 by the Schola Cantorum, which Guilmant himself had helped to found, in their newly established journal, *La Tribune de Saint-Gervais*:

In our services, the *grand-orgue* is called upon generally to make itself heard in alternation with the choir: at mass, at the *Kyrie*, *Gloria*, *Sanctus* and *Agnus Dei*; at vespers, after the psalms; at the hymn, at the *Magnificat*. A certain number of organists have the habit . . . of playing small pieces [in *alternatim*] which have nothing in common with that which the choir chants, and that seems to me bad from a musical point of view because the melody ought to follow [the chant] in its rhythm and tonality. . . . It is necessary that, in the pieces which alternate, the organist play the Gregorian melody, or at least some versets which are based on these themes. I think that there are some very interesting things to write in the polyphonic style with the ancient tonalities [modes], and on these chants which are so beautiful. The German organists have composed some pieces based on the melody of chorales, forming a literature for the organ which is particularly rich; why should we not do the same with our Catholic melodies?[10]

The desire for a distinguished body of Roman Catholic organ music was not a new one: the call for a parallel achievement in contemporary Roman Catholic liturgical organ music to that of the Lutheran Baroque was sounded by François-Joseph Fétis early in the nineteeth century, echoed at mid century by his student Jaak Nikolaas (Jacques-Nicolas) Lemmens and critics of the state of liturgical organ music such as Jean-Louis-Félix Danjou, and is here reiterated at the end of the century by a student of Lemmens. More than Lemmens, and more than any other Lemmens student, it was Guilmant who honored that call with substantial collections of service music.[11] While he incorporated several examples of liturgical organ music based on chants in his earliest collections [the *Pièces d'orgue dans différents styles*, series 1 (ops. 15–20: twenty-four pieces composed between 1861 and 1866) and series 2 (ops. 24–25, 33, 40, and 44–45: twenty pieces composed between 1869 and 1875)], later in his career his organ music that was based on chant tunes and appropriate only for specific services was increasingly segregated in his publications not only from the concert repertoire but also the church pieces such as preludes, communions, and finales which did not employ chant tunes—what Gastoué called "pieces of religious inspiration"[12]—and thus had no intrinsic reason to be linked to particular feast days. (That whatever dividing line there might be between a "secular" slow movement and, say, a communion, or between a concert show piece and a "sacred" *sortie* was at best vague could not have escaped Guilmant's attention. Moreover, Guilmant never incorporated liturgical melodies into any of his eight organ sonatas, composed between 1874 and 1906, although Lemmens in his own sonatas had provided examples of this procedure in 1874, and in the 1890s Widor, who had also studied with Lemmens, based two of his organ symphonies—essentially his version of the organ sonata genre—on chant tunes.) A few chant-based pieces found their way into *L'Organiste pratique*, ops. 39, 41, 46–47, 49–50, 52, and 55–59 (fifty-one pieces useful in church services, composed between 1861 and 1883, but mostly in the 1870s). But in *L'Organiste liturgiste*, op. 65, that genre came into its own.[13]

The full title of Guilmant's op. 65 is "The Liturgical Organist, a Collection of Pieces based on Liturgical Chants, for Use in the Church, Composed for Organ (or Harmonium)." As the title implies, all its sixty items (and some are sets of pieces) are based on chant. All are suitable for church use, and Guilmant indicates precisely the service (or services) for which a particular work is intended. Like *L'Organiste pratique* (and the third series of the *Pièces d'orgue dans différents styles*, ops. 69–72 and 74–75), it is a retrospective collection: music from Guilmant's youth (from as early as the first years of the 1860s, that is, up to a decade before his arrival in Paris) is intermingled with works from the 1870s and beyond. For the most part, however, its contents are the work of the 1880s and 90s—years which mark the height of his career at La Trinité—and as such it can be understood as something of a successor to *L'Organiste pratique*, which was largely the product of the 1870s, and was destined for the same audience, the church organist of less than virtuoso rank. The significant difference between the two projects is Guilmant's definitive turn from a largely generic approach to liturgical organ music to one based on specific chant melodies creating music which was appropriate, in many cases, on perhaps just one or only a few days a year.

Guilmant's comments in "Du rôle de l'orgue dans les offices liturgiques" are also interesting because they give a specific idea of his conception of ideal *alternatim* organ music: that in which is heard the chant melody, its rhythm and modality. Because Guilmant almost always dated his organ compositions, and included those dates in his publications, it is relatively easy to construct a chronology of his published organ works; such a chronology reveals not only that his earliest chant-based organ pieces were modest versets suitable for *alternatim* use (rather than large-scale paraphrases suitable for concerts), but that while elements of this late ideal were present from the beginning of his compositional career, in his early years they were not often brought together in one piece. Furthermore, understanding how Guilmant's ideas regarding the use of chant in his organ music changed over the course of his career is significantly complicated by the fact that the prevailing conception of chant underwent profound changes during those years. Virtually all aspects of chant, including whether or not it should be made to conform to contemporary tonality, the speed at which it was sung, and the flexibility of its rhythm, came under intense scrutiny in France during the second half of the century. Benjamin Van Wye's assessment of Guilmant's chant-based organ works highlights the changing background against which they must be understood:

> Taken chronologically, they reflect the transition in French churches during the late 19th century from the corrupt and often unauthentic liturgical melodies performed in a slow and heavy manner to the textually authentic and rhythmically revivified plainsong restored by the Solesmes Benedictines.[14]

Thus to incorporate into an organ verset the rhythm and modality—even the notes—of a given chant tune might well mean working with strikingly different material in the 1860s and 70s as opposed to the last years of the century.

Compositions of the 1860s

The earliest pieces in *L'Organiste liturgiste* are the two versets and amen on a chant which serves a variety of texts including *Gallicæ custos* (for vespers for the Feast of St. Geneviève) and *Sæpi dum Christi* (hymn for vespers for the Common of a Confessor) from 1865 and the two versets on *Christe, sanctorum decus Angelorum* (for vespers for the Feast of St. Gabriel) from 1866. These works are the collection's only music from the 1860s and are the earliest examples of Guilmant's chant-based music organ which can be reliably dated. The first verset of *Gallicæ custos* proudly presents its chant tune, conceived in a firmly metrical guise, in a canonic layout; a hint of modal harmony at the close of its chant tune clouds an otherwise tonal context. The second verset begins as a trio with the chant theme in the bass and whiffs of canonic imitation in the accompanimental voices. But the commitment to trio texture is indecisive and the verset concludes, after more than its share of awkward moments, with a cadence in five voices. While it begins with harmonies, voice leading, and dissonance treatment typical of the Baroque, these traits eventually give way to a cloying chromaticism which lies outside those norms. The first verset of *Christe, sanctorum decus Angelorum* is another trio setting, this time one with a Baroque-like walking bass line, and the second verset a fugue with a dense concluding stretto. Both versets share with *Gallicæ custos* the prominent presentation of chant tunes in obvious, strongly metrical patterns, within an essentially tonal framework.

What are probably additional chant-based works from the 1860s—all *alternatim* versets for hymns and psalm antiphons—survive in the first series of *Pièces d'orgue dans différents styles*, ops. 15–20. While all of the contents which are dated in this series were composed from 1861 to 1865, it is precisely the four works which are based on chant (and the one set of modal amens) which are undated. Indeed, the earliest published organ works of Guilmant which are dated are from 1861 and more are found in this collection than anywhere else. While this first series of *Pièces d'orgue dans différents styles* shows that Guilmant was actively engaged in writing various genre pieces such as meditations, marches, and *pastorales* as early as that year, the chant settings of *L'Organiste liturgiste* demonstrate that he was writing chant-based works at least by the middle of the 1860s. There seems, then, no reason not to believe that the chant-based works in this first series of the *Pièces d'orgue dans différents styles* date from the same period as the other items in the collection.[15] That these undated pieces might be even earlier, perhaps from a time before which Guilmant began systematically to date his music, can only be conjectured.

The liturgical pieces in the first series of *Pièces d'orgue dans différents styles*, hymn versets for *Crudelis Herodes* (for vespers for Epiphany), *Iste Confessor* (two versets, each on a different chant tune, the first for vespers for the Common of a Confessor not a Bishop and the second for that of a Confessor Bishop), *Nunc Sancte nobis Spiritus* (for Quasimodo Sunday), and a psalm antiphon, *Alleluia* (for vespers for Quasimodo), demonstrate a variety of techniques. Each displays its chant tune prominently: the opening phrases of *Crudelis Herodes* and *Nunc Sancte nobis Spiritus* are the subjects of fughettas, while one complete statement of the chant is heard in each of the *Iste Confessor* settings (the first in the pedals as a tenor cantus firmus, the second as a *Récit en taille*). *Alleluia* combines both methods: beginning in a fugal texture based on its opening phrases, it concludes with a complete statement of the antiphon. In each case the chant material is conceived in a strongly metrical fashion. For the most part, these pieces are more tonal than modal: some of the chant fragments (as the opening phrase of *Nunc Sancte nobis Spiritus*) adapt with ease to a tonal setting; others, such as the two *Iste Confessor* chants, conform with more awkwardness; though the opening of *Crudelis Herodes* establishes a tonal style its chief cadence is Phrygian; the cantus-firmus style presentation of the complete *Alleluia* chant—a melody whose ending formula does not readily suggest tonal harmonization—in a tonal setting already established by the opening fugal passage necessitates some rather unexpected cadential harmonies. Some of these pieces, like the first of the *Iste Confessor* settings with its tight, busy counterpoint, are as evocative of Baroque style as their counterparts in *L'Organiste liturgiste*. But a work like *Nunc Sancte nobis Spiritus*, with its jaunty syncopations, full-fisted staccato chords, and virtuoso pedal part, declares its allegiance to the modern world of the festive *sortie*.

The earliest chant-based organ piece in *L'Organiste pratique* is the *Ite missa est*, op. 55, no. 5, dated 1861.[16] Ostensibly the earliest of Guilmant's dated chant-based organ pieces, there are many reasons to suspect the accuracy of this date. Guilmant usually inscribed alongside the date of composition the place as well; for all the works composed before his appointment to La Trinité in 1871 that place is Boulogne-sur-mer, except in the case of *Ite missa est* which was written in Paris. While it is perhaps not impossible that Guilmant was in Paris in 1861, his first Paris performance was in 1862 at the inauguration of the Cavaillé-Coll organ at Saint-Sulpice. That the date of this work is actually 1871 rather than 1861 is suggested by its place of composition and made more than likely by its dedication to "my friend Théodore Salomé," who became the chancel organist at La Trinité in 1869 and in 1871 was Guilmant's new colleague. Stylistically as well the work suggests an origin later than 1861. With its melody (from the mass *Orbis factor*) not made to conform to a modern D minor but in its original first mode and with a clearly modal final cadence, it is a more rigorous exercise in archaism than can be found in any of Guilmant's comparable works of the 1860s. Moreover, as such it looks forward to even more uncompromisingly modal pieces in the 1870s, such as the Mixolydian verset from the *Quatre Versets* of 1876 in *L'Organiste pratique*. Yet however old-fashioned the style of *Ite missa est* might be, its atmosphere is a peculiar one, for not only its fussy fugal texture but also its voice leading and dissonance treatment recall Baroque styles rather than genuinely modal medieval or Renaissance ones.

None of this music from the 1860s is particularly praiseworthy and cannot be excused merely as the fruits of Guilmant's youth, for by 1867 he was thirty years old. While it is perhaps surprising that Guilmant published this music, and at that alongside works from the 1870s, 80s, and even 90s (by 1900, did any of his organ music from his years in Boulogne-sur-mer still remain unpublished?), this curious penchant for promoting early works is a way in which Guilmant resembles his fellow Lemmens student, Widor (who likewise published what appear to be student compositions in his earliest organ symphonies, and did not hesitate to include them with more accomplished movements composed years later[17]). But despite the fact these works seem like student exercises, they do give interesting insights into Guilmant's early conception of *alternatim* organ music. Resembling in striking ways Protestant chorale preludes, with their emphasis on liturgical tune and motivic derivation, they testify to Guilmant's interest in that repertoire and especially that of Bach, undoubtedly encouraged, perhaps even instigated, by his studies with Lemmens, who was internationally famous as a Bach player. While reports of Lemmens's performances of Bach focus on his playing of the great preludes, toccatas, and fugues, it seems certain that some of Bach's chorale preludes were circulating among Fétis, Lemmens, and their circle; Fétis included several such works in his assembled but never published collection, *Le Parfait Organiste*.

Even as late as 1892, Guilmant was one of the few French organists who knew Bach's chorale preludes, according to Louis Vierne, Guilmant's student:

> Because of an inquiry made at the time among my young colleagues in the different schools I can safely state that except for [Widor], Saint-Saëns, Gigout and Guilmant, no one suspected the existence of these incomparable pages, the most original, the most daring, the most miraculously conceived of all the pages produced by the creative genius of the Cantor. Franck was acquainted with them, but did not require them of us any more than anything else.[18]

Vierne's enthusiasm for these works undoubtedly echoes that of Guilmant. In his 1898 article, "Organ Music and Organ-Playing," Guilmant summed up his view of Bach in similarly extravagant terms and also drew special attention to the chorale preludes:

> My admiration for Bach is unbounded. I consider that Bach is music. Everything else in music has come from him; and if all music, excepting Bach's, were to be destroyed, music would still be preserved. People who think of Bach as a composer of fugues, and imagine that because he wrote fugues and pieces belonging to that style of music, he was merely a dry, learned, musical arithmetician, are to be pitied. . . .
> But I find the heart of Bach in the chorales which he wrote for the organ. These combine in a wonderful degree exact musical science with the deepest feeling, and are grand objects of study.[19]

The influence of those "grand objects of study" was only beginning to be felt by Guilmant in the 1860s, and not surprisingly, it is the artifice of musical science rather than the aura of deepest feeling which is first apparent.

Yet Guilmant's debt to the German Baroque in his chant-based pieces is likely less deep than it might appear. Chant melodies in mid-nineteenth-century France were performed, in their tempo and metricality, such that they resembled in some ways chorales, in any case certainly more so than they would if performed, as they are now apt to be understood, as influenced by the Solesmes reforms.[20] Van Wye has drawn attention to French liturgical organ music from the first half of the nineteenth century in which "the chant appears in the soprano or the bass, its monotonous and ponderous succession of long note-values against a lifeless pseudo-contrapuntal texture" and has pointed to the corresponding way in which chant was sung "whereby each note was prolonged for roughly the same duration and the resulting accentuation of each note increased by doubling the voices with a serpent, an ophicleide and, sometimes, even a double bass."[21] Thus when Guilmant's setting of a chant tune seems to be in the style of a German chorale, this may reflect his native conception of chant as well as whatever notion of chorales he might also have acquired.

Moreover, Guilmant's knowledge of German chorale preludes—with their dogged concentration, as if by definition, on the presentation of their chorale tunes—is not the only way to help explain his preference for presenting the chant tune in each of his versets, nor is his likely ignorance, during the 1860s, of the many potential French Baroque models of *alternatim* organ music which even in their most distinguished examples by François Couperin and Nicolas de Grigny do not quote chant tunes in every verset.[22] Rather, Parisian liturgical requirements and traditions for *alternatim* organ music during this time suggest that Guilmant was closely following prescribed formats.[23] The first organ verset in the *alternatim* performance of a hymn, for example, was expected to present the chant tune while succeeding ones were not. This helps explain, as Van Wye has pointed out, why Guilmant often presents only a few, and perhaps even just one, such verset for a particular hymn.[24] As further versets did not require the presence of the chant tune, Guilmant seems to have assumed they could be drawn from other sources, or more likely improvised. Indeed, only a few of his *alternatim* sets provide enough versets for the complete performance of their chant. Later, to be sure, Guilmant's interest in versets without chant tunes was manifested in his *Soixante Interludes dans la tonalité grégorienne*, op. 68, of 1884. This collection anticipated others of this genre, today better known, by the two other leading organist-composers of this time who directed significant efforts toward liturgical organ music, Franck and Gigout. Franck's collection of fifty-nine short tonal pieces for the *alternatim* performance of the Magnificat, posthumously published as *L'Organiste*, and Gigout's *Album grégorien* and *L'Orgue d'église* (which contain hundreds of modal miniatures) are diverse yet eloquent testimonies from later in the 1880s and beyond of this tradition of *alternatim* music without chants. In retrospect, however, all these collections make Guilmant's abiding interest in the chant-based verset all the more striking. That devotion, already formed in the 1860s, was to endure for the remainder of the century.

Compositions of the 1870s

Guilmant's chant-based organ music of the 1870s which found its way into print appeared more or less equally divided between the second series of the *Pièces d'orgue dans différents styles*, ops. 33, 44 and 45, *L'Organiste pratique*, and *L'Organiste liturgiste*. This genre was not, however, the main focus of Guilmant's attention during the decade. While he likely improvised many such pieces during mass and especially vespers throughout the course of this his first decade at La Trinité, these were the years in which he composed the bulk of *L'Organiste pratique* (devoted chiefly to generic liturgical organ music such as marches, communions, and nöels) and the second series of the *Pièces d'orgue dans différents styles* (with largely similar sorts of works, but, conceived on an grander scale, perhaps even more reflective of Guilmant's own practice at La Trinité). In addition, the 1870s was the decade of Guilmant's First and Second Sonatas, his earliest works in this most ambitious of organ music genres. Nonetheless, Guilmant made a number of crucial innovations in his use and treatment of chant in his organ music during these years. What in the 1860s had looked like a genre restricted to modest versets for *alternatim* use became in the 1870s a widely varied field ripe with new possibilities.

The first chant setting dated in the 1870s appears in the second series of the *Pièces d'orgue dans différents styles*, op. 33; from 1872, this second of three versets for *alternatim* performance of the hymn *Verbum supernam* (for lauds as well as mass for Corpus Christi)[25] exhibits no new techniques but is decidedly more graceful than its predecessors of the 1860s. The modal character of the chant tune, heard as a cantus firmus in the tenor, is clearly compromised: the whole step which closes three of the hymn's four phrases (G-A in its original eighth mode) is consistently rendered as a half step supported by dominant to tonic progressions (G natural-A flat). As in so many cases such as this, what now seems like Guilmant's purposeful undermining of a chant's modality may merely reflect contemporary norms of chant performance.

Most of the chant-based pieces of the mid 1870s are more innovative. The two pieces on *Ecce panis* (the twenty-first verse of the sequence *Lauda Sion* for mass for Corpus Christi, also used in honor of the Blessed Sacrament) of 1873 from *L'Organiste liturgiste* are both modest verset style compositions, but labeled as elevations and not versets for the *alternatim* performance of *Lauda Sion*, they are among Guilmant's first attempts to bridge the gap between the chant-based *alternatim* verset and the other genres of liturgical organ music which were at the time typically not based on chant.[26] The second *Élévation* is also one of the earliest of Guilmant's published chant settings, and one of only a few from the 1870s, to carry harmonium indications in its definitive version. (That the whole of *L'Organiste pratique* was first published in a two-stave format typical of harmonium music but later revised and issued in a three-stave format appropriate for *grand-orgue* obscures the significant degree to which Guilmant was concerned with composing for the harmonium during the 1870s.) But the salient fact about the 1874 *Sortie pour les fêtes de la Ste. Vierge* on *Ave maris stella* (hymn for vespers for Feasts of the Blessed Virgin Mary) from *L'Organiste liturgiste* is not its scoring to accommodate harmonium performance but rather its form: no longer the modest size and scope of an *alternatim* verset, it is a sizeable composition in a musical form—scherzo and trio—far removed from the typical cantus-firmus construction of Guilmant's versets. Moreover, it treats not one but two themes (the trio section elaborates an alternative *Ave maris stella* chant). This significant work, from the year of two of Guilmant's most successful organ compositions, the First Sonata, op. 42, and the *Élégie-Fugue*, op. 44, no. 2, is the first herald of what later became Guilmant's rather frequent practice of combining several chant melodies in the same work; as such, it set the stage for the far grander conception of the *Marche de procession sur deux chants d'église* on *Iste Confessor* and *Ecce sacerdos magnus* (antiphon for vespers for the Common of a Confessor Bishop), subtitled *Fantaisie*, from 1875, published in the second series of the *Pièces d'orgue dans différents styles*. With this *Marche*, for the first time one of Guilmant's chant-based works can be placed, in substance if not in popularity, alongside his other showpieces in that genre, such as the popular *Marche sur un thème de Haendel*, op. 15, no. 2, and *Marche funèbre et chant séraphique*, op. 17, no. 3, both from the first series of the *Pièces d'orgue dans différents styles*. The latter, performed by Guilmant at the inauguration of the Cavaillé-Coll organ at Notre-Dame in 1868, did much to help establish his reputation.

While no new ground was broken with several small versets from 1875 and 1876 eventually published in *L'Organiste liturgiste*,[27] nor in the larger *Sortie pour la fête de l'Assomption de la Ste. Vierge, sur la prose "Induant justitiam"* of 1877 found in *L'Organiste pratique*, 1878 saw the composition of two unusually significant works: the *Grand Chœur en forme de marche, dans la tonalité grégorienne* and the *Communion sur "Ecce panis Angelorum"*, both found in *L'Organiste pratique*. The *Grand Chœur*, although not an actual chant setting, shows with its self-conscious modality the unmistakable influence of chant, and eloquently demonstrates yet another way of building bridges between the world of chant and composition in the modern genres. The *Communion*, another example which unites a standard nineteenth-century genre—the sonata-form slow movement—with chant, is an early but nonetheless polished demonstration of a technique that becomes familiar in Guilmant's later chant settings: the derivation of thematically significant florid passagework from a chant melody contrasted with a more straightforward presentation of the chant. This ostensibly Bachian procedure is here given a thoroughly Romantic realization. The opening arabesque of sixteenth notes in 6/8 time, while based upon the beginning of the chant melody, is not treated as *Vorimitation* but rather as the main thematic material of the first key area, G major, of the sonata form; only after a modulation to the dominant is the chant tune heard, as the "second theme" in D major—with the chant's modal qualities sacrificed for a thoroughly tonal rendition—in a cantus-firmus style presentation in dotted quarters. After a development based upon the opening ideas, the recapitulation brings the return of that material in the tonic as well as, in due course, the material of the second key area. A brief turn to the flat submediant balanced by delicate echoes of the opening of the first theme brings this charming piece to a close. So full of Mendelssohnian grace, it is certainly on a par with, if not actually superior to, the slow movements of Guilmant's organ sonatas; more than any other such work of the 1870s, it marks the maturation of the chant-based genre in Guilmant's hands.[28]

Compositions of the 1880s

In the 1880s Guilmant's fame as a church organist at La Trinité and concert organist in Europe continued to grow; while in these years his interest in composing organ music did not diminish, it gradually took on a different focus. Early in the decade he completed the Third Sonata, op. 56, and L'Organiste pratique, and by 1884 the Fourth Sonata, op. 61, and well as the Soixante Interludes dans la tonalité grégorienne, op. 68. But 1884 also saw a new emphasis: it was the year he took up in earnest the composition of the pieces which would become L'Organiste liturgiste.

This collection is organized into ten livraisons which were issued separately between about 1886 and 1899, and in them Guilmant continues his already established interest in supplying service music for organists of more modest abilities.[29] The pieces of L'Organiste liturgiste leave behind the virtuosic world of the sonatas and many of the Pièces d'orgue dans différents styles with only one exception, the elaborate Variations et Fugue sur le chant du Stabat Mater (in the third livraison), which seems curiously out of place. Guilmant grouped the contents of the livraisons according to liturgical events: for example, five of the eight items in the first one are intended for various Marian feasts and four of the six items in the eighth are for Corpus Christi. While some livraisons are more liturgically unified than others, none is devoted to a single feast or service, and there is no overarching organization which rationalizes the order of the contents. While the collection is not comprehensive—an unlikely project even for a musician as industrious as Guilmant[30]—there is nonetheless some duplication of effort: two offertories on Ave, Maria (in the first and ninth livraisons, written in 1886 and 1898 respectively) are both designated for the same liturgical function. As in Guilmant's chant-based organ music of the 1860s and 70s, the pieces are most often destined for use in the offices, particularly vespers. The majority of the chants set are hymns, with the cantus-firmus style in which the tune is heard once through in one voice (usually the soprano) with reasonably elaborate, sometimes motivically derived, accompaniments remaining the most popular; more unfamiliar genres from simple chant harmonizations (both metered and unmetered) to complex concoctions in which a variety of chants are treated together, and even simultaneously, receive increased attention.

If Guilmant had trouble deciding how to present L'Organiste pratique—for harmonium (or organ) on two staves or for organ on three staves—and eventually opted for the latter, his solution in L'Organiste liturgiste was to mix and match. The collection contains works unquestionably for *grand-orgue* alongside works clearly conceived for harmonium. A few of the works scored for organ even have alternative passages appropriate for the harmonium, and vice versa; one work, the *Sortie sur l'hymne "Creator alme siderum"* (fifth *livraison*), a prelude and fugue, loses its prelude when performed on the harmonium. It is clear, however, that Guilmant's interest in harmonium pieces was at its peak in the mid 1880s: while virtually all the music in the first *livraison* is scored for harmonium, as the contents of successive ones were composed (and in part compiled from earlier compositions) and published throughout the 1890s, the emphasis on harmonium works gradually decreases to the point that the last *livraison* has no such pieces at all.

During 1884, Guilmant composed nine items which were published in the first, second, fourth, fifth, and ninth *livraisons*. (While the ten *livraisons* appear to have been published in numerical order, their contents exhibit only a very rough chronological presentation.) Almost surely the first works since 1876 to figure in the collection,[31] they are virtually all for harmonium and (as would be expected with harmonium music) not especially ambitious. In them appear the same mix of *alternatim* versets and more extended pieces such as offertories and postludes familiar from Guilmant's earlier chant-based works.

The first work of the first *livraison*—also the first of the pieces from 1884— sets the tone of its collection. An immediately appealing, gracious work playable on either harmonium or organ, it sets an antiphon for the Feast of the Purification of the Blessed Virgin Mary, *Lumen ad revelationem gentium*, heard during the blessing of the candles before mass. This is not a work for *alternatim* use with the chant itself—an unlikely practice with such an antiphon—but rather an *offertoire*, presumably for the mass which follows the singing of the antiphon. Ingeniously cast in sonata form with the first two phrases of the chant treated as the first theme group and the remaining two phrases as the second theme group, it is altogether more substantial than Guilmant's typical *alternatim* verset. Rather, it embodies the approach to the use of chant already seen in more substantial works such as the *Sortie pour les fêtes de la Ste. Vierge* of 1874 and especially the *Communion sur "Ecce panis Angelorum"* of 1878, but in a smaller frame. There is no liturgical reason why this offertory should set this chant; it was Guilmant's idea to tie the antiphon, which belongs to a liturgy which anticipates this particular mass, to music for the mass itself. Instead of setting the actual offertory chant for the mass, Guilmant turns to one of the most melodious—and as the music heard during the lighting of candles, ceremonially one of the most memorable—of the chants for the day. Moreover, the second piece in the *livraison* is a *sortie* on the same chant (whose wooden Baroque-style metricalization of the chant melody only makes us value more highly the smoother rendition it receives in the *Offertoire*). Guilmant here only hints at an approach to service playing in which various more or less unrelated parts of the organist's duties—offertories, communions, and postludes as well as *alternatim* hymn versets—might be united through a kind of musical cyclicism reminiscent of Renaissance vocal masses in both elegance and arbitrariness. Dubbed "suites liturgiques"[32] by Gastoué, likely the first scholar to call attention to them, the use of such a liturgical *idée fixe*—what Gastoué in 1911 called a "thème générateur,"[33] with obvious overtones of Vincent d'Indy and the Schola Cantorum (which Guilmant helped to found in the 1890s)—yields more extended, and persuasive, examples in later *livraisons*.

The simplest *alternatim* versets of 1884 are also the most interesting: two new kinds of versets, both four-part harmonizations with the cantus in the soprano, appeared during that year. When the chant is heard in a strongly metrical rendition in quarter notes, set with common-practice tonal harmonies, voice leading, and dissonance treatment, they are evocative, in both sound and notation, of Bach's chorale style.[34] The first verset of the set on *Pater superni luminis* (hymn for vespers for the Feast of St. Mary Magdalen, ninth *livraison*), in a vigorous 3/4 time, is a striking example. Indeed, a few examples of this type from later years are even labeled "dans le style de J. S. Bach." Others find their inspiration elsewhere. Impossible to mistake for a Bach chorale, they are set apart aurally by harmonies consisting of virtually all root position chords heard in an unconventional syntax and visually by notation in old-fashioned half notes.[35] Only vaguely metrical, sometimes even without meter signatures and using bar lines as phrase marks, they mimic chant accompaniment in the style of Gigout's examples in the treatise on that topic by Louis Niedermeyer and Joseph d'Ortigue;[36] these sounds were typically associated with the modest *orgue de chœur*, and it is not surprising that the first example of this practice, the short unmetered first verset of the set on *Ad regias Agni dapes* (hymn for vespers for Quasimodo, fifth *livraison*), is scored for harmonium (see Example 1). Nonetheless, it points the way to much more impressive realizations of this ideal destined for the *grand-orgue* just two years later.

But not all the *alternatim* versets of 1884 are so starkly conceived. Surely

Example 1a. Gigout, beginning of harmonization of *Panis Angelicus* from Louis Niedermeyer and Joseph d'Ortigue, *Gregorian Accompaniment: A Theoretical and Practical Treatise upon the Accompaniment of Plainsong*, trans. Wallace Goodrich

Example 1b. Guilmant, beginning of first verset of *Ad regias Agni dapes* from *L'Organiste liturgiste*

the most sumptuous is the second of two versets on *Pange lingua gloriosi* (hymn for vespers for Corpus Christi, fourth *livraison*): unmistakably cast in French overture style with all its usual pomp and splendor, its likely model—the shorter *Wir glauben all' an einen Gott*, BWV 681, from Bach's *Clavierübung III*—is far more obvious today than in the 1880s. Gastoué, for whom this Maestoso movement was "very remarkable," accorded this work more attention than any other *alternatim* verset in his appraisal of Guilmant's liturgical organ music, seeing in it a valued example of Guilmant's inspiration reaching the realm of pathos.[37]

Guilmant took up the composition of *L'Organiste liturgiste* again in 1886, the likely year that the first two *livraisons* appeared in print, and contributed more pieces to the collection in that year than in any other. This burst of compositional activity was almost exclusively concerned with *alternatim* versets, and Guilmant's new sensitivity to the potential rhythmic subtlety of chant can be seen in several ways. The first verset of the set on *Sanctorum meritis* (hymn for vespers for the Common of Two or More Martyrs, fifth *livraison*) shifts back and forth between 3/2 and 4/2, its bar lines indicating the phrases of the chant rather than a regularly recurring pulse. Yet Guilmant's presentation of the chant melody is still quite metrical, clearly alternating strong and weak notes. Altogether more striking, the versets on *O quot undis lacrymarum* (hymn for the Feast of the Seven Sorrows of the Blessed Virgin Mary, third *livraison*) are expansive examples of the style observed in the first verset of *Ad regias Agni dapes*. Stark, rigorously modal harmonizations in half notes, with irregularly placed dotted halves and occasional quarters and bar lines restricted to indicating the ends of phrases, they not only carry no meter signature but, more importantly, genuinely avoid any reference to standard metrical patterns. While the first verset is essentially chant accompaniment, the second adopts that style to a *Récit en taille*. Eerily archaic, it resembles no actual past style of organ music.

The versets from 1886 demonstrate that, if during the 1860s and 70s Guilmant's versets were usually tonal in character with only occasional modal touches, by the 1880s the reverse is the case. In both versets on *Deus tuorum militum* (hymn for vespers for the Common of one Martyr, first *livraison*), for example, the prevailing Mixolydian mode is only momentarily disturbed by the introduction of a few accidentals; not even one such foreign element can be found in the entire set on *Exultet orbis gaudiis* (hymn for vespers for the Common of Apostles and Evangelists, first *livraison*), so pure is its Dorian mode. Indeed, to surround the chant melody with modern, chromatic chord progressions, albeit cleverly conceived, as in the second verset on *Ave maris stella* (first *livraison*), is now the exception rather than the rule.

The most remarkable of the all the sets of *alternatim* versets from 1886 is that on the sequence *Stabat Mater dolorosa* (for mass for the Feast of the Seven Sorrows of the Blessed Virgin Mary, third *livraison*).[38] At ten versets the largest such set Guilmant ever published, this most obvious of features—size—is not the most compelling reason for its distinction. Rather, a quality less easy to discern ultimately deserves more attention: unlike any other of Guilmant's *alternatim* sets, the *Stabat Mater* contains striking examples of text painting. This is in some ways surprising, for it is at odds with Guilmant's overwhelmingly conservative musical style, one based firmly upon the intrinsic qualities of music such as rhythm, harmony, form, and above all melody. Moreover, text painting is not a memorable characteristic of his earlier *alternatim* compositions. In other ways, however, it seems almost expected, a predictable reflection of Guilmant's intense—according to Gastoué,[39] in France unprecedented—engagement with Bach. Guilmant did not fail to notice the obvious examples of text painting in the cantatas and passions:

> His "Passion" music, for instance, is full of emotion. The expression in such recitatives as that describing the rending of the veil of the temple [in the *St. Matthew Passion*] is marvellous. At the same time, the music is extremely realistic. In fact, throughout the "Passion" music, recitative and chorus follow the action closely and give exact expression to the emotions suggested by the text.[40]

Guilmant gives a further example from the cantatas:

> Another dramatic number in Bach's works, to which I always like to call attention, is the F Minor chorus in the cantata entitled "Actus Tragicus" [BWV 106: "Gottes Zeit ist die allerbeste Zeit"]. In this chorus the alto, tenor, and bass chant a sad and solemn reflection on death, while above them the soprano part soars like a prayer breathing hope in the Saviour. In fact, in everything relating to the Saviour, Bach's musical expression is exquisitely tender.[41]

That Bach's consummate skill in the musical expression of a text should influence Guilmant's approach when setting a text so rich in emotion as the

Example 2. Guilmant, second verset of *Stabat Mater dolorosa*, mm. 1–4, from *L'Organiste liturgiste*

Stabat Mater, not to mention when facing the task of composing a set of so many verses to one chant melody, should not, then, seem unexpected.

Noteworthy examples of text painting can be found in many versets of the set. The unassuming first verset, which substitutes for the singing of verse two of the sequence, is in the unmetered, chordal style which resembles chant accompaniment; notated in half notes, it gives a simple yet solemn harmonization of the melody. The next verset, heard in place of the singing of verse four, "The Holy Mother, who was mourning and grieving, while she was seeing the punishment (pain) of [her] famous son,"[42] conjures up an ostinato sighing pattern, perhaps in response to "mourning and grieving" (see Example 2). The verset for verse six is the only one in the set to lie outside the prevailing F-major tonality; its quiet, chordal setting in D minor, heightened by the use of the Unda maris, may reflect the increased sadness—and more personal tone—in its text, "Who would not be able to be saddened to gaze upon the Mother of Christ grieving with her Son?"[43] More powerfully indicative is the chromaticism at the ends of phrase one ("saddened") and two ("to gaze upon"), for like all the rest, this verset is predominately diatonic. The next verset, for verse eight, "She saw Her own dear Son forsaken in dying while He released [His] breath (spirit),"[44] also exhibits similar word-specific chromaticism in the single, rather startling "purple patch" at "forsaken" ("desolatum" at the end of the second line of text, corresponding to the second musical phrase; see Example 3). The sentiment of the text changes dramatically in verse ten, and Guilmant's lush setting takes note: for "Make my heart burn from loving Christ, so that I may be pleasing to Him,"[45] a delicate Voix humaine as the cantus, accompanied by a soprano obbligato on the luxurious Flûte harmonique. The following verset, again a bold contrast, is a rugged, motivic *Grand Chœur* for a text which returns to themes of pain and suffering. For verse fourteen, in which the poet wishes to stand near the cross and to unite in lamentation with Christ, the verset recalls Guilmant's reference to the F-minor chorus in the *Actus Tragicus*: Bach's lower voices sing about death

Example 3. Guilmant, fourth verset of *Stabat Mater dolorosa* from *L'Organiste liturgiste*

while his soprano floats above in a song of hope; Guilmant's cantus is heard in the pedals on an ominous Basson while his soprano and alto are scored in sweet parallel thirds and sixths on the *Jeux doux*. The gently pounding ostinato in verse sixteen suggests the reference to wounding by blows in verse seventeen (which would have been sung by the choir). The most striking aspect of the verset for verse eighteen, "Having been set on fire, lest I be consumed by the flames, through You, Virgin, may I be defended on the Day of Judgment,"[46] is the arpeggio texture Guilmant made famous in the "Chant séraphique" portion of his celebrated *Marche funèbre et chant séraphique* (see Example 4). With the same dynamic level (*pp*) and highly unusual registration (Bourdon, Viole de Gambe, Voix céleste, Voix humaine, and tremulant), this memorable figuration and timbre evoke in both cases a beatific image not unrelated to the *In paradisum* of Fauré's Requiem. The final verset, reflecting its text, "When the body dies, grant that the glory of Paradise be given to the soul. Amen,"[47] returns to a simpler style, its calm perhaps suggesting that when death comes, the soul will find that peace with Christ in Paradise of which the text speaks.

Perhaps one reason Guilmant held Bach's chorale preludes in such high regard was the vibrant way they reflect the imagery of the texts they elaborate. While it is clear that Guilmant's colleague, Widor, was not aware of the text-painting aspects of Bach's chorale preludes until his student, Albert Schweitzer, pointed them out to him in 1899,[48] the evidence of these *Stabat Mater* versets makes clear Guilmant could posit a relationship between a word-specific style of text painting and liturgical organ music at least by the mid 1880s. (A relationship between scenic illustration and organ music, even liturgical organ

Example 4a. Guilmant, "Chant séraphique" from *Marche funèbre et chant séraphique*, mm. 1–2, from *Pièces d'orgue dans différents styles*, series one

Example 4b. Guilmant, ninth verset of *Stabat Mater dolorosa*, mm. 1-3, from *L'Organiste liturgiste*

music, was, as in the case of the notorious organ "storm" piece, altogether too easy for Guilmant to imagine, and one he avoided.) It is not only attractive to think, but reasonable to believe, that Guilmant understood Bach's use of text painting in the chorale preludes by the time he wrote these versets, and that his awareness of this crucial aspect of those works predated that of Widor by more than a decade.

Guilmant's registrations also deserve attention in these versets, for his careful indications for using the distinctive voices of the French Romantic organ enhance the text-painting power of his music. Vierne gives a telling description of his teacher's sensitivity to registration as professor of organ at the Conservatoire:

> Certainly the greatest thing he did for us was to draw our attention to the study and rational use of the different timbres. He was a "colorist" of the first water. . . . he discoursed endlessly on the all absorbing question of color.[49]

These *Stabat Mater* settings are Guilmant's most important demonstration that the "rational use" of the various tonal resources of the organ can include their role in helping to project the textual meanings standing behind the chant melodies, stripped of their words yet nonetheless eloquent, of *alternatim* versets. As with all the contents of *L'Organiste liturgiste*, Guilmant presents them as a tasteful model for the coming generation of Roman Catholic organ composers.

In the last years of the 1880s, Guilmant's interest in *L'Organiste liturgiste* shifted away from *alternatim* versets toward larger forms. The *Offertoire pour la fête du Sacré Cœur de Jésus* (fourth *livraison*) from 1888 is an especially noteworthy work: based on a fragment of an otherwise unidentified offertory chant in the sixth mode, another chant, *Auctor beate sæculi* (which Van Wye has speculated is an eighteenth-century Gallican office hymn[50]), makes an unexpected entrance; the two chants are treated in alternation but not combined with each other. Reminiscent of the earlier *Sortie pour les fêtes de la Ste. Vierge* which treated two different *Ave maris stella* chants, this work is another small step toward the more complex combinations of chants which characterize Guilmant's large liturgical organ works of the 1890s.[51] The surprising appearance of *Auctor beate sæculi*, however, is of more than local interest, for this *Offertoire* is the first item in a four-part "suite liturgique," one of only two in the collection which reach that size, based on *Auctor beate sæculi*. Dominating its *livraison*, this suite, consisting of an offertory, elevation (or communion), *alternatim* versets, and postlude, first plants its "thème générateur" in the unlikely locale of the contrasting middle section of the offertory. After this unexpected intrusion, the *Offertoire* recovers its poise as the opening material returns in predictable fashion, but the restatement grows increasingly epigrammatic as *Auctor beate* soon returns in a more fragmentary appearance. Tiny hints of first the opening motif and then of *Auctor beate* create an infinitely gentle close of which Guilmant must have been proud. The ending of the 1889 *Sortie sur l'hymne "Creator alme siderum"* (for vespers for the Third Sunday of Advent[52]), the conclusion of a three-part "suite liturgique," is special for a simpler reason: this noisy prelude and fugue calls for an unexpected diminuendo from *ff* to *pp* in its final measures, the only such gesture in a postlude by Guilmant. As such, this work looks ahead to Charles Tournemire's well-known penchant for postludes with quiet endings.

The sizeable Variations and Fugue on *Stabat Mater* (third *livraison*) from

1888, a work which would have been more at home in the *Pièces d'orgue dans différents styles* were it not for the fact that it, too, is part of a "suite liturgique," is the largest piece in *L'Organiste liturgiste* and seems downright enormous in context.[53] Its debt to Baroque music is evident from the outset: the chant tune, in a strongly metrical 3/4 version with an alternating strong (half note) and weak (quarter note) pattern, is announced monophonically in the manner of Bach's Passacaglia and Fugue in C Minor, BWV 582, and a ground bass format is soon securely established together with the key of E-flat major. Succeeding variations introduce more complex rhythmic figures, with Bach's Passacaglia never far from view. By the sixth variation triplet motion takes control; this climactic gesture happens much sooner than in Bach's example, and not only signals Guilmant's first important departure from his Bachian model but his impending shift to another: Buxtehude's Passacaglia in D Minor, BuxWV 161. (Guilmant, likely the first organist to play Buxtehude in France,[54] could have known this work, and others like it, from Spitta's edition published in the previous decade.[55]) After seven statements of his ground, Guilmant introduces a short modulatory passage exactly in the manner and at the same point in the form as in Buxtehude's Passacaglia; as in that work, the ground is now heard pitched a fifth higher (but Guilmant's placement of it outside the bass derives from Bach, not Buxtehude). The third variation in the dominant is especially archaic: a *bicinium* complete with sighing motive and old-fashioned slurring techniques, in which short slurs mark small note groupings in the manner of the Baroque "imitatio violistica" (which Guilmant examined in his momumental article on organ music for the *Encyclopédie de la musique et dictionnaire du Conservatoire*[56]) underneath long slurs to mark the phrases. The classical poise of Buxtehude's elegant scheme—seven variations in the tonic, seven in the dominant, seven in the mediant, and a final seven again in the tonic—is only fragmentarily reproduced by Guilmant; after just four statements in the dominant, another modulatory passage is heard, one which by way of some slippery chromaticism leads to the very Romantic gesture of a return of the theme at its original pitch but harmonized in the submediant. This subtle renunciation of Baroque models is soon made blatant as elaborate *a piacere* flourishes suddenly evoke the altogether modern sound of the nineteenth-century violin concerto. The ensuing fugue recasts the chant theme in 2/4, yet the parallel with Bach's Passacaglia and its concluding Fugue remains unmistakable. As in the Variations portion of the work, the Fugue begins in the Baroque only to escape its norms: by the dominant pedal, all pretense of historical pastiche is abandoned; a cadence hopefully fresh to Guilmant's ears but, despite its thematic justification, today tainted by Hollywood brings this muddled work to an end. Ultimately a potpourri of styles rather than a sustained exercise in conscious archaism, it establishes an uneasy balance between delicately `expressive figuration and gross rhetorical gestures. Harvey Grace was not the only observer to claim that "the composer's real strength lay in the smaller forms."[57] While this remains true if, as with Grace, one has in mind Guilmant's sonatas, it is even more true when considering the problematic genre of the historical copy.

Compositions of the Early 1890s

The last decade of the century saw the conclusion of Guilmant's activities as a composer of chant-based organ works; while his career as a composer of organ music extended nearly until his death in 1911, with the publication of the last *livraison* of *L'Organiste liturgiste* in 1899 this aspect of his creative life appears to have come to an end. Without question, however, this decade was the richest of all for Guilmant in the chant-based genre. Striking new techniques can be found in his music of these years as he responded to the radically new methods of chant singing advocated by Solesmes which began to come into their own at this time. Indeed, Van Wye has pointed out that it was only during the 1890s that French liturgical organ music was first influenced by the Solesmes ideas about the rhythmic interpretation of chant.[58] In 1894, Guilmant assisted Charles Bordes and d'Indy in founding the Schola Cantorum, and the activities of this new organization were an impetus for Guilmant's continuing composition of chant-based organ music. The Schola's journal, *La Tribune de Saint-Gervais*, not only provided Guilmant a place to air his views on liturgical organ music (as in his article, "Du rôle de l'orgue dans les offices liturgiques"), but also provided a forum for others to draw attention to Guilmant's own music. No other decade saw Guilmant experiment with so many different ways of setting chant tunes in organ music, and no other decade saw him produce as many notable results. Despite the fact that the Fifth Sonata for organ from 1894 (one of two organ sonatas Guilmant wrote during this decade) is not only one of his most successful but arguably his finest, it is only in the 1890s that the chant-based pieces occupy as large a place in Guilmant's *œuvre* as the free works. Moreover, the best of these chant-based works are not only Guilmant's best work from the decade, but in many ways his most original and significant contributions to the organ repertoire.[59] That virtually all the chant-based works of the 1890s appear in *L'Organiste liturgiste* is the most important reason why this collection is central to any consideration of Guilmant's accomplishments as a composer of organ music.[60]

The year 1890 is memorable in Guilmant's organ music chiefly for one highly unusual work, the *Élévation ou Communion dans le style de J. S. Bach*, a veritable *Choralvorspiel* in Bach's most melismatic style on the hymn in honor of the Blessed Sacrament, *Adoro te devote* (eighth *livraison*). The centerpiece of a large "suite liturgique" (one of the two biggest, including *alternatim* versets in the style of Bach's four-part chorales), it stands out as one of Guilmant's most expressive chant-based works. Indeed, the anonymous reviewer of the eighth *livraison* in *La Tribune de Saint-Gervais* found it to be "a marvelous page of profundity and delicacy of sentiment."[61] Historically significant as "the first nineteenth-century organ work to treat plainsong after the manner of Bach's chorale preludes with ornamented *cantus firmus* in the soprano,"[62] this work is an extreme example of Guilmant's urge to compose in archaic styles. As with the *Variations et Fugue sur le chant du Stabat Mater*, actual models lurk very close to the surface. Unmistakably reminiscent of the *Orgelbüchlein* chorales in size and scope, with a concentration typical of that collection the cantus of *Adoro te* is not anticipated by *Vorimitation* but begins immediately; while brief interludes in the accompanimental voices separate the four ornamented phrases of the chant, none foreshadows the coming phrase of chant. Since the chant itself (although classified in the fifth mode) adapts without alteration to the major scale, Guilmant's fully tonal setting is a logical, pragmatic solution. Its richly conceived harmonies, consisting largely of diatonic progressions with occasional chromatic passages of unusual poignancy, bring to mind the most celebrated piece in the *Orgelbüchlein, O Mensch, bewein' dein' Sünde groß*, BWV 622. So too does Guilmant's tempo of Molto Adagio and request for a rendition *Con grand' espressione*. Yet what looks on the page concise—*Adoro te* has only fifteen measures (most of which are in common time)—in performance is revealed to be more expansive. The extremely slow metronome mark (eighth note equals fifty) is plausible because both the prevailing harmonic rhythm at the sixteenth note (Bach's harmonic rhythm in these kinds of pieces is usually at the eighth note) and the frequent ornamental flourishes in thirty-seconds give the work what is, for Guilmant, an unprecedented density. As a result, *Adoro te* is more than a mere miniature.[63] Indeed, the opening of its second phrase is a direct echo of a memorable moment in one of Bach's largest such works, *Allein Gott in der Höh sei Ehr*, BWV 662 (see Example 5). While an embarrassment today, few organists would have recognized this similarity in the 1890s; it is more likely that this affecting work, which during the last years of the century may well have circulated more widely among French organists than Bach's chorale preludes, served to stimulate interest in its distinguished models.

This combination of chant with Bach's most ingratiating style of chorale prelude composition, successfully demonstrated by the *Élévation ou Communion*, did not engender subsequent examples; rather, Guilmant's two larger-scale chant-based compositions of the following year, the *Offertoire sur l'hymne "Rex gloriose, præsulum"* (for the Commemoration of all the Holy Sovereign Pontiffs) and the *Marche religieuse (Offertoire) sur l'hymne "Iste Confessor"* (both from the sixth *livraison*), took a radically different—and surprising—turn. They are among the only examples of Guilmant's chant-based works to call to mind the noël, a popular genre which occupied

Example 5a. J. S. Bach, *Allein Gott in der Höh sei Ehr*, BWV 662, mm. 9–10

Example 5b. Guilmant, *Élévation ou Communion dans le style de J. S. Bach*, mm. 3–4, from *L'Organiste liturgiste*

Guilmant's efforts throughout his career, from the two early offertories on noëls in the *Pièces d'orgue dans différents styles*, ops. 19 and 33, through the four volumes of *Noëls*, op. 60, to the two very late examples found in the *Chorals et Noëls*, op. 93. Of Guilmant's earlier works, the best example of this approach to chant is found in the middle section of his impressive *Offertoire sur "O Filii"* (hymn for Easter Sunday), op. 49, no. 2, from *L'Organiste pratique* (a work selected by Guilmant's student, Joseph Bonnet, for publication in his well-known *Historical Organ-Recitals* series).[64] Curiously, the chants set in these 1891 works—written within just days of each other during July—have nothing to do with Christmas; nonetheless, the chant tunes are made to sound like noëls and the pieces unfold as do noël variations. In the case of the *Marche religieuse*, Guilmant gives the *Iste Confessor* tune a gracious yet strongly metrical sense of movement, with a squareness of phraseology typical of noëls; gently vacillating with antique charm between modality

224

and tonality, the melody captures the naive, slightly wistful aura so characteristic of many noëls. Moreover, the textures of the work are reminiscent of the noël genre in Guilmant's hands and its variation procedure is standard for noëls both old and modern. In *Rex gloriose*, the chant, whose treatment is again reminiscent of noëls, becomes the motivic basis for a vigorous scherzo. More ambitious than the *Marche religieuse*, it charts unusually broad modulations, with a sense of security uncharacteristic of Guilmant, by the deft handling of chromatic harmony. One of the few instances in which a work by Guilmant calls to mind the music of Saint-Saëns, it is surprisingly similar in style to the seventh of Saint-Saëns's *Sept Improvisations*, op. 150, published some twenty-five years after the composition of *Rex gloriose*. As experimental in their own way as the *Élévation ou Communion dans le style de J. S. Bach*, neither did these two unusual works lead to further examples of their type.

The early years of the 1890s saw the last flowering of Guilmant's composition of *alternatim* versets in the styles which he had been cultivating since the 1860s, and these years contain what can be considered the culmination of that aspect of his career. (The all too few *alternatim* versets which Guilmant wrote, due to the activities of the Schola Cantorum, from the middle of the decade on reflect a radical new turn in his compositional style; examples of a new aesthetic of liturgical organ music more directly influenced than ever by the Solesmes reform of chant, they mark a daringly fresh start and demand evaluation on their own terms.) In 1890 and 1891, Guilmant wrote from one to five versets for six different hymns. As part of the "suite liturgique" that includes the *Élévation ou Communion dans le style de J. S. Bach*, the five versets on *Adoro te devote* (eighth *livraison*) not surprisingly feature versets marked "Choral dans le style de J. S. Bach." Written in 1890, the first of these in particular is a convincing evocation of Bach's four-part chorale style, and makes a noble verset for a hymn which, as in the case of the *Élévation ou Communion* which was written during the same year, is especially apt for Baroque style treatment because of its frankly tonal melody. The five versets from 1890 and 1891 on *Sanctorum meritis* (seventh *livraison*), like previous modal versets, approximate a common practice diatonic style—mostly in four-part chordal texture—but within a modal framework; in a transposed Dorian mode, there is only one momentary accidental in the entire set. The chant tune, however, whether notated predominantly in halves, with mostly quarter-note motion, or in quarters, with mostly eighth- and sixteenth-note motion, is as metrically square and rhythmically stiff as in the verset on the same hymn from 1886 in the fifth *livraison*. Yet, while no more pretentious than previous versets, they are especially smooth and refined; even in the canonic versets, Guilmant is completely at ease with this style of modal harmonization. Such mastery yields its most memorable results in the ninth *livraison* with the three versets for either *Quis novus Cœlis agitur triumphus?* (hymn for vespers for the Feast of St. Vincent de Paul) or *Iste Confessor* from

1891. With its majestic first verset and noble second and third versets featuring a variety of canons, this richly conceived work stands at the summit of Guilmant's achievement in the *alternatim* hymn verset.

By the end of 1891, the first six *livraisons* of *L'Organiste liturgiste* had appeared, and in the next few years, Guilmant's attention turned mainly to other activities: 1892 saw the completion of the third set of the *Pièces d'orgue dans différents styles*, ops. 69–72, 74, and 75, and 1894 the Fifth Sonata, while in 1893, he made his first concert tour of America, the first European organist to do so. Of the works which would later constitute the last four *livraisons*, only a few, such as the *Élévation ou Communion dans le style de J. S. Bach*, were already written, yet Guilmant apparently composed no chant-based organ music in 1892. In the following year he wrote only one work destined for *L'Organiste liturgiste*, a single verset and amen on *Salutis humanæ sator* (hymn for vespers for Ascension, ninth *livraison*). Returning to this chant which during 1875 and 1876 had been given two verset settings in an altogether simpler style for *L'Organiste pratique*, Guilmant composed a densely figural piece—as much "dans le style de Bach" as the *Élévation ou Communion*—redolent of the *Orgelbüchlein* and even more so of Alexandre-Pierre-François Boëly's copies of that style, especially as found in some of his *Quatorze Préludes sur des cantiques de Denizot*, op. 15, both of which collections Guilmant knew well. As is the case with several examples in the *Orgelbüchlein* itself, this quintessentially Baroque style here adorns a modal chant tune. An effective setting, it is a far more rigorous—and convincing—copy of German models than *alternatim* versets from the 1860s and 70s which, in comparison, only hint at eighteenth-century Lutheran forebearers. The amen which follows this verset is interesting, too, for it is the first case in *L'Organiste liturgiste* in which Guilmant ends a chant piece with an open fifth chord, evoking with this solemn sonority a very different past from that of the verset. All this suggests that Guilmant was far from settled at the beginning of the 1890s regarding an appropriate style for *alternatim* versets. A remarkable variety of genuine and fabricated archaic styles had been or were being explored, their common ground not only the effort to evoke the past but also the conception of chant as essentially a cantus firmus rather than a swiftly flowing melody.

Compositions of the Late 1890s

After a hiatus of six years, Guilmant returned to the publication of *L'Organiste liturgiste* in 1897 with the seventh *livraison*. It opens with the *Vêpres de la fête de Ste. Cécile*, a set of five contra-antiphons for the psalms, two *alternatim* versets and an amen for the hymn *Jesu corona virginum*, a contra-antiphon for the Magnificat, and an ambitious *Sortie dans le style de Bach sur l'antienne*

"*Cantantibus organis*" (the antiphon of the first of the five contra-antiphons). Only the *Sortie* is given a date: 6 November 1896. The proximity of 6 November to Saint Cecilia's Day, 22 November, suggests that it marks the conclusion of the composition of the *Vêpres* as a whole, for the anonymous reviewer of the seventh *livraison* in the September 1897 issue of *La Tribune de Saint-Gervais* claimed that this group of pieces was written for a special Saint Cecilia's Day vesper service sung by the Chanteurs de Saint-Gervais at Honfleur.[65] Some or all of these pieces, however, may owe their inspiration to another Saint Cecilia's Day vesper service, this one at Saint-Gervais in 1895, given in honor of the Schola Cantorum, which was reported in the November 1895 issue of *La Tribune de Saint-Gervais*:

> Our First Vespers of Saint Cecilia and Benediction
> The ceremony which was given at Saint-Gervais for the benefit of our work, on the eve of the Feast of Saint Cecilia, was as remarkable for the demeanor of the interpretation as for the choice of the pieces which were performed.
> After the *Deus in adjutorium* of Vittoria, the Gregorian antiphons of first vespers of the Feast of Saint Cecilia alternated with the psalms sung in fauxbourdon, borrowed from formulas of the old masters. The contra-antiphons were played on the *grand-orgue* by M Guilmant.[66]

The reviewer of the seventh *livraison* characterized these pieces as "constituting in themselves an entire doctrine" for as a didactic example of the Schola Cantorum credo, "the improvement of the repertoire of organists, from the point of view of its union with Gregorian melodies and its adaptation to various services,"[67] the *Vêpres* clearly was geared toward the aesthetic principles of that newly-founded organization. Moreover, its allegiance is made even clearer by its dedication to Bordes, chief instigator of the Schola Cantorum, the choirmaster of Saint-Gervais, and director of the Chanteurs de Saint-Gervais (a group essentially independent of Saint-Gervais itself); Bordes participated in both the services which have been linked to Guilmant's creation of the work.

Guilmant's five psalm antiphons are to be heard in place of the repetition of the psalm antiphon after the singing of the psalm itself and thus, as Van Wye suggests, are best termed contra-antiphons. They are all based on the chant tune of the antiphon they replace and represent, as Van Wye has pointed out, a new role for the chant-based verset, for ceremonial directions as well as the published repertoire of antiphon versets strongly suggest that psalm antiphons were not usually based upon chant tunes.[68] Indeed, only one of Guilmant's chant-based pieces before the 1890s, the early *Alleluia* from the *Pièces d'orgue dans différents styles*, op. 17, elaborates a psalm antiphon. Stylistically, these pieces also announce a new direction; indeed, for Gastoué, Guilmant in these pieces "resolutely broke" with his previous practice.[69] Van Wye has drawn attention to the fact that in these works "the rhythmic shape of each plainsong is always fairly supple . . ."[70] and this suppleness is noticeably more sophisticated than in Guilmant's earlier chant-based works, featuring a new kind of vocality which begins to capture the gracious lyricism of the Solesmes interpretation of chant. Harmonically, these pieces are also innovative, for while as in many earlier versets the modality of the chant melody is maintained and the chords remain within the modal scale, here Guilmant explores a new approach to modal composition. His standards of part writing—strict and supremely correct—so evident in his other versets, here occasionally give way, despite the fact that all five of these contra-antiphons are imitative in style, to a more casual treatment. The results are striking. In the first contra-antiphon, *Cantantibus organis*, heard *ff* on the *Grand Chœur* registration, Guilmant abandons the integrity of the part writing, securely established by its four-part fugato style, during the final pedal point with a wash of harmonies unimaginable in his earlier versets. This breathtaking climactic gesture—a final block chord harmonization of the first phrase of the chant—breaks free of traditional harmonic syntax and, with daring parallel ninths which tantalizingly hint at the harmonic style of composers like Debussy and Ernest Chausson, casts an unexpected element of awe over the work (see Example 6). More remarkable still is the fifth contra-antiphon, *Triduanas*, which, while also rigorously imitative in style, never properly establishes the integrity of its part writing; in this verset, like the first a *Grand Chœur*, voices even move in majestic parallel octaves. With diatonic scales of extraordinary scope charting its heights and depths and an imposing open-fifth cadence at its close, this miniature work despite its size reaches for the sublime (see Example 7).

The two *alternatim* versets for the hymn *Jesu corona virginum* are an even more radical departure. Van Wye has aptly summed up their salient qualities:

> In them, the plainsong—first in the soprano, then in the tenor—is notated with eighth notes, the beaming of which corresponds to the neumatic groupings of the original, and a dotted eighth or quarter note for the end of each phrase. The rhythmic freedom of the melody thus notated defies a regular metrical scheme and closely approximates chanting according to Dom

Example 6. Guilmant, *Cantantibus organis*, mm. 18–24, from *Vêpres de la fête de Ste. Cécile* from *L'Organiste liturgiste*

Example 7. Guilmant, *Triduanas* from *Vêpres de la fête de Ste. Cécile* from *L'Organiste liturgiste*

Example 8a. Guilmant, *Jesu corona virginum*, mm. 1–3, from *Vêpres de la fête de Ste. Cécile* from *L'Organiste liturgiste*

Example 8b. Lhoumeau, chant harmonization from "De l'accompagnement du chant grégorien"

Pothier's rhythmic interpretation. The resultant harmonies of these contrapuntal settings are derived exclusively from the mode of the liturgical melody (Hypodorian), and the harmonic rhythm follows the characteristic grouping of two and three notes.[71]

These two eloquent versets surpass the psalm contra-antiphons as reflections of Solesmes style chanting, and establish an altogether new ideal for *alternatim* hymn versets. Moving beyond chant accompaniment in the Niedermeyer style, they suggest comparison with contemporaneous methods such as Fr. A. Lhoumeau's Schola-sanctioned approach which appeared in the October 1898 issue of *La Tribune de Saint-Gervais* (see Example 8).[72]

The contra-antiphon for the Magnificat is perhaps the least radical of all these versets. While it resembles the psalm contra-antiphons in size, scope, and a striving for splendor, its busy sixteenth-note passagework, absent in the psalm contra-antiphons, betrays the influence of the Baroque figural style. Yet another *Grand Chœur*, could the prevalence of that registration, along with the indication for a Nazard in the second psalm contra-antiphon and a Cromorne in the second hymn verset, be a result of a connection between this music and Saint-Gervais with its eighteenth-century organ?

The *Sortie dans le style de Bach*, which concludes the group for the Feast of Saint Cecilia, like the *Élévation ou Communion dans le style de J. S. Bach*, is another pastiche of Bachian procedures. By elaborating the same chant, *Cantantibus organis*, as does the first of the psalm contra-antiphons, this large-scale fugue ties together the extremities of the set and creates something of a "suite liturgique." But unlike the contra-antiphon, the *Sortie* does not feature a modal setting; rather, the fugue subject outlines A minor. Perhaps because this piece is not obviously modeled on a specific Bach work, it is full of the most predictable kinds of Baroque routines. (The minor ninth and its resolution over the extended dominant pedal does, however, bring to mind the parallel moment in the Fugue in A Minor, BWV 559, from the so-called *Eight Little Preludes and Fugues*.) Predictable, too, is how by its close the level of rhetorical power exceeds Baroque norms; the thickly scored chords, heard *fff* in a high register, demonstrate what is effective on a Cavaillé-Coll rather than on a Silbermann, or even on the Clicquot at Saint-Gervais. But more importantly, this piece, in which that aura of elegant discourse which Baroque fugal texture provides is abandoned in favor of the sort of blunt affirmation which only block chords can deliver, appears thereby to abuse, as well as merely use, early styles. Yet this very stylistic inconsistency also signals that Guilmant was interested in something more than the blind worship of old materials, for precisely because of its bombast this ending declares that the *Sortie*, while in an antique style, is not actually of the antique world. What is disappointing is that Guilmant was obviously satisfied with a result this vulgar, an example of the pomposity which all too often characterizes his big organ works not based on chants. More sophisticated ways of uniting old styles with modern composition, such as the ironic detachment of Saint-Saëns's engagement with fugue, let alone the transforming power of Franck's engagement with chorales, were apparently beyond Guilmant's reach.

Regretably, Guilmant composed few subsequent versets in the new style of the *Vêpres de la fête de Ste. Cécile*: the only example in *L'Organiste liturgiste* is the beautifully crafted miniature verset and amen from 1898 on *Miris modis repente liber* (hymn for vespers for the Feast of St. Peter's Chains, ninth *livraison*). Guilmant's last published *alternatim* verset, it is a precious clue suggesting that the impressive sounds first heard in the *Vêpres* were not confined to special Schola Cantorum services but became a feature of his service playing in the last years of his tenure at La Trinité. Perhaps it was hearing works like *Miris modis* there in 1901 that made Guilmant's "impressive church-like style" so memorable to Henderson; and while Carl's claim that *L'Organiste liturgiste* "was written while at La Trinité" is largely but not completely accurate, there is no reason to doubt his report that its contents were used there by Guilmant.[73]

The Schola Cantorum, however, took note of Guilmant's achievement in the *Vêpres* and in 1897 announced a competition for a similar set of versets for Feasts of the Blessed Virgin Mary; though apparently no work was published as a result of this particular call, the Schola did begin a notable series of publications of vesper organ music along the lines of Guilmant's collection, entitled *Les Vêpres du commun des saints*, with one by Guilmant, the *Premières Vêpres des apôtres et des évangélistes*, composed in December of 1897 in New York during Guilmant's second American concert tour, leading the way.[74] This unjustly obscure work joined sets by more distinguished composers, including those by Chausson and Guy Ropartz from 1898 and d'Indy from 1899, to form a rarified group of liturgical organ music based on the ideals of the Schola Cantorum. Somewhat smaller in scope than the *Vêpres de la fête de Ste. Cécile*, the collection contains the usual five psalm contra-antiphons plus one for the Magnificat. While none of its movements quite achieves the grandeur of the first or fifth such contra-antiphons from the earlier vesper set, they are fully the equal of the earlier second, third, and fourth antiphons. Indeed, the third contra-antiphon of the *Premières Vêpres*, *Vos amici mei estis*, with its free treatment of sevenths, is perhaps the most poetic of all these contra-antiphons. Interesting also are the registration schemes shared by these two sets of five contra-antiphons: in both cases the first contra-antiphon is heard on the *Grand Chœur*; the second on Flûtes 8 and 4 (or with the addition of the Nazard); the third on Gambes (or Gambe and Bourdon); the fourth on Flûtes 8 and 4 (or *Fonds doux* 8 and 4); the fifth on the *Grand Chœur* or the *Plein Jeu*. The striking similarity of these registrations suggest the possibility that they might preserve—at least in their broad outline—something of Guilmant's habitual practice.

Another product of Guilmant's American tour during 1897 and 1898 was the *Offertoire pour le commun des confesseurs non pontifes*, op. 87, written in Chicago in January of 1898. This work is noteworthy chiefly because in it Guilmant brought his new style of setting chant in organ music—as illustrated above all in the second, third, and fourth psalm contra-antiphons of the *Vêpres de la fête de Ste. Cécile* (as well as their counterparts in the *Premières Vêpres des apôtres et des évangélistes*)—into the significantly larger frame of the *offertoire*. With its accent on the sensitive rendition of chant in a gracious, lyrical style alternating duple and triple movement, this work looks ahead to the more significant offertories of the ninth and tenth *livraisons*, and in particular to that based on *Ave, Maria*, which Guilmant composed during the remainder of 1898 and 1899.

During the last years of the century Guilmant continued to compose important new organ works as his professional stature, already immense, was further enhanced by his appointment in 1896 as professor of organ at the Conservatoire. Responding to the ascendancy of the Solesmes style of chant singing, he reformed the chant-related portion of the Conservatoire organ examination, requiring students to improvise on chant tunes "accompanied at first as in church, no longer 'note-for-note,' but in a broader style, admitting melodic ornaments, such as embellishments and passing notes, with chords falling on the principal notes." Moreover, reflecting his own recent compositions such as the *Vêpres de la fête de Ste. Cécile* and the *Élévation ou Communion dans le style de J. S. Bach*, students could "choose between a free prelude built on one or more fragments of the chant and a chorale embellished in the style of Bach."[75] In 1897 he completed the Sixth Sonata, op. 86, the same year he began his second American tour. It was also during that year that the publication of *L'Organiste liturgiste* resumed with the seventh *livraison*; the first issued since 1891, by 1899 all ten of the collection's *livraisons* were in print. In order to complete *L'Organiste liturgiste*, Guilmant turned for the last time to the composition of chant-based works, and a half-dozen sizeable pieces—four offertories, a postlude, and a *Deo gratias* (likely intended as a postlude)—were written during 1898 and 1899. Gastoué saw in these works the crown of Guilmant's achievement in liturgical organ music; while his prediction that it would be by these pieces that Guilmant's reputation would survive has not proven true,[76] these last pieces of op. 65 do contain some of Guilmant's most original and provocative organ music.

The first of these works, from March 1898, is the *Offertoire* based on two fragments of *Afferentur regi virgines* (offertory for mass for the Common of a Virgin Martyr, ninth *livraison*). With its chant melodies heard in lyrically flowing eighth notes, it provides continuing evidence of the impact of the Solesmes reforms on Guilmant's liturgical organ music. That influence, which characterizes the versets of the *Veprês de la fête de Ste. Cécile*, is first observable in the larger genres (offertories, communions, and sorties) in the *Communion sur le chant de l'hymne "Placare Christe servulis"* (for vespers for the

Feast of All Saints, seventh *livraison*), written in 1895, the same year as the Saint Cecilia Day's vesper service at Saint-Gervais. Despite its theatricality, the *Communion* is important not only as an instance of an extended work treating chant in the new style but also as the immediate predecessor of the *Offertoire*.

Afferentur is not only a more complex case of the kind of chant setting found in the *Communion* but is also a more sophisticated example of the technique, observed earlier in the 1874 *Sortie pour les fêtes de la Ste. Vierge* (based on two different *Ave maris stella* chants) and the 1888 *Offertoire pour la fête du Sacré Cœur de Jésus* (also based on two chants), in which an expansive A-B-A form is used for a work with two chant themes. In those two earlier examples, each chant melody is relegated to its own section of the form, with the ending of the 1888 *Offertoire* the only exception to that practice. That passage, in which fragments of the two chant melodies are heard several times in close proximity (but not contrapuntally combined) is a precedent for the procedure in *Afferentur*, where both chant fragments are heard in each section. As in the 1884 *Offertoire sur l'antienne "Lumen ad revelationem gentium"*, in which within a sonata design one phrase of chant was treated as a first theme and another as a second theme, the first chant fragment in *Afferentur* opens the work in the tonic (D minor) and after a bridge passage the second chant fragment is heard in the dominant (A minor). Significantly, however, in *Afferentur* this "second theme area" is not the exclusive domain of the second chant fragment; the first chant fragment is soon heard, and the impression of sonata form fades. Indeed, this first large section of *Afferentur* ends in the tonic, with a very brief yet haunting recall of the second chant melody over a tonic pedal which makes the close especially stable (in fact, Guilmant indicates the possibility of concluding the piece at that point). The second section features the motivic development of both themes, here juxtaposed much closer than before, as the second theme in augmentation in the pedal is pitted against the opening motif of the first theme. These thematic manipulations ride upon restless, occasionally preposterous, chromatic progressions and sway back and forth throughout the texture. (Could it be that this section was inspired by the work's composition "à bord de 'la Normandie'?") The abbreviated return of the opening section is predictably more stable harmonically (both themes appear in the tonic); predictable also is the return of the plaintive recall of the second theme with which the first section ended and with which *Afferentur* draws to its close. Important not only for the lyric style in which the chant is presented but also its formal manipulation of more than one chant theme, this uneven work sets the stage for the remaining large liturgical pieces of 1898 and 1899.

The *Offertoire* based on two fragments of *Ave, Maria* (offertory for mass for Feasts of the Blessed Virgin Mary, ninth *livraison*) written in May, is a less pretentious but more successful composition than *Afferentur*. Notable chiefly for its lyricism, it finds new ways to capture a yet more subtle rendition of chant. Within a prevailing eighth-note motion in 3/4 meter, Guilmant introduces occasional triplets (to be performed "very equally and tranquilly, more by holding back than by speeding up the movement") to enhance the fluidity of the chant melody. Formally more compact than *Afferentur*, it shares that work's overall three-part form, but with less clearly drawn formal articulations: beginning as a fugue on the first chant fragment, the tonic key is set up and the second fragment enters at the arrival of the dominant, by which point fugal procedure has permanently disappeared in favor of a more homophonic texture; the first chant fragment joins the second in the new key area, and modulatory developmental passages follow in which both themes appear; the return features both themes joined together without intervening material for the first time (though, following the example of *Afferentur*, they are not contrapuntally combined). *Ave, Maria* differs significantly from *Afferentur*, however, in the articulation of its tonality. In *Afferentur*, Guilmant treated the tunes with enough freedom to obtain clearly tonal thematic material and set that material in a well-defined tonal framework; in *Ave, Maria*, for the Hypomixolydian melody Guilmant proposes neither a modal setting nor an obviously tonal one, but instead an approach based on ambiguity. The first chant fragment, which begins on an F and ends on a G, using in addition only A, D, and E, does not convincingly outline any particular key; with its (real) fugal answer beginning on a C and including B natural, the unfolding fugue suggests Lydian mode rather than a major or minor key. It is only as the fugal rigor relaxes that an actual key (C major) is implied, but before it can be securely established, the modulation to its dominant is already underway. While not fugal, the recapitulation nevertheless reflects the opening of the work and begins as if in F major; it is not until the very end of the piece, with its concluding seven-measure pedal point on C, that the tonic is fully enjoyed. One of Guilmant's more sophisticated tonal structures, *Ave, Maria* suggests yet another solution to the chant-based work by its demonstration of how tonal ambiguity can be suitable for setting chant. Indeed, its shifting tonal implications produce a floating quality which is a particularly apt counterpart to the novel degree of rhythmic flexibility and grace found in its presentation of chant.

The *Sortie* (from the ninth *livraison*) on the last phrase of *Jerusalem et Sion filiæ* (an eighteenth-century Gallican sequence) and the opening phrase of *Terribilis est* (introit for mass for Dedication of a Church) written in July, is as forceful as *Ave, Maria* is tender. Guilmant, once again treating two chant themes in the same work, begins with a portentous if theatrical Andante maestoso introduction of nine measure's duration in which both chant fragments are heard *ff*; the first theme, with its opening pedal solo majestically reiterated in the manuals by block chords of traditional tonal harmony, is effectively contrasted with the second chant tune, in which, taking a cue from its text, "Terribilis est," modal harmonizations with barbaric parallel octaves evoke faux-medieval awe. This prepares a long tonal fugue, *alla breve* and at a faster tempo than the introduction, on the first theme; concluding with numerous stretti, it leads to a chordal harmonization of the entire *Jerusalem et Sion filiæ* sequence. The second theme, complete with its characteristic harmonization, returns as an epilogue ending a work which is imposing to the point of overbearing.

This work's most important model, however, appears to have been neither *Ave, Maria*, nor *Afferentur*, nor any other of Guilmant's pieces on two or even just one chant tune, but rather Gigout's *Sortie sur l'antienne "Adoremus in Æternum"* from the *Dix Pièces*, published in 1892.[77] Gigout's collection could not have escaped Guilmant's attention, for its opening work, the large *Prélude-Choral et Allegro*, is dedicated to Guilmant; while today the most famous of the *Dix Pièces* is surely the *Toccata*, Guilmant may well have been more interested in this *Sortie*, the one chant-based piece in the collection. Though based on only one chant (an antiphon for Benediction of the Blessed Sacrament) the format of Gigout's *Sortie* is remarkably similar to Guilmant's work: a solemn Grave chordal introduction, based on a fragment of the chant tune, sets up an Allegro *alla breve* fugue on the chant melody with notable contrapuntal manipulations; the fugue dissolves, after nearly the same number of measures as in Guilmant's *Sortie*, in favor of more homophonic textures; moreover, the closing gesture of the work is a powerful recall of the opening chordal passage. Guilmant's work is predictably less virtuosic, for unlike *L'Organiste liturgiste*, some of Gigout's *Dix Pièces*, including the *Sortie*, were conceived with a virtuoso organist in mind. Nonetheless, Guilmant's *Sortie* achieves as much splendor, if of a more rugged kind, as Gigout's piece, and, like few other works of *L'Organiste liturgiste*, brought to the world of the church organist of modest capabilities a taste of the musical pomp—as opposed to the mere practice—of the fashionable churches of the *grands boulevards*.

Written in December, the *Offertoire* (for the Feast of the Circumcision) on *Lætare puerpera* (a sequence to the Virgin, tenth *livraison*) is the most successful of all these works from 1898. In this spacious three-part piece, an opening "introduction" in sixteenth-note motion develops a motif based upon the opening pitches of the chant melody; a middle section, entitled "sequence," presents a harmonization of the chant tune in flowing eighth notes (the characteristic repetitions in the sequence's musical form—*aabbccdd* . . . —are omitted by Guilmant); a final section features the first four phrases of the chant in augmentation heard on the Trompette of the Récit amidst the opening sixteenth-note figuration. From the opening measure, this figuration insists upon the modal inflection of the chant's first three notes, G-F natural-G, within the tonal context of G minor, and from this tiny idea Guilmant spins forth an unusually suave melody of remarkably haunting lyricism. Remarkable, too, is the work's thematic integration. The opening diminution in sixteenth notes of the chant's head motive followed by the definitive statement of the entire chant melody at an appropriately slower pace calls to mind a similar procedure in the 1878 *Communion sur "Ecce panis Angelorum"* from *L'Organiste pratique*; this is despite the fact that in the *Communion* (like *Lætare puerpera*, marked Andante) the prevailing dotted quarters of the main statement of the chant move at a metronome mark of one chant note equals forty, reflecting earlier styles of chant singing, while in *Lætare puerpera* the chant in its definitive presentation moves in eighth notes at a metronome mark of one chant note equals 120, exhibiting the influence of the Solesmes reforms.[78] As with the *Communion*, the techniques of Baroque chorale preludes are suggested as well, though neither of these works looks back to a specific eighteenth-century model.

Yet *Lætare puerpera* calls to mind more strongly than any of Guilmant's other chant-based works one of Widor's remarkable compositions of these years, the *Salve Regina* from his Second Symphony, op. 13, no. 2. Like *Lætare puerpera* a striking mix of modality and tonality, this work was first published in the 1901 edition of op. 13 in which there appeared for the first time several new movements, this *Salve Regina* being the most notable; its exact date of composition is not known, but it was in all likelihood written during the 1890s as it exhibits Widor's most mature style, best defined by the *Symphonie romane*, op. 73, of 1899.[79] Whether Widor's work served as a model for Guilmant, or vice versa, cannot be determined; but there are so many similarities between these works that one seems very likely to have influenced the other. In both compositions, opening figural sixteenth-note motion is effectively contrasted with subsequent homophonic texture, and both works end with the chant tune heard as a solo line on a Trompette amidst sixteenth-note figuration. While these textural contrasts define a modest A-B-A plan for Guilmant and a more expansive A-B-A-B-A layout for Widor, the more important point is that both composers draw every section into the elaboration of each piece's chant tune. Revealing a deeper connection between these works is the uncanny similarity between certain parallel passages, such as the ending of Guilmant's first A section and the ending of Widor's second A section (see Example 9). Moreover, can it be sheer coincidence that Guilmant's "introduction" and Widor's opening A section each have seventeen measures? Although both formally and affectively more straightforward, and intentionally more modest, than *Salve Regina*, *Lætare puerpera* remains the best point of comparison in *L'Organiste liturgiste* with Widor's chant-based organ music of the same decade. That it is comparable at all with even one of the smaller examples of those works—music which, at its best, stands with Franck's *Trois Chorals* at the summit of the fin-de-siècle repertoire—is a telling indication of its accomplishment.

As for the two works of 1899, if on the one hand there is nothing particularly noteworthy about the extensive *Fugue et Oraison* on the *Deo gratias*

Example 9a. Guilmant, *Lætare puerpera*, mm. 10–17, from *L'Organiste liturgiste*

Example 9b. Widor, *Salve Regina*, mm. 32–37, from the Second Symphony

237

(tenth *livraison*) save perhaps its unusual title which anticipates comparable ones for several of the *pièces terminales* of Tournemire's *L'Orgue mystique*, on the other hand the *Offertoire (Fantaisie)* for the Feast of Pentecost which opens the tenth *livraison* is a very remarkable work indeed. Based on four rather than just one or two chant tunes, this *Offertoire* manipulates a greater variety of chant material than any other work in its collection: *Veni Sancte Spiritus*, *Factus est repente*, and *Confirma hoc Deus* (the sequence, communion, and offertory, respectively, for mass for Pentecost), and *Veni Creator Spiritus* (hymn for vespers for Pentecost). Writing three years after Guilmant's death, A. Eaglefield Hull called this piece "one of the most masterly of Guilmant's plainsong treatments."[80] This view remains a reasonable one for in this work an unusually rich array of thematic material is matched with an exceptionally powerful formal conception—for *L'Organiste liturgiste*, one of heroic proportions—yielding unexpected emotional depth.

As Van Wye has noted, the four chants, of which only the opening motives of those for mass are used while the hymn is heard in its entirety, "are stated individually, in pairs, and finally combined."[81] In the 1888 *Offertoire pour la fête du Sacré Cœur de Jésus*, Guilmant for the first time published, in Gregorian notation, the chant theme upon which the work is based inscribed just below its title (although for this particular piece, which is actually based on two chants, only the first is so given); when in 1898 Guilmant turned decisively to writing pieces based on two chants (or chant fragments) with works such as the offertories on *Afferentur* and *Ave, Maria* and the *Sortie* on *Jerusalem et Sion filiæ* and *Terribilis est*, not only did he include such quotations of the chant themes, but also labeled them by letter so that their first appearance could be noted in the score. No doubt because the four interwoven chant themes create an unparalleled intricacy as well as appear in an unusually complex design, in the Pentecost *Offertoire* Guilmant continued to label the themes throughout the work. In this way the contrapuntal combinations are announced (only the first two chants are actually heard simultaneously, first in fugal texture as subject and countersubject and then climactically within more homophonic texture); the labeling also points out the occasional fragmentary quotations in diminution which are tucked into the texture, as well as the whispers of the first, second, and fourth chants in the last three measures. Curiously, the various chants are quoted in different styles: *Confirma hoc Deus* is in the Solesmes-influenced manner of the *Offertoire* on *Ave, Maria* with lyrically flowing eighth notes (at metronome mark of one chant note equals 132, the melody is within a typical tempo range for chant settings of this type) while *Veni Sancte Spiritus* has too strong a triple-time swing to claim allegiance to the Solesmes reforms; exhibiting the most versatility, *Factus est repente* is heard both ways, and *Veni Creator Spiritus* is set like a chorale. As in *Ave, Maria*, triplet motion occasionally lends nuance to the lines, but unlike in that and previous works, a single chant melody can exhibit a bewildering variety of tempi (*Veni Sancte Spiritus*, for example, appears at five different speeds plus a final rallentando rendition during the closing Un poco Adagio). With the meter and tempo shifting between Allegro 3/4, C, and 3/2, and Andantino 2/4 so frequently—ten times in 168 measures not counting a Più mosso and the Un poco Adagio—the Pentecost *Offertoire* permanently establishes no single meter and the metrical flow is in flux to a degree unknown in any other piece from its collection.

Standing as a counterpart to the variability of the rhythm and tempo of the *Offertoire* is its freedom of form and harmony. The opening could not be bolder: a *fff* pedal solo statement of the opening fragment of *Veni Sancte Spiritus* whose pitches, B flat, C, D, and E flat, do not sufficiently establish a key; Guilmant appends a continuation that by introducing an A flat defines the excerpt as in E-flat major, but immediately gives the pedal line a wholly unexpected turn landing on an F sharp. At this moment, the manuals enter *fff* with a dazzling D-major block chord statement of *Factus est repente* with the sort of pseudo-medieval parallel motion and modal harmonization observed in the corresponding place in the introduction of the 1898 *Sortie*. Entered through a surprising chromatic motion, this harmonic parenthesis is left in a similar fashion as it twists to cadence on E-flat major. The whole passage is then repeated a fourth higher: *Veni Sancte Spiritus* now implies A-flat major but is deflected to a B natural which initiates a second statement of *Factus est repente* harmonized with G-major chords. This time the passage is extended and, with the collapse of the sequence, G major is firmly established as a dominant. With their exaggerated rhetorical level, these opening measures sound like an introduction despite their expository function and Allegro tempo. With the opening of the 1898 *Sortie* clearly its model, this passage remakes that gesture on a far grander scale and with an unexpected harmonic daring.

With a change of tempo to Andantino and dynamics to *mf*, *Confirma hoc Deus* enters in C minor as if a sonata-form first theme. This impression of sonata procedure is suggested by the power of the preceding massive dominant preparation, strengthened by the melody-dominated texture (very similar to the opening of the sonata-like *Offertoire* on *Afferentur*), and confirmed by the restatement of *Confirma hoc Deus* which, in typical sonata style, becomes a bridge to a new key area. This new area first appears to be G minor, but is then contradicted by the entrance of *Factus est repente* in B-flat major; this key is not established either, and by the time it becomes the the dominant of E-flat major the impression of sonata form weakens.

The surprising return of E-flat major is a springboard to a lively Allegro fugue with *Veni Sancte Spiritus* as its subject; a Più mosso soon adds *Factus est repente* as a countersubject. The prominence of E-flat major in these passages, which recalls that key's important role in the opening of the work, throws into question the tonal primacy of C minor; yet this impression is only temporary, for as one long crescendo full of intense working out of these two chant fragments, this fugue is formally a not too distant echo of a sonata-style development section. Harmonically unstable, it continues the swing toward flat keys until, with stirring sequences, G flat is reached and then reinterpreted as F sharp. A long dominant pedal on G ensues, pointing powerfully toward a return of C minor. But at the last possible moment a strategically placed A natural turns that goal into C major.

The formal gesture of the extended dominant pedal makes a recapitulation predictable, yet when C major appears (crucially weakened by its arrival in first inversion) so too does a new theme, *Veni Creator Spiritus*. Heard not on the expected *Grand Chœur* of the Grand-Orgue but rather on that of the Positif, it articulates a return to the opening Allegro tempo and leads to the definitive climax on the Grand-Orgue in which *Veni Sancte Spiritus* and *Factus est repente* are again heard simultaneously but in a different fashion: *Factus est repente* dominates the texture in its characteristic block chord harmonization with modal inflection as first heard at the opening while *Veni Sancte Spiritus* is woven into the texture as the tenor voice of a double pedal passage. While hardly a standard recapitulation (where is *Confirma hoc Deus*, the putative first theme?), this passage is nonetheless an harmonic resolution, in the sense that both *Veni Sancte Spiritus* and *Factus est repente*—the protagonists of the opening dialogue where they were heard in E-flat major and A-flat major in the pedals, and in D major and G major in the manuals, respectively—appear in the tonic. Fragments of *Confirma hoc Deus* and *Veni Sancte Spiritus* alternate with the remaining phrases of *Veni Creator Spiritus* as the climactic energy recedes; further diminuendo over a second dominant pedal on G finally leads to the brief yet definitive return of *Confirma hoc Deus* in its C minor Andantino guise, fulfilling its sonata-form destiny but unable to share in the major mode climax. An epilogue, Un poco Adagio, shifts one last time back to C major; in an evocative gesture of which the altogether paler close of the *Offertoire* on *Afferentur* provides but a remote precedent, it gently presents fragments of three of the four tunes—all but *Confirma hoc Deus*—in close succession: *Veni Creator Spiritus* is heard on the sweet sonority of the Récit's Voix céleste, *Veni Sancte Spiritus* on a Positif Flûte, with the last word going to a delicate echo of *Factus est repente*, the chief agent of the now-distant climax, on the Pédale Bourdons.

To Guilmant, the form of this *Offertoire* must have seemed radical indeed; today, what is striking about the piece is its testimony that Guilmant was capable at least once of aiming beyond his usual target—a style more or less indebted to Mendelssohn—and of trying out procedures characteristic of more progressive composers. If there is something vaguely Beethovenian about the piece's fugal development, there is more than a little trace of Chopin's *Ballades* in its treatment of sonata form, and a sizeable debt to Franck—from the *Pastorale* of the *Six Pièces* to the last of the *Trois Chorals*—

in its simultaneous combination of themes which were originally presented in sharp juxtaposition. Moreover, the oscillations between C minor and C major enrich the larger question of the precarious balance between C major-minor on the one hand and E-flat major on the other and their respective claims as the actual tonic of the piece; such harmonic ambiguity brings to mind procedures in Schumann and Wagner.[82] While the juxtaposition of Guilmant and Wagner might seem unexpected, Guilmant's affection for that music is documented by Carl:

> He was a frequent visitor to Bayreuth, where he gave two recitals. For years he would take the greatest delight in playing selections from "Tristan," "Parsifal," and the "Ring" to the friends who were entertained at his villa in Meudon. This all had its bearing on his writings, and kept him abreast of the times.

This *Offertoire*, however, is one of only a few of Guilmant's pieces which substantiate Carl's claim that "The influence of Wagner in his later compositions was apparent."[83]

Yet the most important innovation in the *Offertoire* is not its formal liberty nor even its harmonic license but rather the end result of those features, its genuine sense of drama. With histronic rather than dramatic qualities typical of Guilmant's large-scale music, the dramatic conception of this work takes on special significance. Moreover, to achieve its drama it does not rely on models so far afield as Wagner, but rather, more closely at hand, on progressive French organ music of the day and on another *offertoire* in particular: the *Offertoire pascal* of J. Guy Ropartz. Written in 1889 and published in 1895 in the second volume of the *L'Orgue moderne* series edited by Widor (which he later co-edited with Guilmant), this piece by a devoted disciple of Franck brings to the chant-based organ repertoire a sure handling of Franck's style as it was extended by the *Franckistes* like d'Indy and Ropartz—heirs not only of Franck's chromaticism but also his formal procedures—in the last years of the century. Ropartz treats only one chant tune, *Haec dies* (the gradual for mass for Easter Sunday), and like three of the four chants in Guilmant's Pentecost *Offertoire*, only the opening motive is heard. Ropartz's conception of chant is that of the slower cantus-firmus style which was still the norm in 1889; his conception of how to lead a composition to a powerful climax and artfully retreat from it reflects as well the norms of his day. Guilmant, for the most part a composer at least a generation behind his own time, seems to have found this unusual combination of an advanced compositional style and chant stimulating, for in his Pentecost *Offertoire* he mimicked Ropartz's piece in a number of important ways. Of comparable size and scope, the two works, after introductory passages, each engineer a long, broad drive to a powerful climax, followed by an extended, touching afterglow in which the music delicately fades away. Conceived like a big wave of musical energy, this syntax of gestures calls to mind, in its grandest realizations, Wagner and Bruckner but here appears in a comparatively miniature context. That Guilmant had Ropartz in mind, rather than those more illustrious German composers, is betrayed by the very curious four-measure passage which leads into his fugue: a sudden "purple patch" of Franckian chromaticism which would have been more at home in Ropartz's *Offertoire* than his own; despite the unimpeachable craftsmanship, it stands outside the harmonic style of his work. That this wave-like procedure was new to Guilmant is likewise divulged by how he handles the climax. Unlike Ropartz, who knew how to balance convincingly the accumulated power of a climactic preparation with the force of the actual climax, Guilmant tipped the scales: his climax, though heroic, seems truncated; too short for the accumulated tension generated by its extensive preparation, the climactic moment is not played out to its full potential. Only a mere four-and-one-half measures stand at Guilmant's summit, while Ropartz has eight (plus an additional two more of extension). As a result, the role of Ropartz's last page is unambiguous, but a cloud of uncertainty is cast over Guilmant's post-climactic passages. Threatening under even the best of circumstances to come across as a concoction of odds and ends, they simultaneously search for an additional climactic gesture while providing a dénouement. Yet the fact that how they find what they do, namely the quiet return of *Confirma hoc Deus*, heightens the sense of resignation already implicit in the turn to minor mode caused by the reappearance of that theme still does not satisfy the unfulfilled implications of the vigorous climactic preparation. The epilogue, nonetheless, is as peaceful as Ropartz's, surpassing it in richness of content and capturing the same magical sense of withdrawal and evaporation.

Overall a successful experiment, the Pentecost *Offertoire* stands at the head of a group of Guilmant's chant-based organ pieces from the 1890s which Gastoué called "grandes *fantaisies*," and in these pieces he discerned the composer's true originality.[84] This view that the "large plainsong-based composition was perhaps Guilmant's most original contribution to French liturgical organ music" has been echoed by Van Wye.[85] It is perhaps best confirmed by the fact that works such as the Pentecost *Offertoire* in particular are a clear formal anticipation of compositions as impressive as Tournemire's *fantaisies* based on several chant themes in *L'Orgue mystique*. While sadly enjoying no successors after the turn of the century from Guilmant's own hands (neither the Seventh or Eighth Sonatas, ops. 89 and 91, of 1902 and 1906, nor the *Dix-huit Pièces nouvelles*, op. 90, of 1904, continue the progressive style of these works), they did find worthy heirs in the next generation.

What might well have been the apogee in the history of Guilmant's chant-based organ music was reached in June of 1911—Guilmant had died the previous March—when Bonnet performed as a *sortie* the *Marche de procession* on *Iste Confessor* and *Ecce sacerdos magnus* and, in *alternatim*, the versets on *Verbum supernum* (both from the second series of the *Pièces d'orgue dans différents styles*) as part of services held at Saint-Eustache, where Bonnet was organist, during a lavish four-day Parisian church music congress.[86] It was also in that decade that Harvey B. Gaul could write:

> The only man in the Arts who neglects Italy is the organist. Tradition tells him France and Germany, or to sum it up in two names, Bach and Guilmant, offer the greatest opportunity for his peculiar study.[87]

To be sure, Guilmant's stature has fallen a good deal since the early years of the twentieth century when Bach and Guilmant could be enshrined together on coequal pedestals. Today, Guilmant's pieces "dans le style de Bach" likely sound less like Bach than they did in 1900, and are now more accurately placed in the arcane tradition of Boëly's more ambitious attempts at recapturing Bach's style rather than next to Bach's own music. That the *Élévation ou Communion dans le style de J. S. Bach* found a direct descendent in the third of the versets on *Ave maris stella*, "ornamented in the style of J. S. Bach," from the *Fifteen Pieces* by Marcel Dupré, a student of Guilmant, is more the exception than the rule.[88] While a few of Guilmant's more daring pieces—the Pentecost *Offertoire*, for example—seem to have been noticed by younger progressive composers for the organ, the music in his usual style was old-fashioned in its own day and found few followers of note.[89] Moreover, Guilmant's trenchant repudiation of the splashy French toccata found even fewer adherents. Upon Guilmant's death, Gastoué discerned three phases in his career as a composer of liturgical organ music (the "Mendelssohnian" period from ca. 1860 to 1875, the era of *L'Organiste pratique* from 1871 to 1881, and the final phase from 1884 on),[90] but the most crucial boundary now appears to be the impact of his association with the Schola Cantorum and the chant reforms of Solesmes, strongly reflected in his chant-based organ music beginning in the middle of the 1890s. In the late twentieth century, Guilmant looms largest as someone who tried to raise the standards of his profession, and it is neither the fruits of that endeavor as a composer nor as a church musician but rather his accomplishments as a promoter of the whole of the organ repertoire as he knew it, as a concert organist of international fame and as an editor of distinction, for which he is most respected. But for Gastoué, Guilmant's most essential aspect was his place as "the great *liturgical* organist of his time."[91] *L'Organiste liturgiste* powerfully recalls that forgotten aspect of this multi-talented man.

NOTES

[1] Amédée Gastoué, "Al. Guilmant organiste liturgique," *La Tribune de Saint-Gervais* 17, numéro spécial (1911): 15.

[2] *The Forty Programs Rendered by M. Alexandre Guilmant at Festival Hall, World's Fair, St. Louis* (1904; reprint, Richmond, Va.: The Organ Historical Society, 1985).

[3] For the life of Guilmant see Rollin Smith, "Alexandre Guilmant: Commemorating the 150th Anniversary of His Birth," *The American Organist* 21 (March 1987): 50–58; François Sabatier, *Pour une approche d'Alexandre Guilmant . . .*, L'Orgue: cahiers et mémoires, no. 35 (Paris: L'Orgue, 1986); and Wayne Leupold, "Chronology of Guilmant's Life," in *The Organ Music of Alexandre Guilmant*, ed. Wayne Leupold, 12 vols. (Melville, N. Y.: Belwin-Mills, 1984–1993), 6:vii–xi.

[4] William C. Carl, "Alexandre Guilmant; Noted Figure Viewed 25 Years After Death," *The Diapason* 27 (June 1936): 4.

[5] Frederic B. Stiven, *In the Organ Lofts of Paris* (Boston: Stratford, 1923), 62; Gastoué described Guilmant as "un vrai chrétien" ("Al. Guilmant," 15).

[6] A. M. Henderson, "Memories of Some Distinguished French Organists," *The Musical Times* 78 (1937): 978.

[7] Wallace Goodrich, "Alexandre Guilmant and His Methods," *Jacob's Orchestra Monthly* 2 (May 1911): 25.

[8] "Editorial," *The New Music Review and Church Music Review* 10 (1911): 301–5. The anonymous author claims to have been a student of Guilmant.

[9] André Cœury, "Present Tendencies of Sacred Music in France," *The Musical Quarterly* 13 (1927): 594.

[10] Alexandre Guilmant, "Du rôle de l'orgue dans les offices liturgiques," *La Tribune de Saint-Gervais* 1 (September 1895): 11–12.

[11] A chronological list of Guilmant's chant-based organ works, with correlations to the *Liber usualis* when possible, is given in the appendix of Benjamin Van Wye, "The Influence of the Plainsong Restoration on the Growth and Development of the Modern French Liturgical Organ School" (D.M.A. diss., University of Illinois, Urbana-Champaign, 1970).

[12] Gastoué, "Al. Guilmant," 16–17.

[13] Much of Guilmant's organ music is now available in *The Organ Music of Alexandre Guilmant*, ed. Wayne Leupold, 12 vols. (Melville, N. Y.: Belwin-Mills, 1984–1993). The three series of *Pièces d'orgue dans différents styles* are in vols. 1–3, *Dix-huit Pièces nouvelles* in vol. 4, *L'Organiste pratique* in vol. 5; *L'Organiste liturgiste* in vol. 6; and the sonatas and other works in vols. 7–12; these important reprint editions make modern Guilmant scholarship possible. The contents of *L'Organiste pratique* as found in the Leupold edition do not match the contents as given in Sabatier's work list in *Pour une approche*, 31–35. A *Catalogue des compositions de Alexandre Guilmant*, ca. 1905, which appears with some of Guilmant's publications, lists the version of *L'Organiste pratique* as described by Sabatier as for "grand orgue ou harmonium"; the version published by Leupold is listed as both *The Practical Organist: New Edition in three staves* (in English) and *L'Organiste pratique transcrit pour le grand orgue avec pédale obligée*. The contents of these two collections are very similar, but the ordering in which the pieces appear is quite different. Five pieces from the earlier version do not appear in the new edition at all, while two items appear for the first time in it.

[14] Benjamin Van Wye, "Gregorian Influences in French Organ music before the *Motu proprio*," *Journal of the American Musicological Society* 27 (1974): 13.

[15] Van Wye dates them from ca. 1865 ("The Influence of the Plainsong Restoration," 131).

[16] There is an undated verset on *Iste Confessor* (hymn for vespers for the Common of a Confessor not a Bishop) in *L'Organiste pratique* which is reminiscent of examples by Lemmens in his *École d'orgue*; likely an early work, Van Wye has suggested the date of ca. 1865. Two works in *L'Organiste liturgiste* (two versets and amen on *Sacris solemniis* [hymn for matins for Corpus

244

Christi, fourth *livraison*], and a verset and amen on *Creator alme siderum* [hymn for vespers for the First Sunday of Advent, fifth *livraison*]) are also undated; Van Wye has suggested an origin in the mid 1880s ("The Influence of the Plainsong Restoration," 131–34).

[17] On the probable inclusion of early pieces in Widor's symphonies, see John Near, "The Life and Work of Charles-Marie Widor" (D.M.A. diss., Boston University, 1985), 33, 81.

[18] Louis Vierne, "Memoirs of Louis Vierne; His Life and Contacts with Famous Men," trans. Esther Jones Barrow, *The Diapason* 30 (January 1939): 8.

[19] Alexandre Guilmant, "Organ Music and Organ-Playing" (1898; reprint in *The Organ Music of Alexandre Guilmant*, ed. Wayne Leupold, 12 vols. [Melville, N. Y.: Belwin-Mills, 1984–1993], 6:xxv-xxviii). Excerpts of this essay appear in William C. Carl, "Some Reminiscences of Alexandre Guilmant," *The Diapason* 15 (May 1924): 6.

[20] See Walter Hillsman, "Instrumental Accompaniment of Plain-chant in France from the late 18th Century," *The Galpin Society Journal* 33 (March 1980): 8–16.

[21] Benjamin Van Wye, "Marcel Dupré's Marian Vespers and the French *alternatim* Tradition," *The Music Review* 43 (1982): 202.

[22] Guilmant was to have an important role in publishing this repertoire, with André Pirro, in the *Archives des maîtres de l'orgue*.

[23] For a fuller discussion of the history of *alternatim* organ music in France as well as the liturgical regulations which have affected organ playing see Benjamin Van Wye, "Ritual Use of the Organ in France," *Journal of the American Musicological Society* 33 (1980): 287–325; also his "The Influence of the Plainsong Restoration," "Gregorian Influences," and "Marcel Dupré's Marian Vespers."

[24] Van Wye, "Marcel Dupré's Marian Vespers," 203.

[25] It is unclear if the other two versets, which are undated, were also written in 1872; the smooth, even cloying style of the first verset would suggest it might be of a later date; the third verset appears significantly more accomplished than other fugal versets from the 1860s.

[26] Of the numerous pieces included in *La Maîtrise* (edited by Louis Niedermeyer and Joseph d'Ortigue between 1857 and 1861), which features a rich collection of liturgical organ works such as *communions*, *marches*, and the like, virtually none is based on chant.

[27] The first of the six versets for *Iste Confessor* (second *livraison*) and the two versets for *Veni Creator Spiritus* (hymn for vespers for Pentecost, first *livraison*).

[28] Guilmant's debt to Mendelssohn is clear in many of his works, but never more so than in the 1865 Allegretto in B Minor, op. 19, no. 1, from the first series of the *Pièces d'orgue dans différents styles*; Guilmant himself indicates that the main theme is borrowed from Mendelssohn's *Songs without Words*, op. 67.

[29] At the bottom of the last page of the collection is found the inscription, "Fin du premier volume," suggesting further *livraisons* were intended. Indeed, William C. Carl claimed that Guilmant eventually completed twelve *livraisons*, not ten ("Guilmant's Contribution to Organ Music and Organ-Playing" [1912; reprint in *The Organ Music of Alexandre Guilmant*, ed. Wayne Leupold, 12 vols. (Melville, N.Y.: Belwin-Mills, 1984–1993), 6:xxx]). According to Van Wye, there is no further evidence of additional *livraisons* ("Gregorian Influences," 13, n. 38).

[30] Gastoué's claim that the collection is a "veritable *liturgical year*" is something of an exaggeration ("Al. Guilmant," 17).

[31] Only a very few works in *L'Organiste liturgiste* are undated; Van Wye's proposed dates for them are in each case after 1884.

[32] Gastoué, "Al. Guilmant," 17.

[33] Gastoué, "Al. Guilmant," 18.

[34] Benjamin Van Wye's article in this volume points to similar compositions by Boëly.

[35] Sabatier has noted the unusually simple harmonic vocabulary of these settings (*Pour une approche*, 21).

[36] Louis Niedermeyer and Joseph d'Ortigue, *Traité théorique et pratique de l'accompagnement du plain-chant* (Paris: Repos, 1857). Gigout's examples appear in the second edition from 1878, which was the edition translated by Wallace Goodrich as *Gregorian Accompaniment: A Theoretical and Practical Treatise upon the Accompaniment of Plainsong* (New York: Novello, Ewer, 1905).

[37] Gastoué, "Al. Guilmant," 17.

[38] Guilmant labels *Stabat Mater* a prose, to indicate that his setting is of the version in which,

like a hymn, each verse is sung to the same tune; on this distinction, see Fr. A. Lhoumeau, "In festo Septem dolorem B. M. V.," *Revue du chant grégorien* 8 (September 1899): 26–29.

[39] Gastoué, "Al. Guilmant," 15.

[40] Guilmant, "Organ Music and Organ-Playing," 6:xxvi.

[41] Ibid., 6:xxvii.

[42] "Quae maerebat et dolebat,/Pia Mater, dum videbat/Nati poenas inclyti."

[43] "Quis non posset contristari,/Christi matrem contemplari/Dolentem cum Filio?"

[44] "Vidit suum dulcem natum/Moriendo desolatum,/Dum emisit spiritum."

[45] "Fac ut ardeat cor meum/In amando Christum Deum,/Ut sibi complaceam."

[46] "Flammis ne urar succensus,/Per te, Virgo, sim defensus/In die judicii."

[47] "Quando corpus morietur,/Fac ut animae donetur/Paradisi gloria. Amen."

[48] Schweitzer to Widor: "many things in the chorales must seem obscure to you, for the reason that they are only explicable by the texts pertaining to them." See Charles-Marie Widor, preface to the German Edition (1908), in *J. S. Bach* by Albert Schweitzer, trans. Ernest Newman, 2 vols. (1911; reprint, New York: Macmillan, 1964), 1:viii.

[49] Vierne, "Memoirs of Louis Vierne," 9.

[50] Van Wye, "The Influence of the Plainsong Restoration," 132. The chant can be found in *Cantus ad Processiones et Benedictiones SSmi Sacramenti* (New York: J. Fischer & Bro., n.d.), 53–54.

[51] For Gastoué, this work is the first in a series of offertories in which Guilmant refined his treatment of that genre ("Al. Guilmant," 18).

[52] According to *L'Organiste liturgiste*; for the First Sunday of Advent following the *Liber usualis.*

[53] Guilmant also wrote a *Méditation sur le Stabat*, op. 63, for organ and orchestra; this unusual work was also transcribed for organ solo.

[54] Guilmant played pieces by Buxtehude, including the Ciacona in C Minor, BuxWV 159, in at least two concerts at the Trocadéro in 1879 ("Music in Paris," *The Monthly Musical Record* 9 [1879]: 121–22).

[55] Dietrich Buxtehude, *Orgelkompositionen*, ed. Philipp Spitta, 2 vols. (Leipzig: Breitkopf & Härtel, 1875–1876).

[56] Alexandre Guilmant, "La Musique d'orgue: les formes, l'exécution, l'improvisation," in *Physiologie vocale et auditive, technique vocale et instrumentale (voix—instruments à réservoir d'air)*, part 2, vol. 2 of *Encyclopédie de la musique et dictionnaire du Conservatoire*, ed. Albert Lavignac and Lionel de la Laurencie (Paris: Delagrave, 1926), 1155.

[57] Harvey Grace, *French Organ Music Past and Present* (New York: H. W. Gray, 1919), 109.

[58] Van Wye, "The Influence of the Plainsong Restoration," 74.

[59] A view first expressed by Gastoué ("Al. Guilmant," 18).

[60] Two chant-based works of the 1890s which do not appear in *L'Organiste liturgiste* are *Les Vêpres des communs des saints, I: Premières Vêpres des apôtres et des évangélistes*, and the *Offertoire pour le commun des confesseurs non pontifes*, op. 87, both published by the Schola Cantorum.

[61] "L'Organiste liturgiste (huitième livraison), par Alex. Guilmant," *La Tribune de Saint-Gervais* 4 (April 1898): 96.

[62] Van Wye, "Marcel Dupré's Marian Vespers," 203.

[63] Guilmant's metronome markings for the *Orgelbüchlein* are preserved in Johann Sebastian Bach, *The Liturgical Year (Orgelbüchlein)*, ed. Albert Riemenschneider (Bryn Mawr, Pa.: Oliver Ditson, 1933). Guilmant's suggested metronome mark of eighth note equals fifty for *Adoro te* is very similar to his indications for several *Orgelbüchlein* chorales of its type: *Wenn wir in höchsten Nöten sein*, BWV 641, at eighth note equals forty-two, and *Das alte Jahr vergangen ist*, BWV 614, at eighth note equals fifty-two. Guilmant's metronome mark for *O Mensch, bewein' dein' Sünde groß* is eighth note equals eighty.

[64] Noël style treatment of *O Filii* is at least as old as Jean-François Dandrieu and can also be found in Alexandre-Pierre-François Boëly, both of whose works Guilmant edited.

[65] "L'Organiste liturgique [*sic*]. Septième livraison, par Alexandre Guilmant, op. 65," *La Tribune de Saint-Gervais* 3 (September 1897): 141–42.

[66] *La Tribune de Saint-Gervais* 1 (November 1895): 14–15. The service also included, among other musical items, the Stainer *Amen.*

[67] Quoted by Van Wye in "Gregorian Influences," 11.

[68] Van Wye, "Marcel Dupré's Marian Vespers," 206.

[69] Gastoué, "Al. Guilmant," 18.

[70] Van Wye, "Gregorian Influences," 16.

[71] Ibid., 14–16.

[72] Fr. A. Lhoumeau, "De l'accompagnement du chant grégorien," *La Tribune de Saint-Gervais* 4 (October 1898): 237.

[73] Carl, "Guilmant's Contribution," 6:xxx.

[74] See Van Wye, "Gregorian Influences," 14–19, and "Marcel Dupré's Marian Vespers," 207–13, for details of the Schola competition and *Les Vêpres du commun des saints*. The latter includes a helpful catalogue of those works.

[75] Louis Vierne, "Reminiscences of Louis Vierne; His Life and Contacts with Famous Men," trans. Esther Jones Barrow, *The Diapason* 30 (February 1939), 8. Quoted in Van Wye, "Gregorian Influences," 18, and "Marcel Dupré's Marian Vespers," 203; both contain further discussion of this change by Guilmant in the Conservatoire curriculum.

[76] Gastoué, "Al. Guilmant," 18.

[77] The chant tune used by Gigout is not that of the *Liber usualis*; see Fr. A. Lhoumeau, "Adoramus," *Revue du chant grégorien*, 4 (October 1895): 45–47.

[78] The metronome mark of quarter note equals 120 in the Leupold edition of the *Communion* is surely an error; it should be eighth note equals 120.

[79] The *Salve Regina* was revised by Widor after its first publication in 1901, but those revisions consisted of retouching details and did not alter the overall conception of the work.

[80] A. Eaglefield Hull, "The Organ Works of Guilmant," *The Monthly Musical Record* 44 (1914): 300.

[81] Van Wye, "Gregorian Influences," 18.

[82] See Charles Rosen, *Sonata Forms* (New York: W. W. Norton, 1980), ch. 13, for a discussion of Schumann's music which implies two tonics at the same time; Robert Bailey's concept of the "double tonic" is presented in his "An Analytical Study of the Sketches and Drafts," in *Wagner: Prelude and Transfiguration from "Tristan and Isolde,"* ed. Robert Bailey (New York: W. W. Norton, 1985), 113–46, and is further developed in several articles by William Kinderman, such as his "Dramatic Recapitulation in Wagner's *Götterdämmerung*," *19th Century Music* 4 (1980): 101–12.

[83] Carl, "Guilmant's Contribution," 6:xxx.

[84] Gastoué, "Al. Guilmant," 17–18.

[85] Van Wye, "Gregorian Influences," 18.

[86] "Notice historique et pratique des offices religieux du congrès," *La Tribune de Saint-Gervais* 17 (June 1911): 137–43.

[87] Harvey B. Gaul, "Bonnet—Bossi—Karg-Elert: Three Aperçus," *The Musical Quarterly* 4 (1918): 357–58.

[88] Van Wye points out the relationship between these two pieces in "Marcel Dupré's Marian Vespers," 220.

[89] At least to judge by published organ music; Guilmant's music served as a model for liturgical improvisation well past the middle of the twentieth century, even in the hands of Dupré, some of whose extremely conservative Guilmantian service improvisations at Saint-Sulpice have been recorded by the Association des Amis de l'Art de Marcel Dupré.

[90] Gastoué, "Al. Guilmant," 16.

[91] Ibid., 18.

Widor's *Symphonie romane*

LAWRENCE ARCHBOLD

It is simultaneously the privilege and the reward of those who work hard that they know neither weariness nor weakness, and that their talent, far from subsiding, grows stronger and increases with the years. The productions of Widor's maturity constitute a third group of symphonies of an appreciably different character than the preceding ones, with an inspiration perhaps even more elevated and more serene. With these compositions, of which the *Symphonies gothique* and *romane* are the most striking examples, Widor returns to the traditions of yesteryear, to grave and solemn ways, to themes of austere serenity and all imbued with the plainchant of the old organs of bygone days. Certainly he does not abandon any of the hard won modern features, but he imposes on them a classic turn and shape. "With new thoughts, let us make old verses," wrote André Chénier. Widor accomplishes the same sort of task when he performs, on the instruments of Cavaillé-Coll, the dignified musical compositions of the old Sebastian, "our holy father Bach," as Gounod called him.[1]

These words of Louis Vierne, published in 1902 as part of a review of the 1901 revision issued by Charles-Marie Widor of his first eight organ symphonies, call attention to distinctive qualities of Widor's final two contributions, his ninth and tenth organ symphonies, to that remarkable genre of organ music of which he was the creator. Concerning those works, the *Symphonie gothique* of 1894 and the *Symphonie romane* of 1899, Albert Schweitzer, writing in 1906, also noted the quality of "the austere that Widor brings back to sacred art in his last two symphonies."[2] To be sure, most commentators on Widor's organ symphonies—from Paul Locard, who wrote a monograph surveying Parisian organists in 1901 (just one year after the publication of the *Symphonie romane*), to John Near, whose 1985 dissertation presents the most comprehensive biographical study of Widor to date—view the *Symphonie gothique* and *Symphonie romane* as works set apart from Widor's previous organ symphonies, constituting a separate and final stage in the composer's development of the genre.[3] The often repeated opinion that Widor's organ symphonies are better understood as "suites" (or perhaps "symphonic suites") rather than as "symphonies" is an idea not without some justification when considering his earlier compositions; it is less persuasive, however, in reference to the two works of the 1890s which show, at the very least, a heightened degree of thematic integration.[4] Indeed, in many ways these last two symphonies are, in the words of Charles Quef, "the summum" of Widor's œuvre, and that with them, "it would almost be possible to say that a new genre was created."[5]

These two organ symphonies of the 1890s were conceived in what was a particularly crucial decade in Widor's career. Having achieved prominence in the Parisian music scene with his appointment in 1870 as a young man to the prestigious post of organist at Saint-Sulpice with its monumental Cavaillé-Coll organ, in the 1890s Widor entered and solidified his position in the highest levels of the Conservatoire. Despite the fact that he did not hold prizes from that institution—he studied with Jaak Nicolaas (Jacques-Nicolas) Lemmens and François-Joseph Fétis in Belgium rather than with teachers in Paris—he succeeded César Franck as professor of organ there in 1890. By 1890, Widor had also established himself as a noted composer: he began publishing his works in the late 1860s, and by 1890 the list of his compositions exceeded sixty opus numbers, a list that would eventually include, by 1934, eighty-seven. Only several years after his appointment as professor of organ, in 1896 he was named a professor of composition, counterpoint, and fugue, a more prestigious post, and handed over the organ class to his fellow Lemmens student, Alexandre Guilmant. Widor's rise to fame as an educator of note in the 1890s came at a price: at least in part because of these new duties, his output as a composer diminished considerably in these years, and he never regained the productivity he enjoyed in the 1870s and 80s.

Yet, Widor's compositions of the last decade of the century stand out as of special interest, particularly to organists. Indeed, no other decade of his career was as strongly dominated by the composition of organ music as the 1890s, save the very last years of his exceedingly long career. "Seduced," as he himself said, by the Cavaillé-Coll organ of Saint-Sulpice, he had already composed eight organ symphonies, and reportedly considered himself to have finished with that genre.[6] Yet in the 1890s he turned again in that direction, composing the *Symphonie gothique* and *Symphonie romane*. (Though only a small fraction of his large compositional output, various excerpts from the organ symphonies remain the music by which he is best known today.) Besides these two works stands the now largely forgotten Symphony No. 3, op. 69, for organ and orchestra, his largest and most ambitious compositional project of the 1890s, and, interestingly enough, the work with which Widor attained one of his highest honors as a composer: in 1895 its first performance in Paris took place in the prestigious if short-lived Concerts de l'Opéra series.[7] While the Third Symphony was closely modeled on Camille Saint-Saëns's own Symphony No. 3 with organ and as such broke little new stylistic ground, the *Symphonie gothique* and *Symphonie romane* extended the organ symphony into new realms.

The increasing interest in France and elsewhere in the 1890s in liturgical music was perhaps the most important reason for Widor's return to the organ symphony. In particular, chant—its very nature, history, and performance— received new attention as the work of the monks of Solesmes gained wider recognition, and the newly founded Schola Cantorum promoted a new vision of liturgical organ music based closely on chant. Writing in 1892, that is, after the publication of the first eight organ symphonies but before the appearance of the *Symphonie gothique*, Henry Eymieu described Widor's approach to religious music as having "created a style, in agreement with the new resources offered by modern instruments, responding to religious feelings without the aridity that liturgical music ought to have which alternates with the severity of the plainchant."[8] Indeed, Widor's first eight organ symphonies do not employ liturgical themes, despite the fact that some of the most obvious predecessors for those works—the sonatas of Mendelssohn as well as those by his teacher, Lemmens—make prominent use of them. (The sole exception, the *Salve Regina* movement of the Second Symphony, was first introduced by Widor into that work during its revision in 1901.) In the *Symphonie gothique*, however, Widor broke with his previous practice, introducing into the third movement of that four-movement work the Christmas introit *Puer natus est* and continuing with an extensive fourth movement based entirely on the same chant. As the *Symphonie gothique* points toward a more obviously sacred ideal for the organ symphony through the incorporation of liturgical melody, the *Symphonie romane* continues and expands on that trend: in that later work, all four of the movements are based on chant, with two liturgically related chants, the Easter gradual *Hæc dies* and the Easter sequence *Victimæ paschali*, appearing in the work. Yet, demonstrating Widor's commitment to the values of absolute music, neither of these works attempts a picturesque portrayal of the events which these holy days celebrate (events which, musically speaking, not only are ripe with programmatic possibilities but enjoy a history of such treatment in the organ repertoire). Finally, additional aspects of the presentation of both these organ symphonies from the 1890s further increased their spiritual flavor: the *Symphonie gothique* is dedicated to the memory of Saint Ouen, memoralized in the gothic church which bears his name in Rouen, while the *Symphonie romane* is dedicated to the memory of Saint Sernin, likewise remembered in the romanesque church named for him in Toulouse.

The use of chant tunes and the allusion to architectural styles of sacred association (not to mention the evocation of saints) mark these works as having taken paths quite different from Widor's ideal of the organ symphony as developed in his works of the 1870s and 80s. Even if identifying actual "gothic" or "romanesque" qualities—of whatever sort, historical or imaginative—in the music seems problematic at best, the qualities of these works which set them apart from the first eight organ symphonies also suggest links back into history, even if that be a rather murky one. Indeed, François-Auguste Gevaert's *La Melopée antique dans les chant de l'église latine* of 1895 explored what the author believed to be the connections between Roman Catholic plainsong and the music of ancient Greece.[9] Widor remarked in his enthusiastic review:

> The light is therefore lit. Thanks to this admirable *Mélopée antique dans le chant de l'Église latine*, we are now able to follow, in effect, hour by hour, the progress of this slow, but irresistible, current which began in the land of Homer, and has come, little by little, to overtake and revitalize the Western world.[10]

Whatever their value today, such ideas helped to revitalize Widor's own conception of the organ symphony by making chant seem more centrally important in Western musical culture, and, perhaps in addition, making a more self-consciously spiritual modern music seem equally so. Thus a new kind of organ symphony was born, one enriched by ancient chant and historic architecture, yet allied to new organs—both Saint-Ouen and Saint-Sernin had recently received new organs from Cavaillé-Coll—yielding works with a deeper sense of both spirituality and historical evocation if not history itself.

The *Symphonie romane*, composed in 1899 and published in 1900 as opus 73, was singled out by Norbert Dufourcq in 1941 as Widor's masterpiece.[11] Nonetheless, it was largely neglected, especially in the United States, during the years after the Second World War when interest in the Baroque organ and its music dominated the organ scene. It has never been one of his most popular organ symphonies (surely the best known remains the Fifth), nor was it the composer's own favorite (which appears to have been the *Symphonie gothique*, to judge from Widor's own concert programming in his later years), and by no means is it the longest or most complex of Widor's organ symphonies (the Eighth remains by far his largest such work). The *Symphonie romane* is, however, in many ways the most sophisticated, surely the most unified both stylistically and thematically, and more than the *Symphonie gothique*, shows its composer to be meaningfully engaged not only in the search for a more spiritual musical style, but also to be more clearly aware of up-to-date compositional techniques as well as current conceptions of chant.

Of all Widor's organ symphonies, the *Symphonie romane* is in some ways the most orchestral in its treatment of the organ, though not in the more naive sense of the composer's description of the organ, at one point, as "in reality, an orchestra of wind instruments. An organ of thirty, forty, fifty stops is an orchestra of thirty, forty, fifty musicians."[12] In fact, his earlier organ symphonies show more attempts to highlight the imitation of individual orchestral timbres. Rather, this work, at least in its outer movements, features the imitation of the dynamic surge and ebb typical of Wagner's orchestral writing and other late-nineteenth century orchestral composition influenced by him. Closely allied to those techniques is, for Widor's organ symphonies, an unprecedented emphasis on melody and its development. Widor's student, Marcel Dupré, related that Widor often told friends that the theme of this work "stayed on his desk for more than a year before he decided to develop it."[13] Perhaps as a result of what may well have been a long period of contemplation, Widor's treatment of thematic material in the work is unusually elaborate. Indeed, his preface to a revised edition of his earlier organ symphonies in 1887 claimed that:

> Such is the modern organ: essentially symphonic. A new instrument needs a new language, another ideal than that of scholastic polyphony. We no longer invoke the Bach of the fugue; rather, the melodist who so moves us, the supreme master of expression . . . [14]

Widor's "new language" was not always in evidence in the first eight organ symphonies, and "scholastic polyphony" is the kind of charge some critics leveled at the *Symphonie gothique*.[15] Nonetheless, in his last organ symphony, Widor found a melodic style fully worthy of the aims he set forth for his work over a decade before.

In the preface to the *Symphonie romane*, Widor describes the themes of his last two organ symphonies in these terms:

> *Puer natus est*, with its very pure lines and solid construction, is an excellent subject for polyphonic treatment . . . *Hæc dies* is just the opposite, an elegant arabesque embellishing each syllable of its text of several words—about ten notes per syllable—a vocalise as free as a bird's song . . . [16]

Only the first few phrases of the chant in question are actually heard in either of these symphonies. Indeed, both works use only about the first third of their respective chant's refrain sections. In the case of the *Symphonie romane*, Widor uses the chant melody for the opening four words of the text, "Hæc dies, quam fecit," repeatedly drawing thematic material featuring the sizeable opening melisma for "Hæc," the somewhat shorter one for "di-" of "dies," and the larger one for "-cit" of "fecit." While this portion of the chant is indeed a fragment to judge by the text, from a musical point of view this excerpt contains the most distinctive melodic material of the chant. Traditionally notated beginning on A, the opening melisma for "Hæc" begins with decorative motion around that note featuring a striking B flat followed by a rising F-A-C motion; that for "dies" returns to A by way of a B natural which contradicts the B flat of the previous one. Most striking about the setting of "quam fecit" is the falling E-C-A motion, which seems, at least in the context of this short excerpt, to balance the previous triadic gesture. The phrase for "fecit," like that of the chant as a whole, returns to A for its close.[17]

In even this portion of *Hæc dies*, the modal issues which have made this chant a subject of controversy can be observed. It is labeled a second mode

Hæc   di   -   es,   quam fe-cit

Example 1a. Beginning of *Hæc dies* as it appears in the *Paroissien romain*

Hæc   di   -   es   quam fe - cit

Example 1b. Beginning of *Hæc dies* as it appears in Dom Joseph Pothier, "Graduel Hæc dies,' du jour de Pâques"

chant in the *Paroissien romain* as published in Paris in the late nineteenth century, a source which reflects the chant as used in Paris since the seventeenth century.[18] (The more familiar *Liber usualis* of the early twentieth century also classifies it as second mode.) Yet, in an article published in 1896 which surely caught Widor's attention, the French chant authority Dom Joseph Pothier claimed that this chant "has only an accidental similarity to the second Gregorian mode. Its true mode, without ending on its final, is the fifth."[19] Pothier understood this chant, then, to begin and end on the third note of its scale rather than as a chant of the second mode transposed up a fifth. However sympathetic Widor might have been with Pothier's analysis of the modality of *Hæc dies*, he drew his melodic paraphrases of the chant from the version as found in the *Paroissien romain* (or a similar version elsewhere) rather than from Pothier's more recently devised source-critical revision of the chant as published in his article (see Example 1).

Yet Widor clearly must have been intrigued by the modal ambiguity of *Hæc dies*. For him, Western tonality originated in the melodic heritage left by liturgical plainsong, a wealth of music based in turn on the theoretical writings of the ancient Greeks; if chant could be understood to contain the roots of modern tonal practice, *Hæc dies*, then, could likewise be understood to anticipate issues in nineteenth-century harmonic style. Indeed, while discussing the origins of music in his *Initiation musicale*, a little musical handbook of 1923, Widor claimed that *Hæc dies* "is already our modern scale: two relative keys: *D major, F-sharp minor*," quoting exactly the same portion of the chant as is heard in the *Symphonie romane*.[20] In addition, he transposes the quotation down a minor third from where it appears in the *Paroissien romain*—or Pothier's article, or the *Liber usualis*, for that matter. In those sources, the chant suggests (anachronistically) a reading in F major. In his symphony, it appears beginning on F sharp (instead of A) where it suggests first the key of D major and then, as the melody unfolds, a modulation to D major's mediant, F-sharp minor.[21]

Widor's little example is telling in yet one more way: the *Hæc dies* quotation is not presented in chant notation, but rather as it might be found in an organ symphony or any other modern composition, and with an arresting array of rhythmic values: triplets, eighths, quarters, halves, and dotted halves. Also revealing is the seemingly unconscious juxtaposition—on the very same page—of this example with another quotation of chant, the *Lauda Sion*, notated entirely in whole notes. To be sure, the proper rhythmic interpretation of chant was an even more lively topic at the turn of the century than modal analysis. Even as late as the *Symphonie gothique*, Widor held up in that work what was, by the end of the century, an old-fashioned view of chant as a relatively slow, rather stodgy series of notes. If *Puer natus est* in the *Symphonie gothique* sings forth in the style of a cantus firmus, with the *Symphonie romane* Widor charted a new path, outlined in his preface to the work: chant as "a vocalise as free as a bird's song." He even went so far in that preface as to present three different rhythmic interpretations of the opening of his chant excerpt in an attempt to demonstrate how, in various compositional situations in the work, the chant might appear in different rhythmic guises (see Example 2). Interestingly, the version given in the *Initiation musicale* is different still, yet no less rhythmically variegated (see Example 3). What Widor does not discuss in his modest preface is that this approach to chant—for him in his organ works, a new approach—was widely adopted by

Example 2. *Hæc dies* as it appears in Widor's preface to *Symphonie romane*

Example 3. *Hæc dies* as it appears in Widor's *Initiation musicale*

composers of French organ music by the end of the 1890s. Indeed, no better example of the change to a faster, more flowing, more rhythmically free rendition of chant in organ music could be found than in the liturgical organ works of his colleague and friend, Guilmant. While these things were new for Widor in 1899, they show him as much following a trend as setting one.

If any single work might have served as an inspiration for Widor's decision to return yet once again to the organ symphony with a work based on *Hæc dies*, it was probably not one by Guilmant, despite that composer's commitment to liturgical organ music based on chant, but rather a work which Widor edited for publication in 1894: the *Offertoire pascal* by Guy Ropartz, based on *Hæc dies*. The work appeared in the second volume of *L'Orgue moderne*, Widor's then newly established series of recently composed organ music by various (mostly younger, mostly French) organ composers.[22] Written in 1889, Ropartz's *Offertoire* blends into a decidedly Franckian musical language just the opening melisma (for "Hæc") of the chant tune, which is sporadically presented throughout the work as a kind of cantus firmus in various (sometimes rather outlandishly chromatic) harmonic contexts. Like Widor's symphony, it is prefaced by a quotation of the chant tune, but here (as in Widor's own quotation of *Lauda Sion* in the *Initiation musicale*) it appears in undifferentiated rhythmic values, reflecting a more old-fashioned style of chant performance than that mirrored in the *Symphonie romane*.

Widor believed that the rhapsodic quality of *Hæc dies* required an unconventional approach in the *Symphonie romane*: "The only way of fixing the listener's ear on so fluid a theme is to repeat it constantly," he wrote in his preface. Indeed, the first movement of the work called forth special pleading there on that account: "That is the purpose of the first movement . . . sacrificing everything to its subject, the timid attempts here and there at development are quickly abandonned in favor of the original theme." The unfolding repetitions of the opening phrases of *Hæc dies*, or fragments thereof, throughout the opening Moderato movement yield an essentially monothematic effect. Yet, Celia Jones's designation of the movement as a fantasy, while not inappropriate, fails to elucidate the formal principles which give it shape.[23] While the thematic web of recurring quotations of the chant tune is the Moderato's most obvious source of coherence, underlying the theme and its development is a tonal plan which not only reflects the issues of modal ambiguity implied in the chant itself, but also reflects contemporary formal practices articulating tonal ambiguity, marking this movement as one of Widor's most advanced. Curiously, Widor shunned the most obvious applications of sonata form in his organ symphonies. (His colleague, Guilmant, used them frequently in his organ sonatas, and Widor's protégé, Vierne—who also studied with Guilmant—employed them in his own organ symphonies, works which, in many other ways, show Widor's influence.) Nonetheless, certain aspects of sonata form procedures help give a sense of order to the events of the Moderato, while other formal procedures, essentially at odds with sonata style, enrich and individualize the movement.

The Moderato opens with a haunting arabesque of sixteenth-note motion in 12/8 spanning the distance from F sharp¹ to F sharp‴. This gesture prepares a striking inverted pedal point on that high F sharp which serves as an accompaniment to the first statement of the chant tune fragment, which begins on F sharp″. Bearing the extravagant indication of *Quasi recitativo, espressivo, a piacere*, the chant alternates with developmental variants of the opening arabesque which repeatedly return to its original pedal point. In this transposition, the chant tune quotation begins and ends with F sharp, its triadic outline of D-F sharp-A is answered by C sharp-A-F sharp, and the stressed G natural of the opening phrase is repeatedly contradicted with G sharps as the chant continues. With the support of the F sharp pedal, then, the key of F-sharp minor is implied. A further statement of just the chant melody for "Hæc" then appears in the pedal in a richly elaborate texture: in this more conventional context, the tune is treated less as a vocalise than as a cantus firmus. With the chant again beginning on F sharp, again with a pedal point (again inverted, though this time buried in an inner voice) but on A, the passage is poised in D major. A crescendo leads to a pause in that key (m. 16) which sets up another statement of the chant, again at the same pitch level, in a texture more like that of the opening. But in place of the pedal point on F sharp, there is a double pedal point on D and F sharp, reinforcing the preceding harmonic reinterpretation of the chant from F-sharp minor to D major. This time, however, the tune is quoted beyond merely the melisma for "Hæc," continuing into that for "dies," where the G sharps of that portion of the tune (which in the first presentation helped to confirm F-sharp minor) now stand outside the scale, appearing as the raised fourth degree. It is hard to say whether this passage should be understood as a harmonically clarified restatement of the opening (an initial impression of F-sharp minor replaced by a more solid D major), or whether, within the context of an already established F-sharp minor, this passage is an excursion to that key's submediant, its material colored by errant if poignant G sharps. The essential effect in the opening pages of the Moderato is that of tonal ambiguity, an uncertainty which directly reflects the arguments over the modal classification of the chant: is the tonic to be F-sharp minor, reflecting the traditional analysis of the chant as transposed second mode, or is it to be D major, following Pothier's hypothesis of fifth mode? Nonetheless, the movement is in fact notated in two, rather than three, sharps, indicating D major rather than F-sharp minor.[24]

If the thematic statements of the movement so far seem to tip the delicate balance between F-sharp minor and D major as tonal centers towards D major, the passage which appears next (beginning in m. 23) suggests the opposite. A deceptive resolution of a D major seventh chord opens up the unexpected harmonic territory of C-sharp. The pedal ostinato which grounds this passage, a descending figure of A-G sharp-E sharp-C sharp, implies both C-sharp major and C-sharp minor (either of which lies more within the realm of F-sharp minor than D major); the notation in four sharps is contradicted by ubiquitous added E sharps. The melody for the left hand, highlighted on the Grand-Orgue, can be heard as a derivative of the melisma for "dies" with the crucial third expanded to a fourth, as Marmaduke P. Conway claimed.[25] This luxurious passage, so rich in harmonic inflection and contrapuntal density, can best be understood formally as a second theme; harmonic stability argues against its reading as a bridge. That its close, on C-sharp major, prepares a reappearance of the main theme (in a texture clearly derived from that of the opening, for once again, a pedal point serves as accompaniment, but this time it is not inverted) transposed up a fifth—a traditional sign of the opening of a development section—reinforces that interpretation.

The tonal ambiguity of F-sharp minor and D major at the opening is replicated here in this restatement of the entire "Hæc dies, quam fecit" melody (beginning in m. 30) as the suggestion of C-sharp minor is eventually contradicted by A major. As was the case before, this relatively sparse statement of the tune leads to a more contrapuntally complex passage. And once again, that more complex passage presents only the "Hæc" melisma of the chant tune. But this time, the passage is more developmental and more harmonically unstable: "Hæc" appears transposed up a fourth—suggesting G major, the subdominant of D major, but sufficiently clouded by C sharps and A sharps in the accompanimental figures to make any tonal interpretation precarious—followed immediately by a swift crescendo to a *fff* climax articulated by the triumphant presentation of the "Hæc dies" portion of the tune in the pedal in octaves. Strikingly, the chant melody is here transposed down a second (!) from its original presentation (beginning on E rather than on F sharp). Above it is heard shimmering, harmonically fuzzy figuration which at first suggests C major, but veers towards E minor by the conclusion of the chant statement (E minor stands in the same relationship to C major as does F-sharp minor to D major, or, indeed, C-sharp minor to A major.) At this point, an equally quick diminuendo ensues.

The resolution of this climax unfolds with developmental writing which, while devoid of the chant theme, is far from extraneous. In mm. 55 and 56, the third relationships so characteristic of the movement (F-sharp minor and D major at the opening, C-sharp minor and A major at the restatement, and C major and E minor at the climax) are presented with as yet unprecedented boldness: the passage oscillates back and forth between root position chords of F-sharp major and D major.[26] This immediate harmonic juxtaposition is then presented in another way, writ large as it were, as an eight-measure pedal on F sharp (supporting figuration which continues to spin out the energy of the climax but without making reference to the chant) followed by an even longer (twenty-measure) pedal on D, with which the movement closes. Not until the F-sharp pedal falls to the D pedal is chant material heard again: "dies" then returns repeatedly, along with a statement of "quam fecit" (the latter featuring a beautifully crafted extension in mm. 67–68). Conway heard the appearance of the "dies" melody at the beginning of the D pedal as the return of the second theme; this analysis is best defended not, as Conway proposed, because of the second theme's similarity to the "dies" melisma (the material here has the third interval typical of "dies" rather than the second theme's fourth which stood in its place), but rather because of the return at this moment of the pedal ostinato associated with the second theme, which here is heard in D major with its characteristic flat-sixth coloration (B flat-A-F sharp-D).[27] Eventually, it seems, even the energy motivating the statements of the chant tune fragments fades, leaving only enough momentum to motivate more neutral figuration. Only when the B flat foreign to D major has been finally purged from the harmonic context is the first completely uncluttered cadence in D major in the entire movement heard (m. 81); the movement comes to complete repose just three measures later.

The dramatic shape of this remarkable movement derives, then, more from its sense of climax and resolution than from its allegiance (or allusion) to sonata form; once the movement seems really underway, the themes ride the surge and ebb of the dynamic flux, one of several ways in which the Moderato evokes the style of Wagner. This is especially true of the extensive resolution: while the traces of "first" and "second" themes can be discerned, and the signs of a development section are clearly present, what provides a sense of recapitulation—the return of the ostinato transposed to the tonic D major—is quite subtle, and hardly climactic in view of the explosion of sound at the *fff*. Indeed, everything beyond that point of climax is heard in its shadow; the movement ends not so much when, or because, the recapitulatory function is accomplished, but when the energy of the climax has been fully dispelled, the limits of its shadow reached. And the tonic key of the movement secured, for more remarkable still is the fact that the climax occurred outside the tonic. Such a formal strategy goes beyond what can be found in either of the large outer movements of the *Symphonie gothique* (or Franck's *Trois Chorals*, written in 1890) where the climaxes always articulate a powerful tonic arrival. (A movement such as the Adagio of Anton Bruckner's Seventh Symphony for orchestra, first performed in 1884, provides an example of the design employed in the Moderato.) The outer movements of the *Symphonie gothique* do, nonetheless, provide important examples—as do the composer's Variations from the Eighth Symphony and the *Final* of the Third (a movement which originated after the first publication of that work)—of movements which draw much of their sense of form from powerful climaxes followed by extensive resolutions. So too, of course, does Franck's Second *Choral*, and, not unimportantly, so does Ropartz's *Offertoire pascal*, which suggests one more way in which Widor might well have found that work intriguing.

After the single-mindedness with which *Hæc dies* was heard in the Moderato, the fact that the second movement is also built upon the same fragment from the same chant may come as a surprise. The key of the second movement, F Major, is also surprising. The overall tonal plans formed by the keys of the various movements of Widor's organ symphonies show varying degrees of cogency; particularly in his later such works, he favored a triadic outline of the key of the symphony as a whole: in the case of the *Symphonie gothique*, the first movement is in C minor, the second is in E-flat major, the third is in G minor, and the final movement is in C major.[28] The second movement of the *Symphonie romane*, however, appears in a very distant key, remote from D major (and also F-sharp minor). Moreover, the Moderato did nothing to prepare the way for F major; in his two other major mode organ symphonies, the Second in D and the Eighth in B, the second movements are both in the subdominant. F major, however, welcomes *Hæc dies* at its conventionally notated pitch beginning on A, interpreting the opening note as the third step of the scale, as was ultimately the reading offered in the Moderato. Indeed, in the case of the second movement, as opposed to that of the Moderato, the tonal ambiguity of the chant tune is not an issue.

Entitled *Choral*, the movement begins Adagio with the melody for "Hæc dies, quam fecit" set as a soprano melody in a four-part harmonic style which in some ways evokes that of chorales. (Whatever Widor's intention in his choice of a name for this movement, this *Choral* bears no formal similarity to the movement of the same name in his Seventh Symphony—a form later used by Vierne in the *Choral* of his Second—not to mention the *Trois Chorals* of Franck.) The chorale style of the opening precludes a treatment of the chant "as a bird's song," and gone is the *Quasi recitativo, espressivo, a piacere* marking found at the opening of the first movement. Yet, the *Choral* is characterized by thematic repetition at least as intensive as that of the Moderato, and Widor's comment, "The only way of fixing the listener's ear on so fluid a theme is to repeat it constantly," applies at least as well to the *Choral* as it does to the Moderato.

The *Choral* maintains an emphasis on the chant fragment despite the introduction, reiteration, and development of a second lyrical melody, frequently heard in combination with the chant itself. (Since the second melody's first hearing in mm. 5–6, where it begins in A minor, seems anticipatory to its full statement and repetition in mm. 11–15, where it appears in the tonic F major like *Hæc dies*, it might better be understood as a contrasting or "counter-theme" rather than an actual "second" theme.[29]) The head of this counter-theme is shortly thereafter transformed into a bass ostinato (m. 18), high above which is heard the melody of "fecit"—the curiously disembodied quality of the chant melody in this passage is as close as the *Choral* gets to vocalise—and the developmental writing in this passage, in which Widor treats the melisma for "fecit" as surprisingly malleable, is some of the most impressive in the entire symphony. A deceptive cadence (m. 28) closes this section, opening the way to a contrasting interlude (whose initial material is even more fancifully drawn from "fecit" than the preceding passage).

The harmonic excursion begun by the deceptive cadence is finally drawn back to F major to begin a section which functions as the reprise (m. 41). Yet if the thematic material of this return is familiar, its layout is entirely new: high in the texture is heard a melody spun from the opening of the counter-theme, the pedal sings the entire chant melody in augmentation beginning with "Hæc dies" and then (at the introduction of double pedal scoring) "quam fecit," while the inner parts provide arpeggiated accompaniment. Later, the chant tune finds its way to the soprano, and eventually this passage deflects to the subdominant where it stops (but hardly cadences). The movement resumes with yet another announcement of the melody of "Hæc" (mm. 52–53), beginning a passage which includes some of the most slip-and-slide chromaticism to be found in the symphony, culminating with an affective pause, as Near has pointed out, on the sonority known as the "Tristan" chord (m. 54).[30] By the magic of a modal progression the passage returns to F major and a restatement of the counter-theme in its entirety, again featuring some melodic motions reminiscent of *Tristan und Isolde* (m. 58), as Jimmy Jess Anthony has noted.[31] As a concluding gesture, the ostinato texture heard earlier in the movement returns, still in F major, this time with the melody of "Hæc dies" rather than "fecit" soaring above (m. 60) before the final "purple patch" of cadential extension (mm. 65–66).

Widor, one of the few French musicians present at the premiere of Wagner's *Ring* cycle at Bayreuth in 1876, apparently thought the sounds of *Tristan* were not incompatible with the prevailing sacred mood of his work. (*Tristan*, indeed, was finally performed in Paris in a staged version in 1899, the very year in which the *Symphonie romane* was composed.) The same conclusion can be drawn regarding the opinions of his contemporaries, at least to judge from commentaries about the work from the first decades of the century: what influences of Wagner the symphony demonstrates were apt to pass by unnoticed. Conway characterized the *Choral* with these words: ". . . many think it the finest [movement] of the whole symphony, since nowhere else are we conscious of a deeper religious atmosphere or of higher sincerity of ideal."[32] How much of these Wagnerian evocations are conscious creations of the composer is not easy to say. Richard Taruskin has drawn attention to the many "involuntary Tristanisms in *fin-de-siècle* French music."[33] So too has Scott Messing:

> The chromatic harmony of Wagner's music was both new and fascinating to Parisian composers and an example not easily outdistanced. The recurrence of even so obvious a case as the opening motive from *Tristan und Isolde* . . . is striking for the subtle variety of its appearance in otherwise very different French compositions.[34]

In any event, *Tristan* was a well-known composition; Ropartz's *Offertoire pascal*, however, was not, and it is thus perhaps even less surprising that the striking similarity between that work and Widor's *Choral* has likewise not been stressed. At the climactic moment of the *Offertoire*, Ropartz introduces a bass ostinato, F-E-F-C, high above which is heard the chant melody of "Hæc." Could this passage have been the inspiration for Widor's own bass ostinato, F-E-D-C, above which was also heard—albeit in a much more relaxed and flexible way—first the melody of "quam fecit" and then, just before the close of the movement, "Hæc dies" itself?

For all the attention Widor drew to *Hæc dies* in the preface of his symphony, it seems peculiar—even bizarre—that the chant heard in the third movement, *Victimæ paschali laudes*, received no mention there whatsoever. Indeed, the composer's presentation of the *Symphonie romane* seems to suggest that no chant but *Hæc dies* appears in the work. Not surprisingly, then, various commentators have claimed that *Hæc dies* does in fact appear in all four movements. In 1922, Quef's analysis of the symphony located *Hæc dies* in each of the movements, claiming in particular that in the third movement that chant "was not forgotten"; shortly after Widor's death, Gustave Bret asserted that "The *Romane* [is] entirely constructed on the *Hæc dies*"; and as late as 1964, Jean Piccand made the same claim.[35] However, Widor's title of the third movement, *Cantilène*, is a term which, indicating a non-Biblical text, is often associated with sequences. Widor himself in the *Initiation musicale* pointed to *Libera me, Victimæ paschali, Inviolata, Salve Regina, Ave verum, Veni Sancte Spiritus, Lauda Sion,* and *Stabat Mater* as the most popular chants of this type.[36] As his presentation there makes clear, he was well aware that these chants date from the high or late middle ages and constitute a very different repertoire from graduals like *Hæc dies*; moreover, most of the items on his list are, like *Victimæ paschali,* sequences. Thus, a discerning observer would likely be surprised to encounter a movement entitled *Cantilène* based on a gradual such as *Hæc dies*.

Widor did not treat *Victimæ paschali* with the same intensity as he had *Hæc dies* in the first two movements of the symphony; the constant repetition of the chant melody which characterizes the Moderato and the *Choral* is strikingly absent here. Indeed, this Lento movement opens with a freely-invented melody; heard on the suave Clarinette against an accompaniment of foundation stops, it is memorable for its swooping (and swooning) leaps. With A minor established as tonic, the passage continues with a modulation to the minor dominant: it is at this point that *Victimæ paschali* makes its first appearance as the Clarinette continues with the melody of the first line of the chant text, "Victimæ paschali laudes immolent Christiani" (m. 11). The tune is pitched one step higher (on E) than its usual notation in chant books (on D). Moreover, once again nineteenth-century editions of chant reveal that Widor clung to the chant tune as he knew it more closely than comparisons

Vi- cti- mæ Pas- cha-li laudes Immolent Chri-sti- a - ni.

Example 4a. Beginning of *Victimæ paschali laudes* as it appears in the *Paroissien romain*

Vi- cti- mæ paschá- li láudes * ímmolent Christi- á - ni.

Example 4b. Beginning of *Victimæ paschali laudes* as it appears in the *Liber usualis*

Example 4c. Widor, *Cantilène*, m. 12, from *Symphonie romane*

with more recent publications revised in the light of nineteenth- and twentieth-century chant scholarship would indicate. For example, Widor's stepwise pitch pattern corresponding to "immolent" (B-A-G in m. 12) reflects the reading (A-G-F) found in the *Paroissien romain* of the late nineteenth century rather than that of the *Liber usualis* (A-G-E) and the same is true for Widor's choice of rhythmic values (see Example 4). The chant melody of the opening phrase of the second line, "Agnus redemit oves," is then heard repeatedly in E major, closing the first section of the *Cantilène*. (Were the repetitions of this memorable portion of the chant suggested by the fact that, unlike the melody for "Victimæ paschali laudes immolent Christiani," that for "Agnus redemit oves" returns several more times in the chant as a whole?)

Overall, then, the formal layout of the *Cantilène* thus far resembles that of a sonata form exposition. The following short interlude can be understood as a miniature development section, for it contains several varied repetitions of "Agnus redemit oves" in which that melody is reharmonized (and set apart from the preceding by a four-part chorale-like texture similar to that of the opening of the *Choral*). Sonata form is even more strongly evoked by the reprise. The opening Clarinette melody returns in its original key followed by "Victimæ paschali laudes immolent Christiani" and "Agnus redemit oves" both a fourth higher than before, pitched now on A (the tonic of the movement) rather than E (the dominant). The close of the exposition (which had been in the major dominant) is repeated without alteration other than transposition, thus turning A minor to A major. A short coda presents once more the melody for "Victimæ paschali laudes immolent Christiani," balancing the appearances of "Agnus redemit oves" in the developmental interlude. As "Agnus redemit oves" there reappeared in a subtly new rhythmic guise, even more so does "Victimæ paschali laudes immolent Christiani" here: departing for the first time from the prevailing compound meter of the *Cantilène*, this final appearance of the chant melody is recast in a duple meter rhythmic pattern.

The two slow movements of *Symphonie romane* exhibit different formal patterns and different methods of elaborating chant tunes. The *Choral* is a one-of-a-kind chant paraphrase, intent on "fixing the listener's ear on so fluid a theme" as *Hæc dies* through its constant repetition. While the movement employs a contrasting theme not derived from chant, that theme seems chiefly destined to be woven into the presentations of the chant tune as a counter-theme, and never undermines the primacy of *Hæc dies*. Shorter, less episodic, and more conventional in its formal plan, the *Cantilène* relegates its own chant, *Victimæ paschali*, to the status of the secondary theme in a sonata form; the chant emerges with no little surprise out of an otherwise independent melody line of striking beauty. Moreover, the pitch level of *Victimæ paschali* shifts according to the dictates of the tonal plan of the *Cantilène*. If the key of the *Choral* seems particularly appropriate to *Hæc dies* (allowing it to appear at its standard notated pitch), the key of the *Cantilène* has nothing to do with the traditional notation of *Victimæ paschali*; rather, the movement's key is the minor dominant of the symphony as a whole, poised in obvious preparation for a tonic finale.

Quef remarked that Widor's way of handling the organ in the *Final* resembled "a gigantic orchestra, and, as in an orchestra, the initial theme returns in different rhythms, with the most diverse sonorities, low, high . . ."; and the composer's method of treating *Hæc dies* through continual repetition, observed in the first two movements, does return in this movement with even greater intensity.[37] To be sure, in no other movement of the *Symphonie romane*—in no other organ work by Widor—is a chant tune so freely, imaginatively, and dramatically developed. Moreover, in the *Final*, elements of the Moderato and the *Choral* (the two previous movements based on *Hæc dies*) reappear in new contexts. And in some cases, these aspects of those previous movements find a new and deeper sense of resolution. As in the Moderato, the repetitions of the chant melody fragments dominate the thematic discourse, their varied appearances creating the impression of a fantasy-like form—yet one which owes much to the generalized outline of the sonata—all focused by, and subordinated to, the sweeping rise and fall of dynamic levels as powerful climaxes are approached, attained, and dissipated. In the *Final*, however, these techniques are all realized on a significantly grander scale.

The movement, marked Allegro, begins *fff* with the melody of "Hæc dies" transformed into a rapidly unfolding, breathless swirl of figuration, a presentation of the chant melody in sharp contrast to the ways in which chant had been heard previously in the symphony: as vocalise or as cantus firmus. After an elaborate continuation eventually transforms the opening monophonic texture into polyphony, this burst of energy begins to fade. The dynamic level falls as the reeds and mixtures of the Grand-Orgue and the Positif are retired and the passage, which began in D major, modulates to F-sharp minor, where it finds a temporary cadence, recalling by its tonal plan the opening statement of *Hæc dies* in the Moderato. Again as in that movement, the opening thematic idea is restated with an enriched accompaniment; with a return to *fff*, the "Hæc dies" motive is again heard, this time with a chordal backdrop. Again like the Moderato, this second statement leads to a contrasting, "second" theme. In the *Final* the dynamic level again falls just as in the first statement while a more extensive developmental passage, this time modulating more widely, leads to the movement's first pedal entrance. It announces the melody of "quam fecit," not in the figural style in which "Hæc dies" has been heard in the movement, but rather, in a way which is more typical of the work as a whole, that of a florid cantus firmus. (The remarkable variety of its rhythmic values—eighths, dotted eighths, quarters, dotted quarters, and dotted halves—bears eloquent witness to Widor's efforts in this symphony to capture, as he put it in his preface, the "inexpressible suppleness" and rhythmic liberty of chant.) The "quam fecit" melody is pitched beginning on G, its continuation implying a harmonization in A minor; at this pitch level, the preceding melismas for "Hæc dies" (if they had appeared here) would have begun on A, suggesting a harmonization in F major. This is, of course, the pitch level at which the entire chant fragment was heard in the *Choral*, and its presentation here leads immediately to an extensive pedal point on F. Remaining at that same pitch level, "dies," again as in a cantus-firmus rather than in a figural style, appears in the top voice over the pedal point, solidifying the arrival in F major. Finally, "Hæc dies," in its fast-moving figural guise, is also heard in that key (m. 44). Thus, the presentation of the various phrases of "Hæc dies, quam fecit" in F major in the "second" theme area connect the *Final* and the *Choral* just as the chant theme, formal layout, and key areas of the "first" theme area link the *Final* to the Moderato.

The return of the opening motive in F major initiates new variants of the "Hæc" motive through fragmentation and sequencing (m. 47), suggesting that "exposition" has given way to "development." Increased harmonic instability, a rapid crescendo leading to *fff*, and a rich chordal climax of extravagant harmonies continue to suggest that impression. Out of this awesome passage, at its moment of greatest tension, emerges a twisted version of the opening of the "Hæc" melisma: (A flat-G-B flat-A flat-G-A flat in mm. 54–55). This striking gesture is the most convincing confirmation yet of the developmental quality of this portion of the movement. After a swift decrescendo, the figural motive derived from "Hæc dies" reappears, first in D-flat major (which, emerging enharmonically from C sharp, could be understood as a subtle reference to that key area in the Moderato) and, passing through F minor, on the surge of another crescendo arrives at D major via a diminished chord.

This second *fff* climax combines the figural version of "Hæc dies" in the manuals with "Hæc dies, quam fecit," in florid cantus-firmus style in the pedal, both in D major (beginning in m. 72). Such a dramatic superimposition strongly suggests that this passage performs a recapitulatory function. What had been heard as the "first" theme in D major (the figural version of the chant) and the "second" theme in F major (the chant in a florid cantus-firmus presentation) are not only here heard simultaneously but, above all, the "second" theme is now reconciled to the tonic key. (This technique is a sign of recapitulation in many progressive nineteenth-century compositions including the finale of Beethoven's Ninth Symphony and Wagner's overture to *Die Meistersinger*; as for French organ music, it is most notably associated with Franck, and can be found at the climaxes of the Fantasy in A Major and the *Choral* in B Minor, among other works.) As for the *Final* as a whole, however, this "recapitulation" is clearly a way station rather than the ultimate goal (and in this way Widor's treatment of dramatic superimposition is quite different from Franck's): its approach is too indirect—and too sudden—to be a convincing climax for the *Final* at this point. Rather, it is better characterized as a recapitulatory gesture, a recapitulatory moment. Indeed, the pedal statement of the entire chant fragment is once again harmonized with a modulatory key plan with D major eventually supplanted by F-sharp minor, recalling yet again the work's characteristic harmonization of the *Hæc dies* fragment and the tonal ambiguity of the Moderato. Yet, neither D major nor F-sharp minor is established at the conclusion of "quam fecit" in the pedal; the passage, deflected away from its expected goal, is extended with impressive developmental variations of the first theme (beginning in m. 82) in what soon becomes a highly unstable harmonic context. Eventually, this climactic passage also loses momentum, but not before achieving a substantially longer duration than the first *fff* climax.

As immediately following the first climax, a decrescendo to *piano* and a few measures of elegant Andante noodling provide a moment of calm before another drive toward climax begins. In one of Widor's most memorable passages, fast-moving figuration derived from the three notes of "quam fe-" (E-F sharp-A) murmur near the bottom of the Grand-Orgue (with coupled

Récit) while high above enters "Hæc dies" in the florid cantus-firmus style on the Récit alone. As Conway noticed, this is yet "another instance of the wide separation of theme and accompaniment" in the *Symphonie romane*; it recalls striking passages in both the Moderato (beginning in m. 30) and the *Choral* (beginning in mm. 18 and 60).[38] This time, however, the effect is even more arresting, indeed, in some ways cinematic. "Hæc dies," presented *pp* against a louder accompaniment, is heard as if far away (just out of sight?) with a clear sense of expectancy; the ensuing crescendo, created by a surge of energy from the "quam fe-" motive, not only brings the music as if closer (fully into view?) but, sweeping even the opening motive of "Hæc" into its swirl of sixteenth-note motion, over a sizeable dominant pedal powerfully reinforces the sense of anticipation. Unlike the approach to the first *fff* climax, which was abrupt, and unlike that of the second *fff* climax, which relied on a sense of surprise, this passage provides a full measure of climactic preparation: the four measures preceding the arrival of the climax, in which the dominant pedal is decorated with upper neighbor-note motion (mm. 108–11), is a fine example of the musical prolongation of climactic inevitability.

Unlike either of the two preceding climaxes of the movement, this third try at a climactic gesture is convincingly prepared. Further, unlike the previous climaxes, a significantly slower new tempo is introduced as it arrives: Andante quasi adagio, quite exceeding the A tempo ma meno vivo indication for the first climax. (No slowing of the tempo was indicated for the second climax at all.) This *fff* passage, then, arrives as a potentially convincing climax for the movement, and its effect more than meets those expectations. A majestic four-part chorale-like texture is heard on the manuals, with "Hæc dies" in the lowest voice in a new, slower moving transformation which is even more like a cantus firmus than any previously encountered in the movement. A brief pedal entry underlines the migration of the chant melody to the alto where it is restated. Once again a pedal entry signals a change in the voice part of the melody, and "Hæc dies" is now found in the soprano as the pedal fills out an even fuller five-part (and in spots even denser) texture. Coming to a sudden stop on the diminished chord A sharp-C sharp-E-G (m. 129), E-G is first isolated and then harmonically reinterpreted as C major, making possible in that key yet another statement in the soprano of the chant melody. This most emphatic moment of the *Final* recalls in its tonality the C major climax of the Moderato; "Hæc dies," however, does not force a modulation to E minor as before. Widor instead gives the theme a new continuation, dramatically twisting it back into the realm of D major where the climax of the climax, so to speak, is reached on a massive six-four chord above a double D pedal (m. 133).

"Colossal" was T. Carl Whitmer's word for this summit of the *Final*; continuing, he drew attention to this remarkable portion of the movement:

The construction of such a climax is worth study. There is no slipshod piling up of ordinary chords which can suck all of the wind out of an ordinary organ; there is something more than mere banks of tone piled up. A careful examination reveals that the tonal intensity is the result of more than vertically placed chord masses; the management of individual voice-parts in such passages is done in a freely polyphonic way; so that, although to the eye there is horizontal movement, to the ear the bigness of the passage, its freedom, is not interfered with, but has the mighty ponderousness that is not elsewhere met outside the domain of orchestral writing.[39]

These remarks draw our attention to the sheer size of this passage: while the second of the preceding climaxes was longer than the first, the third is far longer than either of them. But "bigness" is more than length; it is also a question of density and weight. With its contrapuntal ingenuity and "mighty ponderousness" this passage far exceeds the norms of the preceding climaxes, establishing itself not only as the grandest climax of the movement, but of the entire symphony as well. Indeed, an essential quality—perhaps *the* essential quality—of this passage is its unsurpassability: a yet grander climax later in the work seems inconceivable.

Various aspects of this section of the *Final* suggest its interpretation as a coda, including the chorale-like transformation of the main melody of the movement and the concomitant disappearance of the the figural "first" and florid cantus-firmus "second" themes. Moreover, the passage can be understood as an apotheosis, both in the more everyday sense of the word as exaltation—certainly this is the crowning point of the work—and also in the more technical sense proposed by Edward T. Cone: what was originally heard (at the opening of the Moderato as well as the opening of the *Final*) in a thin texture here appears in a thick one.[40]

The resolution of this culmination is more leisurely than those of the previous two climaxes (though less extensive than the unusually long such section in the Moderato). Unlike any of those previous passages, however, it leads to a gesture so far unprecedented in the work: the actual recall of a passage from a preceding movement. The beginning arabesque of the Moderato is heard, as is its opening statement of "Hæc dies," returning the symphony to that style of chant which Widor described as "a vocalise as free as a bird's song." This time the quotation is heard *pp* rather than *ff*, as if a distant memory, lending a dream-like quality to the remainder of the movement. The chant tune's barest hint of a modulation from D major to F-sharp minor is gently countered by a lushly chromatic final cadence in D major, drawing the movement and with it the symphony to a serene conclusion.

The rounding of the *Symphonie romane* as a whole, with the return of the opening of the symphony at its very end, provides not only a poetic gesture of touching beauty but highlights yet once more Widor's emphasis on the "inexpressible suppleness" of chant which that passage epitomizes. (The *Final*, with its highly elaborate formal structures, did not foreground that quality of *Hæc dies* to the degree found in preceding movements.) It also serves, by implication, to draw attention to the ways in which the *Final* amplifies the previous movements of the composition, reintroducing thematic and harmonic elements: the opening monophonic "first" theme suggests the nearly monophonic presentations of *Hæc dies* in the Moderato; the F major tonality of the *Choral* is reflected in the "second" theme which, following sonata form, later resolves to the tonic of the movement and the symphony as a whole; *Hæc dies* in C major, the tonality of its climactic statement in the Moderato, returns at the peak of the climax, this time to be drawn back into the tonic, resolving, in a sense, the non-tonic climax of the first movement; the final appearance of *Hæc dies* as remembered from the Moderato also presents one last time of the tonal ambiguity of the chant with its opposition of D major and F-sharp minor. The sense that the finale recalls aspects of the work as a whole is, like the climax of the Moderato outside the tonic, broadly characteristic of later nineteenth-century symphonic composition, and particularly characteristic of Bruckner. So too is the wave-like construction of the *Final*; even more than in the Moderato, the articulation of form in the *Final* depends on the rise and fall of dynamic levels and the drive toward, and relaxation from, climactic moments. It was not for nothing that Widor was once called "a brother of Bruckner."[41]

According to Dupré's report, Widor thought about *Hæc dies* extensively before beginning to compose the *Symphonie romane*; details of Widor's early ideas about the work are not known, but a letter from him to Wallace Goodrich, dated 2 November 1898, states that the composer was at that time beginning to work out the *Symphonie romane* in his mind.[42] Regarding Widor's efforts to perfect his performance of the symphony, Schweitzer provides this touching remembrance:

> And when one May Sunday, still striving with technical problems, he played for the first time in St. Sulpice the *Symphonie Romane*, I felt with him that in this work the French art of organ playing had entered sacred art, and had experienced that death and that resurrection that every art of organ playing must experience when it wishes to create something enduring.[43]

Although Schweitzer does not specify the year in which this experience took place, it was almost surely 1899: in January 1900, Widor was reported to have performed the as yet unpublished *Symphonie romane* in concert (along with Bach's Fantasia and Fugue in G minor) at the Gedächtniskirche in Berlin.[44]

Soon after the publication of the *Symphonie romane*, both Vierne and Schweitzer noted in it something they each also observed in the *Symphonie gothique*: the quality of austerity. This austerity derives from the overall tone of these works—one of grandeur, solemnity, and serenity—and more specifically from their employment of sacred melodies. Yet neither Vierne nor Schweitzer could have known in the first decade of the twentieth century that austerity would reach new heights in Widor's next publication of music for the organ: the *Suite latine*, composed in 1927. Several of that collection's six movements are based upon chant tunes. There, nearly thirty years after composing the *Symphonie romane*, Widor turned away from the extremes of the rhythmically fluid rendition of chant melodies, as well as their intensive repetition, characteristic of his last organ symphony. Indeed, *Ave Maris Stella*, the movement in *Suite latine* most indebted to a chant melody, more closely resembles the *Salve Regina* of the 1901 revision of the Second Symphony than any movement in the *Symphonie romane* (not to mention the *Symphonie gothique*). Yet, the final five bars of the *Ave Maris Stella* do unmistakably recall the *Symphonie romane*: the final quotation of the chant melody in *Ave Maris Stella* is reminiscent of that of the *Final* where (recalling the distinctive passage near the opening of the Moderato) *Hæc dies* is heard as a vocalise accompanied by nothing more than a pedal point; in addition, the final cadence of *Ave Maris Stella*, immediately following the chant quotation, exhibits a similar harmonic extravagance as that of the *Final*, which follows from its own chant tune statement in the same way. In addition, the *Beatus vir* of *Suite latine* exhibits a melodic profile in its first section which is in some ways similar to that of the *Cantilène* of the *Symphonie romane*.

However much the *Symphonie romane* influenced Widor's later organ music, it did not go unnoticed by other French organ composers: the climax of Charles Tournemire's ambitious *Triple Choral* of 1910, despite the work's obvious allegiance to the Franck of the *Trois Chorals*, is clearly modeled on that of the *Final*. Moreover, the outer movements of the *Symphonie romane*—examples of large-scale movements based on chant tunes—must surely have been inspirational for the Tournemire of *L'Orgue mystique*, composed between 1927 and 1932. Moreover, the echo of the *Symphonie romane* is unmistakable in several other chant symphonies for organ which appeared in France in the first half of the twentieth century. In different ways, these works are logical extensions of Widor's conception: the *Symphonie d'après "Media Vita"* of Joseph Ermend-Bonnal from 1932 treats a single chant melody—but in its entirety, not merely its incipit—over the course of a multi-movement work while the *Symphonie mariale* of Léonce de Saint-Martin, completed in 1949, is a multi-movement organ symphony with each movement based on a different, but liturgically related, chant tune. (The monophonic, arabesque-like opening of its first movement seems a conscious evocation of the opening of that of the *Symphonie romane*; so too, for that matter, does the opening of the first movement of Vierne's Sixth Symphony, a work which, however, is not based on chant tunes.) Surprisingly, perhaps, the *Symphonie-Passion* by Widor's protégé of his later years, Dupré, composed in 1924, stands noticeably farther away from Widor's conception: its four movements each treat different chant tunes, not liturgically related but rather ordered for programmatic effect (Advent, Christmas, Good Friday, and Easter); perhaps paradoxically, given its altogether more advanced harmonic vocabulary, the treatment of those chants is more conservative, more in the style of the *Symphonie gothique* than of the *Symphonie romane*.

Schweitzer reports that around the turn of the century Widor remarked to him:

> that except for Bach's preludes and fugues—or, rather, except for certain preludes and fugues of Bach—I can no longer think of any organ art as holy which is not consecrated to the church through its themes, whether it be from the chorale or from the Gregorian chant.[45]

This may seem an extreme, even perplexing, view today: after the 1890s, Widor certainly continued to play at sacred services excerpts from his symphonies which were not based on chant tunes. Yet, as the words of Vierne which opened this essay indicate, such a view is not unrelated to Widor's idea—even more startling—that "since Cavaillé-Coll, the study of Bach has begun."[46] Widor's twin projects, the resurrection of Bach's organ music using the great French organs of his own time, and the development of a contemporary sacred organ music, likewise grounded in the attributes of those remarkable instruments, largely define, in their very broadest outline, his distinctive contributions to the art of organ playing and organ music. While Widor's style of Bach performance is today a curiosity in the history of the reception of that composer's music, his own organ music retains a significant place in the repertoire. And of his organ music the most important example—as well as the most impressive—remains the *Symphonie romane*.

I would like to thank Jimmy Jess Anthony for his help in the early stages of the formation of this essay; I am indebted in particular to his unpublished study, "The *Symphonie Romane* as *Art Nouveau*: An Interdisciplinary Structure," regarding several aspects of the work of François-Auguste Gevaert and Dom Joseph Pothier, as well as for a specific quotation noted below.

NOTES

[1] Louis Vierne, "Les Symphonies pour orgue de Ch.-M. Widor," *Le Guide musical*, 6 April 1902, p. 320.

[2] Albert Schweitzer, "The Art of Organ Building and Organ Playing in Germany and France," in *Music in the Life of Albert Schweitzer*, ed. Charles R. Joy (Boston: Beacon, 1951), 174.

[3] Paul Locard, *Les Maîtres contemporains de l'Orgue* (Paris: Fischbacher, 1901); John Near, "The Life and Work of Charles-Marie Widor" (D.M.A. diss., Boston University, 1985).

[4] Félix Raugel's comments (*The New Grove Dictionary of Music and Musicians*, s.v. Charles-Marie Widor) are typical; less characteristically, Jean Piccand refers to Widor's organ symphonies as "vast symphonic poems" (Jean Piccand, "Trois Organistes français," *Schweizerische Musikzeitung* 104/5 [1964]: 299). Indeed, an organ symphony might be considered "symphonic" for a variety of reasons, including form, effects related to timbre and scoring, and even character and tone: for Marmaduke P. Conway, "Widor no doubt uses the term ["symphony"] as implying breadth and loftiness of treatment . . ." (Marmaduke P. Conway, "Widor's Organ Symphonies," *Musical Opinion* 55 [1932]: 534).

[5] Henri Eymieu, "Nos Grands Organistes: Ch. M. Widor," *Revue pratique de liturgie et de musique sacrée* 6 (July-August 1922): 45.

[6] Charles-Marie Widor, "Les Orgues de Saint-Sulpice," in Gaston Lemesle, *L'Église Saint-Sulpice* (Paris: Bloud & Gay, 1931), 138.

[7] Elinor Olin, "The Concerts de l'Opéra 1895–97: New Music at the Monument Garnier," *19th Century Music* 16 (1993): 257.

[8] Henri Eymieu, *Études et Biographes musicales* (Paris: Fischbacher, 1892), 123.

[9] François-Auguste Gevaert, *La Mélopée antique dans le chant de l'église latine* (Ghent: Ad. Hoste, 1895).

[10] Charles-Marie Widor, "La Musique grecque et les chants de l'église latine," *Revue des deux mondes* 131 (1895): 706.

[11] Norbert Dufourcq, *La Musique d'orgue française de Jehan Titelouze à Jehan Alain* (Paris: Floury, 1941), 182.

[12] Interview with Pie Meyer-Siat, p. 62, in "Fonds Montpensier (Widor)," Bibliothèque Nationale. I am indebted to Anthony for this quotation.

[13] Marcel Dupré, "M. Charles-Marie Widor," *Les Nouvelles musicales*, 1 March 1934, p. 2.

[14] Charles-Marie Widor, avant-propos to *Symphonies pour orgue* (Paris: Hamelle, [1887]).

[15] Concerning the *Symphonie gothique*, Clarence Eddy remarked that Widor "has overladen it with contrapuntal design. It is full of canon and fugue and all that sort of thing, exceedingly difficult and not particularly interesting. Alfred Hollins, the celebrated blind organist of London, calls this symphony 'dry bones.'" (Clarence Eddy, "Great Frenchmen of Organ World in 1897 Are Pictured by Eddy," *The Diapason* 28 [May 1937]: 14.)

[16] Charles-Marie Widor, avant-propos to *Symphonie romane* (Paris: Hamelle, 1900).

[17] *Hæc dies* refers to the melody of the chant, while "Hæc dies" indicates its text.

[18] *Paroissien romain noté en plain-chant* (Paris: Adrien Le Clere, [1874]). Richard H. Hoppin maintains that *Hæc dies* is a second mode chant transposed up a fifth; see his *Medieval Music* (New York: W. W. Norton, 1978), 70.

[19] Dom Joseph Pothier, "Graduel 'Hæc dies,' du jour de Pâques," *Revue du chant grégorien* 4 (1896): 115. During the first decade of the twentieth century, Widor published several contributions to the debates concerning the editing and performing of chant (for example, "La Revision du plain-chant," *Correspondant*, 10 July 1904, pp. 55–66), while during those years Amédée Gastoué's "Autour de l'édition vaticane: lettre de Dom Pothier à M. Widor sur les éditions ponctuées" (*La Tribune de Saint-Gervais* 12 [January 1906]: 1–9) further drew Widor into the discussion; Widor's views on chant were still the subject of an impassioned article as late as 1927 (Dom L. David, "M. Widor, l'édition vaticane et le Te Deum," *Revue du chant grégorien* 31 [1927]: 81–90). Widor's positions in these controversies are summarized by Andrew Thomson in

272

The Life and Times of Charles-Marie Widor, 1844–1937 (Oxford: Oxford University Press, 1987), 67–68.

[20] Charles-Marie Widor, *Initiation musicale* (Paris: Hachette, 1923), 109.

[21] There can be no question but that he had the *Symphonie romane* in mind here: the reference to *Hæc dies* is paired with one to *Puer natus est* which appears in the *Symphonie gothique*.

[22] *L'Orgue moderne* first appeared in 1894. Volume two, which contains works by Boëllmann and Vivet in addition to Ropartz's *Offertoire pascal*, also dates from that year. By the end of the 1890s, Guilmant was a co-editor of the series with Widor; after Guilmant's death, Widor was once again the sole editor. The series was still appearing as late as 1929, having reached forty-two issues.

[23] Celia Grasty Jones, "The French Organ Symphony from Franck to Langlais" (D.M.A. diss., University of Rochester, Eastman School of Music, 1979), 63.

[24] Exactly why Widor chose D major as the tonic for the *Symphonie romane* is impossible to say, but the way his first eight organ symphonies appeared in their collections in stepwise rising keys is highly suggestive: the first four symphonies, op. 13, are in C minor, D major, E minor, and F minor, respectively; the second four, op. 42, are in F minor, G minor, A minor, and B major, respectively. With his Ninth, the *Symphonie gothique*, Widor returned to C minor; by placing his next such work, the *Symphonie romane*, in D major, Widor continued an already well established practice. This ordering does not, moreover, reflect the exact chronology of the composition of these works: Near has demonstrated that the Sixth, in G minor, was written before the Fifth, in F minor (Near, "The Life and Work of Charles-Marie Widor," 119–20). Additional support for the reading of the opening of the *Symphonie romane* in D major is provided by the fact that themes featuring the raised fourth degree are not unusual in Widor's organ music of this period; indeed, he demonstrates a particular fondness for this effect, as in the first theme of the first movement of the *Symphonie gothique* (F sharp in the context of C minor) and, even more tellingly, in the opening roulade of the *Salve Regina* movement of the Second Symphony (G sharp in the context of D minor).

[25] Marmaduke P. Conway, "Widor's Organ Symphonies," *Musical Opinion* 59 (1936): 530.

[26] Andrew Thomson has pointed to Widor's use of third related chords; see his "C. M. Widor: a Revaluation," *The Musical Times* 125 (1984): 170. His example there is drawn from the *Final* of the Third Symphony; Thomson does not, however, point out that this movement did not appear in the earliest edition of that symphony, and thus represents a somewhat more mature phase of Widor's compositional style than most of the other movements of that work. (The *Final* itself was also significantly revised several times after its first printing.)

[27] Conway, "Widor's Organ Symphonies," 530.

[28] The tonal plan of the Fifth Symphony is very similar: the first two movements are in F minor, the third in A-flat major, the fourth in C major, and the fifth in F major. Those of the Seventh and Eighth Symphonies—the two such works which were composed between the Fifth and the *Symphonie gothique*, the Sixth having been composed before the Fifth—also exhibit triadic organization, but in a more complex way: the Seventh, in A minor, outlines the triad of F-sharp minor, while the Eighth, in B major, includes a movement in the subdominant (and originally had an additional movement in A minor, a short movement which was linked thematically to, and appeared in the dominant of, a larger one following immediately in D minor).

[29] The term "counter-theme" was proposed by Conway ("Widor's Organ Symphonies," 531).

[30] Near, "The Life and Work of Charles-Marie Widor," 216. Interestingly enough, this was yet another passage of Widor's organ symphonies retouched in later editions. The first edition of 1900 spelled the chord C-G flat-B flat-E flat while a later version gives C-F sharp-B flat-D sharp, probably because of the changes made to the figuration in the following beat. (As late as the 1920 revision of Widor's organ symphonies, the *Symphonie romane* still presented the original version.)

[31] Jimmy Jess Anthony, "Charles-Marie Widor's *Symphonies pour orgue*: Their Artistic Context and Cultural Antecedents" (D.M.A. diss., University of Rochester, Eastman School of Music, 1986), 262.

[32] Conway, "Widor's Organ Symphonies," 531.

[33] Richard Taruskin, "Back to Whom? Neoclassicism as Ideology," *19th Century Music* 16 (1993): 289. Taruskin also draws attention to Scott Messing's comments quoted here.

[34] Scott Messing, *Neoclassicism in Music: From the Genesis of the Concept through the Schoenberg/Stravinsky Polemic* (Ann Arbor: UMI Research Press, 1988), 6.

[35] Quef is quoted in Eymieu, "Nos Grands Organistes: Ch. M. Widor," 47; Gustave Bret, "Les Symphonies pour orgue de Ch.-M. Widor," *Bulletin trimestriel des Amis de l'Orgue* 10 (September 1938): 16; Piccand, "Trois Organistes français," 299. Dufourcq apparently also believed this to be the case (*La Musique d'orgue française*, 182).

[36] Widor, *Initiation musicale*, 106.

[37] Eymieu, "Nos Grands Organistes: Ch. M. Widor," 48.

[38] Marmaduke P. Conway, "Widor's Organ Symphonies," *Musical Opinion* 59 (1936): 709.

[39] T. Carl Whitmer, "Widor's Organ 'Symphonies': A Series of Analytical Essays for Those Who Would be Composers or Who Would Better Understand and Interpret Their Works," *The American Organist* 17 (1934): 363.

[40] Edward T. Cone, *Musical Form and Musical Performance* (New York: W. W. Norton, 1968), 84.

[41] *Le Ménestrel* 94 (1932): 335.

[42] The letter is in the library of the New England Conservatory, Boston (see Near, "The Life and Work of Charles-Marie Widor," 211).

[43] Schweitzer, "The Art of Organ Building," 174.

[44] *Le Ménestrel* 66 (1900): 14. In November of 1899, Widor was reported to have completed a "twelfth organ symphony" during his vacation; this is surely a reference (despite the error in numbering) to the *Symphonie romane* (*Le Ménestrel* 65 [1899]: 359).

[45] Schweitzer, "The Art of Organ Building," 174.

[46] Charles-Marie Widor, preface to *Johann Sebastian Bach: The Organist and his Works for the Organ* by André Pirro, trans. Wallace Goodrich (New York: G. Schirmer, 1902), xix.

The Organ of the Trocadéro and Its Players

ROLLIN SMITH

The nineteenth century's greatest celebrations of commerce and industry, agriculture, science, and the fine arts were the five Universal Expositions held in Paris usually every eleven years: 1855, 1867, 1878, 1889, and 1900. (A sixth was held in 1937). Before the third Exposition it was decided to build a permanent headquarters in which all future events could take place and the site appropriated for the building was that area known as the Trocadéro. It was directly opposite the Champ-de-Mars—the broad expanse from the École Militaire to the Seine—which was used as the fairgrounds and the site upon which the Eiffel Tower was erected for the 1889 Exposition. The Champ-de-Mars was connected to the Trocadéro by a bridge, the Pont d'Iéna.

The original Trocadéro was a small fort on the Bay of Cadiz captured in 1823 by the Duc d'Angoulême, son of Charles X. To commemorate this Spanish campaign the king envisaged erecting on Chaillot Hill, then a beautiful terraced tree-shaded slope on the right bank of the Seine, an obelisk placed in the middle of an architectural ensemble which would be called La Villa Trocadéro. Later in 1856, Napoléon III planned a monument to the glory of the Italian army. Although neither of these projects was ever realized, the area came to be known as the Trocadéro.

On 4 April 1876, a commission was appointed to plan the Exposition headquarters. With only two years before the opening of the Exposition, the designs for the hall and the architects' plans were quickly approved and construction was under way. The completion of so great an edifice within a few months was a miracle of modern engineering. The Palais du Trocadéro, a gigantic Moorish-pseudo-Byzantine structure built by Bourdais and Davioud, was 1,411 feet wide and covered 42,653 square feet, with a colossal statue of Fame surmounting the great dome. The central building was a circular hall, the Salle des Fêtes, about 197 feet in diameter and 164 feet high. Above its northern facade (see Plate 1) rose two 230-foot high towers—like square minarets—intended as observation platforms, or belvederes, which were

275

Plate 1
The Northern Facade of the Palais du Trocadéro
Viewed from the Place du Trocadéro

equipped with remarkably advanced hydraulic elevators. On the south the palace was flanked by two-story high galleries with arcades which contained thirty statues representing the arts, science, and industry—many illustrating somewhat less than classical activities, such as La Pisciculture, La Télégraphie, and La Photographie. From the Trocadéro a great waterfall flowed down to the Pont d'Iéna, carving out a series of gardens bordered by smaller cascading waterfalls. Two great sloping flowerbeds surrounded by lawns decorated with statues framed the lowest eighty-nine-foot-wide expanse. At the bottom an immense pool was fed by still more waterfalls. A powerful hydraulic machine on the bank of the Seine brought water necessary for the fountains and sprinklers from the reservoirs at Passy.[1]

The principal building of previous Expositions had always been the Palais de l'Industrie in which all the exhibits were displayed; now a Palais des Fêtes was available for concerts, theatrical productions, and meetings. The great Salle des Fêtes, or Festival Hall, was an enormous 5,000–seat auditorium, an impressive capacity considering that the Paris Opéra seated only 2,100; the Théâtre du Châtelet, 3,600. The imposing interior (see Plate 2) was described in *The New York Times*:

> On the ground floor, arranged as a parquet—here called orchestral stalls,—there are 1,500 seats. In the first two there are 42 boxes, in the form of *baignoires*, with pilasters of black and gold supporting the balcony, which is divided into 50 opera boxes. The appearance of the pilasters is melancholy and funereal, and is not sufficiently relieved by the hangings of dark crimson velvet. Above the balcony is a vast amphitheater for 2,000 persons. Pierced in the wall, like the windows above which they are placed, are nine spacious tribunes. On the right and left of the stage, which is double the size of that of the Grand Opera, are two large proscenium boxes, one intended for the president of the Republic, the other for the minister of agriculture and commerce. The ornamentation of the hall is showy, if you except the black and gold pilasters. On the ceiling is a rose, divided into twelve parts by alternate branches of palm and laurel, with an immense "R. F." in the center. From the cupola extend gilded newels, each ending in a sphinx supported on a bracket, decorated with a scroll bearing the names of Bach, Handel, Haydn, Mozart, Beethoven, Cherubini, Weber, Mendelssohn, Berlioz and Félicien David. At the extreme end of the hall are two triumphal columns surmounted by statues of Fame distributing crowns, with escutcheons entwined in laurel leaves and inscribed with "Honneur aux Sciences! Gloire aux Arts!" These are the work of the sculptor, Carrier Belleuse, as those on the other side of the proscenium boxes are due to the genius of Mr. Blanchard, who has taken for his subject "Law" and "Strength." The frieze above the stage, painted by Charles Lameyre, represents France summoning to her throne all the nations of the earth.[2]

By January 1877 a Committee for the Admission of Musical Instruments, on which Aristide Cavaillé-Coll was the only organbuilder, was appointed and in August, Camille Saint-Saëns, Alexandre Guilmant, and Théodore Dubois

Plate 2
The Salle des Fêtes

were among those appointed to the Exposition Music Committee. An organ was evidently not one of the immediate priorities of those charged with the hall's appointments. Cavaillé-Coll, his biographers contend, was approached by the committee to build an organ but because of the price—200,000 francs—his proposal was rejected.[3] When the committee changed its mind at the last minute, it was too late to build an organ large enough to fill so vast a space in time for the opening of the Exposition. The solution:

> Cavaillé-Coll had just finished an organ for the new church in Auteuil which had hardly begun to go up. . . . The pastor [was] the same Abbé Lamazou who, since 1854, had been unceasingly devoted to the organ and to Cavaillé-Coll. An agreement was easily reached to loan the forty-five-stop organ to the Trocadéro.[4]

The village of Auteuil was annexed to the City of Paris in 1860. When the parish church of Notre-Dame was rebuilt in the seventeenth century its original tower, dating from the twelfth century, was incorporated into the new structure. Voltaire's brother and Anatole France's father were buried in the parish cemetery; Charles Gounod was married in Notre-Dame-d'Auteuil in April 1852. César Franck's younger brother, Joseph, was organist there from 1861 to 1866. Pierre-Henri Lamazou, one of Saint-Saëns's curates at La Madeleine, was appointed pastor of Notre-Dame-d'Auteuil in 1874. The church, which had become too small for the size of its congregation, was torn down in 1877.[5] The new building was not free of debt and was not consecrated until 1892. Cavaillé-Coll's first connection with the church seems to have been his two-manual, thirty-two-stop organ delivered to Notre-Dame on 3 December 1884. (It was inaugurated 11 February 1885.) In the meantime, in 1881, Abbé Lamazou had been named Bishop of Limoges.

The question, then, is why would Cavaillé-Coll have built a three-manual, forty-five-stop organ for a church that was admittedly too small for its parish's needs—and for which its sixteen-stop Stoltz organ was adequate—if, indeed, Cavaillé-Coll's organ was for the old church; or, why would an organ have been completed for a church whose old building had not yet been demolished? How, indeed, had Notre-Dame-d'Auteuil become connected with the organ of the Trocadéro?

A reasonable hypothesis may be constructed from the available, though disparate, facts. It is obvious that Cavaillé-Coll had a three-manual organ completed. There is no reference in his opus list to the Trocadéro, save the eventual installation, and no mention of the church of Notre-Dame-d'Auteuil until 1884.[6] The purchaser (now unknown) of the recently finished organ had undoubtedly cancelled the contract. Abbé Lamazou seized the opportunity to acquire a fine organ for his new church with two advantages in the bargain: he would have gotten it for a good price and also would have the new organ completed and installed at the time of the completion of the church—a notably rare occurrence—schedules of building contractors and organbuilders rarely coinciding. Lamazou would have given Cavaillé-Coll a retainer but, due to delays in construction schedules and price increases, the pastor found himself financially overextended and realized that it would be several years before his church could take possession of the organ. Evidence of this transaction is found in a letter written in Rome from Abbé Lamazou to Cavaillé-Coll on 29 September 1877 in which he mentions an audience with Pope Leo XIII at which he "did not dare remind him of Suspendiumus Organa nostra and tell him of the unfortunate incident at Auteuil."[7]

The Trocadéro's demand for an organ presented a solution for both the financially embarrassed priest and the organbuilder anxious to make a sale. A propitious set of circumstances converged to enable Cavaillé-Coll, a member of one commission, to use the influence of his friends on other committees, to have the syndicate acquire his organ. The new organ delivered to the new Exposition headquarters seems to have been on a kind of permanent loan: its price was neither agreed upon nor paid for another four years.

The Organ

To the original organ Cavaillé-Coll added a fourth manual, augmented the pedal division, and added 32' towers at either end of the case. The sixty-six-stop organ contained 4,070 pipes and was ideally situated in the front of the hall stretching forty-nine feet across the width of the stage. The case was thirty-three feet deep. The specification of the organ is given in Figure 1; the console layout is in Figure 2.

Two undated manuscript diagrams drawn by Marcel Dupré and Joseph Bonnet provide the basis for the schematic diagram of the organ console.[8] Dupré's diagram, dating from well before 1920, is the earliest source and is a replica of the knobs as they were symmetrically arranged on the console. He played the organ for the first time publicly on 23 April 1911, but had pulled stops for Guilmant previously. Bonnet's more schematic diagram is less precise than Dupré's, being drawn in uniform squares always starting from the left. Most of the names are abbreviated and, hastily executed on the back of a program, it might even have been reconstructed from memory. The only discrepancy between these two specifications is the inside Positif drawknobs. Bonnet designated the left knob *Comb. Gde. Péd.* while Dupré wrote *Combinaison Pédale*, perhaps a kind of "free combination" device added at a later date. The right drawknob was labeled *Récit au Positif* by Dupré; Bonnet omitted it altogether, beginning the side with the *Flûte harmonique* and ending with two blank squares at the right. Wind for the organ always having been supplied by steam engine, there were no *Sonnette*, or bellows signal, drawknobs.

Tonally, the Trocadéro organ was an ideal vehicle for French symphonic organ music and a worthy companion to Cavaillé-Coll's great instruments at

Figure 1

Specification of the Trocadéro Organ[82]

I. Grand-Orgue (56 notes, C-g''')
Montre 16
Bourdon 16
Montre 8
Flûte harmonique 8
Bourdon 8
Violoncelle 8
Prestant 4
Flûte douce 4
Doublette 2
Dessus de Cornet V
Plein jeu V
Bombarde 16
Trompette 8
Clairon 4

II. Positif (56 notes)
Bourdon 16
Principal 8
Flûte harmonique 8
Salicional 8
Unda maris 8
Flûte octaviante 4
Quinte 2 2/3
Doublette 2
Plein jeu harmonique III-IV
Basson 16
Trompette 8
Cromorne 8

III. Récit (56 notes)
Quintaton 16
Flûte harmonique 8
Cor-de-nuit 8
Viole de gambe 8
Voix céleste 8
Flûte octaviante 4

Octavin 2
Cornet V
Carillon I-III
Basson 16
Trompette 8
Basson-hautbois 8
Voix humaine 8
Clairon harmonique 4

IV. Solo (56 notes)
Bourdon 16
Diapason 8
Flûte harmonique 8
Violoncelle 8
Flûte octaviante 4
Octavin 2
Tuba magna 16
Trompette harmonique 8
Clarinette 8
Clairon harmonique 4

Pédale (30 notes, C-f')
Principal basse 32
Contrebasse 16
Sous-basse 16
Grosse Flûte 16
Violon basse 16
Grosse Flûte 8
Basse 8
Bourdon 8
Violoncelle 8
Contre-bombarde 32
Bombarde 16
Basson 16
Trompette 8
Basson 8
Clairon 4
Baryton 4

(Stops in italics are controlled by the *anches* pedals.)

282

Pédales de Combinaison

From left to right:
Orage
Tirasse Grand-Orgue
Tirasse Positif
Tirasse Récit
Anches Pédale
Grand-Orgue Octaves Graves
Positif Octaves Graves
Récit Octave Graves
Solo Octave Graves
Anches Grand-Orgue
Anches Positif
Anches Récit
Anches Solo
Grand-Orgue sur machine
Positif au Grand-Orgue
Récit au Grand-Orgue
Solo au Grand-Orgue
Récit au Positif
Tremblant Positif
Tremblant Récit
Expression Positif
Expression Récit
Combinaison du Solo

Figure 2

Trocadéro Console Layout

Left Side	*Right Side*
Top Row, Left to Right:	Top Row, Left to Right:
Solo	Solo
Clarinette 8	Violoncelle 8
Tuba magna 16	Flûte harmonique 8
Octavin 2	Diapason 8
Flûte octaviante 4	Trompette harmonique 8
Bourdon 16	Clairon harmonique 4

283

Left Side	*Right Side*
Second Row, Left to Right:	Second Row, Left to Right:
Récit	Récit
Basson 16	Flûte harmonique 8
Cornet V	Cor-de-nuit 8
Octavin 2	Viole de gambe 8
Voix humaine 8	Voix céleste 8
Carillon I-III	Basson-hautbois 8
Flûte octaviante 4	Trompette 8
Quintaton 16	Clairon harmonique 4
Third Row, Left to Right:	Third Row, Left to Right:
Positif	Positif
Basson 16	Récit au Positif
Doublette 2	Flûte harmonique 8
Quinte 2 2/3	Principal 8
Flûte octaviante 4	Unda maris 8
Salicional 8	Plein jeu harmonique III-IV
Bourdon 16	Trompette 8
Combinaison Pédale	Cromorne 8
Fourth Row, Left to Right:	Fourth Row, Left to Right:
Grand-Orgue	Grand-Orgue
Bombarde 16	Montre 8
Dessus de Cornet V	Violoncelle 8
Doublette 2	Flûte harmonique 8
Flûte douce 4	Bourdon 8
Prestant 4	Plein jeu V
Bourdon 16	Trompette 8
Montre 16	Clairon 4
Bottom Row, Left to Right:	Bottom Row, Left to Right:
Pédale	Pédale
Clairon 4	Contrebasse 16
Trompette 8	Violon basse 16
Bombarde 16	Grosse Flûte 8
Contre-bombarde 32	Violoncelle 8
Basse 8	Bourdon 8
Sous-basse 16	Basson 16
Grosse Flûte 16	Basson 8
Principal basse 32	Baryton 4

Sainte-Clotilde, Saint-Sulpice, and Notre-Dame with two celestes, two Cornets, two expressive divisions, a Clarinette in addition to the traditional Cromorne, and 16', 8', and 4' chorus reeds on every division. All of these appointments must be considered in studying Franck's *Trois Pièces*, as this is the organ for which they were composed. Although the printed registration reflects Sainte-Clotilde's forty-six-stop organ, we know from the registration written in the manuscript that the composer/organist did not try to duplicate that instrument's sound on the Trocadéro's more varied tonal palette.[9] And while Franck does not indicate crescendos or diminuendos on the Positif, Widor does in his Fifth Symphony, and it is not unreasonable that he had this instrument, rather than that of Saint-Sulpice, in mind when registering his Fifth and Sixth Symphonies.

The Organ's Inauguration

The first official concert of the 1878 Exposition took place on 6 June 1878, when Édouard Colonne conducted an orchestra of 350 and a large chorus in Félicien David's *Le Désert* and Saint-Saëns's cantata, *Les Noces de Prométhée* (see Plate 3). The organ, still being installed, was not inaugurated until two months later when, on 7 August, Alexandre Guilmant (1837–1911), organist of La Trinité, played the opening recital. Among the works he played were:

Fanfare	Lemmens
Gavotte in F Major	Martini
Marche	Chauvet
Marche funèbre et chant séraphique	Guilmant
Concerto in B-flat Major	Handel
Toccata and Fugue in D Minor [BWV 565]	J. S. Bach
Adagio (Sonata No. 1 in F Minor)	Mendelssohn
Grand Chœur alla Handel	Guilmant

It was noted that:

M Guilmant's playing is marked by qualities of clarity and a discerning confidence in the choice and combination of timbres. He employs the expression pedal rather often perhaps, but always to achieve a logical effect.[10]

While the first part of the program was loudly applauded, the music of Bach and Handel made the audience restless. "Too bad for the audience. We are consoled by thinking that little by little it will be musically educated."[11]

The Recital Series

After this dedicatory recital began a series in which, for two months, twice a week at three o'clock in the afternoon, sixteen organists were heard in hour-

Plate 3
The Opening Concert of the Trocadéro

long recitals. These programs were of great importance in the history of the organ in France, for this was the first time a large concert organ had been installed in a public hall. No longer would people listen to the solemn tones of the organ only as it rolled beneath Gothic arches in dim light filtering through centuries-old stained glass. Instead, they sat in the great ovoid-shaped room and looked directly at the imposing organ case which dominated the stage. Admission was free and, as this was the only time the general public could get in to see the celebrated hall without having to pay to attend a concert, the organ recitals drew larger audiences than any other musical program at the Trocadéro during the Exposition. Of course, there was a large turnover in the audience which came and went, but a nucleus of music lovers, estimated at between 1,500 and 2,000 persons, who came to hear, not just to see, stayed for the entire recital. This was particularly phenomenal as the organist was hidden from view. Just as in church, the console was reversed so that the organist (concealed by a wooden screen in the very center of the case) faced into the auditorium.

The programs of the fourteen *Séances d'orgue* have been culled from contemporary issues of *La Revue et Gazette musicale* and *Le Ménestrel*. Any pertinent critical commentary has been included.

II. Samuel de Lange
10 August

Toccata and Fugue in C Major [BWV 564]	J. S. Bach
Fantasia and Fugue in G Minor [BWV 542]	
Canzona	Frescobaldi
Two movements (Sonata No. 6 in D Minor)	Mendelssohn
Adagio	Merkel
Concerto No. 4 in D Major	Handel
Sonata in G Minor	de Lange

Samuel de Lange (1840–1911), professor of organ at the Cologne Conservatory, was the most prominent Dutch organist of the day.

His choice of pieces, as well as the brief time he was allowed to familiarize himself with the organ, prevented him from using certain tonal and expressive effects with which, perhaps, he might have more easily won over his audience.[12]

The critic pointed out that de Lange's program distinguished itself from those of Guilmant and Gigout by its severe and churchly style, cited the necessity for a varied program and use of varied stops, and commented that "while it is not necessary to descend to bad taste, the severity of style necessary for church must be put aside in these concerts—a point understood by Guilmant and Gigout."[13] The most popular piece on the program was the Allegretto from the Mendelssohn Sonata.

III. Eugène Gigout
13 August

Prelude in E Minor [BWV 548]	J. S. Bach
Intermezzo	Gigout
Gavotte (Sonata No. 3)	Padre Martini
Andante religioso (Sonata No. 4 in B-flat Major)	Mendelssohn
Fugue in D Minor	Niedermeyer
Prelude (*Trois Pièces*, No. 1)	Gigout
Andante con moto (Prelude No. 2 in G Major, op. 37)	Mendelssohn
Trio Sonata No. 2 in C Minor [BWV 526]	J. S. Bach
Fantasy in E-flat Major	Saint-Saëns
Prelude (*Grand Chœur*)	Niedermeyer
Pastorale	
Andante con moto (*Trois Pièces*, No. 3)	Gigout
Improvisation	
Finale (Concerto No. 3 in G Minor)	Handel

Gigout (1844–1925) was organist at Saint-Augustin and, as of December 1876, a member of the commission appointed by the city of Paris in charge of selecting builders for new organs, examining them, and inaugurating them. He later opened his own school where he taught organ and improvisation and, in 1911, succeeded Guilmant as professor of organ at the Conservatoire. His playing of the Bach Prelude

> seemed a little confused due to the *trop grande sonorité* of the organist's choice of stops . . . The melodious Andante of Mendelssohn's *Fourth Sonata* was encored. The employment of the Voix humaine and of certain other stops clearly revealed the virtuoso in search of effects, but it cannot be denied that those effects were charming. We would have wished for less *rallentando* and studied refinement in Mendelssohn's *Andante con moto*.

Gigout showed off the organ with an improvisation "whose themes were short and facilely developed."[14]

IV. Théodore Dubois
21 August

Prelude and Fugue in G Minor	J. S. Bach
Allegretto (Sonata No. 4 in B-flat Major)	Mendelssohn
Fantaisie	Dubois
Two canons	Schumann
Two chorale preludes	J. S. Bach
Herzlich tut mich verlangen [BWV 727]	
Allein Gott in der Höh sei Ehr [BWV 711]	
Sonata No. 6 in D Minor	Mendelssohn
Improvisation	
Grand Chœur	Dubois

Dubois (1837–1924) at this time was one of the leading musicians in France. By 1859 he had won first prizes in harmony, piano, organ, counterpoint, and fugue at the Conservatoire and the First Grand Prix de Rome in

1861. He had served as *maître-de-chapelle* under Franck at Sainte-Clotilde and under Saint-Saëns at La Madeleine. He had been professor of harmony at the Conservatoire since 1871 and organist of La Madeleine for a year.

Dubois played the only Bach chorale preludes on the recital series: "a beautiful adagio in B Minor, its theme simply stated, was easily grasped by the audience, and a two-part contrapuntal arrangement in G Major." The opening Bach work was "very correctly played" and the Mendelssohn Allegretto, "decidedly a popular piece among organists," was played in a way to make it thoroughly enjoyed by the audience except that "the left hand sixteenth-note figuration at the beginning was played on soft stops and was difficult to hear." In the improvisation

> two themes in different rhythms were treated stylishly and interestingly; the ending was particularly delightful. This part of the program (more or less prepared, no doubt, but what does that matter to the audience?) brought the artist a well deserved ovation.

The audience turnover was particularly annoying at this concert and the reviewer concluded his remarks by imploring the administration "to ask the ushers to take seriously the notice forbidding the public entrance to the hall during performances."[15]

V. Charles-Marie Widor
24 August

Sixth Symphony (First Performance)	Widor
Chorale and Allegro	
Andante	
Intermezzo	
Cantabile	
Final	
Adagio (Sonata No. 1 in F Minor)	Mendelssohn
Fanfare	Lemmens
Pastorale (Second Symphony in D Major)	Widor
Fugue in D Major [BWV 532]	J. S. Bach
Allegretto (transcription of the Duo for harmonium and piano)	Widor
Final (Third Symphony in E Minor)	Widor

By the time of this recital Widor's (1844–1937) organ career had become firmly established and his "virtuosity legendary."[16] "A brilliant performing talent with scarcely a difficulty standing in his way," nevertheless he sometimes "rushed the tempo, as, for instance, in Bach's *Fugue in D*. We also wished that he had used softer stops in the Mendelssohn *Adagio*."[17]

The program listed the *Cinquième Symphonie* but, from the titles of the movements, it is obvious that what was premiered at this concert was what came to be published as the Sixth Symphony in G Minor. This work, it now seems clear, was composed before the Fifth Symphony in F Minor but, in order to maintain an ascending key sequence for publication, the composer reversed their chronological order.[18] The critic noted the "very gracious

289

Andante which brings to mind, by its descending half steps, the style of Wagner."[19] The same reviewer was uncertain what defined organ style as opposed to piano style. He had previously commented that Saint-Saëns's Fantasy in E-flat Major, played by Gigout, at times seemed to have been conceived "for the piano rather than this grandiose instrument"[20] and was later critical of Liszt's organ works played by Saint-Saëns. Referring to the Intermezzo of Widor's new *Symphonie* he commented that it was "brilliant, but written for the piano rather than the organ, as are other parts of this work in fast tempo and more than one piece of which we have had to speak in the preceding recitals."[21] The absence of an improvisation prompted the writer to ask: "Why, with his virtuosity and talent as a composer, has not M Widor followed the example of his French colleagues who have all reserved a place on their programs for improvisation?"[22]

VI. Alphonse Mailly
28 August

Allegro maestoso and Andante (Sonata in D Minor, op. 1)	Mailly
Prelude (Allegro moderato e serioso from Sonata No. 1 in F Minor)	Mendelssohn
Aria	Handel
Fugue in G Minor	J. S. Bach
Simple Mélodie (*Petites Pièces*, No. 12)	Mailly
Toccata and Fugue in D Minor [BWV 565]	J. S. Bach
Romance in B-flat Minor	Chauvet
Prière	Lefébure-Wély
Petite Marche solennelle	Mailly

Mailly (1833–1918) had succeeded Jaak Nikolaas (Jacques-Nicolas) Lemmens as professor of organ at the Brussels Conservatory. He displayed "perfect mastery of his instrument [and was] very at ease in playing" but, on the other hand, he yielded

to the temptation to temper whenever possible the severities of organ style and to make *everything* he interprets as expressive as possible. Thus can be explained the rather capricious tempo and rhythmic variations introduced in the Mendelssohn and the two admirable Bach works.

The reviewer objected to the obbligato figuration played on a 16' and 2' combination (as printed in the score) heard against the principal theme of the Andante of Mailly's Sonata, and further noted "we should like to see excluded the carillon stop, which is hardly suitable to a sonata."[23]

VII. 3 September
PART I
Victor Nant

Marche nuptiale	Guilmant
Pastorale	Franck
Romance in B-flat Minor	Chauvet
Scherzo	
Vif varié	Lebel
Résurrection (Symphony for Organ)	Nant

The organist of Saint-Jean-Baptiste and professor at the National Institution for Blind Youths,

> by reason of his blindness, excited a lively interest. He proved that without the aid of sight he had acquired quite a serious talent at the organ. His skill was especially evident in Guilmant's *Marche nuptiale* in which the continuous manual changes in no way hindered him.[24]

PART II
Edmond Lemaigre

Prelude and Fugue in C Minor	J. S. Bach
Cantabile	Lemaigre
Communion in G Major	Batiste
Fanfare	Lemmens

Lemaigre was organist of the Cathedral of Clermont-Ferrand where the previous year Guilmant had inaugurated the new Merklin organ. His style, as exemplified in his own Cantabile, was "not very severe. . . . The Bach was well played, the Batiste encored. The concert, a little long, could not have ended more brilliantly than with the Lemmens *Fanfare*."[25]

VIII. Clément Loret
10 September

Another former student of Lemmens, Loret (1833–1909) was organist of Saint-Louis-d'Antin and professor of organ at the École Niedermeyer where he numbered among his former pupils three organists who appeared on this Trocadéro series: Eugène Gigout, André Messager, and Jules Stoltz. Loret presented several of his own compositions.

> Generally conceived in a pleasantly melodious style, they have every chance of pleasing the public: consequently, they were enthusiastically applauded, especially the *Variations sur des Noëls*. The improvisation was, perhaps, a bit dull, but it set off advantageously certain stops of the instrument. M Loret played very well the Adagio of Handel's *First Concerto* and Bach's *Fugue in G Minor* (not the great fugue which follows the famous *Fantasy in G Minor*).[26]

IX. Jules Stoltz
12 September

Allegro (Concerto in G Minor)	Handel
One piece	Couperin
Prelude	Clérambault
Finale (Concerto)	Rinck
Allegro (Finale from Sonata No. 4 in B-flat Major)	Mendelssohn

Jules Stoltz (1848–1906) was the son and brother of Édouard and Eugène Stoltz, the noted organbuilders. He was a pupil of Loret, having won first prize in organ at the École Niedermeyer in 1869. He remained at the school as teacher of solfège and later improvisation and, at the time of this recital, was *maître-de-chapelle* of Saint-Leu. "His performance was good, intelligently shaded, although sometimes a little unfaithful to the text."[27] The Clérambault, perfectly registered, was the highlight of the recital. The Rinck Concerto movement was judged very old-fashioned and no value was seen in restoring it to the repertoire. The Mendelssohn was "a little too overladen with details for the organ."[28]

Guilmant arranged for his former organ teacher, Jacques-Nicolas Lemmens (1823–1881) and his wife, Helen Lemmens-Sherrington, the celebrated English soprano, then visiting Paris, to be heard in a special concert at the Trocadéro. Even though it was not part of the official recital series, and there was a one franc admission charge, Lemmens's program drew a very large audience—but, as usual, "more visitors than listeners."[29] Their program:

Sonate pontificale	Lemmens
M Lemmens, organ	
"Grand Dieu! quel art humain"	Handel
(*Ode to Saint Cecilia*; organ accompaniment)	
"Air du Rossignol"	
(*L'Allegro, il Penseroso*)	
Mme Lemmens, soprano	
Paul Taffanel, flute	
Alexandre Guilmant, piano	
Fanfare	Lemmens
Hosannah!	
Grand Fantasia in E Minor ("The Storm")	
M Lemmens, organ	

"As always, the famous *Fanfare* carried the audience away with enthusiasm and it had to be played twice."[30]

X. Scotson Clark
19 September

Commemoration March	Clark
Mélodie in F Major	
Thème et Variations	
Marche aux flambeaux	
Two pieces	Lemmens
One piece	Mendelssohn
Fugue	J. S. Bach

The unintentional contrast between Lemmens's concert and the one which followed was astounding. The 19 September concert was to have been a joint recital given by Frederick Scotson Clark (1840–1883) and an Italian organist, M Galimberti. The former, an English clergyman, organist, and composer, had founded the London Organ School in 1873 and was the representative English organist at the Exposition. His *Fifteen Marches* enjoyed a certain popularity in the late nineteenth century, particularly the *Marche aux flambeaux.*

An Italian organist M Galimberti was also to have played on this recital. His program was to have been composed of overtures by Verdi, Flotow, and Rossini, and a *Gran Pezzo Fantastico* by Maestro Quirici, *The Catastrophy of Pompey*, for which it appeared the organ of the Trocadéro was insufficiently provided with noisy stops, drums, cymbals, etc. Rather than compromise the effect of the *Gran Pezzo Fantastico*, M Galimberti declined to be heard. It is a great pity.[31]

XI. 24 September
PART I
Auguste Andlauer

Choral	Widor
Canzone	Guilmant
Toccata and Fugue in D Minor	J. S. Bach
Grand Fantasia in E Minor ("The Storm")	Lemmens
Grand Chœur	Andlauer

Auguste Andlauer (d. 1889), a Belgian student of Lemmens, was organist of Notre-Dame-des-Champs in Paris. He was "an artist of very conscientious and correct talent who showed the most serious qualities in the performance of all his pieces, and in particular the Bach, which he took at a tempo a bit too fast."[32]

293

PART II
Jules Grison

Toccata in A Major	Hesse
Morceau pour l'inauguration d'orgue sur un motif de Mendelssohn	Grison
Andante in B Major	Chauvet
Andante in G Major	Batiste
Les Cloches, souvenir	Grison
Prelude and Fugue in E Minor [BWV 533]	J. S. Bach
Improvisation, *en pastorale*	
Marche triomphale	Grison

M J. Grison, organist of the Cathedral of Rheims, does not understand the organ in the same way as Auguste Andlauer. . . . Aside from the *Toccata* by Hesse and Bach's *Prelude and Fugue*, he set himself to playing the kind of compositions most pleasing to the great majority of the audience. Not that it is necessary to cultivate a severe genre exclusively at the Trocadéro, but there are limits to be avoided at the opposite extreme. The improvisation seemed *un peu léger* and we noticed several modifications to the text of the Bach piece: M Grison transposed an octave higher the beginning and other parts of the fugue, whose melancholy character hardly calls for a change. Nevertheless, certain picturesque effects were very well done and he must have been very pleased with the reception he received.[33]

XII. Camille Saint-Saëns
28 September

Trois Rhapsodies sur des cantiques bretons	Saint-Saëns
Prelude to *Le Déluge*	
Prelude and Fugue in E-flat Major [BWV 552]	J. S. Bach
Legend No. 1: "Saint Francis of Assisi Preaching to the Birds"	Liszt
Fantasia and Fugue on "Ad nos, ad salutarem undam"	
Introduction	
Adagio	
Fugue	
Finale	

A large crowd, including all of the illustrious artists of Paris, came for what was one of the rare opportunities of hearing this French master of the organ. Saint-Saëns (1835–1921), who had recently left La Madeleine after nearly twenty years as organist, was one of the leading organists in France. At the conclusion of the *Rhapsodies bretons*, "gems of fine registration and charm of execution,"[34] the audience was warmly enthusiastic and "numerous cries for an encore were heard."[35] The Prelude to *The Deluge* had been added to the original program and "the composer interpreted it very tastefully and skillfully and the organ's various timbres produced a charming effect." Saint-Saëns was given such an ovation that "this time he yielded to the audience's request and played it again."

He concluded the first half of the recital with "a very beautiful and artistic" performance of Bach's Prelude and Fugue in E-flat Major. One critic observed:

> We only would have wished for fewer heavy manual stops in the *Prelude*—16' tone made the playing a bit confused given the size and acoustics of the hall. Besides, the *organo pleno* in Bach's time was not what it is today and the 16' reeds, especially, did not have the intensity of our modern stops on high pressure. On the contrary, the organs were rich in high-pitched stops, mixtures, etc. Above all, clarity of execution is necessary in the *Prelude* which is often written in five parts in a low, rather than a high, register.[36]

It had been publicized that Saint-Saëns would play the Liszt Legend between the *Three Breton Rhapsodies* and the Bach.[37] Other accounts list the entire second half of the program devoted to the music of Liszt. Wherever its place in the program, it was a distinct novelty in 1878 to have the music of Liszt on an organ recital. This was the first performance of the Fantasia and Fugue on "Ad nos, ad salutarem undam" in France, indeed, its first performance outside of Germany. Moreover, a champion of Liszt's piano music, Saint-Saëns was the first French pianist to play the piano works of Liszt. He had played both of Liszt's Legends ("Saint Francis of Assisi Preaching to the Birds" and "Saint Francis of Paola Walking on the Waves") on the organ— the first he played frequently for weddings at La Madeleine. Liszt was delighted with the effect of that piece on the organ and wrote Saint-Saëns:

> I am still quite struck with wonder at your *Prédication aux oiseaux*. You use your organ as an orchestra in an incredible way, as only a great composer and a great performer like yourself could. The most proficient organists in all countries have only to take off their hats to you.[38]

Liszt was later to describe Saint-Saëns as "the most eminent and extraordinary king of organists,"[39] a judgement based, perhaps more than anything else, on Saint-Saëns's performances of the Fantasia and Fugue on "Ad nos." This work, composed in 1850, was one Saint-Saëns played frequently for the rest of his life. He described it in 1911 as:

> . . . the most extraordinary organ piece in existence. It lasts forty minutes and the interest doesn't lag for a moment. Just as Mozart in his *Fantaisie* and *Sonata in C Minor* foresaw the modern piano, so Liszt, writing his *Fantaisie* more than half a century ago, seems to have foreseen today's instrument of a thousand resources.[40]

When Saint-Saëns brought these two works before the general public in 1878 they were still contemporary music; then as now, they were criticized as being too pianistic. One reviewer wrote that:

> It would take nothing less than the great talent of this eminent artist to make us accept these two virtuoso pieces, the second of which, although written for the organ . . . seemed to rely chiefly on pianistic devices.[41]

But the writer for *Le Ménestrel* concluded that:

> It is futile to speak of M Saint-Saëns's playing. It is simply prodigious. As for his registration, it is a reflection of the orchestral palette of the composer of the Symphonic Poems. M Cavaillé-Coll, who attended the recital, stated with satisfaction that, after numerous hearings of the organ, it was still possible to draw new effects from his superb instrument.[42]

There was disappointment only in not hearing Saint-Saëns improvise. After so many illustrious musicians had visited La Madeleine to hear his improvisations, "for no apparent reason, none found a place on the very meaty program of this recital."[43]

XIII. César Franck
1 October

Fantasy in A Major	Franck
Grande Pièce symphonique, op. 17	
Cantabile	
Improvisation	
Pièce héroïque	
Improvisation	

Perhaps the single most important reason the name of the Trocadéro has survived in the organ world is that César Franck's *Trois Pièces* were composed expressly for his organ recital there. They were completed within seven days, two weeks before the recital. By October 1878 Franck (1822–1890) had been organist of Sainte-Clotilde for twenty years and professor of organ at the Conservatoire for six. His *Six Pièces* had been in print for ten years and his reputation was well established among organists, so well established it seems that it was not untoward for him to give a recital of only his own music—the only such program on the Trocadéro series.

Of the new *Trois Pièces*, the critic found the Fantasy in A Major a beautiful, very skillfully wrought piece,

> but all the details were not well brought out: the soft stops lacking presence and distinctness in the hall. The *Cantabile* in B Major, an impressive melody of noble character, was more effective thanks to the telling Récit stop employed. The *Pièce heroïque*, although containing some excellent things, seemed less interesting than the two other works. As for the *Grande Pièce symphonique* in F-sharp minor, it has long been known and justly appreciated. The Andante, as always, was warmly welcomed.[44]

Perhaps because of the negative criticism, Franck never played the *Pièce héroïque* in public again (although, ironically, it later became his most popular organ piece). He did play both the Fantasy and the Cantabile twice more.[45]

Franck's first improvisation was based on themes by French masters: the first chorus of Félicien David's *Le Désert*, two themes from Hector Berlioz's *L'Enfance du Christ*, and two themes from Georges Bizet's *L'Arlésienne*. "He brought out charming details in his free-style treatment of these themes,

296

especially those of Berlioz." Franck concluded his recital with another lengthy improvisation on Russian themes (two popular motifs), first treated separately, and then superimposed upon Swedish, Hungarian, and English themes.

> The themes were too numerous and it would not have been possible to take advantage of each one sufficiently without fatiguing the audience. With this slight reservation, we happily pay hommage to the most elevated and complete talent known. Once again we are to be congratulated that so peerless an artist is at the forefront of organ teachers in France.[46]

XIV. Carl Locher
5 October

Carl Locher (1843–1915) of Berne is remembered today as the author of *An Explanation of the Organ Stops*, an 1888 English edition of his *Die Orgel-Register und ihre Klangfarben*. His recital at the Trocadéro offered little of interest and, although a talented amateur, "he is neither a virtuoso nor serious composer and there is undoubtedly in Switzerland another artist who could better represent his country."[47] H. Moréno observed that:

> . . . the program left a little to be desired. For the secular, the pièce de résistance was a *fantaisie* on Swiss national airs with an accompanying obligatory storm. These sorts of organ pieces—tourist attractions—have a certain degree of success in Switzerland. It can even be said that they are one of the artistic attractions of that country. In France, where everything passes quickly, storms are no longer in fashion. From an elevated artistic point of view there is no cause for regret.[48]

XV. André Messager
8 October

Allegro (Sonata No. 3 in A Major)	Mendelssohn
Rhapsodies sur des cantiques bretons, Nos. 1 and 2	Saint-Saëns
Intermezzo	Gigout
Musette	Chauvet
Passacaglia [BWV 582]	J. S. Bach
Improvisation	
Prelude in G Major	J. S. Bach

The final organ recital in the inaugural series was played by the twenty-four-year-old André Messager (1853–1929). He had studied at the École Niedermeyer with Gigout (composition) and Loret (organ) and had been *organiste-du-chœur* at Saint-Sulpice since 1874. Messager became conductor at the Opéra-Comique, London's Covent Garden, and the Paris Opéra. Debussy's *Pelléas et Mélisande* is dedicated to him and he conducted its premiere in 1902. Messager wrote numerous popular operas and ballets and by the time of his Trocadéro recital his 1875 Symphony had been awarded a gold medal by the Société des Compositeurs and, together with his first opera, *François-les-Bas-Bleus*, had been performed at the Concerts Colonne on 20 January 1878.

This young artist knew his instrument and there was much to commend in his musical and expressive performance. However, preoccupation with putting feeling into his playing often leads him to be negligent in rhythm and accuracy. This is a very evident shortcoming on the organ which M Messager should persevere to correct. His improvisation had some extremely fine moments if only he would take care neither to mix a measure of four-four time with one of three-four nor to abuse such special stops as the Voix humaine.[49]

At a time when at least half of the organ recital repertoire in the United States and England consisted of transcriptions, it is worthy of note that the fifteen Trocadéro programs were made up of practically all original organ music. Only six transcriptions appeared on this series—two were arrangements from the organist's own works:

Widor: Allegretto, a Duo for harmonium and piano
Gigout: a Gavotte by Padre Martini
Saint-Saëns: Prelude to Le Déluge and Liszt's Legend No. 1
Chauvet: Romance in B-flat Minor (played twice) and Musette, two of the
    Quatre Morceaux de genre for piano published posthumously in 1876

The most frequently played composers were Bach (thirteen works), Mendelssohn (eight), and Handel (six). As was customary, each organist included some of his own works, but Franck was the only player who drew exclusively from his own music. The most popular piece was Lemmens's Fanfare with three performances. As had been noted in Le Ménestrel, "storms were no longer in fashion," and, whereas but a few years before, no recital was considered successful without a storm, only three were played at the Trocadéro—two being performances of Lemmens's Grand Fantasia in E Minor ("The Storm"); the other, improvised.

The generally high calibre of players and music was reflected in the intelligent and precise press notices which appeared in the two major weekly Parisian music journals. Criticism was no longer limited to the standard phrases, "he played in a very severe way" or "he showed off the stops of the organ in a magisterial way," but specifically detailed various aspects of the musical performances.

At times the reviews are contradictory. The same critic who felt de Lange's program was too severe for his audience noted that Loret and Grison played pieces in a melodious style which had every chance of pleasing the audience. It seemed necessary to make a distinction between organ style and piano style but no one was sure just what the distinction was or how to define it. Music in a "severe" style was either serious (that is, contrapuntal) and/or religious; i.e., suitable organ music. Logic failed to describe concert organ music: Lemmens's Fanfare, the first all-staccato piece in the organ repertoire, was acceptable and praised, but the Intermezzo from Widor's Sixth Symphony, Saint-Saëns's Fantasy in E-flat Major, and Liszt's organ music were "too pianistic." Dubois's Mendelssohn slow movement was too soft, but Widor's was too loud.

Moreover, organists exemplifying the new "expressive" style of playing were reprimanded by critics adhering to the "severe" style. Guilmant was reproached for using the swell pedals too often, Gigout for applying too much rallentando in Mendelssohn's Andante con moto, and Mailly for tempering the severities of organ style to make everything as expressive as possible resulting in "rather capricious tempo and rhythmic variations" in the Mendelssohn and Bach works. The young Messager was understandably called to task for overindulgence in "expressive playing" at the expense of rhythmic stability and accuracy.

Textual fidelity was expected and Stoltz was cited for his liberties and Grison for transposing an octave higher certain parts of Bach's Prelude and Fugue in E Minor. Whatever the criteria of the journalists for Bach tempi may have been, a moderate tempo must have been expected for Widor was accused of rushing the Fugue in D Major and Auguste Andlauer of playing the Toccata and Fugue in D Minor too fast.

Except for the criticism of a detail in Mailly's registration, illogically considered by the writer to be unsuited to a sonata, comments on the players' use of the organ were constructive, and even a bit austere (the Voix humaine was deemed unsuited to Gigout's Mendelssohn Andante and Messager's improvisation). Gigout and Saint-Saëns both over-registered their Bach works: the former's was found to be confused and the latter's was marred by too liberal employment of 16' tone and chorus reeds.

It is unfortunate that more often than not the reviews were unsigned. They were astute and posterity honors their anonymous authors who held the organ in such high regard as a concert instrument and not as an imitator of the orchestra or of meteorological phenomena.

To thank all of those involved in the Trocadéro organ recital series, Cavaillé-Coll gave a banquet in the great hall of his factory. In addition to his numerous personal employees and workmen, he invited Saint-Saëns, Franck, Guilmant, Widor, and Gigout. During the course of the evening each played one of the organs set up in the hall and spoke briefly.[50]

Acoustics of the Hall

Unfortunately, the Trocadéro's acoustics were never satisfactory and the hall, used more often for theatrical performances than for concerts, soon acquired a reputation as an acoustical disaster.[51] Over the organ and stage was a dome which acted as a parabolic reflector or "sound shell." Cavaillé-Coll had been right when he cautioned the architect that curved surfaces almost always generate poor sound.[52] Jean Huré was later to write that "the hall was designed so poorly and the echoes were so numerous that not one sound could be heard distinctly."[53] These echoes were particularly apparent if the sound were the least bit dry or percussive, as those of a piano, drum, or speech. For instance, each note played on a piano sounded twice and to those seated in the orchestra it sounded as though each of a speaker's words was repeated.[54] Other sounds had trouble reaching the hearer and others, after having lost their intensity in the upper reaches of the hall, arrived late.[55] But the organ, curiously, seems to have been unaffected by any of these acoustic phenomena due, it was maintained, to its placement in the focal point of the curve.[56] "The annoying echoes which have so often, indeed, too often, been heard during the official concerts, do not exist, as such, with the organ."[57] It was immediately apparent the first time the organ sounded that "the hall is more favorable to the deployment of every organ sonority than to orchestral effects."[58] Marcel Dupré concurred that "although the acoustics of the hall were defective for speech and orchestral music, the organ spoke clearly and splendidly."[59]

Guilmant's Recital Series

The Universal Exposition closed in November 1878. The following summer Guilmant instituted an annual series of concerts, usually one half organ solo and the other half vocal and instrumental works. Gigout frequently alternated with Guilmant and of the many organists who appeared on the inaugural series, only Widor, Gigout, and Guilmant ever played at the Trocadéro again (see Plate 4).

Guilmant's programs were generally of historical interest and brought to the public organ music by the finest composers of all periods and all schools.[60] On 5 June 1879, he played what was quite possibly the first performance in France of a work by Buxtehude. The same month Widor played his new Symphonies (either Five or Six, or both) at a private audition for the Minister of Fine Arts and several public officials.[61] Gigout played recitals on 2 and 10 July and on 19 October Widor premiered his Fifth Symphony. This performance was not reviewed in Le Ménestrel but, as the work had been published four months previously, there is little doubt that this was the premiere of the Symphony in F Minor—and its celebrated Toccata.[62]

The Trocadéro remained the property of the state and in 1880 was somewhat modified. A Museum of Comparative (cast) Sculpture, a Cambodian and Indochinese Museum, and a Museum of Ethnography replaced galleries, lecture halls, and reception rooms used for the Exposition. The great waterfall was preserved and the 197–foot-diameter basin into which all the water flowed was surrounded by four colossal animal statues, and an aquarium was built nearby.

Cécile and Emmanuel Cavaillé-Coll wrote that "it was due to Widor and Guilmant's intervention and political connections that the hall was saved and

Plate 4
Alexandre Guilmant at the Trocadéro Organ Console

the organ acquired by the state" on 16 March 1882, when a sum of 188,000 francs was voted for the purchase of the Trocadéro organ.[63] The opus list quotes a price of 168,900 francs for the organ and, although lower than the previously mentioned price of 200,000 francs, the Trocadéro organ was still Cavaillé-Coll's most expensive organ to date.[64]

On 20 May 1880, Guilmant began a series of the complete Handel organ concertos. The program for the first concert:[65]

Concerto No. 4 in F Major	Handel
A string quintet and two oboes were conducted by	
Édouard Colonne.	
Tempo di menuetto	Guilmant
Communion	
Prelude	Clérambault
Prelude and Fugue in E Minor [BWV 548]	J. S. Bach
Fugue	Frescobaldi

The next week he played Handel's Concerto No. 7 in B-flat Major, Mendelssohn's Sonata No. 2 in C Minor and a Buxtehude Fugue and Gigue (probably the "Gigue" Fugue) among other works by Lemmens and himself.

These concerts were hardly a popular success, the public being unaccustomed to hearing serious organ music. Even during the Exposition when there was "always a full house," Gigout wrote that:

Little by little the audience is getting used to classical organ music. It still runs out as soon as a serious name appears on the program but this only prevents an important majority from letting itself go to listen to even the works of Sebastian Bach.[66]

Charles Mutin, Cavaillé-Coll's successor, remembered a concert around this time when half of the audience walked out as Guilmant began Bach's Toccata and Fugue in D Minor.[67]

The concerts continued, played to a select audience and administered by Guilmant, a master at publicity. Unconcerned about the success of his "severe" programs, he almost singlehandedly carved out a place in France for concert organ music, and the Trocadéro was the perfect setting. Eventually, in collaboration with the Chanteurs de Saint-Gervais, conducted by Charles Bordes, Bach cantatas and oratorios were heard, assisted by famous singers. Thus an assembly of great talent presented to the Parisian public "the masterpieces of great music for organ solo, organ and orchestra, and choral and organ music from Buxtehude to César Franck."[68]

During the next Universal Exposition Widor premiered his Eighth Symphony when on 3 July 1889, with Jules Delsart, cellist, he played:[69]

302

Symphony No. 8 in B Major		Widor
	Widor, organ	
Aria		J. S. Bach
	Delsart, cello	
Symphony No. 5 in F Minor		Widor
	Widor, organ	
Sarabande		J. S. Bach
	Delsart, cello	
Toccata and Fugue		J. S. Bach
	Widor, organ	

On 11 June 1896, Widor conducted at the Trocadéro his Symphony No. 3, op. 69, for organ and orchestra; Louis Vierne played the organ. On the same program Widor played the organ for the Trio from Saint-Saëns's *Oratorio de Noël* and Harold Bauer was soloist in Saint-Saëns's Piano Concerto in G Minor.[70]

On 28 April 1898, Albert Mahaut (1867–1943), a blind student of Franck and lifelong champion of his organ music, gave an all-Franck organ recital. His two-hour program included the *Pièce héroïque*, *Prière*, Fantasy in C Major, *Grande Pièce symphonique*, and the Prelude, Fugue, and Variation. The following May he played four works of Franck at the Trocadéro—including the recently published *Choral* No. 1 in E Major. Two weeks earlier, Guilmant had given an all-Franck recital and of that event Adolphe Jullien reported in the *Moniteur universel*:

> There is at present a steeplechase among organists as to who will manifest the most enthusiasm towards one of the incontestable masters of the organ and who will better serve the belated glory of César Franck.[71]

By the turn of the century the Trocadéro organ was already evincing mechanical problems. Infrequent maintenance and lack of funds were ever present problems. The instrument underwent numerous repairs in 1900 at the time of the Exposition and Guilmant played concerts on it for several more years. The fact that he could keep the series going as long as he did is a tribute to his industry and perseverence. But Guilmant died in 1911, and by then the Trocadéro organ was in a pitiful state of disrepair. Widor said at the time of the International Music Congress in 1914 that "the workmen not only took it upon themselves to hang decorations and draperies from the small pipes but used the large pipes for water closets!"[72]

After the First World War attempts were made from time to time to rejuvenate interest in the organ. In 1920, Saint-Saëns conducted the Paris premiere of his latest work, *Cyprès et Lauriers*, op. 156, for organ and orchestra, with Gigout at the organ. Also in 1920 Marcel Dupré played from memory the complete organ works of J. S. Bach in a series of ten recitals in the Conservatoire's small concert hall; he had first considered giving these concerts at the Trocadéro but had confided to Alfred Cortot that "my financial means will not permit me to take such a risk. It would be costly to rent the Trocadéro for ten recitals."[73] But the success of the Bach recitals had so firmly established his reputation and, in turn, so improved his financial situation that the next year he was able to repeat his Herculean achievement and to give ten all-Bach recitals at the Trocadéro, two a week, from 5 April to 6 May. Furthermore, in the spring of 1922 Dupré played a series of eight recitals devoted to the music of Bach, Franck, Mendelssohn, Saint-Saëns, Vierne, and Widor, along with his own.

Nevertheless, the organ continued to deteriorate. In 1924 Vierne wrote:

> The magnificent Trocadéro organ is falling to ruin. Almost half the stops are dead and mechanical troubles abound. The last overhaul was in 1900 and since then the instrument has been defaced by hanging props and decorations on the facade, littering among the pipework and mistreating the claviers and pedalboard.[74]

Jean Huré suggested subscriptions of 100 francs "giving contributors one seat for all recitals in the Trocadéro for a period of ten years. Four hundred subscriptions would suffice."[75]

Incredible as it may seem, in 1925, just a month after the American organist, Hugh McAmis, wrote from Paris that the Trocadéro organ "has fallen into bad repair so that most of the reeds cannot be used,"[76] Dupré played a recital on it before 3,000 persons! The program on 30 April included the Paris premiere of his *Symphonie-Passion*:

Fantasia and Fugue in G Minor [BWV 542]	Bach
Prelude and Fugue in D Major [BWV 532]	
Symphonie-Passion, op. 23	Dupré
Improvisation	

The themes for the improvisation had been submitted by Paul Dukas, Maurice Ravel, Henri Rabaud, Arthur Honegger, Widor, and Gabriel Pierné. After having created a Sonata-Allegro first movement, Andante, Scherzo, and Passacaglia, Dupré ended with a fugue in D Major on a theme by Pierné, and

> appeared to be working up a stretto wherein he was bringing together all the themes when an accident occurred with one of the bellows treadles (when will they finally decide to use electrical power for that organ?) and, obliged to save wind, he had to quickly adopt an alternative plan and bring his improvisation to a hasty conclusion.[77]

In February 1926 Dupré succeeded Gigout as professor of organ at the Conservatoire and began to use his influence to have the great organ of the Trocadéro restored. When he discussed the matter with Paul Léon, minister of public instruction, he was turned away because of lack of necessary funds. Then, when he received from Frederick Mayer, organist of the Cadet Chapel of the United States Military Academy at West Point, a $500 check to be used for maintenance of Parisian organs, the idea of using the money for the Trocadéro occurred to him. Organizing a fund raising committee composed of Widor, Paul Bruneau, Pierné, Édouard Monet, and the publisher, Alphonse Leduc, he quickly collected 30,000 francs.[78] The firm of Mutin-Cavaillé-Coll had estimated 66,000 francs for the work and Dupré raised the remainder through benefit concerts (see Plate 5). He gave one of these "Profit Trocadéro" recitals on 29 April 1926, playing works by Bach, Daquin, Clérambault, Franck, Widor, and his own *Trois Préludes et Fugues*, op. 7. At the end of the concert Widor wryly addressed the audience:

> Marcel Dupré, who asked me to come before you to plead the cause of this noble instrument, is the worst advocate for this cause. He conceals with such fiendish skill all of its deficiencies that I risk not being believed by any of you were I to describe its pitiful condition.[79]

With the money raised (1,700 francs contributed by Dupré himself), the organ was overhauled that winter and on 2 March 1927, Dupré inaugurated it with music of Bach, Mozart, Franck, Widor, Guilmant, Gigout, and his own *Suite bretonne, Résurrection* from his *Symphonie-Passion*, and an improvised prelude and fugue.[80] With the restoration of the great Trocadéro organ completed it is astonishing that it was only played by Dupré (and perhaps by no one else) only six more times. On 18 March 1932, Dupré played the premiere of his *Le Chemin de la Croix* and on 14 August 1935, shortly before the hall closed, an "Adieu à l'orgue du Trocadéro."

The Trocadéro was demolished in 1935 to make way for the Palais de Chaillot built for the 1937 Paris Exposition. The organ was dismantled and rebuilt by Victor and Fernand Gonzalez and revoiced along neoclassic principles. The key and stop action was electrified, the manual compass extended to sixty-one notes, and the pedal to thirty-two notes; the addition of fourteen ranks, principally mixtures and mutations, brought the total number of stops to eighty. The entire organ was built on a platform on wheels which could be rolled about the stage. The console was movable, connected by a cable to the center of the case. This rebuilt Gonzalez-Cavaillé-Coll was not completed for the Exposition but was inaugurated on 10 March 1939 by Dupré.[81]

When, in 1975, it was decided to renovate the hall completely and dispense with the organ, it was offered to the city of Lyon. There it was rebuilt by Maison Danion-Gonzalez: the Positif expression box was removed, the 32' Montre discarded, mixtures added, the other pipework seriously revised, and installed in the amphitheater Maurice Ravel. Enlarged to eighty-two stops it was inaugurated in 1977 by Pierre Cochereau.

All that remains of the original Trocadéro are several pieces of statuary which once adorned the lawn. They have recently been relocated, in a fitting gesture of remembrance, to the entrance of the Musée d'Orsay.

Plate 5
Marcel Dupré, Charles-Marie Widor, and Gabriel Pierné
at the Console of the Trocadéro Organ, 1926

NOTES

[1] Jacques Hillairet, *Le Colline de Chaillot* (Paris: Minuit, 1977), 77–80.

[2] *Dwight's Journal of Music*, 6 July 1878, p. 264. (This is basically a translation of two descriptions which appeared earlier in *La Revue et Gazette musicale* 45 [1878]: 8, 140; the latter was written by Charles Blanc and first appeared in *Temps*.)

[3] Cécile and Emmanuel Cavaillé-Coll, *Aristide Cavaillé-Coll* (Paris: Fischbacher, 1929), 117.

[4] Ibid.

[5] Eugène Duplessy, *Paris religieux* (Paris: Roger et Chernoviz, 1900), 171.

[6] Gilbert Huybens, *Aristide Cavaillé-Coll: liste des travaux exécutés* (Lauffen/Neckar: ISO Information, 1985), 18, 24.

[7] Cavaillé-Coll, *Aristide Cavaillé-Coll*, 134.

[8] Joseph Bonnet, *Diagram*; Marcel Dupré, *Disposition*.

[9] See Rollin Smith, *Playing the Organ Works of César Franck* (New York: The American Guild of Organists, 1994), chs. 9–11. (Marie-Louise Jaquet-Langlais's article in this volume also discusses the registration of the *Trois Pièces*. Ed.)

[10] *La Revue et Gazette musicale* 45 (1878): 255.

[11] *Le Ménestrel* 44 (1878): 295.

[12] *La Revue et Gazette musicale* 45 (1878): 261.

[13] Ibid.

[14] Ibid.

[15] Ibid., 270.

[16] *Le Ménestrel* 44 (1878): 342.

[17] *La Revue et Gazette musicale* 45 (1878): 285–86.

[18] John Near, "The Life and Work of Charles-Marie Widor" (Ph.D. diss., Boston University, 1985), 121.

[19] *La Revue et Gazette musicale* 45 (1878): 285.

[20] Ibid., 261.

[21] Ibid., 285.

[22] Ibid., 285–86.

[23] Ibid., 286.

[24] Ibid.

[25] Ibid.

[26] Ibid., 297.

[27] Ibid.

[28] Ibid.

[29] Ibid., 305–6.

[30] Ibid.

[31] Ibid., 306.

[32] Ibid., 313.

[33] Ibid.

[34] Louis Kelterborn, "A Few Reminiscences of Camille Saint-Saëns," *The Musician* 12 (1907): 250.

[35] *La Revue et Gazette musicale* 45 (1878): 321.

[36] Ibid.

[37] *L'Art musical* 17 (1878): 311.

[38] Letter from Liszt to Saint-Saëns, Weimar, 14 May 1882 (Chateau-Musée de Dieppe).

[39] Letter from Liszt to Mason & Hamlin Co. in Boston, Weimar, 12 June 1883 (*Letters of Franz Liszt*, ed. La Mara [Ida Maria Lipius], trans. Constance Bache, 2 vols. [London: H. Grevel, 1894], 2:438).

[40] Camille Saint-Saëns's, "L'Orgue," *L'Écho de Paris*, 1 January 1911. (Reprinted in Camille Saint-Saëns, *École buissonnière: notes et souvenirs* [Paris: P. Lafitte, 1913], 173.)

[41] *La Revue et Gazette musicale* 45 (1878): 321.

[42] E. G., "Concerts et soirées," *Le Ménestrel* 44 (1878): 363.

[43] Ibid.

[44] *La Revue et Gazette musicale* 45 (1878): 321.

[45] See Smith, *Playing the Organ Works of César Franck*, ch. 10. (Marie-Louise Jaquet-Langlais's article in this volume also discusses the revisions of the *Trois Pièces*. Ed.)

[46] *La Revue et Gazette musicale* 45 (1878): 321.

[47] Ibid., 342.

[48] H. Moréno in *Le Ménestrel* 44 (1878): 373.

[49] *La Revue et Gazette musicale* 45 (1878): 342.

[50] *Le Ménestrel* 44 (1878): 404.

[51] Pascal Ory, *Les Expositions universelles de Paris* (Paris: Ramsay, 1982), 86.

[52] Cavaillé-Coll, *Aristide Cavaillé-Coll*, 116.

[53] Jean Huré, *L'Ésthetique de l'orgue* (Paris: Sénart, 1923), 187.

[54] Cavaillé-Coll, *Aristide Cavaillé-Coll*,117.

[55] Norbert Dufourcq, *Le Grand Orgue du Palais de Chaillot* (Paris: Floury, 1943), 1–2.

[56] Cavaillé-Coll, *Aristide Cavaillé-Coll*, 117.

[57] *Le Ménestrel* 44 (1878): 295.

[58] *La Revue et Gazette musicale* 45 (1878): 255. At the first official concert it was noted that the effects of Berlioz's *Marche troyenne* "were lessened by the unfortunate echoes and by the want of sonority of the hall. The pedal, underscoring, as it were, the ensemble, could be scarcely distinguished and the seven hundred voices were confused." (*Dwight's Journal of Music*, 6 July 1878, p. 264.)

[59] Marcel Dupré, *Marcel Dupré raconte* . . . (Paris: Bornemann, 1972), 120.

[60] See Rollin Smith, "Alexandre Guilmant: Commemorating the 150th Anniversary of His Birth," *The American Organist* 21 (March 1987): 53.

[61] *Le Ménestrel* 45 (1879): 270.

[62] Ibid., 384.

[63] Cavaillé-Coll, *Aristide Cavaillé-Coll*, 118.

[64] Huybens, *Aristide Cavaillé-Coll: liste*, 18.

[65] *La Revue et Gazette musicale* 47 (1880): 165–66.

[66] *Le Ménestrel* 44 (1878): 342.

[67] Charles Mutin, "Alexandre Guilmant," *S. I. M. (Société internationale de musique, Revue musicale)* 7 (May 1911): 38.

[68] Louis Vierne, "Alexandre Guilmant," *La Schola Cantorum* (Paris: Bloud et Gay, 1927), 27–38.

[69] *Le Ménestrel* 55 (1889): 207.

[70] *Le Monde musical* 8 (July 1896): 72.

[71] Albert Mahaut, *L'Œuvre d'orgue de César Franck* (Paris: Chez l'auteur, 1923), 29.

[72] Jean Huré in *L'Orgue et Les Organistes* 2 (May 1925): 28–29.

[73] Dupré, *Marcel Dupré raconte* . . ., 75.

[74] Louis Vierne, "L'Orgue chez les Anglais et chez nous," *L'Orgue et Les Organistes* 1 (May 1924): 6.

[75] Jean Huré in *L'Orgue et Les Organistes* 1 (Novembre 1924): 13.

[76] Hugh McAmis, "Paris Impressions," *The American Organist* 8 (1925): 210.

[77] Henri Potiron, "Marcel Dupré au Trocadéro," *Les Orgues et Les Organistes* 2 (May 1925): 2–5.

[78] A photograph of this committee appeared in *The Diapason* 17 (September 1926): 3.

[79] Dupré, *Marcel Dupré raconte* . . . , 121.

[80] H. B., "Le Récital d'orgue de Marcel Dupré au Trocadéro," *Le Monde musical* 38 (March 1927): 114.

[81] André Marchal played a series of ten concerts on the organ during 1942 and 1943; the programs along with Norbert Dufourcq's extensive commentaries were published as *Du prélude et fugue au thème libre* . . . (Paris: Floury, 1944).

[82] [Aristide Cavaillé-Coll], *Orgues d'église et de salon*, Exposition universelle de Paris, 1878: classe 13—instruments de musique (Paris: Privately printed, 1878). This volume contains the "Composition des Jeux" of his organ in the Salle des Fêtes of the Palais du Trocadéro (as well as the specification of an *orgue de salon* exhibited in the Galerie des instruments de musique in the Palais du Champ-de-Mars).

LIST OF CONTRIBUTORS

LAWRENCE ARCHBOLD is Associate Professor of Music, Enid and Henry Woodward College Organist, and Chair of the Music Department at Carleton College. He received the Ph.D. degree in Music from the University of California, Berkeley, and specializes in both the performance and scholarship of organ music. He has presented papers at national meetings of both the American Musicological Society and the American Guild of Organists, at various other conferences, and has published articles on French organ music in *19th-Century Music, The American Organist*, and *The Organist as Scholar: Essays in Honor of Russell Saunders*.

CRAIG CRAMER is Associate Professor of Music at the University of Notre Dame, and also serves as Organist at First English Lutheran Church in Mishawaka, Indiana. He is a magna cum laude graduate of Westminster Choir College and earned the M.M. and the D.M.A. degrees from the Eastman School of Music where he was awarded the Performer's Certificate. He has studied with Russell Saunders, William Hays, and André Marchal. Named the winner of several competitions, including the National Competition in Organ at First Presbyterian Church in Fort Wayne, Indiana, he has appeared as a featured recitalist for conventions of the American Guild of Organists.

MATTHEW DIRST is a candidate for the Ph.D. degree is Musicology at Stanford University, where he is completing work on his dissertation, "The Well-Tempered Clavier in Music History and Aesthetics: Case Studies in Bach Reception." Winner of the 1990 American Guild of Organists National Young Artists Competition, he has appeared as an organist and as a harpsichordist in concerts across North America and Europe. His publications include several articles on the keyboard and organ music of J. S. Bach. His first recordings feature harpsichord music of François and Armand-Louis Couperin and organ music of J. S. Bach.

JESSE E. ESCHBACH is Coordinator of Organ Studies at the University of North Texas and holds the D.M.A. degree from the University of Michigan where he was a student of Robert Glasgow. His previous degrees are from

Indiana University where he studied with Oswald Ragatz. He has studied early French music and the works of Jehan Alain in the class of Marie-Claire Alain at the Conservatoire de Reuil-Malmaison, during which time he was awarded the Prix d'Excellence and the Prix de Virtuosité, and later studied organ with Marie-Madeleine Duruflé and piano with Christiane Devos. He has appeared as a recitalist and lecturer throughout Europe and the United States, recorded for Centaur, and, with organ builder Gene Bedient, co-founded the Summer Institute for French Organ Studies.

DAVID GRAMIT is Assistant Professor of Musicology at the University of Alberta. A graduate of Carleton College, he received the Ph.D. degree from Duke University. His primary research interests include biographical, contextual, and stylistic issues surrounding Franz Schubert, the reception of Schubert's music, and, more generally, the social construction of musical meaning, particularly in Germany and Austria in the late eighteenth and early nineteenth centuries. His article, "Schubert and the Biedermeier: The Aesthetics of Johann Mayrhofer's *Heliopolis*" (1993), won the American Musicological Society's 1994 Alfred Einstein Award.

KAREN HASTINGS-DEANS is University Organist and Carillonneur at the University of the Pacific, where she teaches organ, harpsichord, and piano, and is also Organist and Director of Music at Covenant Presbyterian Church in Palo Alto, California. She holds a D.M.A. degree from Stanford University, where she has served as Assistant University Organist. She studied with Herbert Nanney, Sandra Soderlund, John Walker, Philip Simpson, and Colin Ford, and has studied and coached in Paris with Jean Langlais, Gaston Litaize, and Marie-Louise Jaquet-Langlais. She has given numerous recitals in the United States and France, presented several lecture-demonstrations on the music of Jean Langlais, and published articles concerning César Franck's organ music in journals in the United States and France.

MARIE-LOUISE JAQUET-LANGLAIS is Professor of Organ at the Schola Cantorum and at the Conservatoire Supérieur de Paris-CNR. She holds a Doctorate in Musicology from the Sorbonne; her thesis, "Jean Langlais, l'homme et l'œuvre," has recently been published by Combre. She received the Diplôme de Virtuosité in the class of Jean Langlais from the Schola Cantorum, has taught at the Conservatoire of Marseille, was organist of the Silbermann organ in Mulhouse from 1969–1979, and was Co-titulaire de l'Orgue de Sainte-Clotilde from 1979–1987. She has published various articles, a monograph on Jean Langlais, issued several recordings, and presented research at a wide variety of conferences. She is the widow of Jean Langlais.

KIMBERLY MARSHALL is Dean of Postgraduate Studies at the Royal Academy of Music, and previously was University Organist and Assistant Professor of Music at Stanford University. She maintains an active career as an organist/scholar, performing regularly in the United States and Europe and publishing in academic journals. Winner of the St. Albans Competition in 1985, she has been invited to play in prestigious venues, recorded for Radio-France, the BBC, and the ABC, and issued several recordings. She received the D.Phil. in Music from the University of Oxford; her thesis, "Iconographical Evidence for the Late-Medieval Organ," was published in 1989. Her *Rediscovering the Muses*, an edited collection of essays about female musical traditions, recently appeared. She has presented her research to the American Musicological Society, the Schola Cantorum in Basel, the Sydney Conservatorium, and a variety of other institutions.

WILLIAM J. PETERSON is Thatcher Professor of Music, College Organist, and Chair of the Department of Music at Pomona College. A graduate of Oberlin College and Conservatory of Music, he holds a Ph.D. degree in Music from the University of California, Berkeley, and is active as a performer and scholar. As organist, he has given several complete performances of J. S. Bach's *Clavierübung III* and has been heard on "Pipedreams." As scholar, he has read papers for the American Musicological Society, the American Organ Academy, the American Bach Society, and the Third International Romantic Organ Music Symposium. With Lawrence Archbold he is co-founder of The Institute for Critical Studies of Organ Music, which recently sponsored two conferences.

DANIEL ROTH has been Titulaire du Grand Orgue de Saint-Sulpice in Paris since 1985; previously he was Organist of the Basilique du Sacré-Cœur for twenty-two years. He has been Professor at the Musikhochschule Saarbrücken since 1988, after having taught at the conservatories in Marseille, Strasbourg, and from 1974 to 1976 at the Music School of the Catholic University in Washington, D.C. He has given recitals, masterclasses, radio broadcasts, and been a jury member in competitions all over the world. His many recordings have been issued on labels such as Arion, Erato, Phillips, EMI Pathé Marconi, and Festivo; since 1986, he has recorded exclusively for Motette-Ursina. Among the publishers of his compositions for organ are Leduc, Novello, and Bärenreiter. He has been named a Chevalier de l'Ordre des Arts et de Lettres.

ROLLIN SMITH is the author of *Toward an Authentic Interpretation of the Organ Works of César Franck* (1982), *Saint-Saëns and the Organ* (1993), *Playing the Organ Works of César Franck* (1994), *The Aeolian Pipe Organ and*

Its Music (1995), numerous essays on organ performance, articles in organ journals, and editor of a distinguished collection of musical editions. As a concert organist he has played throughout the United States, appeared at national conventions of the American Guild of Organists, the Organ Historical Society, the American Liszt Society, and made twenty-five organ recordings. He studied in Paris with Jean Langlais and holds a Doctor of Musical Arts degree from the Juilliard School.

BENJAMIN VAN WYE resides in upstate New York where he serves as Lecturer in Music at Skidmore College. His investigations into the organ's role in historic liturgies have been productive of a doctoral dissertation, undertaken at the University of Illinois, Urbana-Champaign, on the French liturgical organ school—the first scholarly treatment of the subject in English—and essays published in the *Journal of the American Musicological Society*, *The Music Review*, and *L'Orgue*. Musicological pursuits also inform his work as keyboardist and choral conductor in which capacity he frequently shares with fellow performers and audiences the musical treasures yielded by his research.

EDWARD ZIMMERMAN is Assistant Professor of Music and College Organist at Wheaton College-Conservatory of Music, where he teaches organ, harpsichord, church music, and music history. He is also Director of Music-Organist at First United Church of Oak Park, Illinois. He holds the D.M.A. degree from the Eastman School of Music, where he studied with Russell Saunders. He also holds philosophy degrees from Hampden-Sydney College and the University of Virginia. He concertizes extensively throughout both the United States and Europe, and has performed and lectured for a number of professional organizations, including the Third International Romantic Organ Music Symposium and The Institute for Critical Studies of Organ Music.

INDEX